RED ODYSSEY

An FC Bayern Fan Journey

Rick Joshua

Congratulations!

[signature]

01.08.2020

Watch out for the sequel!

Content Copyright © Rick Joshua, 2017
Cover Design © Rick Joshua, 2017

Typeset in Constantia

Rick Joshua has asserted his right under the Copyright, Designs and Patents Act 1988 to be identified as the author of this work.

This book is sold subject to the condition that it shall not, by way of trade or otherwise, be lent, resold, hired out, or otherwise circulated without the writer's prior consent in any form of binding or cover other than that in which it is published and without a similar condition, including this condition, being imposed on the subsequent purchaser.

First published in the United Kingdom in February 2017
bulibook.com, 24 Peplow Close, West Drayton, Middlesex UB7 7XN, United Kingdom

ISBN 9 781540 647382
www.bulibook.com

For my long-suffering partner Caroline.
Not the world's biggest football fan, but somebody who has always appreciated a hefty tome.

CONTENTS

Introduction	7
The Early Days	13
My First Trophy	21
The Bundesliga Black Hole	31
It means nothing to me	48
The Nearly Men	64
The Lowest of the Low	76
Danke, Bitte und Vestenbergsgreuth	99
Ottocracy comes to FC Hollywood	111
Caught in a Trap	123
So close, and yet so far	140
Two out of three ain't bad	152
The Four-Minute Championship	167
The Pain is washed away	183
Back down with a bump	197
The Changing of the Guard	211
A Fond Farewell	220
Qualität kommt von quälen	233
The Return of Der General	247
The Green Shoots Of Recovery	263
Hype, Hysteria and Hubris	278
Going Dutch	298
Das Feierbiest	328
Vize-, Vize-, Vizemeister	344
Oans, Zwoa, Drei, Gwunna!	376
Project Pep	413

INTRODUCTION

It is sometimes hard to believe that I have been a supporter of FC Bayern München for close to thirty-six years, having first acquainted myself with the club during the late spring of 1981. I was not even ten years old at the time and living in the dark old days of non-existent Bundesliga highlights on British television and sporadic European appearances on late-night midweek sports shows – light years away from the wall to wall football one can find on digital television today.

Over the best part of four decades I have experienced the ecstatic highs and painful lows of being a supporter of Bavaria's and Germany's most famous football club. I have lived through the successful but ultimately unfulfilled 1980s, the barrel-scraping depths of the early 1990s and the period where the club had been dubbed by the unforgiving German media as *FC Hollywood*, the unforgettable and unspeakable pain of the Champions League defeat against Manchester United in 1999, the nerve-shreddingly crazy final Saturday of the 2000/01 Bundesliga season and, ultimately, the glory of the landmark treble of 2012/13 – marking the end of my thirty-third season as an FC Bayern fan.

The seeds for this project were sown on a hotel balcony in Catalonia on the morning after the Champions League final victory at Wembley, the result of one of those unique moments of clarity. Surrounded by blissful silence, I reflected on those thirty-three years, the significance of what had been achieved the night before, and the very realistic prospect of Bayern winning an unprecedented treble.

Following the DFB-Pokal final victory over VfB Stuttgart in Berlin the following week, the path had been set: it had taken just a moment of inspiration on a quiet Sunday morning in Spain to set things in motion, and before I knew it the project had started to gather momentum. I quickly found myself unable to stop as all of the memories started to come flooding back.

My initial mission had been to write a short "fan history" piece for the excellent Bundesliga Fanatic website, but after less than a day at my keyboard I realised that it was never going to be possible to keep everything down to a mere couple of pages. In fact, I very quickly concluded that such a plan was completely ridiculous. I then considered writing a longer article and serialising it, but once I hit and then passed the twelve-thousand word mark when not even a fraction of the way through, I decided that I might as well flesh things out properly and turn it into something bigger.

The short article had been turned into a feature-length magazine article, then finally a book project.

It was never my intention to plan things out item by item, and once things really got going I decided to stick firmly to this approach. The content therefore developed organically and via a stream of consciousness mechanism, and rather than turning into yet another dry football club history it first and foremost remained a written record of my relationship with FC Bayern as a fan rather than as a reporter or journalist.

Hundreds of important games had been played in the past four decades, but my intention from the beginning was to focus the attention on those moments that I had actually remembered well enough to write about without having to start rummaging too deeply through the reference books and websites.

The first real struggle was that of sticking to this approach while at the same time maintaining a steady chronological narrative to glue everything together and provide a little context; this explains why some seasons have ended up being distilled into a couple of pages, while others have taken up entire chapters. Essentially, the mission was to concentrate specifically on those memorable matches I had actually seen and the events I had followed closely at the time – while filling in the gaps to blend it all together into something readable.

My "fan history" approach will also hopefully help to explain what some may consider a serious imbalance in the narrative: while in the mid to late 1980s I would have limited access to Bundesliga matches, the latter part of that decade was something of a black hole on account of my only getting to see potted highlights of a handful of European fixtures. Conversely, after the satellite television revolution of the early 1990s the content rises exponentially, given that today it is entirely possible to watch every single match in every single competition.

Whether it was down to budgetary constraints or just the inability to take time off work, my getting to see Bayern live had always posed a problem. Living in another country certainly didn't help. I had managed to see a couple of matches at the Olympiastadion during the mid-1990s and a small handful of away matches where I conveniently happened to be in the immediate vicinity, and on one occasion also got to see the team at one of the Hallen-Masters indoor tournaments in Berlin – in the days before Bundesliga teams chose to escape the cold weather and jet off to Asia and the Middle East during the *Winterpause*.

Back when I was an impoverished student, and after that a freelance web developer with a high-maintenance client base, there were plenty of potential opportunities to see Bayern play at the Olympiastadion; local fans didn't appear to love the ground that much, and there were times when matches had been massively undersold. One could even find large empty spaces at Champions League matches, something that is hard to imagine happening at the hi-tech Allianz Arena today.

On many occasions an opportunity presented itself, only for any best-laid plans to be immediately defeated by the lack of quickly-available accommodation, extortionate flight prices or simply the possibility of a high-value client or customer calling that their website was down or their email wasn't working.

The massive irony was that no sooner had I found a better paid, permanent job that offered a lot more flexibility Bayern decided to up sticks and move to a state of the art ground that was almost permanently sold out.

The opening of the ultra-modern Allianz Arena in the quiet northern suburb of Fröttmaning in 2005 would make the fan experience a whole lot better – but getting to see Bayern play a home match without the right contacts had become close to a logistical impossibility. Season memberships are like gold dust with a mass of new applications every year, and individual match tickets are like hens' teeth. The only chance one might have is ordering a ticket a long time in advance and creating a holiday around the event – though the upside is that if you don't end up getting one you'll always have plenty to see and do over a weekend in Munich.

The only alternative is getting a ticket at the last moment, and then embarking on a desperate hunt for available accommodation and affordable travel costs. The days of simply turning up at the ground on the morning or afternoon of a match and buying a ticket at the box office on the off-chance are long gone, even at some of the smaller and supposedly less popular Bundesliga clubs. Across Germany, attendances are booming.

The popularity of German football had been on the rise ever since the 2006 World Cup and the rebirth of the national team under first Jürgen Klinsmann and then Joachim Löw, but following the 2013 Champions League final between Bayern and Borussia Dortmund the Bundesliga has quickly become one of the more fashionable and marketable leagues in Europe.

I had always planned to put something like this together at some point, but the treble of 2013 would come just at the right time. In a sense, it was the perfect catalyst for the project. With German football and the Bundesliga gaining large numbers of fans all around the globe and with Bayern arguably the best football club in the world at that moment, things just couldn't have fallen into place any better.

The domestic game in Germany has undergone a massive transformation over the course of the last thirty years, and today both the Bundesliga and FC Bayern München are recognised and highly respected global brands.

When I bought the first of my forty or so FC Bayern replica *Trikots* back in the 1980s it was something of a niche item; today, every new kit design is introduced to the watching world with something approaching a media fanfare after long periods of anticipation and leaked prototypes on the Internet. Thirty years ago one would have been lucky to find a club shirt or scarf; today, there is an encyclopaedic catalogue containing a wide range of items from towels and bedding to egg cups, tablecloths and waffle makers. You can even have the FC Bayern logo on your toast.

Back when I started following FC Bayern, one probably could have counted a handful of overseas supporters; now, the team has a growing network of fan clubs all over the world, from the United States to Brazil and from the UK to the Middle and Far East. The team now takes its annual winter training sessions in the Middle East and Asia, and have opened offices in New York City and Shanghai. More recently, the club changed its website domain from fcbayern.de to fcbayern.com, showcasing its global credentials. The website itself, including the extensive FC Bayern shop, is in nine languages including Arabic, Russian, Spanish and Japanese.

Serendipity is a wonderful thing: not long after I had started on this work, I discovered an FC Bayern fan club that had been established in London in the weeks following the Champions League triumph at Wembley. Set up by a couple of young German expatriates fed up of watching matches in a foreign country on their own, the Red Dragons London had quickly attracted a collection of supporters from far and wide. It was like discovering a whole new world.

My first Saturday afternoons with the Red Dragons were spent regaling many of my new friends over a chilled *Weizen* or two with tales of matches played before some of them had even been born, though I was pleasantly surprised to find other British FC Bayern supporters even older than me. Unsurprisingly, their early experiences in following the club's fortunes had been almost identical to mine.

Fate sometimes has this knack of delivering very pleasant surprises. Having spent my first thirty-three years as an FC Bayern fan largely in isolation, I had suddenly found a group of fellow Bavarian travellers right on my doorstep here in London.

During my first three decades following Bayern I had only managed to attend a handful of matches, and just as I had decided to put all of these memories together I suddenly found myself watching matches at the Allianz Arena and joining the travelling *Südkurve* on trips to the Emirates, Old Trafford, the Stadio Olimpico in Rome and one of the great amphitheatres of world football, the Camp Nou in Barcelona.

It has taken me just over three years to put this work together, a process that has involved far too many late nights rewatching dozens of matches and hundreds of intensive one-page-at-a-time lunchtime writing sessions. In the past I have often found myself getting tired or bored of one massive project and shelving it for another, but this time I was finally able to see things through to the end.

I would like to thank all of the many people who offered their help and encouragement with the project, in particular Wolfgang Steiner and Terry Faulkner for wading through the proof copy and picking out the typos and mistakes. I guess there are not many occasions when you can do an otherwise painstaking job while taking a journey down memory lane, even if not all the memories are particularly pleasant.

If you may happen to encounter any old ghosts from Carrow Road or Vestenbergsgreuth and end up having horrible nightmares as a result, please remember that I too had to subject myself to many hours of painful mental torture. Until sitting down to put this work together, I had not watched the 1999 Champions League final in its entirety for over fifteen years. Yes, really.

I would like to think that much of what I have written here will help in stoking and stirring the memories – both good and bad – of every fan of FC Bayern München, and at the same time offer a unique personal insight on what it was like to be a supporter of an overseas club in a time when information had been seriously limited.

While older readers will be reminded of some of the great moments and names from the past, more recent fans will hopefully get an idea of what we would have to go through in trying to follow the game in the days before satellite television and the Internet.

Thank you for sharing it with me.

THE EARLY DAYS

I was first drawn to FC Bayern München at the beginning of the 1980s, through a combination of a deeply entrenched Germanophilia and the fact that almost everybody around me at the time supported another Champion team that also sported an all-red kit – Liverpool FC. (I also have a part-Dutch background though would never at any point be drawn to Ajax, Feyenoord or NAC Breda).

Given that I was already by then a fairly established supporter of the German national side and was never going to be a Liverpool supporter at any cost – "my" English team had always been Ipswich Town – the event that swung me towards *Die Münch'ner* was the closely-contested European Cup semi-final between the German and English champions that took place in the spring of 1981.

Of course, had this development happened a year earlier with everybody else supporting 1980 European Champions Nottingham Forest, I might well have ended up going down a slightly different path in choosing to follow Hamburger SV – a situation which, when I think of it now, would have been just a little bit unfortunate.

Bayern went on to lose the semi-final on away goals: after a goalless draw at Anfield, a late equaliser from Karl-Heinz Rummenigge at the Olympiastadion in Munich would not be enough to turn things around. While the Bavarians had to be content with just the domestic Bundesliga crown, Liverpool went on to win their third European title in five years by defeating Real Madrid 1-0 in Paris. Meanwhile, my desire for a European trophy was finally assuaged with Ipswich's 5-4 aggregate defeat of Dutch side AZ67 Alkmaar in the UEFA Cup final.

The 1-1 draw against Liverpool in Munich was the first and only time I would actually get to see Bayern in action that season, but I was immediately smitten: sucked into a footballing love affair that has now safely entered its third decade.

The following season – my first as a "proper" FC Bayern supporter – provided the first chapter in what would quickly become be a recurring theme: European Cup final defeat. Living on a Royal Air Force base on the southern coast of Cyprus at the time, I had managed to keep up to date with the weekly Bundesliga highlights programme *Football Made in Germany* and the popular weekly magazines *Shoot* and *Match*, where I studied the line-ups and quickly familiarised myself with the team. The magazines often arrived a month after the issue late and I wasn't even aware of the existence of Teletext, but somehow I managed to make do.

As a fan of the *Nationalmannschaft* I was already well acquainted with superstars Karl-Heinz Rummenigge and Paul Breitner – collectively known at the time in the German media as *Breitnigge* – but soon got to know other club legends including Klaus "Auge" Augenthaler, Wolfgang Dremmler and Dieter Hoeneß as well as less heralded figures such as Bertram Beierlorzer, Bernd Dürnberger, Udo Horsmann and Reinhold Mathy.

As the 1981-82 season progressed and my knowledge of the team started to develop, Hungarian coach Pál Csernai's Bayern side were a clear second fiddle to Hamburger SV in the Bundesliga. In what was a strange season the Bavarians had won their opening five matches to storm to the top of the table, but after that fell away into the mire of inconsistency punctuated by some heavy away defeats. A particularly bleak October saw *Die Roten* go down 4-0 and 4-1 against title rivals Köln and HSV, and their inconsistency was best summed up by their 7-0 defeat of Fortuna Düsseldorf being immediately followed by a 4-1 thrashing at the hands of strugglers Karlsruher SC.

While HSV stormed to the title and scored a staggering ninety-five goals in the process, Bayern slipped, staggered and stumbled throughout, eventually finishing in third place behind Köln. While the Bavarians had won more games than all of their rivals and had the best home record of any of the eighteen teams with a record of 13-3-1, their poor form on the road – with just seven wins and a staggering ten defeats – would ultimately be their undoing.

	P	W	D	L	Goals	GD	Pts
Hamburger SV	34	18	12	4	95:45	+50	48:20
1. FC Köln	34	18	9	7	72:38	+34	45:23
FC Bayern München	34	20	3	11	77:56	+21	43:25

While Bayern's domestic campaigns were covered by the ever so small reports in *Shoot*, I had occasionally managed to catch a glimpse of that famous all-red *Trikot* whenever big European big games were played. For the most part the local television commentary was quite literally all Greek to me, but for some reason – unless my memory is playing tricks – *Football Made in Germany* was in English, retaining the famous voice of narrator Toby Charles.

In the wake of Ipswich Town's disappointing elimination at the hands of Aberdeen in the first round of the UEFA Cup in the autumn of 1981, I began to follow Bayern's progress in the European Cup far more closely.

While the progress of English and Scottish sides in the three European competitions was fairly well covered on the British Forces Broadcasting Service (BFBS) radio station, the only practical way of keeping up to date with Bayern's progress was by deciphering the Greek text at the end of the late local news bulletin every Wednesday evening, and failing that a copy of any decent English newspaper that would usually arrive a couple of days late. Then there was the weekly *Shoot* magazine, which usually arrived at the small YWCA-run newsagent on the base – sometimes more than a month after the date of issue. More often than not, I'd be seeing the results and team lists for first round matches at the time the second round games were being played – and when I think of it today I still cannot understand how I managed to keep up.

Bayern easily made their way into the European Cup quarter-finals with a 6-0 aggregate win over Swedish champions Östers IF before recording a resounding 4-1 thumping of Portuguese league winners SL Benfica, and a 3-1 triumph over Romanians Universitatea Craiova was good enough to see them through once again to the last four where they were drawn against Bulgarian champions CSKA Sofia.

Both Greek and Bulgarian teams were very popular in Cyprus, and Bayern being drawn against CSKA meant that I would finally get to see at least a little footage of the match – even if it were just scratchy highlights. The combination of Bulgarian state television camera work – light years from today's wondrous world of Sky Sports HD – and the small fourteen-inch black and white television screen made for some interesting viewing, as Bayern – in all white – found themselves three goals down in the space of the first twenty minutes against their Bulgarian opponents – kitted out in all grey – before fighting back to eventually go down 4-3.

The return leg looked much the same, though with a slightly better quality picture. It was now Bayern's turn to be kitted out in the all-grey *Trikot* with CSKA playing in all-white, an entertaining encounter at the Olympiastadion where *Breitnigge* shared all of the goals in a resounding 4-0 triumph for the Bavarians as the Bulgarian champions were ruthlessly swept aside. Awaiting the Munich side in the final were English champions Aston Villa.

Now, if some of you are aware of what had happened the previous season in the English league - the then Division One - you will know that unfashionable Villa had surged through at the end of the season to pip a tiring Ipswich Town and take the title. When Bayern lined up at the De Kuip in the European Cup final against the aptly-named "Villains", I saw it as the perfect opportunity to gain some measure of revenge – a sort of payback by proxy.

The 1982 European Cup final also assumed a deeper significance for me personally: it was the very first time I would get to see Bayern play the full ninety minutes in a live televised match. It may have been in Greek on a small black and white television set, but it was a special moment all the same. Bayern were kitted out in their now famous all-grey outfit with white trim, while their English opponents were in a change strip of all white with dark grey pinstripes. All played on a dark grey pitch.

All that remained now to complete the picture was the right result.

It was one of those games that had been written in the stars however, even after Villa had lost their first choice goalkeeper Jimmy Rimmer through injury just nine minutes into the contest. Right from the outset Pál Csernai's team dominated the match, but try as they might that elusive opening goal just wouldn't come. A world-class Bayern team that included Breitner, Dieter Hoeneß and two-time European Footballer of the Year Rummenigge had been scoring for fun in the earlier rounds, but appeared to have left their shooting boots in the locker at home for the most important match of the season.

Chances continued to come and go for the Bavarians, and Rimmer's twenty-four year old replacement Nigel Spink - making only his second first team appearance in what had been five years at the Birmingham club – ended up having a fairytale match. Bayern had by far their best spell in the period either side of half-time with Klaus Augenthaler narrowly missing the target, Bernd Dürnberger forcing Spink into making a fine save and Augenthaler then having a shot cleared off the line by Kenny Swain; they kept knocking on the door, but as the clock ticked by there was no answer.

With sixty-seven minutes on the clock striker Villa winger Tony Morley turned sweeper Hans Weiner inside out on the left, drilling in a low cross towards the lumbering Peter Withe who was lurking at the far post. With Bayern 'keeper Manfred Müller left completely helpless as the ball fizzed across the six yard box, Withe – never the most elegant of centre-forwards - did his best to miss what was an open goal from less than three yards by scuffing the ball towards the goal, sending it spinning almost apologetically into the net having bounced off the inside of the upright. Having offered next to nothing for most of the game, the English champions had taken the lead.

Hoeneß then had the ball in the back of the Villa net only to have it chalked off for offside, which made it clear once and for all that it was going to be one of those sad European evenings for Bayern with the opposition pulling off what was little more than a snatch and grab to claim the prize. The defeat was only Bayern's first European Cup defeat in their fourth final appearance, yet nobody knew back then how often this story would repeat itself over the course of the following three decades.

Defeat in Rotterdam and failure to retain their Bundesliga title meant that Bayern would miss out on European Cup football the following season, but an emphatic 4-2 victory over Bavarian rivals Nürnberg in the final of the DFB-Pokal earlier in the month had ensured that at least one piece of silverware was safely locked away in the trophy cabinet at the Säbenerstraße.

While the final scoreline might have suggested an easy Bayern win, it was in actual fact anything but. First, midfielder Bertram Beierlorzer was forced off injured and striker Dieter Hoeneß suffered a nasty blow that saw him return to the field sporting a massive bandage on his head. Then, Austrian Reinhold Hintermaier thumped a thirty-five yard goal-of-the-season candidate blockbuster to give *Der Club* the lead with just over half an hour on the clock.

With Bayern struggling to find any sort of rhythm, a fast break from their opponents just a minute before half-time saw Hintermaier find the fast-moving Werner Dreßel in space. After collecting the ball and sprinting half the length of the pitch the blond striker made no mistake as he calmly skipped past 'keeper Manfred Müller and rolled the ball into the back of the net to double his team's advantage.

Die Roten were quite literally bloodied and bruised, yet the team that returned for the second half in Frankfurt was a completely transformed beast. Just eight minutes into the second half Karl-Heinz Rummenigge had halved the deficit with a header set up by the bandaged Hoeneß, and five minutes past the hour mark Wolfgang Kraus swept home the equaliser after the energetic Rummenigge had cannoned a crisp shot against the base of the post.

Striker Herbert Heidenreich – who looked like a Mexican cartoon villain with his wonderfully crafted moustache – struck the woodwork at the other end for Nürnberg, but from that point on everything was up for grabs. Bayern were slightly fortunate to be awarded a penalty following a clear contactless stumble in the box from Kraus, but skipper Paul Breitner made no mistake in his face-off with legendary *Elfmeterkiller* Rudi Kargus to put *Die*

Roten in front for the first time in the contest. It was the battle of the big veteran hairdos: Breitner's dark Afro against ex-Hamburger Kargus and his dishevelled blond mane.

Both skipper Breitner and two-time European footballer of the year Rummenigge had played a major part in turning the game around, but the undisputed man of the moment had been the ever-reliable Dieter Hoeneß. Having set up both the first goal and provided the crucial assist that had led to the penalty award, it was only right that he was given the opportunity to finish the job and put the result beyond any lingering doubt. A minute from time, Breitner broke down the left and floated in a perfectly weighted cross for Hoeneß to head home the decisive fourth goal. Bloodied, bruised but far from broken, the big striker rose like a salmon above his marker and thundered the ball with his head past the flailing Kargus to seal Bayern's triumph.

The 1982/83 season saw Hamburger SV continue their domestic dominance, as they became only the third team after Borussia Mönchengladbach and Bayern to retain the Bundesliga title in the professional era. *Die Rothosen* would claim the *Meisterschale* on goal difference ahead of northern rivals Werder Bremen with an impressive fifty-two points, with Bayern finishing eight points adrift in a disappointing fourth place. Bayern's opening game of the season in Bremen had pretty much set the tone for the remainder of the season: an own goal by newly-signed Belgian international goalkeeper Jean-Marie Pfaff.

Having entered the winter break just two points behind the eventual champions after a *Hinrunde* that had included an eleven-match unbeaten run, Pál Csernai's side endured a torrid *Rückrunde* that saw them take just twenty points out of a possible thirty-four. Two mid-May defeats in two matches including a 1-0 home defeat against bogey side Kaiserslautern proved to be the final straw for the coach: after just over four years in charge, the silk-scarved Hungarian had taken the Bayern board as far as they were prepared to go. With just a couple of weeks remaining in the season, Csernai's assistant Reinhard Saftig took up the reins to see things through to the finish.

	P	W	D	L	Goals	GD	Pts
Hamburger SV	34	20	12	2	79:33	+46	52:16
Werder Bremen	34	23	6	5	76:38	+38	52:16
VfB Stuttgart	34	20	8	6	80:47	+33	48:20
FC Bayern München	34	17	10	7	74:33	+41	44:24

Bayern's progress in the cup competitions had not been any better than their Bundesliga campaign, with a second-round defeat in the DFB-Pokal at the hands of strugglers Eintracht Braunschweig being followed by a quarter-final exit in the now defunct European Cup Winners' Cup.

Having disposed of Russian side Torpedo Moscow in the first round and English FA Cup winners Tottenham Hotspur in the second – the latter coming after an emphatic 4-1 win at the Olympiastadion – Bayern met Scottish Cup winners Aberdeen in the last eight, a highly underrated team coached by a certain Alex Ferguson.

After beating the English FA Cup winners in such convincing fashion the German champions were the clear favourites ahead of their meeting with Ferguson's side, but a well-contested goalless draw at the Olympiastadion helped to set the tone perfectly for what would be an equally close return fixture at a chilly Pittodrie Stadium in Scotland's "granite city".

A trademark long-distance cracker from sweeper Klaus Augenthaler gave Bayern the lead just ten minutes into the match, and with Aberdeen needing two goals to progress the visitors were firmly in control of the tie. Seven minutes before half-time however disaster struck for the Bavarians, as Augenthaler blotted his copybook with a dreadful goal line clearance that allowed midfielder Neil Simpson to bundle the ball into the net for the equaliser.

With the score at 1-1 Bayern were still in front on away goals, and with sixteen minutes gone in the second half looked to have settled the contest. A high looping ball into the Aberdeen box from Paul Breitner was only half cleared, and midfielder Hansi Pflügler positioned himself perfectly at the corner of the eighteen-yard box to deliver a stunning left-footed volley that skidded unerringly past Dons' 'keeper Jim Leighton. The home crowd were silenced, and with Bayern now 2-1 in front Ferguson's side once again needed two goals.

With just under a quarter of an hour remaining things continued to look good for *Die Roten*. All they had to do was maintain their concentration to claim their place in the last four. But then came the sucker punch – indeed, a double sucker punch – with the home side scoring twice in the space of a frenetic minute.

On seventy-six minutes, Alex McLeish met a right-sided free-kick from John McMaster and rose above the white-shirted Bayern defence to pull the home side level, and just moments later substitute John Hewitt nodded the ball home after Bayern 'keeper Manfred Müller could only parry a header from nineteen year old Eric Black against the underside of the crossbar.

With Aberdeen ahead in the tie for the first time, there was no way back for Csernai's side. Knocked out cold by the double blow, Bayern were unable to get back on terms to sneak the win on away goals.

More than twenty-thousand delirious Aberdeen fans had witnessed what had arguably been the Scottish club's greatest single footballing moment at Pittodrie, and in one brutal minute yet another European campaign for Bayern had reached its *Endstation*.

Over the years Bayern had provided a number of smaller and less heralded teams with their greatest ever victories in European competition, and Aberdeen were just one more name to be added to the list.

The Dons would eventually go on to lift their first and only European trophy in a soggy Ullevi Stadium in Göteborg against favourites Real Madrid, but for Bayern there was only more pain as just a week after Aberdeen's triumph as Hamburger SV added the coveted European Cup to their Bundesliga title.

On a warm and dry evening in Athens, Italian giants Juventus were sunk courtesy of a memorable long-distance strike from HSV's diminutive midfielder and future Bayern coach Felix Magath as Bayern's northern rivals claimed European football's biggest prize. In doing so, HSV became only the second German team to be crowned as club champions of Europe, seven years after FC Bayern's last triumph in Glasgow in 1976.

Defeat in the quarter-final of the Cup Winners' Cup had been bad enough, but to see Bayern's Bundesliga rivals lift the famous *Henkelpott* was really a case of having a good dose of salt rubbed deep into the gaping wound. I had been a Bayern fan for just over a year, and already I had developed a firm dislike for HSV – something that has lasted to this day even though they are little more than a pale shadow of the great side they once were.

MY FIRST TROPHY

The beginning of the 1983/84 season saw the return to Munich of Udo Lattek, the coach who had guided Bayern to five trophies including the European Cup back in the early 1970s. The disciplined and taciturn yet much-loved East Prussian would always be remembered as the architect of the first great Bayern team, and having been dismissed in 1975 – unfairly, some might argue – he seamlessly transferred his success to rivals Borussia Mönchengladbach, a team that went on to surpass the Bavarians as Germany's number one side during the latter part of the decade. Two fairly nondescript seasons at Borussia Dortmund followed, but in 1981 Lattek landed the plum job of coach at FC Barcelona where he introduced the likes of Bernd Schuster and Diego Maradona.

Also making his way to Munich at the start of the 1983/84 season was the versatile midfielder Søren Lerby, one of the many young stars in a rapidly improving Danish national team. The talented twenty-five year Dane would be an almost direct replacement for old hand Paul Breitner, who had finally hung up his boots after a glittering career for club and country. Meanwhile goalkeeper Walter Junghans ended a five-year spell in Munich with a move to second division Schalke 04.

Udo Lattek's return to the Bavarian capital in the summer of 1983 had been expected by many fans to bring immediate success, but after a far from consistent season Bayern would miss out on *Meisterschale* for the third year in a row. They could only finish in fourth place once again after yet another frustratingly inconsistent season, but unlike the previous year things had been far more competitive at the top of the table.

A tense and dramatic finish saw the four leading sides separated by just a single point, with surprise team VfB Stuttgart denying Hamburger SV a third successive title on goal difference to win the Bundesliga shield for the very first time.

Bayern had finished as the league's top scorers with eighty-four goals in their thirty-four matches and had racked up some record-setting victories, but close behind each victory was always the poor result that would keep them trailing behind the leaders.

When Bayern won it was usually by significant margins – scoring four goals against Mönchengladbach, Nürnberg (twice) and Köln, five against Leverkusen, Bochum and Kaiserslautern, six against Mannheim and Braunschweig, and a record-setting nine against the division's punchbags Kickers Offenbach. In stark contrast they had also fallen to surprise defeats in places where they would have otherwise expected to win, such as Bochum and Düsseldorf.

Although Bayern's chances of winning the title had disappeared the week before the final round of matches, mathematically speaking just one result had determined the difference between the top four sides: the 2-2 draw at the beginning of April 1984 with eventual champions VfB Stuttgart at the Olympiastadion. In a closely contested match Bayern found themselves 2-1 in front midway through the second half, but with just over twenty minutes remaining Icelandic international Ásgeir "Sigi" Sirgurvinsson ensured Stuttgart a share of the points.

The margins between success and failure were incredibly fine, and I ended up spending far too much time playing around with all of the possible permutations, producing a series of "what if" scenarios. I worked out that if Bayern had managed to hold on to their slender advantage against Stuttgart with all other results unchanged, they would have finished the season level on forty-eight points along with Hamburg and Mönchengladbach – though with a goal difference of +44 as opposed to HSV's +39 and Gladbach's +33. New champions Stuttgart meanwhile would have taken a significant drop back down to fourth place, a point behind.

How things actually finished:

	P	W	D	L	Goals	GD	Pts
VfB Stuttgart	34	19	10	5	79:33	+46	48:20
Hamburger SV	34	21	6	7	75:36	+39	48:20
Borussia Mönchengladbach	34	21	6	7	81:48	+33	48:20
FC Bayern München	34	20	7	7	84:41	+43	47:21

How things could have finished without Sigurvinsson's goal:

	P	W	D	L	Goals	GD	Pts
FC Bayern München	34	21	6	7	84:40	+44	48:20
Hamburger SV	34	21	6	7	75:36	+39	48:20
Borussia Mönchengladbach	34	21	6	7	81:48	+33	48:20
VfB Stuttgart	34	19	9	6	78:33	+45	47:21

There was one final dash of irony: before moving to the Neckarstadion at the start of the 1982/83 season, Sigi Sigurvinsson had played seventeen matches for Bayern during 1981/82, scoring one goal.

The near miss in the Bundesliga was compensated somewhat with an exciting DFB-Pokal campaign, which saw Bayern capture the trophy for the second time in three seasons. A hard-fought season had seen some dramatic games, including one that would be indelibly burned on my memory from an afternoon watching *Football Made in Germany*: a scarcely-believable twelve-goal semi-final encounter with Schalke 04, then in the second division.

After racking up nine goals in straightforward wins over second division KSV Hessen Kassel and third division FC Augsburg, *Die Roten* played almost three hours of scoreless football with Bayer Uerdingen before Hansi Pflügler finally settled the issue in the fifty-sixth minute of their third round replay.

Non-league side Bocholt then restricted the free-scoring Bayern side to just two goals in the quarter-final as Lattek's side claimed an unexpectedly tight 2-1 win, which set up a match that will forever remain one of the great German cup classics – an encounter between two sides from different divisions that over the course of three and a half hours would produce some breathtaking see-sawing drama and a staggering seventeen goals.

When the crowd of just under seventy-one thousand people made their way to Gelsenkirchen's Parkstadion on 2nd May 1984, nobody could have known they would be in for a thriller, one of those rare, once-in-a-lifetime footballing spectacles worth every *Pfennig* of the admission fee.

Sitting in second place in the second division, Schalke had come into the game more in hope than expectation – but they were not by any means a pushover for their more illustrious top flight opponents. Among their starting number the *Ruhrpott* side had former Bayern man Walter Junghans in goal, onetime national team captain Bernard Dietz shoring up the defence, and a precocious midfield talent just one day past his eighteenth birthday: the waif-like midfielder Olaf Thon.

In front of a noisy Gelsenkirchen crowd the Bavarians were first off the blocks, sweeping into a 2-0 lead inside the first twelve minutes. With three minutes gone right-sided wing-back Norbert Nachtweih swung a right-sided free-kick into the box, and the famous Rummenigge brothers did the rest. A nod out to the left from Karl-Heinz, and well-placed return cross from younger brother Michael which Kalle stabbed into the net from six yards. Nine minutes later Reinhold Mathy doubled the lead with a wonderful team goal: sweeping forward from deep inside their own half, Søren Lerby sent a high ball out right for the slender winger, who jinked and twisted inside Dietz and exchanged passes with Michael Rummenigge before sweeping the ball past Junghans.

It was all set to be a goal riot, but nobody in the ground could have ever predicted what sort of goal riot it would be.

Within seven minutes of Mathy's goal Schalke were right back in the game with two goals of their own. Seconds after going two down a free-kick from out of the left was floated into the Bayern box for the unmarked Thomas Kruse who buried the chance, and in the nineteenth minute Thon seized on a poor clearing header from Klaus Augenthaler to level the scores. Having wrong-footed Augenthaler and dragged the ball inside the defender with his left foot, the teenager thrashed the ball past Jean-Marie Pfaff at the near post with his right.

It was end to end stuff, and that was just the beginning.

Mere seconds after Schalke had worked their way back into the match, Bayern were in front yet again. So easy: a long ball from Augenthaler, a botched clearance attempt from two white-shirted Schalke defenders, and a smart right-footed finish from Michael Rummenigge.

With the rain now starting to fall, the conditions started to get increasingly tricky as the home side continued to press. Pfaff just about managed to keep hold of the ball in a frenetic goalmouth scramble and Thon shot narrowly wide, but when the half-time whistle blew Lattek's side kept a hold of their lead. Despite the foul weather in the open and expansive stadium, the crowd were being royally entertained by a hard-fought yet open game.

The second half started in much the same way as the first had finished. The visitors could very easily have extended their advantage as a crisp low drive from Nachtweih veered away slightly before hitting the upright, but a catalogue of defensive blunders allowed the hosts to level things up again at three apiece. A poor clearance from Pfaff allowed winger Mathias Schipper to send in a cross from the left, and with the Bayern defenders all over the place Thon – at just 5' 6" the smallest man on the pitch – was right on the spot to head the ball into the empty net.

Just eleven minutes later the game was turned on its head completely, with Peter Stichler giving *Die Knappen* the lead for the first time. With a tiring and increasingly fragile Bayern defence being run ragged by busy striker Klaus Täuber, Michael Opitz' looping ball into the penalty area was nodded home by the unmarked Stichler, who sent the ball into the bottom left-hand corner of the net past Pfaff's desperate dive.

Diethelm Ferner's side should have really closed the game out, but having taken the lead relaxed ever so slightly – allowing Bayern to not only regain their composure but also build up a final head of steam as the clock ticked into the final ten minutes of the ninety. Udo Lattek meanwhile sent on another striker in form of the lumbering giant Dieter Hoeneß in place of defensive midfielder Bernd Dürnberger, and almost immediately the balding big man had the desired impact. Charging down the left, Lerby swung the ball into the Schalke box, and with the defenders concentrating on Hoeneß the unmarked Michael Rummenigge found the back of the Junghans' net with a terrific diving header to claim his second and level the scores at 4-4.

Bayern were now doing most of the pressing as they took their turn to switch up a gear, but neither side was able to force a winner in the last ten minutes. The final whistle guaranteed a further thirty minutes of rain-soaked entertainment for the seventy-thousand plus crowd, and despite the rain hammering down nobody was going anywhere.

The first period of extra time saw the home side have the first chance as a Michael Jakobs shot was smothered by Pfaff, but this was just the calm before the final storm. Halfway through the second period the two sides were still locked at four apiece, but after that this already crazy game would take an even crazier turn.

With eight minutes remaining, Bayern won a free kick just inside the Schalke half, and the reliable Nachtweih swung it high and long into the opposition penalty area. The towering Hoeneß nodded the ball back inside, but only back to the retreating Dietz who played a gentle pass back to 'keeper Junghans. It should have been an easy ball to collect, but the Schalke *Torhüter* made a complete mess of it. As Junghans scrambled desperately to grasp the slippery spherical object, the ever-alert Hoeneß tapped the ball from under the 'keeper's outstretched hand before bundling it into the net.

With a mix of pure elation and relief, the Bayern players celebrated retaking the lead, but this game had a few more twists in its tail yet. Just three minutes later, a Schalke corner was swung in from the right, and once again the red shirts went AWOL. Dietz made the most of the opportunity to make up for his earlier back-pass, sending in a left-footed volley that took a curious trajectory over Pfaff and into the top right-hand corner of the Bayern net. Amidst the wild celebrations from the men in white and the Parkstadion crowd, the bespectacled and taciturn Ferner remained tight-lipped on the touchline.

Perhaps the Schalke coach knew something everybody else didn't. Just three minutes later, the game had swung back towards *Die Roten* again. With the home side pressing for a winner Bayern broke through the centre of the pitch, and the perfect slide-rule pass from Kalle Rummenigge found Hoeneß in space with just Junghans to beat. The giant centre-forward lumbered towards the goal, and looked to have taken the ball too far before crashing a shot that clattered off the legs of the 'keeper before finding its way into the net.

With just two minutes remaining, it was surely all over.

Not a bit of it. As the final whistle approached, the home side had nothing to lose as they threw everything and the kitchen sink forward. As those on the nervous Bayern bench were starting to look at their watches, a mass of white shirts were swarming inside their penalty area like angry bees. Schalke substitute Hubert Clute-Simon called Pfaff into action with a half chance after his shot nutmegged Augenthaler, and the home side won two free kicks just outside the Bayern box in the space of a minute. As the final seconds ticked by, one could sense something hanging in the air. This thrilling take was not over yet.

I have often found myself reliving those final moments again and again, sitting there transfixed as I watch those 120 minutes compressed into ten minutes of frenetic highlights.

As the rain continued to hammer down with the Bayern players desperately waiting for the final whistle, a ragged looking Norbert Nachtweih stood out from the crowd, looking more like a *Nachtweib* in his untucked shirt that resembled a bright red minidress clinging tightly to his torso. One might have thought that such a disturbing sight would have scared away the men in white, but instead they just kept flooding forward, their relentless passion matched by the Gelsenkirchen crowd.

As the clock ticked towards the end of extra time, each passing second felt like an hour. Then, it happened. The second free kick saw a smart step over from Thon, leaving Bernd Dierßen to swing the ball into the Bayern box. Amidst the wet mass of red and white shirts in the crowded penalty area Klaus Augenthaler attempted to clear the danger, first with his foot and then with his head; unable to get any power on his header, Auge was only able to send the ball in an invitingly gentle arc into space on the left.

Lying in wait was the inevitable Thon, whose impulsive left-footed volley was struck with an almost magical timing and precision that left 'keeper Pfaff no chance. The Belgian could only look on helplessly as the ball rocketed past him and high into the right hand-side of the net.

It was the last kick of the match. 6-6. *Unglaublich! Wahnsinn!*

Back in those days a draw after extra time in the DFB-Pokal – apart from the final itself – would result in a replay. And so the teams gathered again in Munich's Olympiastadion the following week.

While nowhere near as frenetic as the classic first encounter at the Parkstadion, this second meeting was almost as exciting. Bayern had taken the lead through Kalle Rummenigge just after the half-hour mark following a neat through-ball from Lerby, and *Die Roten* doubled their advantage a minute before half-time with a goal that truly showcased the elder Rummenigge's arsenal of skills. From a free-kick just outside the opposition box, the Bayern skipper cheekily lifted the ball over the wall – and Dieter Hoeneß did the rest with a cracking shot on the half-volley.

At half-time it looked as if normal service had been resumed, but just minutes after the break Schalke switched things back into crazy mode. It would be that man Thon in the centre of things again, with his lovely threaded pass finding Michael Jakobs who rounded the fast-advancing Pfaff before sliding the ball just inside the post from the tightest of angles. Upping their game and stunning the home crowd, *Die Königsblauen* levelled things up with eighteen minutes remaining as Michael Opitz was able to wriggle into the Bayern box before sending a skidding shot past Pfaff.

As the final ten minutes approached and extra time loomed once more, Bayern played their final ace of the match. Seizing on a mistake in the middle of the pitch from Schipper, Lerby sent substitute Kalle Del'Haye out on the right – whose sharp cross was met by the flying Kalle Rummenigge. Rummenigge's diving header settled the tie once and for all, and was a suitably fitting end to what had been a fantastic spectacle.

It was also one of the few bright moments in a Bayern *Trikot* for the once highly-rated Del'Haye. Having arrived in Bavaria four years earlier from rivals Mönchengladbach, the blond winger had spent much of his time sitting on the sidelines.

Bayern's final against Mönchengladbach in Frankfurt's Waldstadion provided excitement of a more different kind, as both sides lined up for the competition's first-ever penalty shootout. In stark contrast to the two high-scoring and rather frenetic semi-finals, the final was a cagey affair. Frank Mill's strike would take *Die Fohlen* into a half-time lead, and Bayern would have to wait until eight minutes from the end to level the scores through Wolfgang Dremmler. Until then, it looked as though Gladbach were going to hold out; moments before

Dremmler's goal, substitute Reinhold Mathy had struck the base of the post. The thirty minutes of extra time was largely unmemorable; and the highlight I remember seeing more or less jumped straight from Bayern's equaliser to the penalty shootout.

The *Elfmeterschießen* would have its own dramatic and controversial subplot, as Lothar Matthäus – in his final game for Mönchengladbach having already signed for Bayern – launched a rather ugly-looking spot-kick high and wide of the target. Lerby then put Bayern in front before Norwegian Kai-Erik Herlovsen finally put Borussia on the board. The coolest of kicks from Norbert Nachtweih then maintained Bayern's advantage, and Uli Borowka's poorly-taken shot squirmed agonisingly under Jean-Marie Pfaff – prompting a typically theatrical show of rage from the Belgian 'keeper. Wolfgang Grobe just about beat *Foals* 'keeper Ulrich Sude to push *Die Roten* closer towards the finish line, but Hans-Günter Bruns kept his side in the contest with a well-taken shot that gave Pfaff no chance.

Bayern had one kick in hand with the scores level at 3-3, and Klaus Augenthaler would have the opportunity to put the Bavarians one hit or miss away from the trophy. Instead, the usually reliable sweeper hit the ball straight at Sude.

With the shootout now entering the sudden death phase Wilfried Hannes put Gladbach ahead, suddenly heaping all the pressure on Bayern skipper Karl-Heinz Rummenigge. I need not have worried, as King Kalle nonchalantly stroked the ball home. And so it continued: *Hans-Jörg Criens, 5-4 Gladbach. Wolfgang Dremmler, 5-5. Michael Frontzeck, 6-5 Gladbach. Bernd Martin, 6-6.*

Up then stepped Norbert Ringels to keep Gladbach in front. The kick was just too far away from Pfaff for the 'keeper to make the save, but also too wide to hit the back of the net. The unfortunate Ringels could only watch as the ball deflected wide off the post. Bayern now had the opportunity to wrap things up, and Michael Rummenigge did the rest. Showing the same calmness as his brother, the younger Rummenigge gave Sude no chance as he swept the ball home.

In terms of pure drama, Bayern's cup victory of 1983/84 was right up there with the best of them, with both the semi-final and final being edged by the very finest of fine margins. Having not seen any of the successful 1980-81 Bundesliga season or the 1982 *Pokalfinale* against Nürnberg, the penalty shootout of 1984 was "my" first trophy in my three years as an FC Bayern fan.

Fifteen minutes of poorly-edited highlights may not mean much when taken in the context of today's wall to wall television coverage with its glut of live matches and the wonders of interactive "red button" multi-game technology, but back then catching anything that lasted more than a couple of minutes would be akin to finding hens' teeth before locating that elusive needle located at the bottom of the proverbial haystack. With coverage being so extensive today, I'll often while away a Sunday afternoon watching a couple of live Bundesliga matches after that have some La Liga, Serie A or Eredivisie action as ambient background noise; it is so easy to take things for granted, and forget just how difficult things used to be.

Bayern's cup final triumph over Mönchengladbach in 1984 may not have made up for missing out on the Bundesliga and the continued lack of success in European competition, but it is one of those distinct memories that has stayed with me over all these years as a fan.

Bayern's European adventures in the UEFA Cup once again finished prematurely with a 2-1 aggregate third round defeat at the hands of Tottenham Hotspur, with the English club exacting a measure of revenge for the previous year's 4-1 aggregate defeat.

Having scraped a 1-0 win in the first leg at the Olympiastadion with a late Michael Rummenigge goal, the Bavarians were sunk in the return in typically familiar fashion. Scotsman Steve Archibald had levelled up the tie for Spurs with a fifty-second minute strike, and just as the visitors might have been considering extra time striker Mark Falco completed the Spurs comeback with the winner three minutes from time. Once again, Bayern had been undone right at the death and had lost a game that they arguably should have won.

Like Aberdeen in the Cup Winners' Cup the year before, Bayern's conquerors would go on to win the final – beating defending champions RSC Anderlecht on a penalty shootout after a pair of 1-1 draws.

The first round of the competition had seen Bayern play Cypriot side Anorthosis Famagusta, and my living on the island at the time would give me the opportunity to see locally-produced highlights of both matches. My memories of the first leg in Cyprus remain rather hazy – Bayern had eked out a tighter than expected 1-0 win in Larnaca courtesy of a Reinhold Mathy goal – but in the return leg at the Olympiastadion saw sweeper Klaus Augenthaler score a rare hat-trick as *Die Roten* racked up a record-breaking 10-0 win – a result that remains their best in European competition.

Karl-Heinz Rummenigge had set the rout in motion with an angled shot after just five minutes, and with seventeen minutes on the clock a typically robust long-distance effort saw Augenthaler notch up the first of his three strikes. Michael Rummenigge made it three just two minutes later from a far post header, and utility man Wolfgang Dremmler added goal number four on twenty-six minutes after a bustling run into the box from the industrious

Søren Lerby. Just five minutes later Kalle Rummenigge emulated his younger brother with a far post header to score his second and Bayern's fifth, and with eleven minutes of the first half remaining the excellent Lerby thumped the ball into the back of the Famagusta net to bring up the half-dozen.

There was still time for a seventh goal four minutes before the break, with Augenthaler exchanging passes with Lerby outside the box before cutting inside and unleashing a thunderbolt that was still rising as it crashed into the top right-hand corner.

In my first few years as a Bayern fan the man popularly known as "Auge" had quickly become my favourite player in the squad, mainly due to goals like this. You would hardly ever find the lanky and slightly awkward looking sweeper scuffling about inside the box, and nearly every one of his goals had something of the spectacular about it. More often than not, one could see opposition defenders backing away in trepidation as Augenthaler prepared to swing that ferocious right foot and send another blockbuster travelling at speed towards the goal.

The sparse crowd in the Olympiastadion had been disappointing to say the least, but the eight thousand people who turned up on that late September evening in Munich were given three more goals in the second half as Udo Lattek's side slowly and gradually took their foot off the gas. Augenthaler's firm and low free-kick deflected off the defensive wall for Kalle Del'Haye to score *Die Roten's* eighth goal sixteen minutes from time, and just five minutes later Wolfgang Kraus thrashed the ball home to bring up goal number nine.

Nine minutes before full-time Augenthaler scored his third, a very un-Auge like header from close range. The goal completed the sweeper's hat-trick, and took the Bavarians into double figures for the first time in any competitive European tournament match.

At the time I simply enjoyed the goal-feast – in spectacular grainy monochrome on a fourteen inch screen with Greek commentary – but little did I know that it would be the first of many records I would witness as a supporter of FC Bayern. Anorthosis Famagusta may not have been the most testing opponents, but seven goals in the first half of a European tie wasn't something that you'd get to see very often – even in the days when teams from smaller and less heralded countries were little more than cannon fodder.

THE BUNDESLIGA BLACK HOLE

Leaving Cyprus with my family in the early summer of 1984 brought us back home to the UK, but for an FC Bayern fan it was not what one could call a particularly productive move. Just like that, what had been a fairly consistent if small stream of *Deutscher Fußball* had been reduced to a mere trickle. The very basic television service in Cyprus – even with their own domestic teams offering little – had offered a far more healthy diet of European football than any of the four British terrestrial channels, and to make matters worse I'd no longer have the recordings of *Football Made in Germany* to provide me with what had become my regular if infrequent diet of domestic league action.

It was like entering a Bundesliga black hole.

I was still able to catch the highlights from the latter stages of the European club competitions, but as far as the Bundesliga was concerned I quickly found myself thrown right back in the dark zone. To make up for this, I subscribed to both *Shoot* magazine as well as its rival *Match*; my favourite feature in both publications was the small section of European league tables, scoreboards and statistics tucked away in between all of the colour photos of English First Division players, though on occasion one could find an interesting feature article on a Bundesliga star such as Karl-Heinz Rummenigge, Paul Breitner, Pierre Littbarski or Felix Magath.

Bayern striker and two-time European player of the year Rummenigge was by far the most well-known German *Fußballspieler* in England, and as I discovered some years later there had even be a song dedicated to him by a little-known British pop duo.

A rather cringeworthy country-twang ditty by journeyman performer Alan Whittle and his wife Denise, the simply-titled "Rummenigge" had been inspired by the German striker's one-man show in the *Nationalmannschaft's* 2-1 defeat of England in a 1982 friendly at

Wembley – and his "sexy knees". "Rummenigge" unsurprisingly bypassed British audiences completely, but managed to reach number 43 in the German charts in the spring of 1983. It later proved to be particularly popular on the terraces of Hamburg's Volksparkstadion, where it was sung with somewhat ironic glee by the HSV faithful when Bayern came to visit. Having been initially irritated by the song and its being put to use by rival supporters, Rummenigge was soon able to see the funny side – even arranging a meeting with the artists.

What I lacked in visual highlights I made up with what could only be described as extreme football geekery – the sort of time-consuming project that would be lost on most young football fans today. I ended up spending way too much time locating and cutting out any Bayern-related match report from every newspaper I could get hold of, as well as photocopying the relevant pieces from *Match* magazine's fairly comprehensive (at the time) "Match Facts" section – which were then also carefully cut out.

This varied assortment of clippings, scribbles and statistical nuggets were then carefully pasted in my "Bundesliga season diary" – a small exercise book – and at the end of every week I totalled up the points and drew up an updated league table. Unfortunately, all of these items were lost in the many house moves we made, along with the colourful report I had created on the 1986 FIFA World Cup in Mexico and Germany's progress to the final.

Every Monday in between my morning lessons (Thursdays for European midweek matches) I made my way to the school library, where I sifted through the newspapers brought in by the school secretary. The *Daily Telegraph* and the fledgling *Independent* proved to be the most useful sources, and one usually found a small section containing the results from the major European leagues tucked away in some dark and unread corner of the sports pages. Information on midweek matches was far more comprehensive, and if a British team had been involved there was often a decent match report and even the occasional photograph.

These details were very basic but more than enough for me to update the Bundesliga table, and the scrapbook was supplemented with additional information from *Match* or *Shoot*, both of which were sent on later by my parents. Occasionally, I stumbled across a photograph of a Bayern star – usually Rummenigge or Paul Breitner, though I did once find some decent action shots of Klaus Augenthaler, Dieter Hoeneß and Reinhold Mathy – and for major European tournament matches there were additional statistical treats on offer such as goalscorers, attendances, red and yellow cards and even the names of the officials.

It is hard to believe in these days of mass satellite television and easily accessible online resources, but this collection of sorry scraps of paper and snippets of information was like gold dust. Children these days are truly spoiled with all of the easily accessible information they have at their disposal.

German football was at a particularly low ebb at the start of the 1984/85 season, with average attendances falling below the twenty-thousand mark for the first time since the early 1970s and morale being heavily sapped following the failure of the national team to progress beyond the group phase of the 1984 European Championships. Europe as a whole had been going through something of a malaise with the game being riddled with corruption, mismanagement and violent hooliganism, and while Germany would not suffer from these afflictions as badly as Italy, Spain or England, there would clearly be a falling out of love for the game among many.

While today the Allianz Arena in Munich is sold out for every single Bundesliga match, back in the mid- to late-1980s attendances had fluctuated wildly dependent on the opposition. While the likes of Hamburger SV and Borussia Mönchengladbach remained major draws with fixtures pulling in 70,000 plus crowds at the Olympiastadion, matches against less fashionable opposition often saw *Die Roten* performing in front of a stadium that was barely a tenth full. Given the vast expanse of the ground and the presence of the athletics track that separated the spectators from the playing area it often made for a depressing sight, especially on a bleak afternoon in late November or December. It is worth remembering that only eight thousand spectators had turned up for the record-breaking 10-0 UEFA Cup first round victory over Anorthosis Famagusta in the previous season.

The most significant new arrival at the start of the 1984/85 season was course Lothar Matthäus, who finally arrived at the Säbenerstraße in the summer following his much-discussed DM2.4 million move from Borussia Mönchengladbach. The talented midfielder was joined in the first team by a number of players from the Bayern youth and amateur squads, while defender Norbert Eder made the short journey south from Nürnberg. Having scored thirty goals in thirty-five games in the second division for MSV Duisburg, promising twenty-one year old striker Roland Wohlfarth also made his way to the Bavarian capital.

Among those leaving Bayern were Hans Dorfner, Wolfgang Kraus and veteran goalkeeper Manfred Müller, but by far the biggest blow came with the news of the departure of much-loved skipper Karl-Heinz Rummenigge to Serie A side Internazionale. Having started out as a raw teenager at the beginning of the 1974/75 season, "Kalle" – and, of course, his sexy knees – had become part of the furniture in Munich. For many, the Lippstadt-born striker had become the personification of the club following the retirement of Paul Breitner at the end of the 1982/83 season.

It is no exaggeration to say that Rummenigge's decision to leave Bavaria after ten successful seasons was a crushing blow to many Bayern fans.

While the Bundesliga had dominated European club football along with the English First Division during the mid to late 1970s and the early part of the 1980s, the mid 1980s had seen the resurgence of a far more powerful Italian league. Serie A clubs suddenly had plenty of money to throw around, and very soon the cream of world football could be seen plying their trade south of the Alps for the likes of Inter, AC Milan and Juventus. Karl-Heinz Rummenigge was just short of his twenty-ninth birthday when he made his decision to leave Munich, and for him it would be the perfect career move.

The Italian giants paid Bayern what was then a record sum for a Bundesliga player - DM10.5 million, today around €5.6 million – which was also at the time the second-highest transfer fee in the world after Diego Maradona's eye-watering €13 million move from FC Barcelona to Serie A with SSC Napoli. For Bayern, it was a case of adapting to life without "Kalle"; Roland Wohlfarth was a promising signing, but it would take more than just goalscoring potential to fill the boots vacated by a man rightly seen as an FC Bayern legend.

Udo Lattek's side opened their Bundesliga campaign with a comfortable 3-1 win in Bielefeld against Arminia which would take them to the top of the table. Five more straight victories then followed including a 4-2 demolition of rivals Werder Bremen, and by the end of September Bayern were a healthy five points clear of the chasing pack.

A 2-1 home defeat to an in-form Waldhof Mannheim broke the winning streak and a four-game winless spell culminating in a 3-0 defeat in Leverkusen allowed the chasing pack to close the gap down to a point, but it was as if Bayern were teasing the rest. No sooner had the chasers taken a nibble at their heels, *Die Roten* simply switched up a gear and moved away again. At the winter break, Bayern were on twenty-five points, two clear of Bremen in second place.

The second match of the *Rückrunde* saw Werder take revenge for their earlier defeat with their own 4-2 win to once again get within a point of top spot, only for Bayern to embark on an eight-game unbeaten run. Bremen continued to maintain the pressure however, and even after this eight-game stretch Bayern's lead was still only three points. A 2-1 defeat in Hamburg in late April allowed Werder to once again get within a point, but then Bayern gave up with the constant teasing and finally put their foot down as they approached the final straight.

With four wins from five matches including a 4-0 thrashing of third-placed Borussia Mönchengladbach, Bayern were two points ahead of Werder ahead of the final afternoon, needing just a draw against bottom side Eintracht Braunschweig to secure the title. The encounter at the Städtisches Stadion an der Hamburger Straße was far from pretty, but a goal from Dieter Hoeneß four minutes into the second half was enough to take the points and the coveted *Meisterschale* back to Munich. No doubt aware of Bayern's goal in Braunschweig, Bremen then went on to concede two second half goals in Dortmund to leave Lattek's side clear at the top by four a slightly flattering four points.

	P	W	D	L	Goals	GD	Pts
FC Bayern München	34	21	8	5	79:38	+41	50:18
SV Werder Bremen	34	18	10	6	87:51	+36	46:22

Bayern's football during 1984/85 had not been the most spectacular, but nobody involved with the club cared too much. Udo Lattek's disciplined and slightly conservative approach had garnered results, and even without Kalle Rummenigge Bayern had won its first Bundesliga title after four years – finally breaking the stranglehold that had been established for much of the early part of the decade by Hamburger SV.

The campaign to retain the DFB-Pokal in 1984/85 would not start auspiciously for Bayern as they struggled to see off non-league BV 08 Lüttringhausen with ten men in the first round of the competition, but they would show far less mercy in the second round with part-timers TSV Friesen Hänigsen being subjected to an eight-goal thrashing. 1-0 and 3-1 wins against Waldhof Mannheim and Bayer Leverkusen were enough to secure their place in the semi-finals, and a replay of the previous year's final showpiece against Borussia Mönchengladbach saw *Die Roten* once again taken into extra time before Søren Lerby settled the issue from the penalty spot four minutes from the end of the first fifteen-minute period.

In reaching the final, Bayern were not only hunting down their eighth DFB-Pokal, but also their first domestic double since 1969. Their opponents were Karl-Heinz Feldkamp's solid but unspectacular Bayer Uerdingen, a workmanlike team that had largely flown under the radar in finishing in a respectable eighth place in the Bundesliga. Not surprisingly, Bayern would start the match as red-hot favourites.

The two league meetings between the two sides earlier in the season had seen Bayern come out on top with a 3-1 win in Krefeld and a far more competitive 2-1 result in Munich, but despite Uerdingen's reputation as a robust unit nobody was expecting anything other than a

Bayern victory when the two teams lined up in West Berlin on the last Sunday of May 1985. Having been played in a number of different stadiums since the Second World War the final of the DFB-Pokal had finally returned to Berlin, signalling a new era with the veritable Olympiastadion being touted as "Germany's Wembley".

In my ongoing mission to keep up with Bayern's progress I had decided to experiment with longwave radio, and more by luck than design I stumbled across what was a rather scratchy sound coming from a German station. Amid the beeping, buzzing, scratching and hissing I was able to pick up the words "München", "Berlin" and "Pokal", and with everybody else out and about I retreated to my dormitory to spend the afternoon with my Walkman. Even if I could pick up a fraction of what was going on, it was better than nothing at all – and I could always verify things later on the teletext and the following week in that small section of the sports pages reserved for European results.

I joined the match after around a quarter of an hour, with the score already at 1-1. Dieter Hoeneß had opened the scoring in the eighth minute for Bayern with a cracking left-footed effort, but within a minute skipper Klaus Augenthaler had inadvertently helped on a left-wing cross from Uerdingen winger Werner Buttgereit, setting up midfielder Horst Feilzer who cracked the ball past 'keeper Raimond Aumann – in the starting eleven as a replacement for the injured Jean-Marie Pfaff – into the Bayern net.

The underdogs were first to find their rhythm and quickly set the pace with *Libero* and captain Matthias Herget in particularly fine form, and Icelandic international Lárus Guðmundsson would have the ball in the Bayern net only to have his effort disallowed for offside – a really bad decision from the linesman, as I later discovered. Udo Lattek's side had been largely outplayed, and were perhaps rather fortunate to be going into the break with the score level at 1-1.

In the meantime I had managed to get a steady if faint signal on the radio, and dared not meddle around with the tuning during the break. Both in Berlin and deep in the Quantock forest in Somerset, everything was finely balanced.

Less than three minutes into the second half Bayern received a major blow, with Wolfgang Dremmler sent off for a late challenge on the dangerous and highly mobile Wolfgang Schäfer. Being unable to see what was going on I would have no real idea whether the dismissal had been merited or not, but it must have been bad as Dremmler was shown a straight red card. Playing against an energetic and committed Uerdingen side that had more than held their own during the first half had been difficult enough, but now Bayern found themselves having to play the remaining forty or so minutes with just ten men.

Things didn't get any better. With the radio commentator getting increasingly excited as Uerdingen continued to press, I felt that a genuine shock was in the offing. Six minutes past the hour another Uerdingen attack initiated by the classy Herget saw Buttgereit release the dangerous Schäfer, who easily beat a lumbering Norbert Eder before tucking the ball past a grounded Aumann as the team from Krefeld retook the lead.

The Bayern coach responded by replacing defender Holger Willmer for another attacker in Michael Rummenigge, but there was to be no comeback from a beleaguered Bayern. Indeed, their opponents could easily have won by a bigger margin. Friedhelm Funkel sent the ball flying high over the crossbar with the goal at his mercy, and substitute Peter Loontiens did all of the hard work to create a shooting chance only to scuff his shot straight at Aumann. With Feldkamp's side dominating every facet of the game in the second half, there was only ever going to be one winner, and as I sat back to scribble the details into my scrapbook there really wasn't much to write about.

At the time I thought about Bayern being reduced to ten men and whether it might have made any difference to the outcome, but having watched the game with a slightly clearer head some years later I don't think it would have made any difference. Dremmler's red card was perfectly justified, Bayern had been completely out-thought and outplayed, and Uerdingen's first major trophy had been well deserved. I would just have to wait a little longer to see the domestic double.

The 1984-85 European campaign is one I'll remember for all the wrong reasons as an FC Bayern fan. After three years in Cyprus I was now back in the UK and resident at a boarding school in the south-west, tucked away in the forest in deepest Somerset – where many a late night was spent sneaking into the common room to get a glimpse of those all-important midweek European games. Risking punishment – which meant anything from washing up hundreds of filthy plates after dinner through to chopping logs and receiving a couple of hefty blows across the palm of the hand with a heavy duty nautical ruler - was no great deterrent. Quite simply, if there was even the slightest chance that Bayern would be on the television, it just could not be missed.

Bayern's victory in the previous year's DFB-Pokal had won them a place in the European Cup Winners' Cup, and they eased into the competition with a straightforward 6-2 aggregate victory over Norwegian side Moss FK. *Die Roten* were given a far sterner test in their second round encounter with understated Bulgarians Trakia Plovdiv, who after going down 4-1 in Munich had threatened a comeback by taking a two-goal lead thirteen minutes either side of half-time in the return leg. Plovdiv had needed just one more to level things up at 4-4 on aggregate and snatch the tie on away goals, but Bayern just about did enough to hold firm and make their way into the last eight.

The quarter-final pitted Lattek's side against Italian cup winners and the previous year's European Cup runners-up AS Roma, providing me with my first sighting that season – courtesy of a sneaky night-time visit to the common room at the end of the corridor. In watching the late night football highlights during the 1980s you never had any idea what matches were going to be shown when – or if at all. More often than not I found myself waiting for a less interesting match to end, only for it to be followed by another even less interesting match. It was all part of the fun – well, it was fun until you got caught red-handed by a patrolling housemaster who made Argus Filch from the *Harry Potter* books look like a paragon of kind-hearted generosity.

Bayern had created plenty of chances throughout the first half of the first leg in Munich, but had to wait until a minute before the break for the opener. It was worth the wait, as Norbert Nachtweih rolled the ball into the path of skipper Klaus Augenthaler, who thumped a thirty-yard piledriver into the top left-hand corner of the Roma net.

More opportunities were created in the second half, and the pressure from the home side finally paid off with a second from Dieter Hoeneß thirteen minutes from time. The big blond striker collected an inswinging cross from the left, and showed great skill that defied his reputation as clumsy finisher as he calmly rounded 'keeper Franco Tancredi before stabbing the ball home from six yards. Quietly ecstatic at the result, I carefully made my way back to my dorm. From my night-time tactical operation through to the result, everything had gone perfectly to plan.

It was much the same scenario for the second leg. I had quietly sneaked out of my dormitory – trying desperately to avoid making too much of a noise with the squeaking door – before making my way to the common room. It was a relatively short walk along the darkened corridor, but one that was filled with danger: should the housemaster have been lurking around the corner, there would be no place to hide. Thankfully, the unmistakable flash of light from his torch offered a clear signal of any impending danger.

Having made it inside – opening the door ever so slightly to squeeze inside and avoid making too much of a noise, I carefully made my way towards the television, weaving my way in the darkness past the pool table and through a maze of sofas and armchairs. There was no remote control, but the advantage was that you could turn down the volume before actually switching the thing on – avoiding a sudden burst of noise that would have brought the operation to a premature end. Despite being tempted to raise the sound a little, I stood by the television and watched in silence, my index finger hovering over the off button.

I tuned into BBC1, and *Sportsnight* – the midweek sports show that would, among other things, feature potted highlights from all of the European club tournaments and, if I was lucky, a few minutes of the Bayern match. (This would only really work from the quarter-finals onwards, unless Bayern were playing a British team in one of the earlier rounds). Of course, not knowing what was actually going to be in the potted highlights package was one of the biggest problems: one could stand there in front of the television in stomach-churning fear of being rumbled for well over an hour without actually getting to see anything.

Having seen highlights of the first leg I lived in hope of seeing the return, and waited patiently. Liverpool versus Austria Wien, followed by highlights of some of the other European Cup matches. Then – if my memory serves me correctly – Manchester United's UEFA Cup quarter-final against Hungarian side Videoton, which resulted in a penalty shootout. Then, finally, the Cup Winners' Cup, and Everton's meeting with Dutch outfit Fortuna Sittard. I waited as patiently as I could for highlights of the Bayern match, but nothing came.

The programme ended, and found myself sloping disappointedly back to bed, trying not to drag my feet too much along the way. I found out the next morning that Bayern had triumphed 2-1 in Rome with goals from Lothar Matthäus and Ludwig Kögl, completing a 4-1 aggregate win and sealing a place in the semi-finals against the previous season's FA Cup winners Everton.

I had been able to watch the first leg of the semi-final at home during the Easter holidays, which had finished goalless - not a bad result to take to Goodison Park a fortnight later. The second leg on the other hand quickly turned into something of a nervy encounter - for me, in more ways than one as I found myself sneaking once again into the common room to catch that unmissable quarter of an hour of *Sportsnight* on BBC1. As I carefully switched on the television set, like a ghost appearing out of the darkness emerged the kind and welcoming moon-shaped face of the late Tony Gubba.

After almost getting caught and having to swiftly dive behind the sofa with the score at 0-0 – Sepp Maier, Oliver Kahn, Manuel Neuer, eat your hearts out – I switched the television back on to find Bayern a goal up. *Yes!* I wasn't able to see Dieter Hoeneß' thirty-seventh minute strike until my return home – thankfully, my younger brother had recorded all of the highlights for me – but after that first scare it was a constant struggle to keep silent and at the same time have one eye looking out for a flash of a torch from the corridor.

Half-time arrived, and the Toffees needed two goals to make it into the final. A headed equaliser from an unmarked Graeme Sharp brought the Howard Kendall's side level just three minutes after the restart, but that would be the end of the semi-final for me. Taking my own eye off the ball, I had simply forgotten where I was and the crime I was committing. The door suddenly swung open, the light from the torch catching me almost straight in the face – standing and unable to move like a startled fawn – with my finger glued in panic to the off button.

I had been well and truly rumbled. This time, there was no escape from the punishment that awaited me.

With nary a word, I found myself being frogmarched to the dormitory master's room where I was administered a swift strike across the palm of each hand with a service issue nautical ruler. Now if you haven't seen a service issue nautical ruler, you should try looking one up on the Internet: it is a long, well-made piece of heavy-duty plastic, and some of us service kids would have one. Unfortunately, our dormitory master was equipped with one too.

Each stroke – imagine the sound of a full-blooded Klaus Augenthaler shot cracking against the crossbar – was accompanied by the slightest wince, but no sound. If Bayern were to win the game, it would be more than worth it. I could have tried sneaking in to the common room again to catch the final few minutes of the action at Goodison Park – some braver souls may well have done – but not even I was that suicidal.

With my palms still burning I was hastily sent back to my dormitory to await the remainder of my punishment the following day, but this was the least of my worries. Well, let's just say that I would have happily taken another couple of slapped palms and whole month's washing up in return for a Bayern win after I saw the final result the next day. *Everton 3, Bayern Munich 1.*

Yes, Bayern were out and I ended up spending two evenings of the following week elbow-deep in lukewarm greasy soap suds. I would meet a similar fate during the World Cup finals the following year, but this one would be particularly painful. With every greasy plate and food-encrusted fork, I visualised the annoying Andy Gray putting Everton 2-1 in front, before seeing Trevor Steven deliver the *coup de grâce*.

With the defeat at Goodison Park, all of the talk of a trophy treble quickly disappeared down the memory hole, and yet another European adventure had come to an end. Everton meanwhile went on to win the Cup Winners' Cup final at the De Kuip in Rotterdam – the scene of Bayern's 1982 Champions' Cup defeat – with a 3-1 demolition of Austrian side Rapid Wien.

The end of the 1984/85 season witnessed a catastrophic event that turned European football on his head: the disaster at Heysel Stadium in Brussels on the evening of the European Cup final between Liverpool and Juventus, which resulted in death of thirty-nine people and injury to hundreds more. The horrific events of that balmy and surreal May evening in the Belgian capital would result in all English club sides being banned from the three major European competitions until the beginning of the following decade.

UEFA's controversial but not wholly unsurprising decision changed the face of European club football, which during the late 1970s and early 1980s had largely been dominated by English clubs. Up until Juve's controversial 1-0 victory in 1985 the European Cup had remained in England since Liverpool's victory over Borussia Mönchengladbach in 1977, with the only break in the series coming in 1983 when Hamburger SV had claimed the crown in Athens.

England's loss would of course be the rest of Europe's gain, and Bayern in particular must have fancied their chances of profiting from this unfortunate situation. Four of the previous five seasons had seen *Die Roten* beaten by English sides, all of which would go on to win the competition: Liverpool (European Cup, 1981), Aston Villa (European Cup, 1982), Tottenham Hotspur (UEFA Cup, 1984) and Everton (European Cup Winners' Cup, 1985).

In contrast to the previous season there were few headline-making transfers, with a number of low-key players heading to Munich. Defender Helmut Winklhofer returned to Bavaria after three seasons with Bayer Leverkusen, striker Frank Hartmann was signed from Hannover 96, and midfielder Hans-Dieter Flick – later to become assistant coach of the national team – was signed from Oberliga Baden-Württemberg champions SV Sandhausen.

Among those on the way out were veterans Bernd Dürnberger and Bernd Martin, but perhaps the saddest departure was that of Kalle Del'Haye, arguably the most famous benchwarmer in the history of the club. Signed right at the peak of his career from Borussia Mönchengladbach in the summer of 1980, the blond winger had already made two appearances for the *Nationalmannschaft* as well as being part of the winning Euro 1980 squad. Touted as one of Germany's brightest young talents, a move to Bayern seemed to be the perfect springboard in a burgeoning career. Alas, it was not to be.

Unable to fit into a suitable role in Pál Csernai's side, Del'Haye quickly found his regular place in the team – on the substitutes' bench. There were a few memorable moments – he was one of the scorers in Bayern's record European victory over Anorthosis Famagusta and had come off the bench to provide the assist for the winning goal in the 1984 cup semi-final against Schalke – but for most part his five years in Munich amounted to little more than stagnation. Having made just seventy-four first-team appearances in five years, Del'Haye, his two international caps a distant memory, departed for Fortuna Düsseldorf on a free transfer.

The 1985/86 season saw *Die Roten* retain the Bundesliga title in truly dramatic fashion, but once again I was unable to catch even a minute of the action. With no Bundesliga highlights on British television and no more access to the life-saver that was *Football Made in Germany*, I continued to use the radio with varying levels of success. Outside of the really big matches searching for something was far more trouble than it was worth, and I often found myself spending time tuning back and forth and find some football commentary, only to then discover that I was listening to Bordeaux versus Sochaux in the French league.

As a result I found myself almost completely reliant on my Bundesliga scrapbook and Teletext, which for me had been a recent and most helpful technological discovery. However, while both Ceefax on the BBC and Oracle on ITV provided a decent enough overview of the results from the major European leagues, that was as far as the level of detail usually went; I quite often found myself using my imagination and making up the goals in my head, even if I had been unsure who had actually scored.

While Bayern had been a constant feature at the top end of the German game from the early 1970s – apart from the drop in form between 1977 and 1979 following the departure of Franz Beckenbauer – their rivals continued to come and go. Local rivals TSV 1860 München had dropped away at the latter end of the 1960s, Borussia Mönchengladbach had turned into a fierce rival during the 1970s only to fade away and be replaced by Hamburger SV, who would challenge for supremacy in the late 1970s and early 1980s. HSV's gradual demise in turn coincided with the rise of their northern rivals Werder Bremen, who under long-time coach Otto Rehhagel quickly became one of Bayern's serious domestic adversaries during the mid to late 1980s.

Coached by the unorthodox and outspoken Rehhagel and managed by the local left-wing politician Wilfried "Willi" Lemke, Werder Bremen developed a reputation as a cult club for many Bundesliga-watchers during the early 1980s: the living antithesis of the all-powerful beast that was FC Bayern. While the two teams became serious and at times bitter rivals on the pitch, ideological blows were also traded off it as well: there was little love lost between the bellicose and highly opinionated Lemke and the larger than life Bayern general manager Uli Hoeneß, and the constant sniping from both sides became a popular sideshow for many observers in the German media.

The 1985/86 Bundesliga season was one that would be particularly memorable, even though I would never get to see a minute of it. Just following and plotting Bayern's progress week by week was fascinating enough, but the final dénouement was something that made all of the photocopying, cutting, pasting and endless scribbling worthwhile. Heavily involved in this intriguing plot was the ugly green creature from the north, Werder Bremen.

Bayern had started the season in the worst possible way with a 1-0 defeat on the road at Bayer Uerdingen, setting the tone for what would turn into a disjointed and inconsistent *Hinrunde*. Although Udo Lattek's side were only three points adrift of leaders Bremen at the end of the first half of the season, they had suffered no fewer than five defeats including an embarrassing 4-0 thrashing at the hands of lowly Fortuna Düsseldorf and a 3-0 reverse at mid-table Bochum.

The start of the *Rückrunde* had seen a little more consistency, with Bayern putting together an eight-game unbeaten spell that saw them climb back up to second spot, though still three points off the lead. The unbeaten run would come to a sudden and inexplicable end however when Fortuna Düsseldorf – by now struggling in the relegation zone – walked away from the Olympiastadion with a 3-2 win to complete a rare home and away double, but this setback simply made Bayern up their game yet again.

The defeat against Düsseldorf sparked Lattek's men into embarking on yet another unbeaten streak, one that saw them gather momentum just at the right time. Bayern scored four times in Mannheim against Waldhof, avenged their earlier 3-0 defeat in Bochum in handing out a resounding 6-1 thrashing at the Olympiastadion, and put five past an off-colour Kaiserslautern. Meanwhile, leaders Bremen had slowly started to buckle under the pressure.

Having not quite touched the summit all season, *Die Roten* had somehow managed to claw themselves to within a point of the league leaders, and the penultimate set of fixtures would throw the top two together at the Weserstadion for what was billed as the ultimate make or break encounter. One couldn't have arranged the fixtures any better: a win for Bayern would take them to the top spot on goal difference, a draw would just about keep them in the hunt with Werder maintaining the advantage, while a defeat would give the northerners their first-ever Bundesliga title. I could only imagine how tense it must have been for both the players and the crowd of just under forty-one thousand people.

	P	W	D	L	Goals	GD	Pts
SV Werder Bremen	32	20	8	4	82:39	+43	48:16
FC Bayern München	32	20	6	6	76:31	+45	46:18

The match could not have been more dramatic – though at the time I wouldn't have known to what extent. When I filled in my scrapbook and carefully scribbled in the match details some weeks afterwards it would simply read as *Werder Bremen 0, Bayern München 0* – enough to keep Bayern in with a shout going into the final week. What I didn't know at the time was that Werder had been awarded a penalty a minute from the end – only for Polish defender Michael Kutzop to send his kick against the the right goalpost.

Soon after coming on for Norbert Meier, Bremen's Rudi Völler had darted towards the Bayern penalty area, chasing down the ball with Søren Lerby. Stumbling slightly as he tried to keep up with the striker, the Dane felt the ball hit his face as Völler attempted to hook it towards the goal – only to see referee Volker Roth pointing to the penalty spot for handball. Replays from all available angles showed that the ball had been nowhere near Lerby's hands, but the protests from the Bayern players were just waved away by the official.

A small crowd of journalists and cameramen had gathered behind the Bayern goal and even the local police were on standby at the edge of the terraces as Kutzop stepped up to address the ball, having one last exchange of words with Michael Rummenigge before his one-on-one with Jean-Marie Pfaff. It was almost the perfect penalty: taking his run-up from the edge of the box, the Pole stroked his kick firmly to his right and Pfaff's left. Completely helpless and almost rooted to the spot, the Bayern 'keeper could only watch as the ball flew past him – and struck the outside of the upright before spinning away behind for a goal kick.

Bremen had been, quite literally, just one spot-kick away from the title; a couple of inches of aluminium had made all the difference. Kutzop had taken more than forty penalty kicks in a Bundesliga career that had spanned eleven years for both Werder and Kickers Offenbach, and this would be his only miss in all that time.

Having maintained their two-point lead going into the final day, Bremen remained marginal favourites to claim their first title. With Bayern facing fourth-placed Borussia Mönchengladbach at the Olympiastadion, the *Green-Whites* were at fifth-placed VfB Stuttgart, a team that they had beaten 6-0 earlier in the season. While Bayern needed nothing less than a win over Mönchengladbach and a Bremen defeat just to be in with a chance of snatching the title, Rehhagel's men just needed a draw.

	P	W	D	L	Goals	GD	Pts
SV Werder Bremen	33	20	9	4	82:39	+43	49:17
FC Bayern München	33	20	7	6	76:31	+45	47:19

By half-time, things were already going Bayern's way. A goal in the opening minute from Lothar Matthäus and a twenty-fifth minute strike from Dieter Hoeneß had given the Bavarians a comfortable advantage at the Olympiastadion, while some two-hundred kilometres to the west at the Neckarstadion in Stuttgart a goal from Karl Allgöwer on twenty-two minutes had put the home side in front. As things stood at that time, Bayern were on top of the table on goal difference.

Things only got better. Roared on by a capacity crowd of seventy thousand, the second half in Munich saw Bayern score four more goals without reply to wrap up a convincing 6-0 win, while Allgöwer scored a second for Stuttgart. Manfred Burgsmüller pulled one back for Bremen eleven minutes from the end to heighten the drama and make for a nail-biting final ten minutes, but Rehhagel's side were unable to score the vital second goal to snatch the title – or rather snatch it back.

	P	W	D	L	Goals	GD	Pts
FC Bayern München	34	21	7	6	82:31	+51	49:19
SV Werder Bremen	34	20	9	5	83:41	+42	49:19

Werder Bremen had floundered when it really mattered, and Bayern – like a racehorse advancing on the inside rail in the final straight – had timed their run to perfection to take the race by a short nose on the line. After being second best for the entire season the Bavarians had snatched the *Meisterschale* right at the death from right under Bremen's nose, adding more needle to the burgeoning rivalry between the two sides.

As had been the case in 1984/85, Bayern's path to the final of the DFB-Pokal had been smooth and relatively trouble-free. Regulation 3-1 wins at both Kickers Offenbach and Saarbrücken in the opening two rounds were followed by a slightly more testing encounter against VfL Bochum, who held the Bavarians to a 1-1 draw at the Ruhrstadion before succumbing 2-0 in the replay in Munich. Bogey side Kaiserslautern were summarily dispatched 3-0 in the quarter-final, and two goals in the semi-final against Waldhof Mannheim were enough to take Bayern to West Berlin, where they would play VfB Stuttgart.

Having failed in trying to pick up even the faintest signal from one of the German radio stations, I had resigned myself to finding out the result that evening on the teletext. There was to be no repeat of the previous year's close-run contest; in what proved to be a fairly gentle workout for Bayern, two goals from Roland Wohlfarth effectively finished the contest before half-time. Michael Rummenigge added two more in the space of seven minutes in the second half, and although Guido Buchwald got Stuttgart on the board with fifteen minutes remaining Wohlfarth completed a memorable cup final hat-trick just two minutes later.

There was enough time for a twenty-one year old Jürgen Klinsmann to score another consolation goal for the Swabians, but Bayern had done enough to secure a record-extending eighth cup victory. Having missed out the previous year against Bayer Uerdingen, Bayern had sealed their second domestic double – their first such success in seventeen years.

Having secured back to back Bundesliga titles and the domestic league and cup double Bayern were head and shoulders above the opposition in Germany, but on their European travels there was more disappointment. Their first Champions' Cup campaign in four years saw Lattek's team fall in the quarter-finals at the hands of Belgian champions RSC Anderlecht, but it was a tie that *Die Roten* could and perhaps should have won.

Bayern's early exit from European competition at the quarter-final stage meant that I didn't get to see any extended match highlights that season, and had to be satisfied with what amounted in total to around four minutes of goals. I had asked my brother back home to record every single European highlights segment on both *Sportsnight* and ITV's *Midweek Sports Special*, in the hope that they might happen to include the goals from the Bayern games.

During the course of Bayern's 1985/86 European Cup campaign, I had only got to see the goals from the 3-3 draw in the second leg of the second round tie against Austria Wien and the first leg of the quarter final against Anderlecht – a closely-contested match that had seen Bayern take a 2-0 first half lead through Dieter Hoeneß and Roland Wolhfarth only for the Belgians to snatch a late away goal that would prove crucial ahead of the return leg a fortnight later in Brussels.

With Bayern unable to find a way through at the Constant Vander Stockstadion, two goals in the space of six minutes just before half-time would be enough for Anderlecht to draw the line under yet another failed European adventure for the *Münch'ner*.

Bayern's quarter-final defeat in Brussels ended what had been an interesting series of results: in every European competition *Die Roten* had played since 1980, they had gone on to be beaten by the eventual winners. With Anderlecht unable to continue the trend as they fell to Romanian champions Steaua București in the semi-finals, the final produced one of the biggest shocks in the tournament's history as the Romanians went on to beat favourites Barcelona on penalties after more than two hours of goalless tedium.

IT MEANS NOTHING TO ME

The 1986/87 season would see a drama-packed year for the *Münch'ner*, with Udo Lattek's side relinquishing their domestic cup title early on at the hands of Fortuna Düsseldorf before confidently marching on to a third successive Bundesliga title – an achievement that added yet one more record to the Bayern coach's impressive resumé.

Lattek had over the years shown himself to be a proven master in building excellent squads, and with the core unit already in place the coach set about fine-tuning the team. Internationally-proven and highly versatile wing-back Andreas Brehme was signed from Kaiserslautern and promising young midfielder Hans Dorfner made his way back to Munich from Nürnberg.

Among these more recognised names was the somewhat unknown young Danish striker Lars Lunde, a summer signing from Swiss side Young Boys Bern. The Swiss league may not have been the most accurate barometer of international quality, but the Bayern scouts, in their ongoing search to find a suitable long-term replacement for Karl-Heinz Rummenigge, had seen potential in the twenty-two year old Dane, who had topped the goalscoring charts in Switzerland.

The end of the previous season had seen the retirement of established squad men Wolfgang Dremmler and Wolfgang Grobe, while the unsettled Bertram Beierlorzer headed west to VfB Stuttgart. Perhaps the most significant loss however was midfield pocket battleship Søren Lerby, who after three successful years in Bavaria headed across the border to join French League outfit AS Monaco.

Bayern started slowly, and a rather unspectacular start to their Bundesliga campaign saw them draw almost as many matches as they would win. An opening eleven-game unbeaten run with six wins and five draws had taken them to the top of the table ahead of Bayer Leverkusen, but a surprise 3-0 home defeat to the *Werkself* at the beginning of November helped create a tight bunching together at the top with four teams tied on seventeen points. With a dozen games played new leaders Leverkusen led the way on goal difference, ahead of Hamburger SV, Bayern and Werder Bremen.

The Leverkusen defeat had fallen in the middle of what turned into Bayern's poorest spell of the season – a four-game winless streak that had included three draws – but two more wins and two more draws saw them move back into second spot on goal difference behind HSV at the end of the *Hinrunde*.

With Lattek's side threatening to break the record for the most draws in a Bundesliga season, the winter break arrived just in time. Having initially picked up where they had left off at the end of the *Hinrunde* the second half of the season would see a massive improvement in the win-draw ratio. Having started with two draws and a win from their first three games in the *Rückrunde* to remain in second place behind new leaders Leverkusen, an inspired eight-game winning streak was the catalyst for what would prove to be a decisive charge for the title. Having managed to see off title rivals Hamburg with a well-contested 2-1 win at the Volksparkstadion courtesy of a late Michael Rummenigge goal, by match day twenty-seven Bayern were comfortable five points clear of the *Rothosen*.

The winning streak came to an end with a goalless stalemate in Leverkusen, but having finally found more consistent form Bayern continued unbeaten to the end of the season. The race for the title was effectively over with three games remaining, with the winning point secured at the Olympiastadion with a 2-2 draw against Bayer Uerdingen.

The final table would see the Bavarians finish six points clear of HSV, with twenty wins, thirteen draws and just the one defeat.

	P	W	D	L	Goals	GD	Pts
FC Bayern München	34	20	13	1	67:31	+36	53:15
Hamburger SV	34	19	9	6	69:37	+32	47:21

Away from home, Bayern finished as the first team to go through an entire Bundesliga season unbeaten – a record that would only be matched by Jupp Heynckes' treble-winning team in 2012/13. As had been the case in 1986/87, in 2012/13 Bayern would only lose the one match – at home to Bayer Leverkusen.

Interestingly, Bayern's 1-0 win at the Bökelberg against Borussia Mönchengladbach in April 1987 kick-started what would be a ten-game winning streak for the *Die Fohlen* – a final charge that saw them climb from eleventh place in the league table to third. This winning streak would remain unmatched for more than twenty years until VfL Wolfsburg achieved the same feat in 2008/09 en route to claiming the title – only for Bayern to once again claim the record for themselves with a run of fourteen successive victories in 2012/13.

Bayern had taken their excellent domestic form into the European Cup, where after a masterful and goal-packed campaign they reached their second final in the space of five years. With no English teams to offer a threat, for many fans the time had surely come for Bayern to reestablish themselves as the continent's leading footballing power and claim a fourth European crown. Udo Lattek had assembled what was arguably the strongest and most talented Bayern squad since his own European Cup winning team of the mid-1970s, and surely the time had come for Matthäus, Augenthaler and co. to finally bring the *Henkelpott* back to Munich.

A 2-0 aggregate first round victory over Dutch champions PSV Eindhoven was followed by a trouble-free 3-1 win over Austria Wien, while a repeat of the previous year's quarter-final encounter with Anderlecht saw the Bavarians exact some brutal revenge as they romped to a 5-0 triumph at the Olympiastadion before drawing 2-2 in Brussels.

For my final year at school I had been moved to another building with no resident housemaster, making the task of sneaking from my dormitory to the common room considerably easier. However, this was still not without its hazards, which included the headmaster making his nightly rounds. This I had discovered to my cost the previous year, when I had been caught watching an otherwise meaningless World Cup first round match between France and Canada – a crime for which I was banned from watching all World Cup matches for a week.

Unlike in the previous common room the television was very close to the door, meaning that the brightness had to be lowered right down to prevent the telltale sliver of light from shining through the large gaps in the old Victorian-era door frame. Standing right next to the screen with my finger hovering over the off button, I tuned one ear to the door, carefully listening out for the distinctive gentle warning squeak of the staircase below and the almost metronomic *click-click* of the paws of the Head's dog – a large and slightly whiffy *Deutsche Schäferhund* called Starsky.

Standing in the darkness in a heightened state of alertness was crazy enough, but having to squint at what looked like little more than a strange silent movie consisting of a collection of faint shadows chasing a dark grey blob around an almost pitch-black background was clearly complete and utter madness. I knew full well that being caught could end up with my being banned indefinitely from watching any football and spending most of my weekend free time chopping logs, but to see even five minutes of condensed highlights of Bayern thrashing Anderlecht was always going to be worth the risk.

Bayern were two goals up before half-time thanks to Kalle Rummenigge and Hansi Pflügler, but it took until the sixty-ninth minute for Dieter Hoeneß to scramble in the third. A convincing victory was turned into a resounding thrashing in the final three minutes, with Hoeneß adding a fourth and Roland Wohlfarth getting on the scoresheet a minute from time. None of the goals had been particularly spectacular, but I for one wasn't complaining as I quietly made my way back through the dark corridor to my room. Barring the biggest turnaround in the history of the European Cup, Bayern were safely into the semi-finals.

Anderlecht took the lead just after half an hour of the second leg when Juan Lozano was gifted a chance by Andy Brehme, but Wohlfarth's equaliser eleven minutes after the break put paid to any lingering Belgian hopes. Needing an impossible six more unanswered goals the home side were left playing for pride, and they looked to have salvaged a win when Luc Nilis worked his way into the Bayern box and scuffed his shot past his countryman Jean-Marie Pfaff. However just two minutes from time Lothar Matthäus capped off a fine run into the opposition box with the smart angled finish to maintain *Die Roten's* unbeaten run in the tournament and round off a 7-2 aggregate victory.

With one more awkward opponent safely out of the way, the draw for the last four would pit Udo Lattek's side against six-time European club champions Real Madrid.

The first meeting between the two teams in European competition had come in 1976 when Bayern won 3-1 on aggregate en route to their third European Cup triumph, but the tie would be remembered more for the post-match scuffles than the result. At the end of the first leg at the Bernabéu that had finished 1-1, Gerd Müller was punched by a home "supporter", who then attacked the referee before finally being grounded by Bayern 'keeper Sepp Maier. Bayern had sealed the tie with a comfortable two-goal triumph in Munich, but the seeds of what would become a bitter rivalry had been sown. During the clubs' second European meeting more than a decade later, the simmering pot would come quickly to the boil before spilling over completely.

With it being the Easter holidays I was now back home, able to watch the midweek football without having to cut the sound, lower the brightness to almost pitch blackness or listen out for the clicking feet of large dogs. With no English clubs in the competition, I knew that I would get to see at least ten solid minutes of the semi-final. I must have seen hundreds of matches involving Bayern over the years, but somehow this one has always stuck in the memory. Having recorded the ten minutes of highlights, I cannot even begin to count how many times I must have watched it afterwards. These days the highlights of many great matches from the past are easy to find on YouTube, but back in 1987 it was like gold dust.

With only eleven minutes on the clock Klaus Augenthaler put Bayern 1-0 up with one of those famous long-range drives. Then, just short of the half-hour mark, Lothar Matthäus doubled the lead from the penalty spot after Roland Wohlfarth was crudely clattered by 'keeper Francisco Buyo. Two became three when Wohlfarth calmly chipped the ball over the hapless Madrid *Torhüter*, and Bayern looked to be safely on their way to the final. Then, all hell broke loose.

Just two minutes after Bayern's third goal, Matthäus and Real midfielder Chendo were competing for a fifty-fifty ball. Having taken a spectacular tumble, the Spaniard leaped back up and shoved Matthäus to the ground. Prostrate on the pitch, the Bayern midfielder could not have even begun to imagine what was coming next. Out of nowhere, the talented but highly temperamental Juanito suddenly charged like a crazed bull into the fray and stamped hard on Matthäus' back, before bellowing an insult and following up with another even more vicious stamp on the Bayern man's face – an offence so blatant that it beggared belief. In all my years I had never seen such a thing take place in a football match.

Juanito was immediately dismissed and would be subsequently banned from the game for five years, and Leo Beenhakker's side were actually lucky not to have Manuel Sanchís sent off as well as he too got in on the act with a sneaky step on the stricken Matthäus' knee while the referee wasn't looking. This wasn't football, but criminal thuggery of the worst sort.

Ten-man Madrid pulled a goal back through the prolific Emilio Butragueño just before half-time, but another Matthäus penalty after a ridiculously obvious handball restored Bayern's three-goal advantage. To really cap off a terrible evening for the Spanish champions, defender Mino also received his marching orders eighteen minutes before the final whistle. Madrid finished the game with nine men, but it could very easily have been seven or less.

The assault on Matthäus by Juanito was an incident that instilled in me a deep and somewhat visceral hatred of Real Madrid that remains to this day. It might sound particularly harsh, but when I heard that the controversial Spaniard had died in a car accident some years later I was certainly not going to be shedding any tears.

The second leg at Madrid's imposing and intimidating Santiago Bernabéu saw Bayern set out to defend their lead in front of over a hundred thousand noisy spectators, and they knew they were going to be in for a rough evening when a variety of objects made their way onto the playing area courtesy of the boisterous Real faithful during the opening minutes. Experienced French referee Michel Vautrot just about managed to keep things under control, and it was clear that Bayern were going to be under attack from forces both on and off the pitch.

Having collected a yellow card in Munich and accumulated enough points to earn a one-match ban, Lothar Matthäus, so influential in the first leg, could only watch helplessly from the stands as his team looked to defend their three-goal advantage. Without their talismanic midfield machine Bayern managed to weather the initial storm, keeping things tidy at the back against a skillful and highly aggressive Madrid team. However, a crazy five minute spell either side of the half-hour mark threatened to turn the tie on its head.

On twenty-eight minutes sweeper Klaus Augenthaler could only turn a scrambled effort from Carlos Santillana into his own net to give Real the lead on the night, and the Bayern captain's evening would get even worse just three minutes later, when he became the third player from either side to be sent off for an early bath over the two matches. There was no doubt that Augenthaler's challenge was a foul and perhaps worthy of a booking, but the painfully elaborate, Oscar-winning theatrics from Mexican international Hugo Sánchez were enough to persuade Monsieur Vautrot to reach for the dreaded straight *Rot*.

In spite of being a man down in front of a fanatical and hostile home crowd, Bayern 'keeper Jean-Marie Pfaff produced an inspired display to keep the hosts – in particular the dangerous Sánchez – at bay. The Belgian was like a rock, remaining firm as the men in white threw everything they could at him. With the defence being rejigged to make up for the missing Augenthaler the Bayern attack had been almost nonexistent for almost two-thirds of the game, but when the final whistle blew *Die Roten* had done enough to progress to their fifth European Champions' Cup final. It had been a solid and highly professional display, against opponents that had not been in the slightest bit concerned with taking the concepts of gamesmanship and foul play as far as they possibly could.

The massive downside of course had been the dismissal of their influential skipper "Auge", whose one-match ban was carried over into the final. It was a major blow both for the player and FC Bayern.

Having disposed of Madrid, Bayern headed down the road to Vienna's veritable old Praterstadion to take on Portuguese champions FC Porto, a team making their first appearance in European club football's biggest showpiece. As in the 1982 final against Aston Villa the Bavarians were again the favourites, even though they would be without midfielder

Hans Dorfner and striker Roland Wohlfarth – both out through injury – and the suspended sweeper Augenthaler.

Everything was set up nicely. Following Udo Lattek's decision to retire at the end of the season, it was the perfect opportunity for the team to see the legendary *Trainer* end his second spell at Bayern on a *Henkelpott*-winning high. Post-match parties were arranged, large numbers of Bayern fans flocked across the border into Austria to make the short journey to the Austrian capital, and I too set about making my own plans for the evening.

Finally, five long years after watching the 1982 final on a small black and white television in Cyprus, I was able to watch Bayern play live in glorious technicolour. Well, not quite.

Being at boarding school had continually got in the way of my wanting to watch the late night European football highlights, and one might have thought that things should have been considerably easier with the match kicking off at a quarter past seven on a Wednesday evening. After all, there were no issues with bed times, even if the match went the distance to a penalty shootout. The problem was instead caused by our daily preparation – boarding school speak for "homework" – which ran for an hour up until eight o'clock. Try as one might, there was no getting out of it. Wanting to watch the European Cup final offered no reasonable grounds for exemption, and the common room was completely off limits.

Thankfully with it being my final year I was able do my "prep" in my own dormitory – though the formation of coral atolls or quadratic equations were the last things on my mind as I tuned into the live commentary on the radio. No sooner had the clock struck eight to signal our release, I charged down the corridor to the common room to get the best seat, turfing out a number of juniors who had been watching *EastEnders* or some other rubbish. Bayern were already one goal up, scored in the twenty-fifth minute by young winger Ludwig Kögl.

As I settled in front of the television the first half was just coming to an end. Most of the 62,000 crowd in the Praterstadion were decked out in red and white, and the atmosphere was like that of a home game at the Olympiastadion. Rather than their traditional all-red ensemble, Bayern were kitted out in red shirts, their "Brazilian" pale blue shorts with yellow trim, and red socks.

During the half-time break I managed to see Kögl's goal. Having won a throw-in out on the left, Norbert Nachtweih had flung the ball into the box, where it took a slight deflection off a Portuguese head towards the diminutive winger. Although not particularly famed for his aerial ability, the 5' 7" "Wiggerl" launched himself at the ball, guiding a diving header that made its way into the net and past the outstretched left hand of Polish 'keeper Józef

Młynarczyk in the Porto goal. From what I could tell, there had been few other opportunities and Bayern had looked more than comfortable.

The opening minutes of the second half appeared to support these thoughts. The Bavarians quickly settled into a steady rhythm after the restart, with their wingers holding sway over the narrow Portuguese 4-4-1-1 formation. Missing their leading striker Fernando Gomes, the Porto attack looked toothless and desperate, and for the Bayern fans that made up the majority of the crowd it was surely just a matter of time until skipper Matthäus would finally get his hands on the famous silver trophy to seal *Die Roten's* first European triumph in over a decade.

As the seconds ticked by, I too had a growing sense of expectation.

But this is a story of my life as a Bayern München fan, and nothing was ever going to be this simple. Indeed, over the years I quickly discovered that nothing could be taken for granted, particularly on European nights like this.

At the start of the second half, Porto coach Artur Jorge replaced holding midfielder Quim with the Brazilian striker Juary, transforming the staid 4-4-1-1 into a more fluid and conventional 4-4-2. The change saw Lattek's side thrown onto the back foot, but despite not being able to exercise the same dominance as in the opening forty-five minutes the time continued to tick away.

As the match entered its final quarter Bayern still held their narrow advantage, but as the increasing pressure from the Portuguese side started to take its toll on the harried red-shirted defence things started to wobble. As is usual watching games like this, my confidence was slowly being transformed into increasing sense of nervousness with each passing second; the one tactical change from Artur Jorge had clearly altered the balance and flow of the game, and having created next to nothing in the previous seventy-five minutes the Portuguese underdogs were suddenly looking the more dangerous of the two teams. The dynamic Paulo Futre had come right back into the game and had started to terrorise the tiring Bayern defenders, while Lattek's side slunk back into their shells and adopted something resembling a siege mentality.

With just twelve minutes remaining in the contest, Porto produced one of the most memorable moments in the history of the tournament – well, unless you happened to be a Bayern fan. As a number of blue and white shirts streamed into the Bayern penalty area, with substitute Juary working the ball past 'keeper Jean-Marie Pfaff and cutting it across the face of the goal. There to meet it was Algerian Rabah Madjer with – in the worlds of the late ITV commentator Brian Moore – a "cheeky little back-heel". Of course, this was the same Rabah

Madjer who had scored Algeria's opening goal in Germany's infamous World Cup defeat at the hands of the North Africans in Spain five years earlier.

Caught completely cold, the Bayern players knew that it was going to be a struggle just to get back into the flow of the contest, let alone restore their advantage. With the hitherto dominant wing-backs completely neutralised and forced into playing a more defensive game, the onus was on movement through the centre and the lumbering Dieter Hoeneß – a superb finisher, but a player who had really never set the world alight with his pace or agility. Crucially, the pendulum had swung completely, and the momentum was now firmly with Porto.

Bayern never had sniff of a chance to retake the lead, for as soon as they had relinquished it the transformed Portuguese side kept their foot firmly down on the accelerator, capping two minutes of mayhem with a second and ultimately match-winning goal. This time Madjer turned provider, setting up Juary who slammed the ball into the roof of the net to complete a stunning turnaround.

Completely floored, there was no way back for Lattek's side. Bayern had fallen at the final hurdle against first-time European finalists for the second time in five years. If the result against Aston Villa in Rotterdam had come as a genuine surprise, the nature of the result in Vienna was quite hard to bear.

I had been watching the game live with a collection of other schoolchildren who had been either neutral or rooting for the Portuguese, and when the final whistle blew everybody else just got up, walked out and simply carried on with their lives. I however just sat there in stunned silence as the post-match analysis went in through one ear and out through the other, with what felt like a cold tear rolling down my fifteen year old face.

At that very moment, I simply hated football.

Never before had I experienced such desperate emotions as a football fan, and having nobody around me to sympathise with just made it hurt even more. When the post-mortem was over I slowly retreated back to the solitude of my dormitory, trying desperately to rewrite the final lines of the nightmarish plot that had unfolded on that dramatic and bitter May evening.

The match had been billed as the final farewell to Udo Lattek, the man who had served FC Bayern so well in delivering two Bundesliga hat-tricks, three DFB-Pokal victories and the club's maiden European Cup triumph in 1974. A second *Henkelpott* would have been the crowning glory in what had been a glittering career, but it was just not to be.

Apart from my sense of upset at the defeat, my not being able to see Lattek walk away with another European triumph was also a poignant moment. Up until 1983 FC Bayern München had simply been my favourite German team, but by 1987 I had become a fully-fledged supporter; it is no exaggeration to say that Udo Lattek had been directly responsible for that transformation.

I could never listen to Ultravox's *Vienna* – one of my favourite tracks of the early 1980s – without thinking of this awful match and the memories it invoked. Perhaps the most famous line of the song is "it means nothing to me", but as hard as I tried I could never make it so – the bad memories will always remain. As far as the 1987 European Cup final defeat is concerned, Joe Dolce's awful *Shaddap You Face* provided a far more appropriate soundtrack.

Having dominated European football with their three successive European titles in the middle of the 1970s, the Bayern team of the 1980s had been transformed into the continent's nearly men during Lattek's second spell as coach. While dominant domestically, they were never able to reach the same heights on the European stage. They remained one of the teams to beat and one of the "big boys", but in the final analysis they were never quite good enough – or perhaps lucky enough – to take the most coveted prize.

The massive disappointment of the European Cup final defeat and the departure of Udo Lattek gave way to an even more disappointing first season under new coach Jupp Heynckes, with Bayern finishing four points behind Werder Bremen in the Bundesliga and exiting the DFB-Pokal at the quarter-final stage against old but fast fading rivals Hamburger SV.

There were few changes in personnel at the start of Heynckes' time in charge. Twenty-three year old striker Jürgen Wegmann was brought in from Schalke 04 to solve the ongoing problems up front, and in a major coup the highly-rated Welsh international Mark Hughes arrived on a one year loan spell from Catalan giants FC Barcelona. Meanwhile the long-serving Dieter Hoeneß finally hung up his boots at the age of thirty-four, and the underused Reinhold Mathy made the move to Bayer Uerdingen after seven seasons in Munich.

Bayern's league campaign during 1987/88 could best be described as schizophrenic, with Heynckes' side supremely dominant at home but continually prone to weakness and inexplicably poor results on their travels – in stark contrast to the previous season where they had gone unbeaten in all of their seventeen away matches. Having started the season with a fine 3-1 win in Dortmund, Bayern failed to register a win away from home for almost two months – a dismal run that included defeats against Mönchengladbach, Köln and unfashionable FC 08 Homburg. In stark contrast the same period had seen the Bavarians win their first five home fixtures, among them a satisfying six-goal demolition of a fast-deteriorating HSV.

Having not managed an away win for the best part of two months Bayern seemingly turned things around with three wins from their next four matches on the road, enough to haul them back into the title race. Meanwhile at home their record would read played nine, won nine. As the season reached its halfway point *Die Roten* were sitting in second place, just two points behind leaders Bremen.

The penultimate match before a shortened *Winterpause* saw the first home match of the *Rückrunde*, and unfortunately the successful streak at the Olympiastadion came to an unexpected end as Dortmund exacted revenge for their opening day defeat by the same 3-1 scoreline. A golden opportunity to put more pressure on the league leaders had been lost, and after a 2-2 draw in Hamburg the Bavarians went into the *Winterpause* in third place, five points adrift of leaders Bremen and one behind Köln.

The remainder of the *Rückrunde* saw much of the same: excellent results at home, and questionably erratic form on the road. With the exception of a 2-2 draw against fellow title chasers Köln Bayern would win all of their remaining matches at the Olympiastadion to finish with a record of 15-1-1, but after winning their first two away matches of 1988 they once again entered a long and frustrating barren spell. Having defeated Nürnberg 3-0 at the Frankenstadion in the first week of March, Heynckes' didn't register a win on their travels until the final week of the season, when they would come back from 3-1 down to beat Bayer Leverkusen 4-3 – just about enough to secure second spot on goal difference ahead of Köln.

	P	W	D	L	Goals	GD	Pts
SV Werder Bremen	34	22	8	4	61:22	+39	52:16
FC Bayern München	34	22	4	8	83:45	+38	48:20
1. FC Köln	34	18	12	4	57:28	+29	48:20

For all their inconsistency, Bayern ended up as the league's highest scorers by a considerable distance – racking up a total of eighty-three goals. Perhaps the most interesting statistic was that a staggering fifty-five of these had been scored in their seventeen home fixtures – an average of more than three goals a match.

Bayern had found the back of the opposition net four or more times on eight occasions: in addition to their 6-0 thrashing of HSV, they racked up another half a dozen against VfL Bochum and subjected poor Schalke 04 to a record 8-1 drubbing at the Olympiastadion – with skipper Lothar Matthäus scoring his one and only hat-trick in the FC Bayern *Trikot*.

In the end however, the final league table actually flattered the Bavarians. They had finished just four points behind new champions Bremen, but any lingering title hopes of snatching the *Meisterschale* had ended two weeks earlier with the Green-Whites holding a decisive seven-point lead with just three matches to play. As the season came to an end and with the *Meisterschale* already safely locked away, the second-time German champions would take it easy, and could even afford to lose their unbeaten home record in being thrashed 4-1 by northern rivals HSV.

Over the course of the season, Bayern had won only seven of their seventeen away matches, which would ultimately be the difference between them and the title.

	P	W	D	L	Goals	GD	Pts
SV Werder Bremen	34	22	8	4	61:22	+39	52:16
FC Bayern München	34	22	4	8	83:45	+38	48:20
1. FC Köln	34	18	12	4	57:28	+29	48:20

The 1987/88 European Cup campaign began with four wins in four matches as Bayern saw off Bulgarian champions CSKA Sofia and Swiss side Neuchâtel Xamax, and a mouth-watering quarter-final pitted Heynckes' side against old foes Real Madrid – reigniting the flame that had been sparked during the previous season's pair of hard-fought and at times brutal encounters. As in 1987 the first leg in a chilly Olympiastadion saw *Die Roten* storm into a three-goal lead by the forty-seventh minute with Hansi Pflügler, Norbert Eder and Roland Wohlfarth getting on the scoreboard, but after that all similarities would end.

With Bayern floating serenely towards what looked like a comfortable victory, the curse of the late double-strike – quickly turning into something of a recurring theme on European tournament nights – struck them once again. What made matters worse was that both Madrid goals had not come from smart counter-attacking moves, but a series of dreadful defensive blunders by the Bavarians.

With two minutes remaining Emilio Butragueno took advantage of a mistimed sliding back pass from Norbert Eder to pull one back for *Los Merengues*, and less than two minutes later 'keeper Jean-Marie Pfaff ended up looking more like Jean-Marie Gaffe as he allowed a weak free-kick from Mexican Hugo Sánchez to bobble and roll straight through him.

It is hard to decide what was actually more hideous: Pfaff's awful blunder or Bayern's bizarre red shorts with a strange horizontal white band running through them that looked like the sort of cheap novelty item a middle-aged Austrian tourist would wear to a Spanish beach resort. Having looked clear favourites to progress through to another European Cup semi-final, two minutes of madness had thrown the advantage straight back to their opponents.

Bayern's failure to hold onto their advantage and take what should have been a comfortable three-goal lead to Madrid would ultimately be their undoing, and in the second leg at the Bernabéu the Spanish champions gained immediate revenge for their defeat the previous year through first-half goals from Yugoslav Milan Janković and local favourite Míchel. Yet again, another highly promising European campaign ended with every Bayern fans thinking in terms of "what might have been" and "if only".

With neutral coverage of the three European club tournaments on British television tending to start at the quarter-final stage, these two occasions were my only sighting of Bayern that season – a season that in the end I could truly say meant nothing to me.

As the 1980s came to a close, Bayern remained strong domestically while continuing to fail at the business end of their campaigns in Europe. The 1988/89 season brought the Munich side a record-stretching eleventh league title – their tenth in the post-war Bundesliga era – but once again their venture into Europe was a familiar case of so near yet so far.

There had been very little change to the squad at the start of Jupp Heynckes' first season in charge, but the start of his second year would see a number of big moves both to and away from Munich. Since his being signed from Borussia Mönchengladbach in 1984 Lothar Matthäus had become the heartbeat of the Bayern team, but after just four years in Munich he was on his way to Italian giants Internazionale for what was arguably a bargain fee of DM8.4 million.

If the loss of the captain was not bad enough, *I Nerazzurri* also snaffled up the just as influential Andy Brehme for the cut-price cost of just over DM2 million. Elsewhere loanee Mark Hughes made his way back to Manchester United after twenty-three games in the FC Bayern *Trikot*, veteran centre-back Norbert Eder headed south across to Switzerland to join FC Zürich, Michael Rummenigge made the switch to Borussia Dortmund and goalkeeper Jean-Marie Pfaff, another much-loved figure in Munich, headed back home to Belgium to join Lierse SK.

Among the new arrivals perhaps the biggest was Schalke 04 midfielder Olaf Thon, a player whose name had first attracted the attention of every Bayern supporter four years earlier in that famous DFB-Pokal semi-final goal fest in Gelsenkirchen. By this time a full German international, the talented twenty-two year old arrived in Munich for around DM4 million – his task being to fill the massive void vacated by the departing Matthäus.

Defender Roland Grahammer and newly-capped German international Stefan Reuter made the short journey to Munich from Nürnberg as Heynckes shored up the defensive unit, while Bayern's growing foreign contingent was boosted with the arrival of experienced Swedish international striker Johnny Ekström from Italian side Empoli FC and twenty-one year old Norwegian centre-back Erland Johnsen from Moss FK.

Having been dogged by poor away form the previous season, Bayern would produce a far better set of results on their travels. They actually ended up with fewer away victories – five as opposed to seven – but had managed to draw nine while losing only three. On their own home ground in Munich Heynckes' side remained the most powerful team in the Bundesliga, going through all seventeen games unbeaten with fourteen wins and three draws.

More than anything else, the key to their success was the welcome rediscovery of their legendary and almost metronomic consistency. Avoiding the silly defeats that had pockmarked and ultimately derailed the previous Bundesliga campaign, Bayern were able to put together the sort of unbeaten spells that their rivals could only hope to match. The title was essentially decided with an unbeaten run that stretched to twenty-three games, with *Die Roten's* first defeat coming in March 1989 at the hands of Borussia Mönchengladbach.

Perhaps the most pivotal encounter of the season would take place on match day 31, when Bayern visited their closest rivals, Köln. With the Rhinelanders only two points behind the Bavarians and just one short on goal difference, it was a genuine four-pointer. Bayern had only been beaten twice all season, but Christoph Daum's team had put together their own impressive unbeaten run, stretching back seventeen matches, to the two teams' previous meeting in Munich.

Bayern were the team to beat, but in front of a packed Müngersdorfer Stadion *Die Geißböcke* were the team in form. Everything was poised perfectly, and surely something had to give.

Roland Wohlfarth opened the scoring for *Die Roten* on twenty-five minutes only for Thomas Allofs to equalise seven minutes later, but this was followed by a tight and well-contested second half. With the score locked at one apiece with just over five minutes left on the clock it looked as though both teams would take a share of the spoils, but the energetic Wohlfarth had other ideas. An inspired four-minute burst saw the Bayern number nine complete his hat-trick, and effectively seal the title for the men from Munich.

With just three matches remaining, Bayern were a comfortable four points clear of Köln with outgoing champions Bremen a further two points adrift in third place.

Any mathematical chance Daum's men might have had to snatch the *Meisterschale* quickly disappeared the following week when they could only scrape a point in Stuttgart against the relegated Kickers, while at the Olympiastadion Bayern turned on the style and provided the home crowd with a magnificent five-star display against Bayer Uerdingen. Johnny Ekström opened the scoring, but it was left to unsung heroes Hansi Dorfner and Hans-Dieter Flick to complete the scoring with a brace apiece.

The green pretenders from Bremen had only managed to hold the *Meisterschale* for a year. With two weeks remaining in the season, the richly-decorated silver "salad dish" was ready to make its journey back home to Munich.

A 2-1 defeat to regional rivals Nürnberg at the Frankenstadion in their penultimate fixture proved to be little more than a minor irritation to the Munich traditionalists, but another 5-0 rout in their final home match against VfL Bochum – with the in-form Wohlfarth banging in four more goals – provided the final seal on what had been a successful league season for Jupp Heynckes' side. In the end, Bayern had finished a convincingly comfortable five points clear of Köln, with Bremen a further point behind in third.

	P	W	D	L	Goals	GD	Pts
FC Bayern München	34	19	12	3	67:26	+41	50:18
1. FC Köln	34	18	9	7	58:30	+28	45:23
SV Werder Bremen	34	18	8	8	55:32	+23	44:24

Competing in the UEFA Cup after their second place Bundesliga finish the previous year, Bayern had begun their campaign in rich goalscoring form, securing a 3-1 win at home to Legia Warszawa before thrashing the Polish side by an astonishing seven goals to three in the return leg. Czech outfit FK DAC 1904 Dunajská Streda were next opponents to be put to the sword, falling 5-1 on aggregate with new signing Olaf Thon – Schalke 04's hat-trick hero in the classic twelve-goal *Pokal* semi-final of 1984 – scoring three in the red of FC Bayern.

The third round then saw one of Bayern's greatest European comebacks as a disappointing 2-0 home defeat to Internazionale – featuring former stars Lothar Matthäus and Andreas Brehme – was followed by a memorable 3-1 win in the San Siro in Milan to clinch the tie on away goals. I had tuned into the two-minute highlights of this match not expecting much, only to see *Die Roten* storm into a three-goal lead before half-time with goals from Wohlfarth, Augenthaler and Jürgen Wegmann. The Italians pulled a goal back before the break to make things interesting and set up a nervous second half, but for once Bayern would avoid any last-minute disasters to squeeze into the quarter-finals.

After years of dismal luck in European competition I truly started to believe that Bayern's fortunes had finally turned in Milan, and a comfortable if workmanlike 3-0 aggregate victory in the last eight over Scottish side Heart of Midlothian would set up an exciting-looking semi-final against Italian outfit SSC Napoli. Having emerged from the shadows of the Milan giants, Juventus and Roma, Ottavio Bianchi's side featured a number of international stars, including Brazilian striker Careca and the man widely considered to be the world's best player at the time, Argentina's World Cup winning captain Diego Maradona.

After the victory at the San Siro I had found it a little easier to put aside the long-held residual fear of Italian opponents. Bayern had beaten the runaway Serie A leaders en route to the last four, and now it was just a matter of beating the team sitting behind them in second place. I slowly began to look forward to the idea of an all-German final, either against Bundesliga rivals VfB Stuttgart or a historic cross-border clash with East German side Dynamo Dresden.

For all the high hopes, the red train once more hit the buffers in the last four. A goal either side of half-time condemned Heynckes' side to defeat in Naples, and once they had fallen behind in the return leg at the Olympiastadion to a Careca strike in the sixty-second minute – set up beautifully with a classic air-shot by defender Norbert Nachtweih – the writing was on the wall. I momentarily thought back to the second leg against Inter, but this was just too much to ask.

Needing to score four goals, Bayern threw everything forward and equalised through Wohlfarth three minutes later, but eleven minutes from time the irrepressible Careca collected a neat Maradona through-ball to double his tally and remove all remaining doubt. It was just a matter of pride now for the Bavarians, and Stefan Reuter quickly levelled things up on the night to complete the scoring on the evening as Heynckes' side went out 4-2 on aggregate.

With Napoli going on to beat Stuttgart in a well-contested final to claim their first European trophy, Bayern had once again ended up losing to the eventual tournament winners.

THE NEARLY MEN

The turn of the decade had seen much change in Germany with the collapse of Communist East and the breaching of the Berlin wall at the end of 1989, but for FC Bayern it was business as usual in the Bundesliga as they secured yet another title in 1989/90.

With their league rivals fighting for the freshly-available players that had started to flood west from the disintegrating East German leagues, Bayern's signings were low-key but well considered. International centre-back Jürgen Kohler was signed from rivals Köln for just under DM3 million, and the strike force was bolstered by the arrival of Yugoslav international Radmilo Mihajlović from Dinamo Zagreb for just over DM1.75 million and Scottish marksman Alan McInally from Aston Villa for DM3.2 million.

Joining these three high-profile signings were VfB Stuttgart's versatile midfielder Thomas Strunz and defensive midfielder Manfred Schwabl who returned to Munich after three years at Nürnberg, while promising young striker Manfred Bender made the short journey from SpVgg Unterhaching in the Munich suburbs.

Among those leaving Munich were Armin Eck who moved north to Hamburger SV, Norbert Nachtweih who after seven seasons in Bavaria was signed by French side AS Cannes, and Jürgen Wegmann who relocated back to the *Ruhrpott* with Borussia Dortmund. Perhaps the most notable departure was that of Swedish striker Johnny Eckström, who after one season with *Die Roten* joined Nachtweih in the south of France. The Swede had started well enough with a goal on his Bayern debut, but an overall return of just twelve goals in thirty-seven league and cup appearances was never going to be good enough as the Bayern board continued to look for the right man to fill the boots of goalscoring legends such as Gerd Müller and Karl-Heinz Rummenigge.

Caught in my Bundesliga black hole I'd have no access to any of the action, but the combination of teletext, newspapers and the weekly football magazines continued to allow me to keep up to date. Bayern's season would get off to a winning start with a tight 3-2 win against Nürnberg with new boys McInally and Mihajlović both getting off the mark, but a series of inconsistent results including a rotten 1-0 defeat against unfancied Waldhof Mannheim kept them away from top spot until week seven. Five weeks at the summit was followed by more inconsistency and a swapping of places with both Köln and Bayer Leverkusen, but by the halfway stage in the season all three clubs were locked on twenty-three points with Heynckes' side in front on goal difference.

With the World Cup being played that summer there was an extended twenty-one week schedule taking in the first four weeks of the *Rückrunde*, with fixtures stretching well into mid-December. Draws against Bremen and Dortmund and an embarrassing 4-0 defeat against mid-table Nürnberg on the first match of the reversed set of fixtures had seen Bayern knocked off top spot for the fourth time in as little as seven weeks, but on match day twenty the Bavarians returned to the top with a 3-1 win in Homburg. A 4-1 win over Karlsruhe SC the following week at the Olympiastadion was enough to see Bayern go into the winter break in first place.

The first twenty-one games had been far from consistent for Heynckes' side, but the break had come at just the right time. Three wins from three in their final three matches of the extended pre-*Winterpause* period had provided the spark for a massive improvement in form, and after that Bayern would never relinquish their place at the top of the table. An unbeaten run spanning sixteen matches saw the Bavarians quickly accelerate away from the chasing pack that had kept in contention for so long, and with two weeks remaining in the season all remaining mathematical possibilities had been exhausted.

In the end Bayern finished a more than comfortable six points clear of second-placed Köln, with Eintracht Frankfurt nudging out Dortmund for third spot on goal difference.

	P	W	D	L	Goals	GD	Pts
FC Bayern München	34	19	11	4	64:28	+36	49:19
1.FC Köln	34	17	9	8	54:44	+10	43:25
SG Eintracht Frankfurt	34	15	11	8	61:40	+21	41:27
BV 09 Borussia Dortmund	34	15	11	8	51:35	+16	41:27

Bayern's domestic cup campaign had started solidly enough with a 1-0 win in Frankfurt followed by a 2-0 defeat of Waldhof Mannheim, but a comprehensive 3-0 third round defeat in Stuttgart at the hands of VfB would put paid to any ambitions of another domestic double. Outside of the Bundesliga Bayern could now focus more on their European ambitions, but once again it was a case of good but not quite good enough.

Jupp Heynckes' side had made their way into the last four of the Champions' Cup unbeaten, and with relative ease: after a 3-1 aggregate win over Glasgow Rangers that had featured a particularly memorable long-range missile from Klaus "Auge" Augenthaler in Glasgow, Bayern continued their unbeaten march into the semi-finals with home and away victories over Albanian champions 17 Nëntori Tiranë (3-1 and 3-0) and 1988 tournament winners PSV Eindhoven (2-1 and 1-0).

In the semi-finals *Die Roten* faced defending champions AC Milan, a side that hosted an array of international talent including the Dutch triumvirate of Frank Rijkaard, Ruud Gullit and the hero of the Euro '88 final, Marco van Basten. With English clubs still excluded from European competition many Bayern fans had expected far greater success on this big stage, but this period would also coincide with the resurgence of Italian club football – and in particular the rise of a richly-talented Milan side that had become one of the dominant forces in Europe during the late 1980s and much of the 1990s.

The European Cup semi-final of 1989/90 was yet another high-stakes encounter that would find a natural place in the memory bank, and Bayern – wearing an interesting combination of white *Trikot*, "Brazilian blue" shorts and red socks – had come away from the first leg in the San Siro with a single goal defeat, courtesy of a highly contentious seventy-seventh minute penalty from van Basten, by then something of a *bête noire* for many German fans.

The outrageous "dying swan" dive by Stefano Borgonovo that resulted in the award of the spot-kick had been truly nauseating to watch – not that this would have bothered one jot to the boisterous home supporters in the seething San Siro. Raimond Aumann guessed correctly in his attempt to keep out van Basten's effort, but the kick was just too well struck as it skidded low to the Bayern keeper's right.

With the Italians holding their slender lead everything was perfectly set up for the second leg at the Olympiastadion, which was to witness the sort of intense, nail-biting, edge-of-the-seat drama that defined many of these special midweek "European Cup nights".

Having been kitted out in that strange colour combination in Milan, Bayern were back in their traditional and wonderfully simple all-red ensemble in front of a seventy-two thousand strong crowd in fine voice - responding to the challenge and providing the inspiration for what would turn out to be their team's best home display of the season. For a large and cavernous open bowl of a ground that had never really been the most inspiring footballing venue, the atmosphere was electric even with the constant springtime drizzle.

With Arrigo Sacchi's side looking to defend their lead and Bayern in turn not wanting to risk giving away an unnecessary away goal, the match opened in a calculated, cagey fashion – effectively a game of chess on grass. Half-time arrived with the score still goalless and Milan hanging onto their narrow aggregate advantage, but the Bavarians continued to keep things under control and wait patiently for the right moment to strike, knowing that a goal at the other end would leave them needing three.

The game suddenly burst into life just short of the hour mark. The alert van Basten robbed Augenthaler of the ball deep inside the Bayern half before sending in an audacious lob that was acrobatically tipped over the bar by Aumann, and when the resulting corner looked to have sparked a fast counterattack from the men in red it was Olaf Thon's turn to be dispossessed. With van Basten again charging towards the Bayern goal, skipper Augenthaler slid in with a perfectly-timed challenge to atone for his earlier error.

Still the drama continued. The next corner came in and Aumann could only punch it away towards the edge of the box, where Augenthaler again lost the ball, this time to Daniele Massaro. Playing a quick one-two with Frank Rijkaard, Massaro made his way into the box with just Aumann to beat, but the Bayern 'keeper stood his ground brilliantly to keep out and collect the Italian's slightly scuffed effort. With order restored as Aumann rolled the ball out to a red shirt, Bayern carefully worked their way up the pitch, winning a free-kick just inside the Milan half by the left touchline.

Taking the free-kick quickly with a short tap to Hansi Pflügler, Hansi Dorfner carefully took the ball inside, exchanging passes with Thomas Strunz before threading a lovely ball through the middle as the midfielder continued his run into the penalty area. Strunz calmly evaded a challenge from Paolo Maldini before rounding 'keeper Giovanni Galli and sliding the ball into the empty net to round off a dramatic couple of minutes and give Bayern the lead on the night.

Having survived two Milan attacks in the space of a minute, the scores were now level on aggregate with everything back in the balance. The almost constant rain couldn't dampen the enthusiasm of the home crowd, and the chorus of cheers as the languid Strunz calmly celebrated his goal was probably the loudest noise I had ever heard at a ground not particularly known for its acoustics.

Roared on by the 72,000 crowd, *Die Roten* continued to press. Strunz sent the ball narrowly over the target as he lost his footing on the slippery turf, and even defender Roland

Grahammer was making swashbuckling runs through the middle of the pitch. This was unlike any Bayern game I had seen before. The 6-6 DFB-Pokal draw against Schalke in 1984 had been full of goals and excitement and even the 1987 European Cup final had had its moments of high drama, but this was the first time I had really felt this amount of almost relentless tension.

This was not just any old cup tie, but Europe's finest slugging it out and throwing everything at each other in search of the continent's biggest prize. It was like Rocky Balboa against Apollo Creed: the solid and dependable slugger against the dancing showman.

The Bayern coach could probably smell Milanese blood as he threw on striker Alan McInally for Thon with eight minutes remaining, but even with the crowd roaring them on *Die Roten* were unable to find the crucial second goal that would have seen them through to the final.

As the clock ticked towards the end of the ninety minutes, everything was intriguingly set for a further half hour of extra time. If the scores remained the same after that, the dreaded *Elfmeterschießen* awaited. As if we could have withstood any more drama.

Seven minutes into the additional thirty Heynckes replaced the tiring Ludwig Kögl with the versatile Manfred Bender, but just four minutes after that - disaster. On as a sixty-eighth minute substitute, first-leg villain Borgonovo struck again. Not with a dive this time, but an equally outrageous looping shot over Aumann from a position that at first sight looked clearly offside. I found myself waiting for the linesman's flag, but it never came. With penalties no longer a factor, Bayern were left needing two more goals to go through.

In a series of red waves, the home side stormed forward. Soaked to the skin, but roared on by the expectant crowd. McInally charged to the byline and whipped in a cross into the box towards the wiry Bender, who despite being slightly wrong-footed managed to get his shot on target but straight at Galli. The men in red were relentless, with both substitutes providing plenty of energy and pace as the Italian side were forced to defend deep inside their own half.

Something had to give, and just three minutes into the second period of extra time the hard-working but unheralded Dorfner picked out substitute Bender down the left, who sent a firm and perfectly directed first-time cross into the penalty area. Sliding in to meet it at the far post was the inevitable McInally, whose shot bounced into the ground before floating up and over Galli and into the back of the net.

With twelve minutes remaining, hope had been rekindled.

2-2 on aggregate but still behind on away goals, Bayern needed another. The red wave continued to flood forward, but with spaces now opening up all over the soggy and slippery pitch it quickly became something of a free for all. Roland Wohlfarth scuffed a shot wide, before Borgonovo at the other end – yes, him again – beat the advancing Aumann at the edge of the box before inexplicably scooping the ball high over the crossbar with the empty goal at his mercy. Then, Bender ended up agonisingly short of the ball, sliding in at the far post as the elusive leather sphere skidded on the slick surface across the Milan penalty area.

When the final whistle blew, it was little more than a victory in vain. The team were loudly cheered off the pitch, but once again they had fallen just short when it really mattered.

This, however, was different. This was not a Bayern side that had simply thrown away their chance of victory, but a team that had punched far above its weight and given everything they had to offer against a team that was rightly considered to be one of European and World football's leading powers.

If anything, the Bayern side of 1989/90 was arguably more competitive than that of 1987 and even 1982, and had been desperately unlucky not to reach the final. Unsurprisingly, Milan went on to win the showcase event against Portuguese champions SL Benfica, thus retaining the coveted *Henkelpott*.

FC Bayern's quest for glory in Europe's showcase tournament would last another decade, when they reached the final in 2001 and overcome Valencia CF to win their fourth title - ironically, in Milan's San Siro. Jupp Heynckes' side may not have reached the final in 1990, but that semi-final second leg in a wet and soggy Olympiastadion remains one of the club's most memorable evenings.

A victory in vain it may have been, but it was one firmly fixed in the memory bank of every fan that had been around to experience it.

In looking to bolster the squad that had come so close to making it into another European Cup final, Jupp Heynckes chose not to seek out established stars, instead signing a number of younger players from the domestic market.

The exciting twenty-one year old Danish international Brian Laudrup was signed from Bayer Uerdingen for just around DM6 million, rising home-grown midfield star Stefan Effenberg made a DM4 million move from Borussia Mönchengladbach, and the highly-rated rock-star lookalike winger Michael Sternkopf made his way to Munich from Karlsruher SC for just under DM3.5 million. In addition, a number of players from the youth team also made the break into the professional first team squad, including defender Markus Münch and highly-rated midfielder Christian Ziege.

Heading in the other direction were the unsettled Hans-Dieter Flick who moved to Köln, while Erland Johnsen moved across to England to join Chelsea and the underused home-grown youth product Thomas Kastenmaier made his way to Mönchengladbach for DM800,000. Perhaps the biggest name on the exit list however was 1987 European Cup final goalscorer Ludwig "Wiggerl" Kögl, who after six seasons in Munich made the short move west to southern rivals VfB Stuttgart for just under DM2 million.

The beginning of the 1990/91 season coincided with the advent of the satellite television revolution in Britain, which for me was a fantastic thing as a Bayern fan. I found myself no longer having to rely on patchy British terrestrial television coverage to see mere snippets of my beloved *Roten*: I could instead tune in to a number of German channels that had suddenly become available to me.

There were live internationals and European club tournament matches on both of Germany's public channels ARD and ZDF, and I very quickly fell into the routine of making sure to tune into the late night football show on 3Sat every Saturday evening to catch the Bundesliga highlights package – and with it selected players and special guest celebrities shooting a ball into a small circular target. Then there were the commercial channels such as Sat 1, which hosted the excellent *Ran*, the German equivalent of *Match of the Day* that is still going strong.

Perhaps the first real difference I'd notice was the way the packages were put together. While in the UK we had long been used to the match highlights being followed by the post-match interviews, in Germany the action was often spliced with post-match interview snippets.

While the two state channels broadcasted live national team and DFB-Pokal matches, live Bundesliga games at that time could only be found on pay-per-view channel *Premiere* – and when things were really desperate I often found myself tuning in and listening to the heavily scrambled footage as if it were a fuzzy radio signal. If you really tried – I mean, *really* tried – you could even make out the almost ethereal figures moving about under the storm of digital fuzz. In a way, it was like watching *Sportsnight* late at night in an empty school common room with the volume and brightness turned right down.

I was, quite literally, in Fußball heaven. After years in the dark and desolate wilderness, here I was with access to what felt like a feast of German matches on television and, in those pre-Internet days, German teletext - or "Videotext", as it was known in Deutschland. Very soon the names Waldemar Hartmann, Gerhard Delling, Bela Réthy and Gerd Rubenbauer had become as familiar to me as Brian Moore, John Motson, Barry Davies, Tony Gubba and Gerald Sinstadt.

We had the new BSkyB satellite system installed in the spring of 1991, and the first Bundesliga highlights I got to see involving Bayern was their meeting with VfB Stuttgart at the Neckarstadion in the second week of March. Jupp Heynckes' side triumphed 3-0, with Roland Wohlfarth grabbing a brace and Olaf Thon putting the seal on things with a late penalty.

My heightened sense of excitement at finally getting to see the *Münch'ner* in domestic league action was sadly tempered by the rather ordinary results in a season that could best be described as inconsistent. The win at Stuttgart was followed by a solid three-goal victory over Karlsruher SC that took *Die Roten* to the top of the table, but a 2-1 defeat in Kaiserslautern the following week saw the Red Devils jump into the top spot.

A disappointing home defeat to Fortuna Düsseldorf saw Bayern drop back into third place behind both FCK and Werder Bremen, and a series of poor results would put them four points behind the leaders as the season entered the crucial final stretch. With their rivals experiencing the occasional slip-up Bayern had more than enough opportunities to claw back the deficit, but their inconsistency continued to haunt them. A 7-3 thumping of bottom club Hertha Berlin – and another Olaf Thon hat-trick - took Heynckes' side into second place just two points behind FCK, but a dismal 3-2 defeat at mid-table SG Wattenscheid 09 the following week only served to undo all of the hard work.

Even at this late stage Bayern retained an outside chance of snatching the title. Needing just a draw at home to eleventh-placed Borussia Mönchengladbach to wrap things up a week early, leaders Kaiserslautern collapsed to a surprise 3-2 defeat. Bayern meanwhile took both points after a hard-worked 1-0 win in Nürnberg to drag themselves back to within two points of the summit – and with a far better goal difference.

The final week of the season saw Kaiserslautern needing just a draw in Köln, while Bayern – up against already relegated Bayer Uerdingen at the Olympiastadion – were hoping for an upset at the Müngersdorferstadion. It was remote, but not impossible: to snatch the *Meisterschale* on goal difference, Bayern needed to beat Uerdingen at home, and hope that Köln might do them a favour in beating Kaiserslautern.

However within the first quarter of an hour all hopes appeared to have been dashed as news slowly started to filter through from the Rhineland. With just fourteen minutes on the clock, Kaiserslautern were already two goals in front. That was pretty much that, and in the end the *Roter Teufel* clinched the title in grand style with an emphatic 6-2 victory over a Köln side reduced to ten men following the dismissal of former Bayern man Hans-Dieter Flick.

With Kaiserslautern already 4-1 up at half-time Bayern had needed more than a miracle, and all that really remained was for them to sign off on a positive note with a final home display against a poor Uerdingen team that had lost its five previous matches. In the end, Heynckes' side served up an abject display as they hobbled to a disappointing 2-2 draw that pretty much summed up their entire Bundesliga season.

	P	W	D	L	Goals	GD	Pts
1.FC Kaiserslautern	34	19	10	5	72:45	+27	48:20
FC Bayern München	34	18	9	7	74:41	+33	45:23
1. FC Köln	34	17	9	8	54:44	+10	43:25

One of the most comical stories of the 1990/91 season – more so to those not supporters of FC Bayern – concerned one of the new players who had joined the club at the start of the season: Stefan Effenberg. Having moved south to Bavaria from Borussia Mönchengladbach, the Hamburg-born midfielder with the furrowed brow and distinctive peroxide blonde mullet hairdo had been asked about his reasons for joining *Die Roten*.

While a standard clichéd stock answer like "I'd like to win trophies" or "I want to take my game to the highest level" would have sufficed, Effenberg instead uttered the memorable line that the other clubs were somehow "too stupid" to win the Bundesliga - *Die andern sind einfach zu dumm, um Meister zu werden.* Effenberg himself was far from stupid, but had clearly left his brains in a jar on his bedside cabinet that morning.

Of course, in winning the league those inconsiderate, stupid fools from Kaiserslautern had forgotten to read Effenberg's memo.

Effenberg's rather crass "prediction" would continue to haunt him for the rest of the season and even beyond that, and no matter where he went his touching the ball was quickly followed by an orchestrated volley of boos, jeers and other derisory noises from opposition crowds. It even followed him when playing in the *Nationaltrikot* for Germany. If anyone at the time could have been described as the epitome of the "FC Hollywood" phenomenon that had started to take hold in Munich in the early 1990s, it was the man popularly known as "Effe".

Both Effenberg's and Bayern's domestic woes had already been compounded with an embarrassing first-round exit in the DFB-Pokal at the hands of non-league FV Weinheim – a team that would eventually finish tenth in the Oberliga Baden-Württemberg – but in Europe they continued to maintain their high standard with another run of impressive results in the European Cup.

After a slow start in their first round first leg match against minnows APOEL Nicosia, which saw Bayern come back from 2-1 down to win 3-2 with two goals in the final three minutes, the Cypriots were beaten 4-0 in the return with Yugoslav import Radmilo Mihajlović grabbing a second-half hat-trick. This glut of goals continued in the second round as Bulgarian champions CSKA Sofia were hit for seven over the two legs with no reply, and a small measure of revenge was meted out against 1987 final conquerors FC Porto in the quarter-finals as Christian Ziege and Manfred Bender took the Bavarians to a resounding 2-0 win in Portugal after a 1-1 draw at the Olympiastadion.

Despite performing well below their own high standards domestically, Bayern had once again earned a position among Europe's footballing elite in making their way into the last four in their latest quest for the coveted *Henkelpott*. Just one more obstacle stood between the Bavarians and another appearance in European club football's showcase final: the stylish and talented but highly temperamental Yugoslav champions Red Star Belgrade.

Bayern were seen as marginal favourites against a Red Star side that had emerged triumphant against SG Dynamo Dresden and their hooligan supporters in the last eight, but after taking an early lead in the home leg through Roland Wohlfarth Heynckes' men found themselves on the sharp end of a highly disappointing 2-1 defeat with Dejan Savićević netting the winner for the visitors with twenty minutes remaining. It was therefore a case of all or nothing in the return meeting in Belgrade, a game that provided the second dramatic semi-final second leg in the space of two seasons.

Knowing they needed to score at least two goals to progress the onus was immediately on Heynckes' side, but the Yugoslav champions would take the lead on twenty-five minutes as Siniša Mihajlović curled a long-range free-kick past Raimond Aumann. The goal made little difference to the overall situation as Bayern still needed to score twice to take the game into extra time, but as half-time came and went things had started to look increasingly grim.

Then, on sixty-five minutes, Bayern finally got a break. Having won a free-kick some twenty-two yards out, sweeper Klaus Augenthaler struck the ball through an opening in the defensive wall. The shot was well directed but lacked "Auge's" usual power and should have been an easy stop and collect for Red Star 'keeper Stevan Stojanović, but somehow he made a complete mess of things as the ball squirmed under his body and into the net. Suddenly, it was game on again – and how.

Just four minutes after Augenthaler's equaliser, Effenberg sent the ball into the Red Star box from out on the left. Somehow it took a helpful deflection of a defender and fell to winger Manfred Bender who made no mistake with a thumping left-footed shot that fizzed past Stojanović. In the space of just four minutes the entire tie had been completely turned on its head, with the home side rocking and reeling as the visitors looked to seize the momentum. Bender had almost been the supersub hero of the previous year's classic semi-final second leg in Milan, and once again he showed that he was the right man for the occasion with his third goal in his last four European starts – a statistic that stood in stark contrast to his Bundesliga record of just five goals in thirty-three games.

Bayern continued to apply the pressure to score the third goal that would have left their opponents needing at least two more, but try as they might it wouldn't come. As the clock ticked by the game appeared to be heading inexorably for extra time, but there would be just one more nasty twist in store – yet another one of those horrible moments that always seemed to crop up at crucial moments during important European games.

Although the statistics appear to refute it, many claims have been made over the years by both opponents and a selection of hostile commentators that Bayern have always been blessed with a unique brand of luck, called *Dusel* – or, more specifically, the phenomenon known as *Bayern-Dusel*. If anyone has been sitting in any Bayern supporter's position have endured some of their campaigns in Europe over the past thirty years, they will know that this is in fact far from true.

Such would be the case in Belgrade, where with ninety minutes on the clock Red Star midfielder Robert Prosinečki cut the ball back for Mihajlović who in turn swung it into the crowded Bayern box. Augenthaler attempted to slide in to clear the danger, but instead caught the ball with his right boot in a way that sent it looping towards the corner of the Bayern net. It was the sort of move where if you tried it a thousand times on the training pitch you'd never get the same result.

As the ball spun off Augenthaler's outstretched boot, it assumed a particularly wicked arc that took it high over Raimond Aumann's head. The Bayern 'keeper managed to get a desperate hand to it as he scuttled backwards towards the goal, but he could no better than give it a gentle tap with his glove, helping it on its way into the net.

Bayern-Dusel? What a load of complete and utter *Quatsch*.

It was scarcely believable, but for a Bayern fan used to such calamitous finales in important European matches the last-minute drama in Belgrade had not been a massive surprise. Rather than get into a rage and throw random objects at the television, I simply sat back and sighed at yet another sorry Bavarian tale of so near yet so far.

Bayern's Yugoslav conquerors would go on and win the final on penalties after a goalless draw against Olympique de Marseille; yes, it was the same old story there too.

THE LOWEST OF THE LOW

If the first full season of the 1990s had been a disappointing one, the following year witnessed the beginning of what was arguably the worst spell in the history of FC Bayern München in recent memory. Thankfully supporters under twenty years old don't have to remember anything about the rubbish that went on at the Säbenerstraße and the countless journeymen who passed through the club's doors during that period, but for those of us who were around then the bad memories would go far beyond the close title finishes and heartbreaking European Cup final defeats.

While Rotterdam in 1982 and Vienna in 1987 had been hard to stomach, at least Bayern had been competitive enough to challenge Europe's elite. In 1991/92, they found themselves not only struggling against the continent's minnows, but floundering among the Bundesliga's also-rans and mid-table floaters.

I would actually go so far to say that the extended 38-game 1991/92 season was the worst season in my entire thirty-three years as a Bayern fan, a year that Bayern ended up finishing in tenth place behind the likes of Eintracht Frankfurt, Karlsruher SC and – horror of all horrors – Bavarian rivals Nürnberg. Perhaps we should have been grateful that TSV 1860 München had not been in the top flight at the time.

It terms of their final league position, it was not Bayern's worst-ever season. In 1977/78 they had finished back down in twelfth place, sixteen points adrift of champions Köln, and had been on the sharp end of a 6-1 aggregate thrashing in the last sixteen of the UEFA Cup by Eintracht Frankfurt. Older supporters may argue that the 1978 vintage was the worst they had ever seen, but the class of 1992 were a whole new definition of dreadful. With football that can best be described as abject, Bayern were unceremoniously bundled out of Europe in circumstances that could best be described as humiliating. It was nothing short of woeful, the lowest of the low.

As if to make up for the few personnel changes in the previous season there were wholesale changes to the squad, with a number of established figures making their way out. Perhaps the most significant exit was that of skipper Klaus Augenthaler who after fifteen years finally hung up his boots to take charge of the FC Bayern youth squad, while Hans Dorfner – like Augenthaler another piece of the familiar furniture at the Säbenerstraße – moved the short distance up the Autobahn A9 back to former club Nürnberg.

While the retirement of the thirty-four year old Augenthaler and the departure of the just as established Dorfner would have a major impact on the squad dynamic, the changes were easily absorbed. The same could not be said of the departure of Jürgen Kohler and Stefan Reuter, two younger players at the peak of their powers in the German national team. Kohler had spent just two years in Munich and Reuter three, before they were both snapped up by Italian giants Juventus. Central defender Kohler – arguably one of the best in the world – departed at a cost of just under DM15 million, while the versatile right-sided defender Reuter was something of a bargain sale at DM5.5 million.

In comparison, the players brought in to fill the holes were nowhere close in terms of quality or experience, while those that did appear to fit the bill were way past their best. To plug the newly-created gaps in the defence, Oliver Kreuzer was signed from Karlsruhe SC for DM4.5 million and Alois Reinhardt was picked up from Bayer Leverkusen, while the space created by the departure of Hans Dorfner in midfield was filled by Brazilian defensive midfielder Bernardo Fernandes da Silva, better known as Bernardo, signed from São Paulo FC for a similar cost. Up front, unknown Brazilian Waldemar Aureliano de Oliveira Filho, or Mazinho, made his way to Munich from local side Clube Atlético Bragantino for DM3.5 million, and the experienced if slightly limited Kaiserslautern striker Bruno Labbadia arrived at Bayern for DM1.5 million.

In addition to these newcomers there were two more well-known arrivals. 1990 World Cup winner Thomas Berthold made his way back to Germany from Italian side AS Roma for around DM2.75 million, while controversial German international goalkeeper Harald "Toni" Schumacher was persuaded out of retirement having returned to Germany after three seasons in Turkey with Fenerbahçe S.K. Following early season injuries to newly-appointed captain Raimond Aumann and second 'keeper Sven Scheuer a serious goalkeeping crisis had developed at Bayern; left with the inexperienced Gerald Hillringhaus and Uwe Gospodarek, the Bayern management set about persuading the thirty-seven year old veteran to come to

Munich as back up to Hillringhaus until Aumann was able to return. While Schumacher was certainly experienced, his recruitment smacked of desperation.

Bayern's patchy season started as it would go on, with a creditable 1-1 draw in Bremen followed by a home defeat at the hands of former DDR-Oberliga club and Bundesliga new boys Hansa Rostock. Just one week later *Die Roten* also exited the DFB-Pokal at the first hurdle for the second season in succession, collapsing in a miserable heap to a 4-2 home defeat after extra time against second tier FC 08 Homburg.

If the defeat against a team from the 2. Bundesliga Süd were not bad enough, the fact that it had been played in an almost empty Olympiastadion provided that final cruel touch. Just nine thousand spectators would bother to turn up to witness the humiliation.

September and October 1991 provided a succession of embarrassing results, particularly at home. Lowly VfL Bochum had come to the Olympiastadion and eased to a 2-0 win, but perhaps the most stomach-churning setback would take place against lowly Stuttgarter Kickers, who put four past a Munich side that was little more than a disjointed rabble in red shirts.

To nobody's great surprise this thumping defeat proved to be the catalyst for Jupp Heynckes' dismissal, though the coach had never really been the problem. Following the departure of a number of key players – among them Kohler, Reuter, Dorfner and club stalwart Augenthaler – what passed as FC Bayern München in 1991/92 was little more than a vague shadow of the great Bayern teams of the past.

Internal strife and bickering, a catalogue of unfortunate injuries and a mix of has-beens and at times unsuitable players being trotted out in front of increasingly frustrated supporters quickly hastened the beginning of a turbulent period where the once proud FC Bayern München found itself being turned into a laughing stock incapable of beating Stuttgart's second-best team. Then there was the almost comical baiting of Stefan Effenberg by opposition fans whenever he touched the ball, with every loud jeer and whistle a stark reminder of the peroxide blond midfielder's mealy-mouthed statement the year before. The nearly men of the 1980s had turned into what would soon be dubbed *FC Hollywood*.

In a move that in hindsight will always be considered desperate by those around to witness it at the time, the club then chose to appoint former player Søren Lerby as Heynckes' replacement. While the highly respected thirty-three year old Dane had been an outstanding player for Bayern during the mid-1980s, he had no previous coaching experience to speak of. Lacking the required coaching licence Lerby would work alongside youth team coach

Hermann "Tiger" Gerland. As an interested fan I found all of these shenanigans difficult to fathom; I had seen Sunday league youth teams run more efficiently.

Lerby's appointment was bizarre at best, and through no real fault of his own he would take the club even deeper into the mire.

More changes were made to the unsettled squad. Veteran Dutchman Jan Wouters arrived from Ajax Amsterdam for just over DM2 million to shore up the worryingly unstable midfield, while Brazilian flop Bernardo – arguably one of the worst international signings to step out in a Bayern shirt – was jettisoned after just a handful of games.

Bernardo was not the first, and would not be the last of a number of overhyped, overrated and unproductive foreign signings. Uli Hoeneß had in the past been prepared to defend the idea of Bayern being solid, dependable and German, but the stagnant performances in European competition and the increased fluidity of the transfer circus saw a complete change in direction. While the Bayern squad of the 1980s were largely Germans with the occasional high-profile international star such as Belgian Jean-Marie Pfaff or Søren Lerby himself, by the early 1990s there were increasing numbers of imports from outside of the European continent – with most being relative unknowns.

Nobody really expected much from the new coach, and things could not have got off to a worse start as Bayern were crushed 3-0 at home by Borussia Dortmund. Defeat against high-flying VfB Stuttgart followed, and although Lerby would finally get off the mark in his third game in charge with a convincing 3-0 win over relegation-threatened Mönchengladbach, three draws in a row saw Bayern slide down the table into thirteenth place – just two points above the drop zone.

Clearly out of his depth, things would not get any better for the unfortunate Lerby as his lack of coaching and man-management skills quickly unravelled. A hard-fought single-goal win over Karlsruher SC was followed by a fourth home defeat at the hands of Werder Bremen, and a dismal 2-1 defeat in Rostock – who completed an historic season double – saw Bayern slip behind the former DDR-Liga side into fourteenth place. With the coach's future right on the brink, a 3-1 win over second from bottom Fortuna Düsseldorf arrested the downward slide – ensuring that Lerby would survive at least until the end of the *Hinrunde*.

One might have thought that the two-month winter break might have helped recharge the batteries in Munich, and a 1-1 draw in Gelsenkirchen against seventh-placed Schalke 04 provided some grounds for mild optimism. However any such hopes were almost immediately dashed the following week, when relegation-threatened Dynamo Dresden came to Munich and eased out of the drop zone with a 2-1 win.

A 5-0 win in Bochum provided yet another false dawn, as just a week later Lerby's side suffered a shattering four-goal thrashing at the hands of bogey side Kaiserslautern. This would prove to be the final straw for the beleaguered Dane, who passed what was quickly becoming a poisoned chalice to a man at the complete opposite end of the coaching experience scale – one-time national team assistant coach "Sir" Erich Ribbeck.

With just eleven games remaining the hope of a top-six finish and a European berth had all but disappeared, and Ribbeck's mission had become the scarcely believable one of keeping Bayern out of the drop zone. The new coach would get off to a decent enough start with a 2-0 win over Hamburger SV, but further defeats including a less than memorable 3-1 drubbing at the Olympiastadion by Bavarian rivals Nürnberg left *Die Roten* floating in tenth place at the season's end, sixteen points adrift of champions VfB Stuttgart and just seven places and five points above the four relegation spots.

	P	W	D	L	Goals	GD	Pts
VfB Stuttgart	38	21	10	7	62:32	+30	52:24
BV 09 Borussia Dortmund	38	20	12	6	66:47	+19	52:24
Eintracht Frankfurt	38	18	14	6	76:41	+35	50:26
<...>							
FC Bayern München (10.)	38	13	10	15	59:61	-2	36:40

In terms of overall results Ribbeck had fared no better or worse than Lerby, but with a record of five wins, one draw and five defeats the veteran coach was at least able to see things through to the end of the season. While Bayern remained poor on the road with just one win from their final half dozen matches, Ribbeck was able to guide the team to three successive home wins in the Bundesliga – a noteworthy achievement given that they had been unable to string together even successive two positive results in the sixteen previous matches played at the Olympiastadion.

Perhaps the most significant statistical feature of the 1991/92 season had been Bayern's home results; in their nineteen matches at the Olympiastadion, they lost no fewer than seven. Only the two bottom teams – Stuttgarter Kickers and Fortuna Düsseldorf – fared worse on home turf. Even more worryingly, Bayern also conceded thirty-two goals at home, three goals more than the next worst, VfL Bochum. Overall, Bayern were the second-worst defence in the entire league, shipping a total sixty-one goals in their thirty-eight games. Only bottom club

Düsseldorf, with sixty-nine, were worse. On the upside Bayern did score fifty-nine goals, a figure bettered only by the top three finishers.

Bayern's European adventures in the UEFA Cup in 1991/92 proved to be even more calamitous than their dismal domestic results. After Jupp Heynckes had cautiously guided the team past League of Ireland champions Cork City 3-1 on aggregate – a 1-1 draw being followed by a scrappy encounter in Munich decided by two late goals including a last-minute Christian Ziege penalty – his successor Lerby was left to pick up the reins for the second round tie against his countrymen from Boldklubben 1903 København.

On paper, there was no comparison between the two teams. Bayern were three-times champions of Europe and one of the continent's biggest and most established names, while the Danish opponents had only ever won two European ties and had never progressed passed the second round of any European competition in their rather undistinguished history. They hadn't even won their own domestic title since 1975/76. However, on 23rd October 1991 every statistic would be thrown out of the window, for what followed was arguably the most woefully embarrassing European match in Bayern's long and distinguished history. To even call it a game of football would be a travesty.

The first half hour passed by with little incident, and given Bayern's established reputation among Europe's biggest and most successful clubs nobody was surprised when Brazilian striker Mazinho gave Lerby's side the lead after thirty-two minutes. In spite of Bayern's poor domestic form, nobody expected anything less than victory over the unheralded – and for many unknown – Danish side.

It proved to be the calm before the storm. Just five minutes later the home side drew level through Michael Manniche, but as the clock ticked towards half-time with the scores level at one apiece nobody could have anticipated what would come next.

Some twelve minutes into the second half the home side won a penalty that was safely dispatched by veteran Danish international Ivan Nielsen, and Bayern suddenly found themselves chasing the game. However just after the hour mark the floodgates opened. On sixty-one minutes Kenneth Wegner made it 3-1, and before the Bayern players and their fans even had time to look at the scoreboard and rub their eyes Manniche had scored his second and his team's fourth. With thirteen minutes remaining Brian Kaus scored a fifth, and two minutes from time Iørn Uldbjerg made it a round half dozen.

1-6. *1-6. Six. Sechs.*

So there we were: the great FC Bayern München, 6-1 down against a Danish side that would be merged with bigger local rivals FC København and rebranded less than a year later.

Of the Bayern fans that had been there at the start among the fourteen-thousand strong crowd in the compact Gentofte Stadion in the northern suburbs of the Danish capital, I doubt that many of them would have remained in the ground long enough to witness defender Markus Münch's long-distance strike in added time to pull the score back to a no less embarrassing 6-2.

A last-minute penalty from Mazinho gave Lerby's laughing stock outfit a narrow 1-0 win in the return leg at the Olympiastadion, but by that time nobody in the paltry 21,000 crowd really cared that much as Bayern huffed and puffed their way out of the tournament. With nothing else to play for, all that remained was the fight to climb up the Bundesliga table in the hope of getting the consolation of European football the following season.

For every Bayern fan who might have been around to witness this disaster, these were darkest of dark days.

Over the course of this one miserable season, FC Bayern's reputation had taken a serious battering. Opponents and critical commentators made the most of the opportunity to take a bite, and the bitter truth was that from every angle the situation in Munich looked horrendous. From the tactics on the pitch and the dismal results through the curious coaching appointments and the embarrassing mid-table finish, the team had become little more than a laughing stock.

Bayern's tenth-place finish and failure to win any silverware in 1991/92 resulted in the team not appearing in European competition the following year – the first and so far only time in my thirty-something years as a fan that this had happened – and the first time since the 1978/79 season. Supporting Bayern had always been a joy, but during 1991/92 I had slowly started to feel what it must have been like supporting Nürnberg, Eintracht Braunschweig or West Bromwich Albion. It would be fair to say that it was something of a sobering experience.

Erich Ribbeck's first full season in charge would be a marked improvement on the previous year – not that this was really saying much – but it would also be remembered for the team being in first place in the Bundesliga right until the penultimate week of the *Rückrunde*, when they fell apart completely in being overhauled by rivals Werder Bremen. New and old names had arrived in Munich as Ribbeck looked to improve and develop the squad, but something never really felt right. Despite being well respected by his peers, the fact remained that in his long career "Sir Erich" had only won one trophy – the UEFA Cup in 1988 with Bayer Leverkusen.

After the previous season's trauma a number of players shuffled towards the exit, among them Brian Laudrup, Alan McInally, Stefan Effenberg and Thomas Strunz. After two years where he was never quite able to fulfil his potential Laudrup moved to Italian side Fiorentina for DM10 million, while McInally moved back to Scotland with Kilmarnock on a free transfer. Effenberg had looked to have established himself in his two seasons in Munich, but he too was lured by the Lire in joining Laudrup at Fiorentina for just under DM7.5 million. The out of contract Strunz meanwhile headed west for a new challenge at VfB Stuttgart.

These four big names were joined at the exit by Markus Babbel, Manfred Bender and old stager Toni Schumacher, while Hansi Pflügler hung up his professional boots to take up a new role with FC Bayern II.

Among those making their way to Munich there were a number of promising younger players, a pair of established internationals, and a returning legend. Twenty-one year old winger Mehmet Scholl was signed from Karlsruher SC for DM5 million to join a number of players from the Bayern youth team including Dieter Frey and Christian Nerlinger, defenders Thomas Helmer and Jorginho were lured away from Borussia Dortmund and Bayer Leverkusen for DM7.5 million and DM5.5 million respectively, and workmanlike midfielder Markus Schupp arrived from SG Wattenscheid 09 on a free transfer.

However the biggest news concerned the return of Bayern and Germany legend Lothar Matthäus, who returned to Bavaria after a successful four-year spell with Internazionale for the bargain price of DM4 million. It was the perfect confidence boost for both the club and the fans, and the popular Matthäus was widely seen as just the man to lift Bayern out of the doldrums and hasten their return back to the top of the German and European game.

The season could not have started any better, with six wins on the bounce – five in the Bundesliga, and the sixth a 6-0 demolition of non-league Borussia Neunkirchen in the first round of the DFB-Pokal – Bayern's first win in the competition for three years. By the second week of September 1992, Ribbeck and his men were the talk of the town: the great FC Bayern were back.

However, the familiar demons soon returned with a vengeance. A defeat on penalties in Dortmund ended the cup run as quickly as it had begun, and the winning streak was ended at the Olympiastadion by Souleyman Sané's last-minute equaliser for Wattenscheid 09.

Bayern remained at the top the following week with a hard-earned win in Dortmund as they quickly avenged their cup defeat, but after that it was back to that familiar inconsistency. Points were dropped at home to struggling Mönchengladbach and at unfancied Saarbrücken, and the undefeated league record met its end against a slowly improving Werder Bremen who had started to climb ominously up the table after a patchy opening month.

Ribbeck's side made its way to the *Winterpause* with just that one defeat, but seven draws meant that they held just a one-point lead over Eintracht Frankfurt, with Bremen a further point behind in third. The top three teams had lost just four games between them, but the number of one-pointers ensured that things were tight at the top when the Bundesliga went into its annual hibernation. No one side had really dominated proceedings at any stage, and whenever they slipped up their rivals often failed to take advantage.

Three straight wins at the start of the *Rückrunde* saw Bayern open up a three-point advantage, but a flat goalless draw against struggling Dynamo Dresden would allow the others to keep themselves in the hunt. Successive defeats in Hamburg and Wattenscheid allowed Bremen to tie things up at the top, with Bayern a whisker in front by virtue of goals scored. Despite their inability to string two decent results together, Ribbeck's men somehow kept their noses in front. Every time they looked to have handed the advantage back to Bremen, Otto Rehhagel's side would themselves slip up.

Bayern looked to have found their form just at the right time with an emphatic six-goal thrashing of relegation-threatened Saarbrücken, with new signing Scholl scoring a fine hat-trick – his first in the famous red *Trikot*. The Bavarians were two points clear of their rivals with a goal difference advantage of +8, and things were set up perfectly for a crucial four-pointer at the Weserstadion – a genuine Bundesliga *Klassiker*

Things could not have started any better when Christian Ziege scored after twenty-nine minutes, but a soft penalty at the cusp of half-time saw New Zealander Wynton Rufer level the scores for Bremen. Another spot-kick from Rufer seven minutes into the second half quickly turned the game on its head, and with Bayern unable to respond Bremen put their foot on the gas. Austrian midfielder Andreas Herzog provided the home side with a two-goal cushion with just over twenty minutes remaining, and as the game entered the final ten minutes journeyman striker Bernd Hobsch netted a fourth to rub salt into Bavarian wounds.

Despite the 4-1 defeat, Bayern had managed to keep their noses in front – but only just. Their two-point lead had been wiped out, and their +8 goal difference had been whittled right down to just +2. As the season turned into the final straight, things could not have been any tighter at the top. Bayern nudged in front once again with an action-packed 5-3 win over defending champions VfB Stuttgart as Bremen dropped the ball in Wattenscheid, but the following week it was *Die Roten's* turn to slip up as they drew a blank against struggling Nürnberg while Bremen eked out a hard-earned two points against third-placed Dortmund.

And so the see-sawing continued. A morale-boosting 4-1 thrashing of fifth-placed Bayer Leverkusen saw Bayern restore their two-point advantage as Bremen slipped up in Mönchengladbach, but just as though it looked like Ribbeck's men had done all the hard work a horror show at seventh-placed Karlsruhe handed the psychological advantage right back to the reviled *Fischköpfe*.

It was like living in a nightmare. The team that had clinically dispatched Leverkusen the previous weekend completely disappeared, and were replaced by a blubbering, uncoordinated mass of red shirts that found themselves three goals down at half-time at the Wildparkstadion.

Egged on by their flamboyant coach Winfried Schäfer – who resembled a bizarre Teutonic whirling dervish with his stonewashed jeans, leather biker jacket, mop of chaotic blond hair and windmill-armed celebration routine – Karlsruhe even had the temerity to score a fourth four minutes into the second half. Late goals from Mazinho and Ziege halved the deficit and ensured that Bayern avoided a complete embarrassment, but a 4-0 win for Bremen at strugglers Saarbrücken had once more closed the gap at the top of the table. As the season entered its penultimate week, Ribbeck's side were still in front on goal difference.

	P	W	D	L	Goals	GD	Pts
FC Bayern München	32	17	10	5	68:41	+27	44:20
SV Werder Bremen	32	17	10	5	55:30	+25	44:20

Bayern should have already had the *Meisterschale* safely locked away at the Säbenerstraße, but the drama would get even more intense with the finishing post in sight. The penultimate set of fixtures saw Bayern at home to relegation-threatened VfL Bochum while Werder took on northern rivals HSV at the Weserstadion, and it was at this point where Werder finally pulled the rabbit out of the hat. For weeks they had trailed in Bayern's wake, but right when it mattered they produced what was arguably their performance of the season.

At half-time, everything was going to plan for Erich Ribbeck and FC Bayern. *Die Roten* had swept into a three-goal lead with goals from Scholl, Ziege and Matthäus, and although Bremen were themselves two goals ahead against HSV, Bayern were still in front of Rehhagel's side on goal difference. However, just forty-five minutes later, the situation had been dramatically twisted in Bremen's favour. While Bochum produced a far more spirited performance in Munich to peg the score back to 3-1, Bremen netted a third. Then, in the final three minutes, they scored a fourth and a fifth. Rehhagel's side had been sitting in Bayern's shadow all season, but right at the death they had edged themselves in front by the slimmest of margins. It was almost like 1985/86 in reverse.

The final day of what had been a dramatic season saw both clubs tied on forty-six points, with Bremen holding a narrow +1 goal difference advantage; while the northerners were hosted by seventh-placed VfB Stuttgart, Bayern were playing their final match against Schalke 04 in Gelsenkirchen's Parkstadion. The equation was simple: Bayern needed to better Bremen's result to win the title, and should both teams win, Ribbeck's side needed to win by at least one more goal to pip Werder on goals scored.

	P	W	D	L	Goals	GD	Pts
SV Werder Bremen	33	18	10	5	60:30	+30	46:20
FC Bayern München	33	18	10	5	71:42	+29	46:20

I had just arrived in the Czech Republic on a summer study tour for this dramatic finale, and ended up spending what was a warm Saturday afternoon in a grey tower block in a quiet suburb of Plzeň tuned in to the radio station Bayern 3.

Things would not start at all well for Bayern with midfielder Ingo Anderbrügge putting *Die Knappen* ahead after just four minutes, and although Mehmet Scholl pulled things level twenty minutes later, Russian striker Alexander Borodjuk restored Schalke's lead eleven minutes before the break to leave Ribbeck's side with a mountain to climb in the second half.

At half-time Bremen and Stuttgart were still goalless, meaning Bayern were two points behind in the overall standings.

As the second half kicked off in both Stuttgart and Gelsenkirchen I sat back, headphones firmly clamped to my ears, hoping for that miracle to happen. However, just a minute into the second half word came through that Werder had taken the lead at the Neckarstadion, meaning that Bayern had to not only win but score at least three more goals in doing so. When Bremen doubled their advantage just four minutes later, even the staunchest Bayern fan would have throw in the towel. Yet with football being what it is, I just kept listening and hoping for one final twist.

Lothar Matthäus levelled the scores in Gelsenkirchen once again on seventy-four minutes and two minutes later Dutchman Jan Wouters scored a third to rekindle those faintest of faint hopes, but at the very same time Werder virtually wrapped things up with a third goal in

Stuttgart. I spent the final few minutes hoping against hope, but at no stage during the final match day proceedings would Bayern ever be ahead of the game. In hindsight, one could comfortably say that it was never going to happen.

With both teams level on points and Bremen ahead on goal difference I kept thinking back to Bremen's two late second half goals in the dramatic encounter at the Weserstadion, but that itself became a moot point when Borudjuk wrapped up the scoring at the Parkstadion with his second and Schalke's third four minutes from full time.

	P	W	D	L	Goals	GD	Pts
SV Werder Bremen	34	19	10	5	63:30	+33	48:20
FC Bayern München	34	18	11	5	74:45	+29	47:21

And that's how it all ended, with Bayern pipped by a single point. Thankfully my being in the Czech Republic helped me get over things relatively painlessly: the cheap golden *Pilsner Urquell* served at the local tennis club in Bory certainly helped. I was also able to digest the end of the season stories with the help of the German press, and unlike in the UK it was just a matter of popping into the local *Tabak* and picking up a copy of *Bild*, *Die Welt*, or *Süddeutsche Zeitung*. When on one of our regular excursions to Prague, I'd also manage to get hold of a copy of the rudimentary but highly informative *kicker*.

Despite it being yet another silverware-free year at the Säbenerstraße, the second place finish in the Bundesliga had at least guaranteed a return to European competition for Erich Ribbeck's side – though a few months into the 1993/94 season one might have wished that it hadn't happened at all after yet another calamitous UEFA Cup second round episode.

Transfer activity during the summer of 1993 was considerably lighter compared to the previous year, and the start of the season saw the arrival of yet another unknown South American in the form of Colombian striker Adolfo Valencia. Signed from local club Santa Fe, the burly Valencia looked to be the perfect fit for Bayern's somewhat lightweight front line; his greatest assets were his strength and pace, attributes that earned him the soubriquet *El Tren* or "the train".

After nine successful seasons in the Bavarian capital, striker Roland Wolhfarth was one of those who headed for the exit door at the Säbener Straße, signing for French club St. Étienne for DM2.5 million. The unsettled Manfred Schwabl made the short journey up to Nürnberg for a third time, while the disappointing Thomas Berthold headed west to VfB Stuttgart.

To compensate for the departure of Wohlfarth, the offensive unit was bolstered by the arrival of attacking midfielder Marcel Witeczek from Kaiserslautern for around DM5 million, while promising teenager Alexander Zickler was signed from Dynamo Dresden for DM2.3 million.

Such a hefty price tag for a nineteen year old with fewer than twenty first-team appearances might have looked slightly surprising to the casual outsider, but there was also a story behind it: Bayern could very easily have acquired Dynamo's star striker for a far smaller fee, but were happy to pay the DM2.3 million in order to help save the ailing Saxon club from financial collapse.

Bayern's league campaign would get off to a slow and somewhat unimpressive start, and after ten games they were sitting far off the pace in tenth place – six points adrift of early pace-setters Eintracht Frankfurt. *Die Roten* had lost only two of these ten opening matches, but disappointing draws against arguably weaker opposition such as SG Wattenscheid 09 – again – and MSV Duisburg had left the coach sitting on the brink. A four-game winless streak that lasted almost all of September was ended with a 4-0 thumping of third-placed Hamburger SV, and another win by the same scoreline in Köln the following weekend looked to have reignited the Bavarians' stuttering campaign.

A 3-1 win over strugglers Mönchengladbach was then followed by a hard-earned point on the road against leaders Frankfurt, and a 4-0 demolition of fourth-placed Kaiserslautern at the Olympiastadion saw Ribbeck's team climb into second place, closing the gap at the top to just three points.

If Bayern's patchy start to the domestic season had not been worrying enough for coach Ribbeck and the club's expectant and demanding supporters, worse was to come in the UEFA Cup at the end of October 1993. Having disposed of Dutch side FC Twente Enschede fairly easily in the first round of the competition, Bayern were then pitted against English side Norwich City, a team with no European pedigree whatsoever.

The first leg of the second round tie was in Munich, and despite Bayern's slow start to the season they started out as firm favourites both on paper and with the pundits to progress to the third round of the competition. Not only were Bayern unbeaten at the Olympiastadion against English opposition, they were taking on a highly unfancied team playing only its third-ever European match.

The visitors from the county of Norfolk had other ideas. Sporting a hideous yellow and green strip that resembled a regurgitated spinach omelette, Norwich took the game to Bayern right from the whistle, and before the home supporters could even draw breath Mike Walker's team had taken the lead. Taking advantage of Bayern's inability to clear their lines effectively and a poor headed clearance from repurposed sweeper Lothar Matthäus, the ball fell perfectly for midfielder Jeremy Goss, whose sweetly-struck right-footed volley flew unerringly past the helpless Raimond Aumann with just twelve minutes on the clock.

Bayern's shock at falling behind was amplified just after the half-hour mark. Having won a free-kick just inside the Bayern half, right-back Ian Crook lofted the ball high into the box. With centre-back Oliver Kreuzer clambering all over striker Chris Sutton, the ball reached left-back Mark Bowen, who calmly guided the ball with his head past Aumann. In the space of thirty minutes Bayern's confidence had been completely shattered, and the home crowd quickly broke into an orchestrated chorus of boos, jeers and whistles.

A fine right-wing cross from Brazilian Jorghino was headed in at the far post by Christian Nerlinger four minutes before the break as Bayern halved the deficit, but the visitors were able to withstand everything the home side could throw at them in the second half.

Ribbeck tried to force the pace by introducing striker Bruno Labbadia and the ineffectual winger Michael Sternkopf, but in front of a frustrated crowd the Bavarians had to resign themselves to yet another embarrassing European defeat. However this was not just any other ordinary defeat, but one in front of a home crowd not used to such poor performances on the European stage.

Canaries' goalkeeper Bryan Gunn was fêted as a hero by the Norwich supporters, and that evening in the Bavarian capital remains one of the greatest moments in the Carrow Road side's history – arguably even more memorable than their League Cup victory in 1985 or the infamous drunken outburst by chairwoman and celebrity chef Delia Smith.

The return leg at Carrow Road saw Bayern take an early lead through Colombian Adolfo Valencia as they looked to turn the tie around, but this early strike was cancelled out six minutes into the second half by first-leg hero Goss. Bayern were unable to find a second goal that would have kept them alive and taken the tie into extra time, and when the final whistle blew Norwich had completed one of the most famous victories in their history. Meanwhile, the Bavarian giants had sunk to their second ignominious European second round exit in the space of two years.

When it rains it pours, and less than a week after the UEFA Cup second round defeat Bayern's season would suffer another hammer blow, this time in the quarter-finals of the DFB-Pokal at the hands of strugglers Dynamo Dresden. Ribbeck's side had fallen behind in the twenty-first minute at a packed Rudolf-Harbig-Stadion, but a Mehmet Scholl goal twelve minutes from time had given them hope of at least taking the game into extra time. However with just a minute remaining Dresden's big-haired centre-forward Olaf Marschall netted the winner for the Saxon side, and Bayern were sent spinning out of their second cup competition in the space of just six days.

In years gone by many smaller teams had been overawed by Bayern's reputation – to the point where the game had often been lost psychologically even before a ball had been kicked – but the performances of both Norwich and Dresden had gone some way towards proving that this was no longer the case.

Just weeks after the cup defeat in Dresden Bayern would meet the same opponent again in the Bundesliga, and this time it was the Bavarians' turn to snatch a late goal as they salvaged a hardly creditable 1-1 draw. It was the last game before the *Winterpause* after what had been an extended twenty-match *Hinrunde*, and during the recess the Bayern board finally decided to draw the line under this latest painful chapter and part ways with the long-suffering Ribbeck. The man called in to save the club's stuttering season was none other than Bayern legend and former *Nationaltrainer* Franz Beckenbauer, who quickly had to remove his critic's cap and replace it with his coaching one.

Ribbeck – who would resurface again at the turn of the millennium as the coach of the German national team – had been one of the most unsuccessful *Trainers* in Bayern's long and rich history. In addition to being a coach who had overseen a number of memorably bad performances, "Sir Erich" had created his own little niche in the history of FC Bayern München; he became the first and only man to be in charge of the team for more than five-hundred days without winning a single trophy – an unenviable record he still holds to this day. Given Bayern's more recent success, it is a record unlikely to be surpassed in the near future.

While the inexperienced Søren Lerby could have been forgiven for his disastrously short spell in charge at Bayern, there could be such no excuses for Ribbeck, who had arrived at the Säbenerstraße as one of the most experienced and widely-respected coaches in Germany. How he had acquired this reputation, for me at least, had always been something of a mystery: in a coaching career that would eventually span close to thirty-five years Ribbeck would only ever win one major trophy – the 1988 UEFA Cup final with Bayer Leverkusen. One could say that even that had more to do with the ability and application of the players on the pitch rather than Ribbeck's tactics and coaching skills off it.

The Lerby-Ribbeck era of the early 1990s is of course now just a bad and distant memory, and looking at the hugely talented and highly successful Bayern side of today it is difficult to imagine just how bad things actually were back then. There had been genuine fears of a total meltdown, and with morale at its lowest point it would not have been beyond the realms of possibility to have seen the great Munich club following the likes of erstwhile rivals TSV 1860, Borussia Mönchengladbach and Hamburger SV into the bleak and barren land of mid-table obscurity, anonymity and meaningless UEFA Intertoto Cup matches. Were it not for the return of long-established heroes Franz Beckenbauer and Karl-Heinz Rummenigge who joined Uli Hoeneß on the board, the history of Germany's greatest club could have taken a completely different course.

The early 1990s would truly mark the club's lowest ebb in the postwar history of the club – the lowest of the low.

The fourteen-match *Rückrunde* would see a marked improvement in both form and fortune for Bayern, as Beckenbauer quickly looked to draw a line under the previous dark chapter and put his own unique stamp on the team. Things had been allowed to stagnate under the laissez-faire Ribbeck, and Beckenbauer's contrasting approach to discipline and his single-minded approach was just the thing the team needed. While the situation was still far from perfect, there was a greater sense of purpose at Bayern. Supporters were also enthused; with *Der Kaiser* at the helm, things could only get better.

Beckenbauer wouldn't get off to the best of starts with a 3-1 home defeat at the hands of VfB Stuttgart as Bayern slipped back down to fifth place, but an easy 3-1 win at bottom club VfB Leipzig quickly got things back on track. Bayern were now just a point behind surprise front runners MSV Duisburg, and a comprehensive four-goal demolition of the league leaders on match day twenty-three saw the Bavarians hit the top spot in the Bundesliga for the first time that season. Following more workmanlike wins over Werder Bremen and Wattenscheid, *Die Roten* edged two points in front of Eintracht Frankfurt at the top of the table. Once again, *Der Kaiser* appeared to be working his magic.

Back to back wins over Hamburger SV and Köln provided Beckenbauer's men with a comfortable four-point cushion, and while Bayern's results continued to be worryingly inconsistent, the inability of their rivals to take advantage of their slip-ups allowed *Die Roten* to remain at the top of the table – just about clear of the chasing pack as the final weeks of the season approached.

Frankfurt's title ambitions were then dealt a severe blow at the Olympiastadion as a second-half penalty from Lothar Matthäus gave Bayern a tight but deserved 2-1 win over Klaus Toppmöller's side in Munich, and despite a 2-0 defeat against mid-table Borussia Mönchengladbach and conceding four second-half goals at the hands of a rampant Kaiserslautern, *Die Roten's* advantage over the in-form Red Devils remained at two points, with the additional cushion of a slightly better goal difference. With two match days remaining Bayern had one hand on the *Meisterschale*, but a dropped point in Karlsruhe combined with a Kaiserslautern win over Dortmund saw their advantage cut back to just a single point.

The final day of the season would see Bayern entertain Schalke 04 – bringing back memories of the last-day drama of the previous season – while in-form Kaiserslautern took on twelfth-placed Hamburger SV at the Volksparkstadion. With just a point between the two teams, it was yet another case of things going right down to the final Saturday showdown.

While a struggling Schalke side that had just managed to escape relegation were not expected to give Bayern too many problems, bogey side Kaiserslautern were clearly the team in form. As all of Germany prepared themselves for yet another dramatic last day battle for the Bundesliga crown, nobody in Munich was taking anything for granted.

The drama began to unfold early on, and with just eighteen minutes gone in Hamburg Kaiserslautern took the lead through Czech international Pavel Kuka. Kuka's goal brought Friedel Rausch's side level on points with Bayern, but two behind on goal difference. So long as the scores remained the same, the *Meisterschale* was set to return south to Munich.

As half-time approached Bayern were unable to break the deadlock, but spirits at the Olympiastadion were raised ten minutes before the break when news started to filter through from Hamburg. Lithuanian striker Valdas Ivanauskas had levelled the scores for the *Rothosen*, and when the half-time whistles blew in the north and south of Germany it was a case of "as you were".

Five minutes into the second half at the Olympiastadion, the pressure was finally lifted as Lothar Matthäus struck to give Bayern the lead. Just ten minutes later, Jorghino scored a second to secure what was surely yet another Bundesliga title. Meanwhile there was no further news from Hamburg, where HSV and Kaiserslautern were still locked at one goal apiece.

Of course, a Bundesliga finale could not be a Bundesliga finale without a little last-minute drama, and as the final whistle approached in Munich news had started to filter through of not one but two Kaiserslautern goals in Hamburg. It was hardly nerve-jangling stuff, but

Bayern fans had suffered so much over the years that nobody would be singing in the stands until the proverbial fat lady got up to trill the opening chords.

When referee Lutz Fröhlich finally blew his whistle, the 63,000-strong crowd at the Olympiastadion could finally find their voice. For me personally, 1993/94 was the first time I had been able to follow a title-winning season properly – a season where I had seen at least highlights of every single match and every single goal rather than just five-minute dribbles here and there. After the abject misery of the 1991/92 season and the painful near miss in 1992/93, the championship shield was on its way back to Munich. It had been four long years, but the waiting was at an end.

	P	W	D	L	Goals	GD	Pts
FC Bayern München*	34	17	10	7	68:37	+31	44:24
1. FC Kaiserslautern	34	18	7	9	64:36	+28	43:25

Bayern had pipped Kaiserslautern by just a single point with a goal difference of +31 as opposed to the Red Devils' +28, which meant even a draw in their final match would have won them the title by dint of an advantage of +1. It was perhaps just as well that things didn't finish this way however, as it may well have opened up a completely new can of worms.

Just two weeks earlier on match day thirty-two, Bayern had played host to Nürnberg in the famous old school Bavarian derby, setting the scene for one of the most controversial moments in the thirty-year history of the Bundesliga. In the twenty-fourth minute after a right-sided corner and a rather chaotic scramble in the Nürnberg penalty area, Thomas Helmer scuffed a backheeled shot that rolled narrowly wide of the post.

The following moments could best be described as surreal. The home crowd groaned, Helmer waited by the post for a couple of seconds, and the rest of the Bayern team started running back to the middle of the field to prepare for the goal kick – only to see linesman Jörg Jablonski flag for a goal and referee Hans-Joachim Osmers point both teams back the centre circle.

Should Helmer have spoken to the referee? Did he, with his back facing the goal, actually know that his shot had been scuffed wide of the target rather than into the goal? If he didn't see what had happened, why would he have thought about questioning the linemans's decision? Either way, Herr Osmers' decision to award the goal stood, and in what were clearly bizarre scenes the red shirts gathered in a celebratory huddle while the Nürnberg players, led by goalkeeper Andreas Köpke, loudly remonstrated with the officials – to no avail.

The legend of the Thomas Helmer *Phantomtor* was born.

Nürnberg equalised in the second half only for man of the moment Helmer to score a legitimate – and far more spectacular – long-distance goal to restore Bayern's advantage, but the defender's influence on the game was far from over. With just minutes remaining Helmer brought down striker Christian Wück in the box, and Herr Osmers had no hesitation in pointing to the penalty spot as he looked to make up for his earlier catastrophic blunder.

To give things an additional twist the man who stepped up to take the kick was ex-Bayern man Manfred Schwabl, whose poorly-struck effort was easily saved by Raimond Aumann.

Having blown their chance of rescuing the game and taking a crucial point, relegation-threatened Nürnberg had nothing whatsoever to lose – and immediately filed a report about the referee's faulty decision with the DFB. Their protest was immediately upheld without any discussion or debate: Helmer's *Phantomtor* just couldn't be allowed to stand and take its place in the official record books. Even the most fervent Bayern fan couldn't disagree with the decision, even if the complainants happened to be from Nürnberg.

A replay was quickly shoehorned into the schedule as a midweek fixture just four days before the final round of matches, adding further spice to what was building up into a classic season finale. In front of a 28,500 crowd at the Olympiastadion the desperately defensive Franconians were able to make it through to half-time with the score at 0-0, frustrating the home team and the expectant home supporters. That was as good as it would get for the visitors, however. Mehmet Scholl finally opened the scoring for Bayern just two minutes into the second half, and things went from bad to worse for *Der Club* when Czech Luboš Kubík was shown his second yellow card three minutes before the hour mark.

With Nürnberg having to chase the game with ten men, the floodgates opened completely. Scholl scored his and Bayern's second two minutes after Kubik's dismissal, and a Dietmar Hamann goal sandwiched between two Bruno Labbadia strikes saw *Die Roten* romp to an emphatic 5-0 win.

Nürnberg's decision to protest the initial result had backfired badly, but in the end it wouldn't affect their position at the bottom end of the table. A point would have seen them edge SC Freiburg into the drop zone, but given their already poor goal difference the margin of their defeat in Munich made little difference to the overall outcome and their eventual relegation to the second division.

This takes us back to the last day top of the table permutations and the number crunching. Had Bayern only managed a draw in their final match with Schalke, they would have ended up level on points with Kaiserslautern but ahead on goal difference by the smallest possible margin of +1 – a margin that would never have existed without the addition of the five second-half goals scored in the replayed "ghost goal" match:

	P	W	D	L	Goals	GD	Pts
FC Bayern München*	34	16	11	7	66:37	+29	43:25
1.FC Kaiserslautern	34	18	7	9	64:36	+28	43:25

*Assuming a goalless draw between Bayern and Schalke 04.

One can only wonder what would have happened had things finished this way. Would Kaiserslautern have protested? Almost certainly, given that it was hardly their fault that they would have ended up at the wrong end of some brutally harsh mathematics. As for how Bayern or the DFB might have responded to such a protest, it is hard to say.

One thing is clear: if Bayern had clinched the title as a result of a goal difference boosted by the replayed fixture, it would have left a bitter taste in the mouth for all concerned. Thankfully, it would have no significant impact on the final standings.

Then there was the issue of the penalty at the end of the original "ghost goal" game. Had Manni Schwabl converted the kick and levelled the scores at 2-2, Nürnberg would have been three points clear of the drop zone and it is unlikely that they would have even protested the result – meaning that Bayern would have gone into the final day level on points with FCK, but two behind on goal difference:

	P	W	D	L	Goals	GD	Pts
1. FC Kaiserslautern	33	17	7	9	61:35	+26	41:25
FC Bayern München*	33	15	11	7	63:39	+24	41:25

*Assuming the scheduled fixture between Bayern and Nürnberg had finished 2-2, with no protest.

Going into the final minute of the final match day with Bayern leading Schalke 2-0 and Kaiserslautern level at 1-1 with HSV, Bayern would have been a point in front:

	P	W	D	L	Goals	GD	Pts
FC Bayern München	34	16	11	7	65:39	+26	43:25
1.FC Kaiserslautern	34	17	8	9	62:36	+26	42:26

At this exact point in proceedings, a second goal for Kaiserslautern in Hamburg would have flipped things around completely, taking the Red Devils back level on points but ahead by a goal differential of +27 compared to Bayern's +26. A third for Bayern would have also taken them to +27, but to the top of the table on goals scored.

As it happens, Kaiserslautern scored a second goal in injury time through Martin Wagner, and then a third soon after that through Stefan Kuntz. In the space of a minute, Bayern would have had the title snatched from them in the cruellest way possible.

	P	W	D	L	Goals	GD	Pts
1. FC Kaiserslautern	34	18	7	9	64:36	+28	43:25
FC Bayern München	34	16	11	7	65:39	+26	43:25

In the final analysis, things had worked out perfectly. Both Jörg Jablonski and Hans-Joachim Osmers could well have ended up as the unwitting poster boys in yet another controversial *Bayern-Dusel* conspiracy theory, but in the end they would end up as little more than interesting historical footnotes.

These days, the *Winterpause* in Germany often sees Bundesliga teams head out to warmer climes overseas for a mix of training, relaxation and the occasional promotional match against Middle Eastern, East Asian or North American opposition. For instance, over the 2012/13 winter break Bayern would travel to Qatar, where they played a series of friendly matches against local team Lekhwiya Sports Club and even league rivals Schalke 04.

Back in the late 1980s and all of the 1990s things had been very different however, with German clubs competing in a number of indoor tournaments across the country.

There were a number of qualifying events through the winter break leading to a final competition and the award of the DFB-Hallenpokal, with the series also being known as the *Hallen-Masters*. FC Bayern had never really bothered that much with this rather random collection of winter-warmer tournaments: the competition had taken place for fourteen seasons between 1987 and 2001, and while the list of champions had included the likes of Bayer Uerdingen, Hansa Rostock and even local city rivals TSV 1860 and SpVgg Unterhaching, Bavaria's biggest team had only ever reached one final in 1997, where they were defeated by Kaiserslautern.

I had been part of a university study group in Berlin in January 1994, and among the sites on our itinerary was the site of the famous wall, the Reichstag and the grey and rather grim environs of Hohenschönhausen – the headquarters of the infamous *Staatssicherheitsdienst* or

Stasi. On my own personal list was the veritable old Deutschlandhalle, which was hosting the Berlin leg of the Hallen-Masters. Finally, I would get to see Bayern play for real. Yes, it wouldn't be at the Olympiastadion or even on a proper pitch, but I didn't really care. I made sure to pack my *Schal* and an appropriate *Trikot* – at the time I had only three to choose from, and picked the white away one.

With my being based at a hostel in the West End close to the Olympiastadion and Theodor-Heuss-Platz, the Deutschlandhalle was perfectly located: it was as if they knew I was coming. In fact, it was so close that I didn't even need to bother with using the U-Bahn. There were no other takers, as everybody else for some bizarre reason had preferred to spend their Friday evening in the dark East Berlin club jungle rather than watch an indoor football tournament – not that this really bothered me that much. I pulled on my *Trikot* and grabbed my winter coat, hat and slightly frayed red FC Bayern scarf.

After a bracing fifteen-minute walk, making my way to the box office and handing over the grand total of thirty-five Deutschmarks, I was in. Bayern were one of six teams in the tournament alongside hosts Hertha Berlin, Bayer Leverkusen, Eintracht Frankfurt, Werder Bremen and guest side Spartak Moscow, and the first instalment of the three-day tournament schedule included six matches, with Bayern – now under the stewardship of Franz Beckenbauer – involved in two of them.

I took my seat alongside a small group of local Hertha fans, who were somewhat surprised to see a lone British FC Bayern supporter at an otherwise obscure indoor tournament right in the middle of the chilly Berlin winter. As I quickly discovered, there were hardly any Bavarians who had made the journey to the German capital, let alone fans from from further afield – I was probably the only one. This is perhaps hard to imagine today with Bayern being such a popular brand with millions of supporters from all around the world, but back then things were a little bit simpler. Bayern had always been a well-known club, but were far from the international phenomenon they are today.

While today one could expect more than a smattering of overseas supporters, it was a very rare occurrence back in the early 1990s. Of course, for me this was a good thing: if such an event were to be held today, it is very unlikely that I would have been able to turn up on the day and buy a ticket at the door.

The tournament's opening match was an exciting 2-2 draw between Beckenbauer's side and Frankfurt, with goals from Jorginho and Christian Ziege for Bayern. I had an excellent view from the *Obergeschoss* or upper tier, though my rather primitive camera was unable to do the event any real justice. Oh to have had my SLR or even my iPhone.

Hosts Hertha then beat Spartak 2-0 to loud applause from the Deutschlandhalle crowd, and after Leverkusen pipped Bremen 3-2 Bayern were back in the arena to take on Spartak. While the opening match had been a tight affair this one gave me plenty of reasons to cheer a little, as Bayern turned out a convincing display to dispatch the Russian champions 3-0. Markus Münch opened the scoring and Jorghino scored his second of the tournament before Marcel Witeczek wrapped things up.

With Bremen beating Frankfurt 3-0 and Hertha going down 2-0 to Leverkusen, the overnight standings saw the *Werkself* at the top with four points, followed by Bayern on three with Berlin and Bremen both on two and Frankfurt on one. Spartak were left propping up the table, with no points and no goals from their two matches.

As I made my way back to the hostel taking in the crisp late evening January air, it felt good. The Bayern team had not exactly set the world on fire, but I had finally got to see them properly. In the end, I wouldn't miss out on the night time entertainment either: when I returned there were a few people milling around, and we all decided to head out to a local *Kneipe* around the corner – where we stayed until at least three in the morning.

DANKE, BITTE UND VESTENBERGSGREUTH

His caretaker job complete, Franz Beckenbauer quickly retreated back to the sidelines at the end of the season. His replacement was former Milan, Juventus and Internazionale coach Giovanni Trapattoni – a man who arrived at the Säbenerstraße in the summer of 1994 with a string of titles and a massive reputation.

Bayern had had a number of foreign coaches over the years, but Trapattoni was the first genuinely big name to take the job. While the likes of Hungarians Gyula Lóránt and Pál Csernai had arrived in Munich with solid domestic coaching experience, Trapattoni was already a multiple winner on the European stage with both Juventus and Internazionale. Alongside the legendary former Bayern *Trainer* Udo Lattek, the man popularly known as "Il Trap" was the only other coach to have won all three major European club trophies.

Trapattoni was not the only high profile arrival in Munich in the autumn of 1994, as three well-established internationals also made their way to Bavaria. Experienced French international striker and *Ballon d'Or* winner Jean-Pierre Papin was signed from AC Milan for around DM5.5 million, Bulgarian centre-forward Emil Kostadinov was acquired on loan from Spanish club Deportivo la Coruña, and following an impressive showing in the World Cup finals in the United States, Swiss midfielder Alain Sutter was signed from Bavarian rivals Nürnberg for DM3 million.

Other new (and not so new) faces included defender Markus Babbel who returned to Munich from Hamburger SV, promising young Ghanaian centre-back Samuel Ossei Kuffour from Italian side Torino, and a twenty-five year old goalkeeper from Karlsruher SC, Oliver Kahn. Following the departure of veteran custodian Raimond Aumann to ten-time Turkish champions Beşiktaş, much was expected of the promising young DM4.6 million *Torhüter*, whose shock of bright blond hair made him look like a cross between his former coach Winfried Schäfer and the hirsute canine character Dougal from the *Magic Roundabout*.

Of those players leaving Munich, perhaps the biggest name was that of Olaf Thon who after six years at Bayern made his way back to hometown club Schalke 04 for DM2.5 million. Bruno Labbadia left to join Köln – also for DM2.5 million – while underused defender Markus Münch joined Bayer Leverkusen for DM1.5 million. There were a number of retirements too, with Roland Grahammer and Alois Reinhardt both hanging up their professional boots.

The build-up to the 1994/95 season and the fresh start with a high-profile and highly decorated coach had been highly optimistic, but it wouldn't take long for things to come crashing down to earth with what had to go down as one of the biggest shocks in the history of German club football.

Located off the beaten track, halfway between the cities of Nürnberg and Würzburg in the northern Bavarian region of Franconia, one can find the small market town of Vestenbergsgreuth – home to just under 1,500 people. A bit of a mouthful even for native German speakers, Vestenbergsgreuth is a place not many people outside of Germany would have heard of. Indeed, until one day in the late summer of 1994 not many people inside Bavaria, let alone Germany, had heard of it.

By 10pm on the evening of 14th August 1994 however, almost everyone with a television set had heard of Vestenbergsgreuth and its little football team, TSV.

While the Bayern starting eleven contained such names as Oliver Kahn, Lothar Matthäus, Jorghino and Jean-Pierre Papin, TSV *Trainer* Paul Hesselbach's side included a selection of part-time players both young and old from a mix of different professions. Thirty-three year old police officer Werner Pfeuffer and thirty-one year old physician Reiner Wirsching lined up alongside twenty-one year old electrician Ralf Scherbaum and twenty year old bank clerk Frank Schmidt. This was not just David versus Goliath, but David's weaker younger brother against Goliath's bigger and scarier uncle.

Many of TSV Vestenbergsgreuth's players would have watched Bayern on the television many times, yet here they were themselves, live on ZDF in a match that was being broadcast across the entire country - as well as on the Astra satellite where I was able to pick it up in the United Kingdom.

As they made their way out onto the pitch alongside their more illustrious opponents, many of these part-time players would have reached the pinnacle of their footballing careers, and nobody would have blamed them if they had simply fallen under the wheels of the

Bayern juggernaut once the pre-match handshakes and pleasantries were over. By simply being there they had in effect already won, and in a sense they knew they had nothing to lose. Just to be on the same field as the star-studded Bayern team was in itself something of a fairytale.

With the home side looking more like Bayern in a classically simple all-red *Trikot* with white trim, Trapattoni's side were wearing a new and rather bizarre gold, black and green combination that made them look a little like Jamaica. In fact, if you watched the game you'd have thought that it was a pre-season contest between a Jamaican XI and FC Bayern München II.

In front of an enthusiastic 24,200-strong crowd at Nürnberg's Frankenstadion, the gold-shirted *Münch'ner* threw themselves forward against an obdurate amateur team who played as if it were the final – but even as the clock ticked towards half-time with no adjustment to the scoreboard nobody would have expected anything but a Bayern victory. It was surely a case of when Bayern would initiate the expected goal avalanche rather than if.

The chances kept coming for the visitors: TSV 'keeper Scherbaum reacted brilliantly to get his hands to a Mehmet Scholl effort from ten yards, and five minutes before the half-time break Papin took his turn to send the ball wide of the target. Meanwhile, the camera frequently switched to the touchline to focus on the irate Giovanni Trapattoni, who was becoming more visibly animated and frustrated – a red-faced blur of characteristically Italian waving arms.

Then, the impossible happened.

Two minutes before the break, defensive midfielder and electrician Bernd Lunz rolled the ball into the Bayern box looking for police officer Werner Pfueffer, who went down at the edge of the box under a firm challenge from Didi Hamann. Eschewing the standard professional tactic of writhing on the ground with his face contorted in faux pain, Pfueffer simply got on with it and stuck out a leg, stabbing the ball forward into the Bayern box.

Seeing nothing untoward, referee Markus Merk waved play on. From the resulting melée, businessman Wolfgang Hüttner broke past a small group of yellow shirts and made his way towards the byline. His well-timed cross was sharply lifted back into the six yard box, and twenty-one year old midfielder Roland Stein arrived at the near post, stooping perfectly to direct the ball with his head past Oliver Kahn from close range.

The crowd erupted as the men in red celebrated, and all the Bayern players could do was look at each other with hands on hips, simply wondering what the hell was going on. Their defence has been turned inside out, and the egg on their faces was as yellow as the shirts on their backs. Meanwhile, Trapattoni was simmering on the touchline, gently rocking back and forth.

One can only imagine what it must have been like in the Bayern dressing room at half-time. The scowling, brooding Kahn. The opinionated team spokesman and amateur tactician Matthäus. The irate Italian coach, babbling incoherently in what would pass for broken German. Oh to have been a fly on the wall at that moment.

An early second half scare sparked Bayern into action, and they picked up where they had left off in the first half as they continued to huff, puff and run hard at the crowd of well-organised red shirts. Trapattoni threw on the lumbering Colombian striker Adolfo Valencia for the ineffective Marcel Witeczek, Scherbaum again did well to thwart the profligate Papin, and after a crazy goalmouth scramble the big-haired mechanic and centre-half Harry Koch hacked the ball clear. As the game entered the final twenty minutes Bayern had truly started to look desperate, to the point where one was unable to differentiate between the highly-paid professionals and the bunch of amateurs who after the match probably had to go to bed early to get ready for work the following morning.

Deep into injury time, Trapattoni's side took their final throw of the dice. Papin flicked the ball over Scherbaum and seemingly towards the Vestenbergsgreuth goal, but Lunz stretched a desperate leg to deflect it against the foot of the post. There to sweep the ball away was the almost ubiquitous Koch, whose presence had been as big as his unsightly mop of dark curly hair.

Bayern kept pressing with an increasing sense of desperation, but there was to be no last-minute equaliser to take the game into extra time. So much for the infamous *Bayern-Dusel*.

In making it to the final whistle with their lead intact, the amateurs had held out against their professional opponents, with Stein – a fitter with the local tea company who still lived in the attic in his parents' house – outdoing the likes of French international star Papin and the much-fêted Colombian Valencia as his club secured an unlikely and historic victory. For FC Bayern, it was just one more miserable tale in the ever-expanding catalogue of embarrassing stories from the early and mid-1990s – a case of new coach, same old *Scheiße*. In the words of the tabloid *Bild*,

> *Über diesen Witz lacht die Bundesliga: Giovanni Trapattoni hat bisher drei Worte Deutsch gelernt: Danke, Bitte und Vestenbergsgreuth... Die Bayern-Schande. Zu überheblich, zu geldgierig und auch noch zu faul!*

("The Bundesliga laughs about this joke: Giovanni Trapattoni has learned three words of German: thank you, please and Vestenbergsgreuth... The Bayern shame. Too arrogant, too greedy and also too lazy!")

With the exception of skipper Matthäus - collared for what would be a painful post-match on-pitch interview - the Bayern players had not hung around on the field after the final peeps of Herr Dr. Merk's whistle, desperate for that hole in the ground to swallow them up. As a result, the victorious Vestenbergsgreuth team would never get the opportunity to swap shirts with their famous opponents. Not that they would have cared too much at the time, as they took the plaudits from the crowd amidst wild celebrations.

Trapattoni warmly praised the amateur side's commitment and discipline, but didn't have much else to say. Perhaps it was just as well that his German was not good enough to articulate what must have really felt. A philosophical Matthäus, meanwhile, flatly stated in his brief interview that Bayern would just have to accept it and live with the shame.

In the wake of the shock result the press had a field day, with the Hamburg-based *Bild* leading the campaign of mockery and the Köln-based *Express* describing Vestenbergsgreuth as "the strongest village in the country" - *dem stärksten Dorf im ganzen Land*. The *Süddeutscher Zeitung* decided to take a slightly more measured and sober approach, stating that "pride comes before a fall". Unsurprisingly, the story of Bayern's embarrassing demise at the hands of the fifth-tier part-timers also made the front page of the sports papers in Trapattoni's native Italy.

Over the years as a fan of FC Bayern, I have witnessed a number of great events. Bundesliga titles, DFB-Pokal victories, and the glittering triumphs on the European stage. Alongside these great victorious moments there have of course been the defeats, from the glorious but ultimately fruitless fight against AC Milan in 1990 and the pain of Champions League defeat, through to the humiliating debacle in Copenhagen and the horror show against Norwich City. Good or bad, these are memories that define us as football fans.

Every football fan will have distinct memories of their team's "worst ever" defeat, but for me that late summer evening in Nürnberg against TSV Vestenbergsgreuth will always stick in the memory. Perhaps it was the combination of many factors: it being my first live Pokal match, Giovanni Trapattoni's nervous fidgeting on the touchline, Harry Koch's scary hair, the horrible egg yolk-yellow *Trikot*. Like any horrific moment, it is simply impossible to scour away, no matter how much brain bleach is poured over it.

During the summer of 2013 I would finally pay a visit to the small village of Vestenbergsgreuth, and get to see the famous *Gedenkstein*, neatly positioned close to the modest team clubhouse overlooking the small Am Schwalbenburg ground. It was something I had intended to do for a while, and it did provide a sense of closure.

Trapattoni's first Bundesliga campaign had started with a steady 3-1 win at the Olympiastadion against VfL Bochum, but any sense of enthusiasm was almost immediately dampened just a week later at the Dreisam-Stadion against SC Freiburg. There had plenty of lamentable Bayern performances in recent seasons, but a 5-1 hiding at the hands of a club that would spend much of the latter part of the season scrapping at the nether reaches of the league table was just to too much to stomach.

While much of the blame was placed on the coach, tales of dressing room disputes and infighting among the playing staff would soon begin to reach the press - with all sorts of stories starting to circulate about the goings on behind the scenes. Amidst this unstable backdrop that gave birth to the derogatory moniker *FC Hollywood*, the team continued to misfire despite – or perhaps because of – its collection of international stars, and a coach who despite being well-meaning often made the headlines more for his non-sequiturs in broken and grammatically poor German than his tactics and team management.

Bayern had found themselves sitting in fourth place in the table a quarter of the way into the season, but a six game winless stretch in October and early November saw them falling back down into ninth, and once more running the risk of missing out on European competition the following season. To make matters worse, skipper Lothar Matthäus was ruled out of the remainder of the season with a crucial ligament injury sustained in the final game of the *Rückrunde* against Werder Bremen, joining a growing list of walking wounded that included goalkeeper Oliver Kahn.

By the end of the *Hinrunde* Bayern had only lost two matches, but far too many draws had left them back in fifth place, six points behind leaders Borussia Dortmund. More of the same followed immediately after the winter break, with a 2-1 win in Bochum being followed by stalemates against Freiburg, Mönchengladbach, strugglers Duisburg and mid-table HSV. This bizarre five-match unbeaten spell saw Trapattoni's side slide out of the top five, still five points behind the leaders despite having lost fewer games.

A very ordinary single-goal win over relegation-threatened city rivals TSV 1860 eventually broke the sequence of stalemates, but the following week a 3-1 reverse against mid-table Köln quickly undid all of the hard work. When this was followed by a 1-1 draw at home to Kaiserslautern – Bayern's thirteenth in twenty-five matches – there would be less talk about the Bundesliga title than making the top five to qualify for the following year's UEFA Cup.

With just a point from their previous two matches and a long list of injuries Bayern headed to Frankfurt's Waldstadion for their meeting with Eintracht, a game that would produce yet another odd chapter in the story of Giovanni Trapattoni's first and at times rather comical season in Munich. A match up between a Bayern side struggling with injuries and poor form and an Eintracht team languishing in thirteenth place was always going to be unpredictable, but nobody could have foreseen what would happen next.

The match itself was both intense and dramatic. Bayern had taken an eighth-minute lead through Markus Schupp, only for the Eagles to turn things on its head two minutes from half-time with goals from Jay Jay Okocha and Thomas Reis. Marcel Witeczek then struck back two minutes later to level things up going into the break, with the Bavarians once again finding it hard to deal with what was on paper far weaker opposition.

The second half was a different story however. Christian Ziege put *Die Roten* back in front three minutes into the second half, and having forced open the floodgates Trapattoni's side looked to have finally clicked in the final ten minutes when Dieter Frey and Ziege wrapped things up to complete a 5-2 rout.

Or so it appeared.

In the twenty-fifth minute with the score at 1-1, the Bayern coach had replaced the injured Thomas Helmer with twenty-two year old debutant Marco Grimm, one of a number of players from the amateur squad. Running onto the pitch, Grimm joined fellow amateur squad team mates Sven Scheuer and Sammy Kuffour. Fast-forward to eighteen minutes from time with the score locked at 2-2, and another personnel change. This time Marcel Witeczek's number was raised by the assistant on the touchline, with twenty-one year old midfielder Dietmar Hamann poised to come on. Due to the long injury list Hamann had become a regular in the first team and had already notched up thirty top-flight appearances, but was still classified as an amateur.

Bayern now had four amateur players on the pitch – one too many for one of the strict rules of the Bundesliga. Trapattoni however was oblivious and Bayern press officer Markus Hörwick quickly made his way down from the stands in a desperate state of panic, but the deed had been done. Bayern naturally lodged a protest – playing an additional amateur squad player hardly constituted an advantage after all – but the rules were the rules, and the letter of the law was pretty clear. Bayern would have to forfeit the match.

The 5-2 result was immediately readjusted to give Frankfurt a 2-0 win, dropping Bayern a massive eight points behind leaders Dortmund and three adrift of fifth-placed Mönchengladbach. While the red-faced Trapattoni had increased his laughing stock share price, poor Marco Grimm's fairytale debut had suddenly been turned into the stuff of nightmares. It was not only his first full Bundesliga game for Bayern, but also his last.

Somehow Bayern were able to pull themselves out of the mire with a 2-1 win at the Olympiastadion against leaders Dortmund, and three further wins saw them squeeze back into fifth place with four matches remaining. All looked set fair again for *Die Roten* as they looked to continue their climb back up the table, but once again they managed to undo all of the hard work with successive defeats at home to Karlsruhe and away in Leverkusen. A last gasp Marcel Witeczek winner in Dresden and a 3-1 win over Bremen in their final two fixtures was not quite enough, and Bayern would finish the season in a dispiriting sixth place behind Mönchengladbach on goal difference. They had won only fifteen of their thirty-four matches, scoring a paltry fifty-five goals.

Even though they were long out of the title race, Bayern ultimately had a part to play in determining the final destination of the *Meisterschale*. Going into the final Saturday a spluttering Dortmund had been supplanted at the top by Bayern's *bête noire* Werder Bremen, and with Dortmund facing Werder's northern rivals Hamburger SV at the Westfalenstadion the Green-Whites lined up for a final showdown at the Olympiastadion.

With the rivalry between Bayern and Otto Rehhagel's side as bitter and as strong as ever, Trapattoni's side would choose that final day to deliver one of their best performances of the season, storming to a convincing 3-1 win sealed with two stunning strikes from Alexander Zickler, one a beautiful curling shot from distance with his right foot four minutes from half-time and the other a bullet header twelve minutes from the end.

Bayern may have been miles off the summit and unsure of even a place in Europe, but there was something fantastic about seeing an irate Rehhagel throwing a series of arm-whirling tantrums on the touchline and the po-faced, glassy-eyed Willi Lemke staring miserably into space in the stands. It may sound mean-spirited and slightly churlish, but it just couldn't have happened to a nicer bunch of guys. It was pure and simple old-fashioned *Schadenfreude* at its best.

Sitting in sixth place in the Bundesliga table Bayern had missed out on the automatic UEFA Cup qualification slots, but there would be yet one more sharp twist in this bizarre tale. With already-qualified Borussia Mönchengladbach playing in the DFB-Pokal final against second division VfL Wolfsburg, there was one last opportunity for Bayern to find a way into

European competition the following season. It was one of those very rare occasions where all Bayern fans found themselves cheering on their onetime rivals.

	P	W	D	L	Goals	GD	Pts
BV 09 Borussia Dortmund	34	20	9	5	67:33	+34	49:19
SV Werder Bremen	34	20	8	6	70:39	+31	48:20
SC Freiburg	34	20	6	8	66:44	+22	46:22
1. FC Kaiserslautern	34	17	12	5	58:41	+17	46:22
Borussia Mönchengladbach	34	17	9	8	66:41	+25	43:25
FC Bayern München	34	15	13	6	55:41	+14	43:25

The equation was simple. If Mönchengladbach won the cup final, they would take their place in the European Cup Winners' Cup, freeing up the last UEFA Cup slot for Bayern. If Wolfsburg won, they would enter the Cup Winners' Cup, leaving Mönchengladbach in the UEFA Cup and Bayern in the wilderness. Thankfully, there were no nail-biting moments in Berlin as *Die Fohlen* secured an easy 3-0 win over the Wolves – their second goal being scored by former Bayern man Stefan Effenberg.

In Europe, things had been slightly better. With the introduction of the new Champions League group format Bayern were able to avoid early elimination off the back of one bad game, as had been the case in their previous two European misadventures that had seen them crash spectacularly against B 1903 København and get turned over in their own back yard by Norwich City. In playing six matches, there were five opportunities to overturn a bad result rather than just the one.

The four-team group pitted Trapattoni's side against Paris St. Germain, Dynamo Kyiv and Spartak Moscow – and despite defeats home and away to the French champions Bayern would do just about enough against their other opponents to secure second spot in the group and with it a place in the quarter-finals.

Having drawn both of their matches with Spartak, Bayern's most encouraging result would come in their final game in the Ukraine, where they faced a Dynamo Kyiv side that also had a chance of making the last eight along with runaway leaders PSG. With the French side away and clear in first place on maximum points, the situation before the final round of matches saw Spartak and Bayern both sitting on four points with the Russians in front on goal difference, and the Ukrainian champions trailing with two points.

Defeat in Kyiv would have eliminated the Bavarians, but a performance where Trapattoni's side finally looked like the Bayern München of old would see them through. After going behind to an Andriy Shevchenko goal seven minutes before half-time, Bayern turned on the style in a chilly Respublikanskiy Stadium with four unanswered strikes. Christian Nerlinger's shot got *Die Roten* back in the game just before the break, and a brace from new signing Jean-Pierre Papin would put the result beyond doubt. Eight minutes from time, Mehmet Scholl completed a convincing 4-1 rout.

Bayern had just about managed to squeeze through to the quarter-finals, where they were drawn against Swedish champions and two-time UEFA Cup winners IFK Göteborg. History made Bayern favourites ahead of the first competitive meeting between the two teams, but nobody was underestimating a Göteborg side that had finished top of its group, finishing ahead of both FC Barcelona and Manchester United. Given Bayern's recent record in European knockout matches there was no little trepidation ahead of the first leg at the Olympiastadion, more so given IFK's record against German opposition. In their previous four meetings with Bundesliga sides, the Swedes had won three and drawn one – including a 4-0 aggregate victory over Hamburger SV in the 1982 UEFA Cup final.

This was far from the Bayern side that had dominated European football in the 1970s and was even a distance away from the team of battlers that had held its own among the continent's elite in the following decade, yet from somewhere they managed to put two decent games together. After a tedious and frankly forgettable goalless draw at the Olympiastadion, an eight-minute purple patch in the second leg in western Sweden proved to be enough to take them through to the last four.

At half-time in the second leg everything had remained in the balance at 0-0, but goals from Alexander Zickler after sixty-four minutes and Christian Nerlinger after seventy-two looked to have sealed the deal for Trapattoni's side. However, this was not the Bayern of old, and rather than calmly seeing things out they very quickly turned to jelly as the Swedes threw everything and the IKEA kitchen sink at them. IFK needed three goals to turn things around, and would get two thirds of the way there through Mats Lillienberg and Mikael Martinsson before the final whistle spared the Bavarians any further agony. IFK had arguably been the better side over the two legs and retained their unbeaten record against German opposition, but Bayern had done just about enough to sneak through on away goals.

Bayern had already surpassed all expectations by winning what had been a tough quarter-final, and nobody was expecting much when they were drawn against tournament favourites

Ajax Amsterdam in the last four. Coached by one Louis van Gaal, the three-time tournament winner had by this time surpassed AC Milan in Europe's pecking order as the team to beat.

As has been the case in the quarter-final Bayern played the home leg first, and managed to withstand long spells of pressure from the free-flowing Eredivisie champions to keep a clean sheet and grind out a creditable goalless draw. In shutting down their more highly-rated opponents Trapattoni's side had kept themselves in with a chance ahead of the second leg in Amsterdam, and despite being up against a team that had suffered just one defeat all season – a 2-1 extra time defeat at the hands of bitter rivals Feyenoord in the quarter-finals of the KNVB Cup – Bayern fans dared to dream of another European Cup final evening in Vienna.

The return encounter started predictably enough when Finnish striker Jari Litmanen opened the scoring early for the home side, but Marcel Witeczek's well-directed header nine minutes before half-time stoked the fires of hope among all of us fans of *Die Roten*. With the score at 1-1 both on the night and on aggregate, Bayern were ahead on away goals and – albeit with more than half of the match remaining – with a toe in the final.

For that short, sweet, fleeting moment, I found myself sitting in front of my television screen counting down the minutes and dreaming of miracles. The Dutch champions had been the better side by a considerable margin over the two hours or so of football I had witnessed, yet what was probably the worst-ever Bayern side to reach the last four in a major European tournament were somehow still in with a chance of making the most unlikely Champions League final appearance in the club's history.

Sadly but not unsurprisingly, that dream didn't last for long.

Five minutes either side of half-time changed the entire complexion of the tie, as Finidi Geoge, Ronald de Boer and Litmanen – again – provided a far more realistic interpretation of the gulf in class between the two teams. Mehmet Scholl pulled one back for the visitors with a seventy-fifth minute penalty after Danny Blind handled in the box, but van Gaal's side would have the final word as winger Marc Overmars netted a fifth.

With Ajax going to defeat AC Milan in Vienna, Bayern would once again end up losing to the eventual winners.

Bayern had endured some truly horrific seasons in the early part of the 1990s, but the first season under Giovanni Trapattoni could only be described as bizarre. The idiosyncratic Italian's time in charge had witnessed what was arguably one of the biggest shocks in the history of postwar German football, which was then followed by a curious Bundesliga campaign defined by the four-man amateur show in Frankfurt. To think that this shambles of a Bayern side would then get to within fifty minutes of reaching the Champions League final makes the story of the 1994/95 season stranger still.

One simply couldn't make it up: as a Bayern fan I often found myself cringing as the team and its hapless coach stuttered and stumbled from one problem to the next, knowing that officials and supporters of every other club in Germany were lapping it all up.

Not surprisingly, Bayern's frustrating and disappointing season resulted in the club parting ways with Trapattoni, who handed the reins to another tried and tested coach after exactly a year in charge. The Italian's replacement was not another premium foreign import however, but a man who had forged a long-held reputation at a club that had over the course of the late 1980s and early 1990s become one of Bayern's biggest domestic rivals.

His name: Otto Rehhagel.

OTTOCRACY COMES TO FC HOLLYWOOD

Since the ill-judged dismissal of Jupp Heynckes in 1991 Uli Hoeneß and the Bayern management had been continually seeking a coach who could truly work with the squad, with their efforts resulting in a series of highly questionable appointments and an ever-increasing trail of disaster. Søren Lerby, Erich Ribbeck and Giovanni Trapattoni had found themselves ushered in and out of the hot seat, with Hoeneß and the board getting increasingly desperate. In the summer of 1995 things had taken an even more bizarre turn, with the sudden arrival of Otto Rehhagel at the Säbenerstraße.

Yes, *that* Otto Rehhagel. The eccentric, intransigent, autocratic Otto Rehhagel from Werder Bremen.

Even now I have to think about the absurdity of it all: after fourteen years with Bayern's bitter rivals, Rehhagel was making his way south to Munich. To draw a direct comparison to English football, it would have been the equivalent of the late and great Brian Clough suddenly upping sticks at Nottingham Forest and taking charge at Manchester United or Liverpool.

Having lived through the gradual development of Bayern's rivalry with Bremen during the 1980s, I automatically questioned the board's decision. Rehhagel was undoubtedly a great and well-respected coach, but he was not just the former coach of Werder Bremen. He *was* Werder Bremen. How he could work at FC Bayern München, I had no idea.

Right up until the end of the previous season and that final match at the Olympiastadion that had denied his side the Bundesliga title, Otto Rehhagel was a man older Bayern supporters had grown to grudgingly respect at best and dislike at worst, and one younger fans had been almost pre-programmed to hate: the green goblin, the *Fischkopf-in-chief*, the best buddy of the universally loathed rabble-rouser Willi Lemke. Yet here he was just weeks later on the training ground at the Säbenerstraße with his coiffed dark hair and gap-toothed grin, nattily dressed in a red and blue FC Bayern tracksuit.

I just didn't know what to make of it. It just felt bizarre, rather like asking your horrible neighbour to feed your cat and water your garden plants. Or, to look at things another way, it was akin to eschewing the *süße Senf* and pouring spicy curry sauce or ketchup on your late-morning *Weisswurst* – having already chopped it up into bite-sized pieces, skin and all.

As well as bringing plenty of baggage from Bremen, Bayern's new coach also brought with him an approach that many had long considered autocratic and provincial – as well as unorthodox and at times eccentric tactics that had over the years raised a number of sceptical eyebrows among his peers. While Rehhagel had become part of the furniture at the Weserstadion to the point where he had become quite literally unsackable, he arrived in Munich as a familiar figure, yet at the same time a completely unknown quantity.

To mark Rehhagel's arrival there was a massive sweeping of the squad too, with those heading for the exit including Brazilians Jorghino and Mazinho and the disappointing Colombian striker Adolfo Valencia. Among the German contingent the departees included journeyman Markus Schupp, veteran Hansi Pflügler, and the much-fêted superstar that never was, Michael Sternkopf. With the possible exception of workhorses Pflügler and Jorghino, none of these players had ever really made the grade in Munich.

While the number of new arrivals wouldn't match that of the exodus, a selection of well-established names made their way to the Säbenerstraße to join Rehhagel's new-look side. Germany's World Cup winning striker Jürgen Klinsmann made his way to Bayern after a successful spell in the English Premier League with Tottenham Hotspur, highly-rated Swiss midfield schemer Ciriaco Sforza moved to Bavaria from Kaiserslautern, and old boy Thomas Strunz made his way back to Munich after three successful seasons with VfB Stuttgart.

Perhaps the most talked about signing however was Austrian attacking midfielder Andreas Herzog, who accompanied the incoming coach from Werder Bremen for what would measure today out at just over two and a half million Euros. Given the number of established big-name players already in the Bayern squad, one had to wonder where Rehhagel's star man would fit in.

In stark contrast to the disastrous start made by his predecessor Giovanni Trapattoni the previous year, Rehhagel was able to hit the ground running. In delivering the right results, the new coach managed to quieten down a number of the doubters and naysayers – at the beginning, at least.

After a well-contested 3-2 opening win over Hamburger SV which saw Andy Herzog score in his first Bundesliga outing in a Bayern shirt, *Die Roten* then put half a dozen past Karlsruhe SC at the Wildparkstadion – banishing the horrible memories of the previous season's poor performances against that side. Two-goal wins against the renamed KFC 05 Uerdingen, city rivals TSV 1860 München and SC Freiburg followed, and match day six saw a tightly-contested 3-2 win against the 1994/95 runners up Kaiserslautern with the game being decided three minutes from the end by defender Markus Babbel.

A last-minute Jürgen Klinsmann penalty was enough to settle a tight 1-0 win over unbeaten Bayer Leverkusen at the Olympiastadion to take Bayern's record to seven wins from their first seven matches – setting a new Bundesliga record – and with the German leagues having adopted the "English" system of three points for a win Bayern found themselves sitting pretty with an impressive maximum quota of twenty-one points – a healthy seven clear of second placed Borussia Dortmund.

On the face of it, the coach had answered all of his critics both among the fans and the media, but behind the scenes a new storm was slowly brewing. Despite the record-breaking start, there were continued rumblings of discontent.

In the week before the win over Leverkusen Bayern had fallen to a surprise 3-1 defeat at the hands of Fortuna Düsseldorf in the second round of the DFB-Pokal, but the first really pivotal match of the league season came on day eight when Bayern made the trip north-west to Dortmund's Westfalenstadion in the season's first "six-pointer". While a win would take *Die Roten* ten points clear of BVB, a win for Ottmar Hitzfeld's side would close the gap right down to just four.

Since Hamburg's Harald Spörl had scored after just two minutes in the season's opening fixture, Bayern had not been behind in the Bundesliga – but just four minutes before half-time BVB striker Heiko Herrlich was bundled over in the box, leaving ex-Bayern man Stefan Reuter to slip the resulting spot-kick low to the right of 'keeper Oliver Kahn.

The second half saw Bayern work themselves back into the contest through Dortmund-born midfielder Christian Nerlinger, but that would be as good as it would get for Rehhagel's side, with the display in the opposition's final third being particularly poor. The starting front two of Klinsmann and Emil Kostadinov were disappointing, with Klinsmann being replaced after seventy-two minutes by the just as ineffective Marcel Witeczek. For Dortmund, the versatile Matthias Sammer turned out yet another polished display.

Just as Bayern may have been thinking about settling for the point, the home team would strike twice in three minutes to settle the issue. Uruguayan Ruben Sosa found the back of the net just two minutes after replacing youngster Lars Ricken, and skipper Michael Zorc wrapped things up for the *Schwarzgelben* before the Bavarians could get themselves off the ropes. Their seven-point advantage had been cut down to four.

Clearly punch-drunk from their defeat in Westphalia, Rehhagel's side were outdone by another Borussia the following week, and by another Bayern old boy. At the Olympiastadion against Mönchengladbach, *Die Fohlen* would take the lead through ex-*Münch'ner* Stefan Effenberg on the twenty-minute mark, before Herzog put through his own net to double the visitors' advantage. A last-gasp Jean-Pierre Papin strike flattered the hosts in front of their increasingly disgruntled supporters, and with two defeats in two matches Bayern's lead at the top of the Bundesliga table had been cut to just three points with chasers Dortmund picking up a valuable point in Bremen.

From that point on, Bayern would be the perfect model of inconsistency as they mixed spectacular victories with some painfully embarrassing defeats. On match day eleven sixth-placed VfB Stuttgart were put to the sword at the Olympiastadion as Bayern strolled to an entertaining 5-3 victory, but just a week later the Bavarians found themselves at the sharp end of an embarrassing 4-1 thrashing by Eintracht Frankfurt, a team hovering just above the relegation zone.

The defeat at the Waldstadion saw Bayern slip into second place behind Dortmund, and after the winter break things would not get any better. In fact, once Dortmund had taken top spot they would not relinquish it for the remainder of the season. Bayern's inconsistent form in the Bundesliga would be in stark contrast to their UEFA Cup campaign – more on that later – and the pressure both from inside the club and the media had started to build on the coach. As the winter break approached, the record-breaking start to the season had been long forgotten.

For many, there was a sense of inevitability as things slowly began to unravel. Rather like the much-maligned former England manager Graham Taylor, Rehhagel had always been seen as the sort of coach best suited to working with young and unknown players – and there had always been serious doubts about his ability to carry this over in dealing with well-established international stars including the likes of Jürgen Klinsmann, Mehmet Scholl and Jean-Pierre Papin.

Rehhagel had more or less been given the authority to select the team and manage the dressing room how he wished in Bremen, but it should have been clear right from the very beginning that this was never going to be the case in Munich. Somebody or something would at some point have to give way.

Bayern's 4-1 defeat in Frankfurt was followed by two more dropped points following a dull goalless draw in Rostock against FC Hansa, and it was at the Ostseestadion where the growing friction between the coach and the players would get its first real public airing. Having been substituted just two minutes into the second half, midfielder Scholl was seen verbally insulting Rehhagel by the dugout – an incident that provided the headline-hungry boulevard press the perfect opportunity to indulge in yet more stories about both the coach and the ongoing shenanigans both on and off the pitch in Munich.

The tempestuous Scholl was clearly out of order in making his personal feelings public, but for many Bayern supporters it was the surest sign that they were not alone in their opinion and criticism of the beleaguered Rehhagel. It was the last thing the club needed as they attempted to concentrate on the simple matter of playing football, and while Scholl's outburst had been no more than the result of pent-up feelings that had taken root on the training ground and had accumulated over time, for the press it was yet another a new chapter in the ongoing saga that was *FC Hollywood*.

Scholl had been the first open dissenter, but others perturbed by Rehhagel's constant meddling with the team quickly followed him out of the woodwork including Papin, Dieter Frey, Oliver Kreuzer and Marcel Witeczek. The unsettled Swiss international Alain Sutter – another player with a particularly strong and outspoken personality who had an opinion on everything from team dynamics to the state of the environment – had by that time already made his way out of the Säbenerstraße, settling for some fresher air at SC Freiburg.

Three wins and a draw from their last four games before the start of the winter break – including a 2-0 win over Bremen – took Rehhagel's side back to within two points of leaders Dortmund and ten points clear of the chasing pack, but by this stage the football was largely a sideshow. From the Ultras in the *Südkurve* through to the big names in the dressing room, the knives were out for the coach, who responded by just digging his heels in further. All of this was manna from Heaven for the yellow press, who didn't even have to rummage around in the dark for stories anymore.

As had been the case before the *Winterpause*, Bayern's form on the pitch during the *Rückrunde* continued to be inconsistent and at times almost schizophrenic. The first two matches of 1996 saw back to back defeats against Hamburger SV and Karlsruhe SC – the latter a particularly embarrassing 4-1 thrashing where 'keeper Oliver Kahn was humiliated by his former teammates including former Bayern striker Manfred Bender – while the following two weeks saw Rehhagel's side scored a combine total of ten goals against Uerdingen and TSV 1860.

Despite this topsy-turvy form and the ongoing in-fighting Bayern remained in second place behind Dortmund. They would actually pull to within a point of the leaders after a hard-earned win over their rivals at the Olympiastadion, but all of this hard work was immediately undone the following week with a disappointing 3-1 defeat in Mönchengladbach. The defeat at a noisy and passionate Bökelberg would signal the beginning of a five-game winless streak, and at the end of April a 1-0 home defeat to Rostock in turn signalled the end of the road for Otto Rehhagel.

Having spent fourteen successful seasons in charge at Werder Bremen, Rehhagel had not lasted even a year in Munich. He left the Säbenerstraße with immediate effect, and into the breach once more would jump Franz Beckenbauer for his second short caretaker spell in the space of five seasons. Der Kaiser fared little better during Bayern's four remaining Bundesliga matches – winning just the one match against struggling Köln – but would arrive just in time to take the credit for the club's first European trophy in twenty years. This was particularly harsh on Rehhagel, who had plotted the path to the final – including home and away victories over Spanish giants Barcelona.

	P	W	D	L	Goals	GD	Pts
BV 09 Borussia Dortmund	34	19	11	4	76:38	+38	68
FC Bayern München	34	19	5	10	66:46	+20	62
FC Schalke 04	34	14	14	6	45:36	+9	56

Despite his long and well-established record of success at the Weserstadion, Rehhagel was never really destined to be a long-term success at Bayern. While his somewhat provincial approaching to coaching and team management had been perfectly suited to a smaller club like Werder, at Bayern he continually displayed a stunning inability to manage and control those considered international stars and established big names. He had been under constant scrutiny from both the management and the media right from the start, and even the perfect run of seven wins from the first seven matches wasn't enough to buy him much breathing space.

While at Bremen Rehhagel had continually found promising youngsters and slowly moulded them into top-class professionals by applying a mix of firm discipline and philosophical mantras, in Munich the established professionals and big egos had been far from impressed. Attitudes to the coach's formulaic, schoolmasterly approach on the training ground had often ranged from raised eyebrows through to laughter and outright derision, and his cod philosophy – seen by many critics as a false veneer of an acquired cultural sophistication – often left his unenthusiastic audience bemused. The promising early start to the season had served only to cover over the festering wounds, and the club's change in fortunes not long afterwards would result in the bandages coming off completely.

The Bayern players, particularly those with the largest heads, had no desire to be part of Otto's orchestra just playing the tune. While the system of *Ottocracy* may have worked in Bremen, it hadn't carried much weight in Munich. Having been used to getting what he wanted in terms of personnel – right down to hand-picking and even interviewing individual players – Rehhagel had found himself all at sea in managing a squad containing some pretty big egos. Even a player like Jürgen Klinsmann – seen by both colleagues and opponents as open and affable – had found it difficult to get along with the at times intransigent coach.

It is hard even now to truly determine whether Rehhagel's dismal failure in Munich had been down to simple cluelessness or a bloody-minded determination to have things his own way, but in later years he would go on to lead unfancied outsiders Greece to the European Championship title in 2004. The clue here of course is in the words "unfancied" and "outsiders" – the perfect description of the sort of squad with which Rehhagel had always worked best.

Having won their first seven Bundesliga matches at the start of the season – a Bundesliga record that would stand on its own until equalled by Kaiserslautern in 2001/02 and FSV Mainz 05 in 2010/11 before being surpassed by the Bayern class of 2012/13 – the Bavarians would win only eleven of Rehhagel's remaining twenty-three games in charge. To say that his tenure was disappointing had been something of an understatement, particularly given the high level of expectation he had brought with him to the Säbenerstraße.

Bayern's quest for glory in Europe in 1995/96 had started poorly with an uninspiring 1-0 home defeat to unfashionable Lokomotiv Moscow, but a five-goal thrashing of the Russian side in the away leg, inspired by a brace from Jürgen Klinsmann, saw the Munich side safely through to the second round. Scottish side Raith Rovers were their next opponents, and another three goals over the two legs by Klinsmann ensured smooth progress to the last sixteen.

Despite their ongoing domestic problems, the Bayern class of 1996 found themselves at ease in Europe – in complete contrast to the team of the 1980s that had dominated domestically but had continually fallen at the final hurdle in Europe. The third round pitted *Die Roten* against the highly-rated Portuguese side SL Benfica, and all of their troubles in the Bundesliga were quickly forgotten. Klinsmann would eventually score a more than acceptable sixteen goals in thirty-two league matches, but in Europe his goal-scoring record during the

1995/96 season had bordered on the phenomenal. Following his five strikes in the opening two ties, he scored all four of Bayern's goals as they steamrollered the Portuguese at the Olympiastadion – and followed this with another couple in an emphatic 3-1 triumph at the Estádio da Luz.

Bayern entertained two-time European Champions Nottingham Forest in the first leg of their quarter-final, with Klinsmann scoring his twelfth goal of the campaign in a tight and somewhat laboured 2-1 win. With a precious away goal on the board, the English side might have fancied their chances at the City Ground in the second leg, but a dominant Bayern calmly strolled to an impressive 5-1 win with the seemingly unstoppable Klinsmann bagging yet another brace. With his second goal, the Bayern striker equalled the fourteen UEFA Cup goals scored by Ipswich Town's Scottish international John Wark – a record set in 1981 when the East Anglian side had gone on to lift the trophy.

Having quite literally swept the floor with the opposition during their march to the semi-finals, the last obstacle between the Bavarians and a place in their first European final for almost a decade was a much-fancied Barcelona side containing legendary names such as Portuguese star Luis Figo, Romanian national team captain Gheorghe Hagi – and a slimly-built defensive Spanish international midfielder called Josep "Pep" Guardiola i Sala. The Catalans had scored no fewer than twenty-eight goals in progressing to the semi-finals – five more than Bayern – and went into the game as the slight favourites.

The first meeting at a wet and soggy Olympiastadion would see the first real challenge to the Munich side since their opening round first leg defeat in Moscow, and the *Blaugrana* – wearing a curious-looking teal outfit adorned with dark blue pinstripes – struck the first blow with just fourteen minutes on the clock. A defence-splitting pass from José Mari Bakero beat the offside trap, leaving youngster Óscar with just Olli Kahn to beat. The Catalans kept hold of the lead going into the break, and there must have been some in the home crowd thinking about it being yet another case of so near yet so far.

They need not have worried. A five-minute purple patch after the restart hauled Bayern back into the tie, as first Marcel Witeczek and then Mehmet Scholl saw the Bavarians turn the one-goal deficit into a 2-1 advantage. Substitute Witeczek had collected a neat through-ball down the left from Christian Nerlinger before beating Barca 'keeper Carles Busquets with a neat angled finish, and the nimble and effervescent Scholl found the back of the net at the second time of asking after Busquets had parried his first effort.

Despite conceding the early away goal *Die Roten* had looked well set to take a lead to the Camp Nou, but the familiar spectre of the European evening defensive blunder reared its ugly head once more. In the spirit of Jean-Marie Pfaff, Norbert Nachtweih and Klaus Augenthaler, fullback Markus Babbel's poor back pass gifted Barcelona with a priceless equaliser. Having nutmegged the referee, Babbel's pass back into the box was way too short for a teammate but perfectly weighted for playmaker Hagi, who coolly clipped the ball past Kahn and into the bottom right-hand corner of the Bayern net.

As the rain turned into a light flurry of snow, it looked like being yet another one of "those" nights.

In between their two matches against Barcelona, Bayern had failed to win any of their three Bundesliga matches, and in front of an enthusiastic crowd of 115,000 at a seething Camp Nou not even the wildest optimist would have given them much of a chance. Both sides created opportunities in the first half, but it was the visitors who would make the breakthrough five minutes before the break. Picking up the ball out on the left, Mehmet Scholl embarked on a mazy run, cutting inside his marker before lashing a right-footed shot that Busquets could only parry. In what was a remarkable moment of redemption, it was none other than Markus Babbel who appeared at the far post to slide the ball into the empty net.

Roared on by the massive crowd, the home team threw every man forward in search of the equaliser that would see them through on away goals, and seven minutes from time Figo managed to wriggle and dance his way into the Bayern box – beating Thomas Helmer before having his shot blocked by Oliver Kreuzer. With spaces opening up in front of them Bayern saw an opportunity to break, and quickly turned defence into attack.

As the move from the Catalans broke down the white-shirted Bavarians launched their counterattack. Having received the ball just inside his own half, the pacy Witeczek charged purposefully down the left and inside towards the Barcelona goal. Expecting the Bayern striker to either send the ball out to Klinsmann to his right or take the shot across him towards the right side of the goal, 'keeper Busquets was left completely flat-footed as Witeczek's shot took a wicked deflection before creeping just inside the near post.

With just under six minutes of normal time remaining, Barcelona needed two goals just to take the game into extra time.

Bayern should have been home and dry after netting their second goal, but no European evening could ever be complete without some of the familiar last-minute jitters. Substitute Iván de la Peña pulled a goal back for the home side a minute before the end of the ninety minutes to tighten the nerves on the Bayern bench, but it would prove to be nothing more than a meaningless consolation as *Die Roten* held on for an expected but hard-fought and well-deserved victory. Top scorer Klinsmann had failed to add to his tally over the two legs, but this had been the perfect team effort. Against all odds and nine years after the European Cup final against FC Porto in Vienna, Bayern were in another European final.

In making their first UEFA Cup final appearance Bayern were also two games away from becoming the first German team to win all of the three major European club trophies, following their three Champions' Cup victories in the 1970s and their Cup Winners' Cup triumph in 1967.

Rehhagel's side were through to face French outfit Girondins de Bordeaux, but little did the coach know at the time that he would no longer be there to share in the glory. Within weeks of the triumph at the Camp Nou, he was yet another name on the rapidly-growing list of former FC Bayern coaches.

The buildup to the UEFA Cup final could not have been any more inconvenient for Bayern. Otto Rehhagel had barely closed the door behind him, leaving Franz Beckenbauer – taking on the role of caretaker coach for the second time in the space of three years – having to prepare the team for their most important fixture of the season. Yet somehow the players responded, looking completely different from the miserable outfit that had slumped to that miserable defeat against Hansa Rostock just three days earlier. While the change of coach had undoubtedly rejuvenated the squad, there was also that little something special about *Der Kaiser*, one of football's born winners.

With a display that belied their Bundesliga form Bayern made short work of an ordinary looking Bordeaux side, securing a deserved two goal lead to take to France. With thirty-four minutes gone skipper Lothar Matthäus sent in an outswinging corner from the right for Thomas Helmer to steal in with a bullet header that fizzed past Bordeaux 'keeper Gaëtan Huard, and on the hour mark the home side doubled their advantage through Mehmet Scholl.

The dynamic Scholl had been one of Bayern's many standout players during their European campaign, and he took his chance with relish. Picking up a short pass out on the right from substitute midfielder Dieter Frey, the Bayern number seven weaved his way into the Bordeaux penalty area and slipped in between two defenders, before drilling a low shot into the bottom left-hand corner of the net with his right foot.

Taking it all in his stride was the calm and sharp-suited Beckenbauer, prowling on the touchline in his uniquely inimitable style.

The return leg in Bordeaux's noisy Parc Lescure saw the home side – including a young and slightly more hirsute Zinedine Zidane and a small left-sided fullback called Bixente

Lizarazu – bravely take the game to the visitors, but despite plenty of pressure the first half finished goalless, leaving Bayern with their two-goal advantage from the first leg still intact. Unfortunately for Gernot Rohr's side they lost the influential Lizarazu just after the half-hour mark after when he had to leave the field on a stretcher after a poor challenge on Emil Kostadinov, and after that their challenge slowly subsided.

With fourteen goals in the eleven games played up to and including the first leg of the final, Jürgen Klinsmann had levelled John Wark's fifteen year old UEFA Cup goal-scoring record – a nice touch for me as a supporter of both Ipswich Town and FC Bayern – but the real hero of this trophy-winning season was winger Mehmet Scholl, who during his seven years in Bavaria had become one of the club's more well-loved if slightly underestimated players. The UEFA Cup run had been no exception: Scholl had done his job quietly and effectively, but with that touch of class that had elevated him above many of his peers.

The usually injury-prone Scholl had missed just one game in Bayern's UEFA Cup run – the first leg of the second round meeting against Raith Rovers – and contributed massively to what was a glorious cup-winning campaign. In ten games leading up to the second leg against Bordeaux, he scored four goals – not at all bad for a winger – as well as contributing a phenomenal nine assists. Marksman Klinsmann may have broken the long-standing tournament goalscoring record, but silent assassin Scholl had more than played his part.

Fittingly, it was Scholl who would put the final itself beyond all reasonable doubt, giving Bayern the lead eight minutes into the second half after Kostadinov had played a smart reverse pass back into the Bordeaux box. The Bayern number seven's right footed effort took the slightest of deflections before beating Huard and creeping inside the left upright, leaving their opponents needing a miracle. Knowing that they now needed four goals to turn things around, the French side simply had nothing left to give.

Thirteen minutes after taking the lead, Bayern doubled their advantage on the night as Scholl this time turned provider for Kostadinov. The winger swung in a corner from the left, and the Bulgarian found plenty of time and space to calmly nod a header downwards and into the net. With Bordeaux now needing an impossible five goals to win the game with just over twenty minutes remaining, it was fairly safe to say that Bayern were not going to be undone by any late drama in this European final. The long wait was coming to an end.

Les Girondins pulled a goal back with fourteen minutes left on the clock as Daniel Dutuel beat Oliver Kahn low to his left with a well-struck free-kick that fizzed into the Bayern net, but the final word would be left to Klinsmann just two minutes later, who stabbed in a cross-cum-shot from Thomas Strunz to make the tournament goal-scoring record his own.

It was a fitting end to what had been a dominant tournament run for the Bavarians, and for Klinsmann in particular who after three barren games finally scored the record-breaking goal with just twelve minutes remaining in the tie. In between the last of his four goals in the quarter-final second leg against Nottingham Forest and Bayern's third in Bordeaux, Klinsmann had waited a minute short of six hours to score his fifteenth goal of the competition.

Bayern's UEFA Cup victory in 1996 was the club's first European tournament success for two decades, but for me personally it would carry a far more significant meaning and resonance. Up to that point I had followed the club for fifteen years and had witnessed numerous near misses, including the two painful European Cup final defeats. While the victory over Bordeaux would always be on the second rung after the European Cup and Champions League successes before and since, for me it will always be "my" first European trophy as a Bayern fan.

Further significant European triumphs in later years would ultimately mean more in the overall history of the club, but the sight of Lothar Matthäus lifting that handle-less silver trophy in Bordeaux would – for me – be one of the greatest highlights in my long and at times painful love affair with FC Bayern München.

Jürgen Klinsmann's UEFA Cup Goalscoring Record

Date	Opponent	Round	Min.	Goal	Res.
07/08/1995	Lokomotiv Moskva (A)	1R. 2nd Leg	26.	1:0	5:0
07/08/1995	Lokomotiv Moskva (A)	1R. 2nd Leg	35.	2:0	5:0
17/10/1995	Raith Rovers (A)	2R. 1st Leg	6.	1:0	2:0
17/10/1995	Raith Rovers (A)	2R. 1st Leg	73.	2:0	2:0
31/10/1995	Raith Rovers (H)	2R. 2nd Leg	50.	1:1	2:1
21/11/1995	SL Benfica (H)	3R. 1st Leg	26.	1:0	4:1
21/11/1995	SL Benfica (H)	3R. 1st Leg	31.	2:1	4:1
21/11/1995	SL Benfica (H)	3R. 1st Leg	44.	3:1	4:1
21/11/1995	SL Benfica (H)	3R. 1st Leg	46.	4:1	4:1
07/12/1995	SL Benfica (A)	3R. 2nd Leg	32.	1:1	3:1
07/12/1995	SL Benfica (A)	3R. 2nd Leg	68.	2:1	3:1
05/03/1996	Nottingham Forest. (H)	QF. 1st Leg	16.	1:0	2:1
19/03/1996	Nottingham Forest (A)	QF. 2nd Leg	65.	3:0	5:1
19/03/1996	Nottingham Forest (A)	QF. 2nd Leg	79.	4:0	5:1
15/05/1996	Girondins de Bordeaux (A)	Final. 2nd Leg	77.	3:1	3:1

CAUGHT IN A TRAP

At the end of 1993, Bayern legend Franz Beckenbauer had jumped in during the *Winterpause* to rescue the club from the failing Erich Ribbeck. Having guided the team to the Bundesliga title as caretaker coach, *Der Kaiser* had then stepped back and returned to the boardroom – paving the way for the much-publicised appointment of Italian Giovanni Trappatoni in the summer of 1994.

Fast forward two seasons, and it would be a case of Groundhog Day at the Säbenerstraße. Following the dismissal of the much-maligned Otto Rehhagel in the spring of 1996 Beckenbauer had once again come to the rescue, guiding Bayern to their first major European trophy in twenty years before before stepping down once more.

His replacement: Giovanni Trapattoni.

Having overseen what had arguably been Bayern's most humiliating defeat at the hands of fifth-tier TSV Vestenbergsgreuth in the first round of the DFB-Pokal and the farcical "game of the four amateurs" in Frankfurt that had resulted in Bayern having to forfeit two precious league points, Trapattoni had hardly covered himself in glory in what had been at times a bizarre first spell in Munich – yet here he was, back in Bavarian capital for a second shot at the job.

After the appointments of the untried and untested Lerby, the overcooked Ribbeck and the hapless Rehhagel, the second coming of the experienced but eccentric Italian was more than a little bizarre; his return to Bayern would be greeted with incredulity by sections of the local press and a number of the club's supporters, and many would wonder if Uli Hoeneß had finally lost his marbles. I for one found the decision just a little absurd.

Clearly, Hoeneß knew something that we all didn't – and while the man known as "Il Trap" would do a lot better the second time around, his appointment only served to provide the hungry media with more headling-grabbing FC Hollywood stories. Trapattoni had always been a decent enough coach, but as far as the German media were concerned he was the gift that just kept on giving.

The start of the 1996/97 season saw a number of personnel changes at the Säbenerstraße, with Emil Kostadinov, Jean-Pierre Papin, Andreas Herzog and Ciriaco Sforza making way for the highly-rated if controversial winger Mario Basler, Italian striker Ruggiero Rizzitelli, and the shaven-headed, towering centre-forward Carsten Jancker. The signing of Basler had been one of the most talked-about transfer stories of the summer, with the player being signed from none other than Bayern's *bête noire* Werder Bremen.

For many looking in at Bayern from the outside, more trouble was brewing. The club was full of big egos already: chairman Beckenbauer and general manager Hoeneß off the field, and star players Lothar Matthäus and Jürgen Klinsmann on it. Both players had been part of Germany's triumph at the World Cup in 1990 and had been teammates at Internazionale, but it was pretty clear that they were not the best of friends. The addition of Trappatoni and Basler only served to add to the catalogue of big egos in Munich.

The second "Il Trap" era would start positively enough. Any lingering memories of the cup defeat against Vestenbergsgreuth were quickly banished with a comprehensive 3-0 away win against Regionalliga Nordost side Tennis Borussia Berlin, and the start of the league season saw *Die Roten* embark on a seven-game unbeaten run including five victories that took them to the top of the table, a point in front of VfB Stuttgart. The highlight of this opening unbeaten run was a 4-2 defeat of potential rivals Bayer Leverkusen, with new boy Rizzitelli scoring his third goal in three Bundesliga starts.

Bayern's fine unbeaten start ended with a 3-0 disappointing defeat in Bremen with former Bayern players Andreas Herzog and Bruno Labbadia netting for the northerners, but another undefeated spell after that saw Trapattoni's side go into the winter break two points clear of Borussia Dortmund with a record of 10-6-1. The football was far from pretty and many of the results were close, but the Bavarians slowly started to edge in front of their rivals.

There were tightly-fought draws at home to Dortmund and in Stuttgart, and at the turn of the year Bayern were two points in front of the chasing pack.

The unbeaten run continued into the *Rückrunde* and as stretched to a dozen matches as Bayern extended their lead over Dortmund to three points, but match day 21 would see *Die Roten* brought back down to earth in Leverkusen courtesy of a 5-2 defeat and a hat-trick from the unheralded Markus Feldhoff. It was a game that had swung violently in both directions, with *Die Werkself* storming into a 3-0 half-time lead before goals from Christian Nerlinger and Basler brought Bayern right back into the contest with nineteen minutes remaining. One might have thought that the momentum was with the Bavarians, but two strikes in the space of four minutes from Feldhoff secured the three points for Christoph Daum's side.

The defeat in Leverkusen allowed Dortmund to creep back to the top of the league table on goal difference, with Leverkusen just two points adrift. Just four days later, things got worse with a 2-0 midweek defeat at the hands of mid-table Bielefeld. With a dozen matches remaining Bayern were three points behind Dortmund, and once again eyes had started to turn towards the coach.

Unlike the previous season however, the team refused to buckle. After back to back defeats on the road, Bayern returned to the Olympiastadion to take on fifth-placed Schalke 04. The final result flattered Trappatoni's side; having taken an early lead through Thomas Helmer, two goals in the final two minutes from Nerlinger and Klinsmann would put the gloss on what was a solid rather than spectacular display. Elsewhere, there was more good news as Dortmund were hammered 4-1 by a resurgent Stuttgart.

Bayern's return to form and Dortmund's defeat really tightened things up at the top. At the end of match day 23 just two points separated the top four sides, with Dortmund and Bayern both on forty-six points, two ahead of Stuttgart and Leverkusen.

	P	W	D	L	Goals	GD	Pts
BV 09 Borussia Dortmund	23	14	4	5	49:27	+22	46
FC Bayern München	23	13	7	3	41:24	+17	46
VfB Stuttgart	23	13	5	5	55:25	+30	44
Bayer 04 Leverkusen	23	13	5	5	46:30	+16	44

Bayern would hit peak form just at the right time, and five wins on the trot between March and early April – coupled with unexpected stumbles from the chasing pack – saw them re-establish their position at the top as the season approached its end.

By match day 27 Dortmund were six points behind Bayern, and were desperate for a win when the two teams met at the Westfalenstadion. It could not have started any better for Ottmar Hitzfeld's men, who took the lead after just two minutes through Karlheinz Riedle, but within a minute Rizzitelli had levelled things up. And that is how it remained, with both teams cancelling each other out for the remaining eighty-seven minutes.

A thumping 5-0 win over strugglers Fortuna Düsseldorf followed, but a 3-3 draw in the Munich derby against TSV 1860 would keep the title race interesting. It was an exciting and incident-packed Sunday evening classic that had all both sides of Munich talking. Bayern were two down inside twenty minutes as Horst Heldt grabbed an early brace for *Die Löwen*, but goals from Klinsmann and Mehmet Scholl either side of half-time looked to have shifted the momentum back towards *Die Roten*.

At 2-2 with an hour played, it was already an action-packed encounter worthy of the occasion. But there were even more twists and turns to come. Bayern were reduced to ten men when Christian Ziege was shown a second yellow card, and when Jörg Böhme restored 1860's advantage with eight minutes remaining the Lions were roaring. Then, if it couldn't get any worse for Trappatoni's men, Matthäus was also sent packing a minute later. Bayern had not had a man sent off all season, yet two had been dismissed in the space of twelve minutes. The coolest head on the pitch, thankfully, was referee Hans-Jürgen Weber. It could only happen in a local derby!

A goal behind, two men down, with just eight minutes left to play. It was all set for another famous rearguard action – or *Bayern-Dusel*, if you might prefer to see it that way. The 1860 fans were all set to celebrate a rare victory against their big city rivals, but two minutes from time Carsten Jancker, a seventieth-minute substitute for Klinsmann, met a cross from Nerlinger to net the equaliser. It was the big and bald striker's first goal of the season.

Bayern appeared to be inching towards the title, turning out performances that wavered between the impressive and the insipid. It was as if they wanted to keep the race open for as long as possible. Forty-two points separated the Bundesliga leaders and bottom club SC Freiburg, and everybody expected that gap to have been increased to forty-five by the end of match day 31. Instead, the headlines were all about Klinsmann, Trappatoni and... a cardboard advertising pillar.

Long since relegated, Freiburg had nothing to salvage but their battered pride. Bayern, in contrast, were all set to be champions. The Olympiastadion crowd were expecting a festival of goals. Well, that was the script anyway.

The match was anything but the expected gala celebration, but a tedious, painful, forgettable affair. Bayern were unable to find a way through a defence that had leaked more than three goals every game, and with ten minutes left, Trappatoni decided to try something, well, a little different. Waiting on the touchline was Carsten Lakies, a young FC Bayern II player. The number eighteen then flashed up on the board. Clearly not satisfied with his team's performance, the coach had decided to haul off the ineffective Klinsmann.

Star players do not appreciate being substituted. With ten minutes still remaining, Klinsmann probably thought that he had more to offer. Usually, a disgruntled player will simply trudge back to the bench, muttering under his breath. Not Klinsmann. That's right, the placid, well-mannered and serene Jürgen Klinsmann. Yes, the same unassuming and amiable Jürgen Klinsmann who enjoyed baking pretzels and pootling around in his old Volkswagen Beetle.

Rather than amble quietly back to the dugout, the blond striker made a concerted point of marching past Trappatoni, shouting incoherently as he went. The coach, meanwhile, his eyes firmly fixed on the pitch, remained oblivious as the irate Klinsmann stomped past him.

Klinsmann was clearly on the hunt for something. He probably wanted to have a swing at the Italian, but instead zeroed in on a large Sanyo advertising pillar standing by the side of the pitch. Klinsmann had not come remotely close to troubling Freiburg 'keeper Jörg Schmadtke, but he gave the pillar an almighty whack with his right boot. He clearly didn't expect it to give way so easily, and if the images were not comical enough, there was a fraction of a second where the striker struggled to extract his foot from now gaping hole he had made in the flimsy structure. With both feet safely back on terra firma, Klinsmann then resumed his stomp-off. It was the perfect FC Hollywood moment.

It is fair to say that Klinsmann was not happy with the decision, or with the coach.

The controversial change didn't have any effect on the result, and the gap between Bayern and Bayer Leverkusen had been cut to just a single point. With just three matches remaining, the pressure was really on.

It was the beginning of the end for Klinsmann, and there was no way he was going to work his way back into the coach's good books even if he wanted to. His days as a Bayern player were numbered, and it was now just a matter of maintaining his professionalism and seeing things through to the end. Young substitute Lakies' ten minutes of fame, meanwhile, would not signal the beginning of a long and successful career at Bayern. He would finish the season with a Bundesliga winner's medal, but then begin an odyssey involving seven more clubs in as many seasons.

As for the infamous advertising pillar, it now stands in the FC Bayern Erlebniswelt alongside the trophies, shirts, pennants and other historical memorabilia. For neutral observers, its presence is probably a little strange.

Leverkusen were still a point behind Bayern with two match days remaining, but a thumping 4-0 defeat against neighbours Köln combined with the Bavarians' 4-2 defeat of Stuttgart meant that Trappatoni's side had clinched the title with a week to spare. A 2-2 draw in Mönchengladbach saw Bayern finish the season on seventy-one points, two ahead of Leverkusen with Dortmund a distant third, a further six points adrift.

Bayern would have the occasional dose of good fortune in their final run in to the title, most memorably the 3-3 draw in the Munich derby, but all in all had deserved to reclaim the *Meisterschale*. Trapattoni's side had only been beaten three times in the Bundesliga all season, with their final unbeaten burst spanning a dozen matches including eight wins.

	P	W	D	L	Goals	GD	Pts
FC Bayern München	34	20	11	3	68:34	+34	71
Bayer 04 Leverkusen	34	21	6	7	69:41	+28	69
BV 09 Borussia Dortmund	34	19	6	9	63:41	+22	63

Bayern's fourteenth league title – their thirteenth of the postwar professional era – was their first in three years, but overall it had not been a particularly memorable season for *Die Münch'ner*. Bayern had exited the DFB-Pokal at the quarter-final stage with a 1-0 defeat in Karlsruhe, but perhaps the biggest disappointment was in the UEFA Cup, where the defence of their title had begun and ended in the first round against Valencia CF.

A resounding 3-0 defeat in the first leg at the Mestalla had effectively ended the contest, and while Trapattoni's side would go on to win the return at the Olympiastadion courtesy of an early own goal from David Navarro, the 3-1 aggregate defeat constituted Bayern's first opening round exit in any European competition since 1969 – a 3-2 loss to Saint Étienne in the Champions' Cup.

What had taken place in that year's Champions League also helped to rub more salt into Bavarian wounds. With the final of the tournament scheduled to take place at the Olympiastadion in Munich, Bayern fans would not only have to put up with their team not being able to take part in the competition, but the fact that the famous *Henkelpott* would eventually be claimed by none other than Borussia Dortmund. In a spectacular display that saw them inflict a surprise 3-1 defeat on favourites Juventus, Ottmar Hitzfeld's side more than made up for missing out on a third successive Bundesliga title.

Bayern may well have ended Dortmund's spell of domestic dominance, but I can honestly say that every single Bayern fan would have happily given up the Bundesliga title just for the opportunity to see *Die Roten* play for Europe's biggest prize on their home ground in Munich.

Despite their falling at the first hurdle in the UEFA Cup, the Bundesliga title and a return to the elite Champions League would guarantee Trapattoni's position at the Säbenerstraße for at least another season. There were a number of key personnel changes during the summer of 1997: Jürgen Klinsmann's itchy feet and even itchier relationship with Trappatoni saw him head back to Serie A in Italy with Sampdoria, defender Oliver Kreuzer moved across the border to FC Basel in Switzerland, while out of favour striker Marcel Witeczek signed for Borussia Mönchengladbach.

Karlsruher SC had always been a popular source for FC Bayern scouts, and joining former KSC players Oliver Kahn and Mehmet Scholl were midfield duo Thorsten Fink and Michael Tarnat. Highly-rated French attacking left-back Bixente Lizarazu made his way from the previous season's UEFA Cup final opponents Girondins de Bordeaux, while arguably the most significant addition to the squad was VfB Stuttgart's highly-rated striker Giovane Élber.

The Brazilian became Bayern's most expensive signing of 1997/98 at 6.5 million Euros, and arrived in Munich having scored twenty goals in thirty-seven league and cup outings for the Swabians. Bayern had been guilty in the past of signing "promising" South American players with little or no established reputation, but Élber was a completely different prospect. Here was a player who was not only comfortable with the conditions in Germany, but a hard worker and proven goalscorer.

The season began brightly enough for Trapattoni's side in the revived DFB-Ligapokal with wins over Dortmund and Stuttgart, with new signing Élber making an immediate impact. The Brazilian scored Bayern's opening goal in the semi-final against BVB with Markus Babbel securing a 2-0 win, and in the final he was on target again against his former club, doubling the advantage provided by Mario Basler. It may have only been the pre-season Ligapokal, but Trapattoni could finally celebrate winning another piece of silverware.

Bayern were firm favourites to retain their Bundesliga crown in 1997/98, but the ultimate combination of dark forces would come together to thwart their title ambitions. In what could only be described as the perfect witches' brew, bogey side Kaiserslautern and former coach Otto Rehhagel would pull off the most perfectly executed coup. Having been relegated from the Bundesliga in 1996, the Red Devils from the Pfalz had bounced back immediately, and in their first season back in the top flight simply continued to gather momentum.

The first match of the season at the Olympiastadion pitted the defending champions against their former coach, with the result effectively determining the destiny of the *Meisterschale*. With a starting line-up that featured another ghost from the past in the form of former TSV Vestenbergsgreuth centre-back Harry Koch, the visitors registered a 1-0 victory courtesy of a strike by Dane Michael Schønbjerg ten minutes from time.

The opening home defeat was a major blow for Bayern and Trapattoni, but it proved to be the perfect springboard for their newly-promoted opponents. Rehhagel's Red Devils had worked their way to the top of the league table just four weeks into the campaign, and after that would never look back. Bayern meanwhile, despite an unbeaten fifteen-match streak that would run through to the end of the *Hinrunde*, remained static in second place until the end of the season as Kaiserslautern became the first club in the history of the Bundesliga to win the second and first division titles back to back.

Perhaps the defining moment of the battle for the Bundesliga title had come in Bayern's second meeting with Rehhagel's side at a packed Betzenberg in the first week of December. Going into the match Bayern were four points off the pace knowing that a victory would take them to within just a point of the leaders, but a disappointing 2-0 defeat – bringing their long undefeated run to an end – saw them fall seven points behind.

Somehow one could imagine the smug, coiffured Rehhagel sprouting a pair of horns and sniggering maniacally in some dark corner at the Betzenberg, and the story was pure gold for the headline-hungry press. The man once rejected and cast out by Bayern had emerged from the shadows to punch the Bavarians hard on the nose; the infamous green goblin from Bremen had been transformed into the fiendishly archetypal pointy-tailed *Rote Teufel* from the Pfalz.

It also didn't help that Kaiserslautern, much like Werder Bremen, were seen as a cult "underdog" club much-loved by the armies of the Bayern-haters both in and outside Germany. It just added another layer to the at times spiky rivalry between the two clubs that had built up over the years.

The league leaders would drop a number of points as the season rolled towards its inevitable conclusion, but Bayern were never able to reestablish their earlier season form to take advantage of their rivals' slip-ups. The Bavarians would actually claw the deficit back to two points by the beginning of February, but a four-game winless spell – including three straight defeats in Berlin, at home to strugglers Köln and in Gelsenkirchen against Schalke 04 – allowed Kaiserslautern to keep their noses comfortably in front.

With eight match days remaining Trapattoni's side were a massive nine points behind, but just four weeks later had managed to pull this back to just two as Kaiserslautern coughed and spluttered with the finishing line in sight. Match day thirty saw the Red Devils visit fifth-placed Hansa Rostock, while Bayern took on bottom side Arminia Bielefeld – a team that had failed to register a victory since the turn of the year. Having fought their way back from nine points behind, this was surely seen as the perfect opportunity for the Bavarians to finally push themselves into top spot:

	P	W	D	L	Goals	GD	Pts
1.FC Kaiserslautern	30	17	9	4	53:34	+19	60
FC Bayern München	30	17	7	6	59:32	+27	58
Bayer 04 Leverkusen	30	13	12	5	58:34	+24	51

Unfortunately for Bayern and their expectant fans, Bielefeld suddenly started playing some football. In what was a ding-dong battle at the Alm, the home side took the lead after ten minutes through Dutchman Rob Maas, only for Michael Tarnat and Markus Babbel to turn things around in a seven minute spell. Former Bayern man Michael Sternkopf levelled the scores five minutes from half-time, only for Christian Nerlinger to restore Bayern's lead going into the break.

3-2 ahead and Kaiserslautern locked at one apiece in Rostock, Bayern would finally get a tiny sniff of the lead at the top of the table on goal difference. All they needed to do was close the door in Bielefeld, and hope that things remained the same in Rostock.

In a match that was essentially a microcosm of Bayern's painfully inconsistent season, they conceded a third with just over a quarter of an hour remaining as Oliver Kahn was beaten by Greek defensive midfielder Thomas Stratos, and with eight minutes remaining Sammy Kuffour found the back of his own net to hand the relegation candidates a scarcely believable 4-3 lead. Meanwhile some 420km to the northeast at the Ostseestadion in Rostock, Hansa and Kaiserslautern had exchanged further goals to find themselves at 2-2.

Lothar Matthäus would save Bayern from complete embarrassment with an equaliser a minute from time, but the 4-4 draw was nothing less than yet another missed opportunity.

Two points adrift of the league leaders with two weeks remaining, Bayern might have hoped to take things to the last day, but a flat goalless draw against mid-table MSV Duisburg in their penultimate match would put an end to any hope of a miraculous finish. A 4-0 win for Kaiserslautern against VfL Wolfsburg ensured the return of the *Meisterschale* to the *Pfalz*, and complete an astonishing two years for the Red Devils and Otto Rehhagel.

The final game of the season saw Bayern storm to a four-goal demolition of Borussia Dortmund as Trapattoni trumped fellow Italian coach Nevio Scala, but despite the fine performance it was a simple matter of too little, too late.

It had been a bizarre season of peaks and troughs for the Munich side, and despite being well off the pace for much of it they had still managed to create plenty of chances to claim the title. The team had shown that it had been more than capable of getting results, only to turn out inconsistent and at times incredibly poor displays that at times bordered on the infuriating.

	P	W	D	L	Goals	GD	Pts
1. FC Kaiserslautern	34	19	11	4	63:39	+24	68
FC Bayern München	34	19	9	6	69:37	+32	66
Bayer Leverkusen	34	14	13	7	66:39	+27	55

For title-winning Kaiserslautern coach Otto Rehhagel, the 1997/98 season was a personal victory over the club that had unceremoniously discarded him just two seasons before. It was as if the perfect script had been written for him, the culmination of a slow rise back to the top after what had been a miserable nine months at the helm in Munich. It was also further proof that while he may have been completely ineffective when managing Bayern's big stars and even bigger egos, Rehhagel remained the undisputed master in getting the very best out of players who on paper didn't necessarily amount to much. For Giovanni Trapattoni meanwhile, his second spell in Munich was coming to an end.

The same infuriating inconsistency that had plagued Bayern's Bundesliga season would be carried over into their Champions League campaign, which saw some excellent results mixed in with a number of insipid and uninspiring displays. At times, it was really getting hard to tell which Bayern side would turn up from one match to the next.

Trapattoni's side had started the group stage well enough with three straight wins against Turkish side Beşiktaş, Swedish champions IFK Göteborg and Paris St. Germain – with the French side being subjected to a brutal 5-1 hammering as Giovane Élber and Carsten Jancker ran riot – but this was then followed by a disappointing 3-1 defeat in Paris.

Two first half goals from Jancker and Thomas Helmer in Istanbul against Beşiktaş were enough to see Bayern safely through to the quarter-finals, but any hope the home fans might have had for a gala finish to the group stage would be dampened by a woefully pedestrian display against Göteborg at the Olympiastadion. To cap off a truly forgettable encounter, defender Markus Babbel would put through his own net to give the already eliminated Swedish side a surprise consolation 1-0 win.

With the Champions League being a considerably smaller competition than it is today the participating teams had to wait the best part of four months before things resumed in the spring of the following year, and Bayern's quarter-final in the middle of March 1998 against domestic rivals and reigning European Champions Dortmund would fall right in the middle of their worst spell of the season. Trapattoni's men were in second place in the Bundesliga with their opponents floundering in mid-table, but this would not at all be indicative of the Bavarians' form coming into the tie, which had taken a dangerously sudden nosedive. The reality was that the contest was always going to be much closer than the two teams' respective league positions suggested.

Trapattoni's side approached the first leg at the Olympiastadion off the back of two successive Bundesliga defeats, and would fail in their attempt to break down a robust Dortmund side that relied more on stodgy defensive tactics and hard work than the free-flowing dynamism that had taken them to their first European title the previous year. Dortmund's leaky defence had conceded thirty-nine goals in their twenty-five Bundesliga games, but together with a helpful crossbar and post they put together a solid defensive performance to bolt the door shut in the face of a determined Bayern attack in front of a crowd of sixty-thousand.

While clearly disappointing, the goalless draw had not been the worst result for Bayern. Despite their poor form, just the one goal in the return leg at the Westfalenstadion would have put them in with a chance of making the last four. With two weeks between matches, there was always going to be a chance that they could turn things around.

Unfortunately it was not to be. Trapattoni's men had been unable to even find the back of any opposition net for more than a month, and this miserable trend continued as the second leg at the Westfalenstadion inevitably ended goalless after the regulation ninety minutes. Something had to give, and it was left to Dortmund's Swiss international Stéphane Chapuisat to settle the tie four minutes into the second period of extra time as the Ruhrpott outfit continued in their quest to retain their European crown.

Having seen Dortmund win the trophy in the Olympiastadion the previous year had been bad enough, but to see the *Schwarzgelben* advancing to the last four at Bayern's expense was particularly painful. To the huge relief of everybody in Munich, Dortmund couldn't make it past semi-final opponents Real Madrid, ultimately failing in their mission to become the first German team to retain the *Henkelpott* since the great Bayern side of the 1970s.

Bayern's domestic cup campaign had begun against fifth-tier Landesliga Bayern-Nord side DJK Waldberg, evoking memories of the ignominious defeat three years earlier against TSV Vestenbergsgreuth during Giovanni Trapattoni's first spell at Bayern. As had been the case in 1994, the mid-August fixture was played at Nürnberg's Frankenstadion – in front of an even bigger crowd of 35,500 people. The Bayern coach was clearly determined not to underestimate the opposition and see lightning strike twice, but it was hard not to look back at the events of August 1994 with a degree of trepidation.

There any similarities ended. There was a sense of inevitability about the massacre that followed, with the non-league team being put to the sword by a merciless Bayern side. The amateurs actually matched Vestenbergsgreuth's goalscoring feat as they breached the Bayern defence in the sixteenth minute to level the scores at 1-1, but either side of this *Die Roten* notched up a record sixteen goals to register the biggest ever victory in the entire history of the competition, and their biggest win in a competitive match.

Giovane Élber ran in a hat-trick inside the first twenty-five minutes, Carsten Jancker scored five goals in just a quarter of an hour either side of half-time, and seven other players also made their way onto what quickly turned into a crowded scoresheet. Jancker's five goals was at the time a DFB-Pokal record; interestingly, it was broken seven years later by the same player at the same stage of the competition – by then in the colours of Kaiserslautern – in a 15-0 triumph over non-league FC Schönberg 95.

Bayern's reward for putting sixteen goals past their hapless amateur opponents was a second round meeting with VfL Wolfsburg at the Volkswagen Arena, a game that had threated to run away from them early on. A seventh-minute penalty from United States international Claudio Reyna put the Wolves in front and a second from Marijan Kovačević a minute before half-time threatened to derail Bayern's ambitions, but a crucial strike just before the break gave Trapattoni's men hope of mounting a comeback in the second half. Alexander Zickler levelled the scores and Michael Tarnat looked to have completed the recovery five minutes from time, but journeyman striker Roy Präger guaranteed at least another thirty minutes of play just three minutes later.

Thirty minutes of extra time couldn't separate the two teams, and it would all come down to a penalty shoot out. It didn't start at all well for Bayern. After Detlev Dammeier had put Wolfsburg in front, Thomas Strunz's effort was well met by 'keeper Uwe Zimmermann, who failed to be put off by the Bayern midfielder's bright peroxide blond hair as he dived brilliantly to his right. The Wolves made it 2-0 before Mehmet Scholl finally got the visitors on the board, but having scored from the spot in the match Reyna was unable to maintain his team's advantage as his poor kick was easily saved by Oliver Kahn. Christian Nerlinger's well-placed shot levelled things up at 2-2, and when a nervous-looking Präger lifted his kick high above the goal and into the crowd the advantage had clearly swung back towards Trapattoni's side.

Bixente Lizarazu thrashed his kick into the top left-hand corner of the net to give Bayern the lead in the shootout, and although Piotr Tyszkiewicz's kick would keep the Wolves just about alive it was left to Michael Tarnat to wrap things up. The utility man swept a well-directed shot low into the bottom right-hand corner to seal a 4-3 victory.

Things didn't get any easier in the the round of sixteen with a trip to Kaiserslautern, where Bayern eked out a hard-fought 2-1 win that Trappatoni and many fans would have happily traded in for one of the two Bundesliga defeats suffered at the hands of the Red Devils. Nerlinger opened the scoring for Bayern with just three minutes on the clock, and although their opponents levelled things up after twenty-five minutes with a free-kick from former Bayern midfielder Ciriaco Sforza, the in-form Jancker settled the match fifteen minutes from time.

After the two tough battles against Wolfsburg and Kaiserslautern, Bayern's run-in to the final at Berlin's Olympiastadion was far more straightforward. Goals from Christian Nerlinger and Giovane Élber were enough to secure a comfortable 2-0 quarter-final win over Bayer Leverkusen, and three goals in the first twenty-five minutes from Dietmar Hamann, Mehmet Scholl and Michael Tarnat guided *Die Roten* to an emphatic 3-0 triumph over VfB Stuttgart. The showpiece final at the Olympiastadion in Berlin would see the Bavarians take on outsiders MSV Duisburg, in their third DFB-Pokal final and first since 1975.

Duisburg had finished in a more than respectable eighth position in the Bundesliga after a solid if unspectacular campaign, and came into the final showpiece in Berlin with nothing to lose. Already assured of a place in the following year's European Cup Winners' Cup, Friedhelm Funkel's team approached the match in the knowledge that they had managed to hold Bayern to a goalless draw just two weeks earlier. For the Bavarians, it would be their last opportunity to provide *Trainer* Giovanni Trapattoni some much-needed silverware after what had been a fairly ordinary season.

While Bayern's start was worryingly sluggish, their opponents were quick off the blocks. As Trapattoni's side struggled to find their feet let alone any sort of rhythm, Duisburg had clearly taken to the field with a sense of purpose. Togolese striker Bachirou Salou was central to the *Zebras'* early dominance, harrying the Bayern defence and pulling them sideways with his power and pace.

Duisburg had been by far the better team during the opening exchanges, and with twenty minutes on the clock they took a deserved lead. Seizing on some slack play in midfield by the *Münch'ner*, the dangerous Salou collected the ball halfway inside the Bayern half, before blitzing past reincarnated sweeper Matthäus and sending a low shot that fizzed past Olli Kahn and into the back of the Bayern net.

Bayern's tactics had been completely shot to pieces. Matthäus was looking like an invalid, Thomas Helmer appeared to be floating around with no great purpose in the middle of the defence, and the midfield looked slow and bereft of any ideas. In desperation, Trapattoni took action with just over half an hour gone as he hauled off Helmer and Bixente Lizarazu, replacing them with the more versatile midfielder Thorsten Fink and striker Carsten Jancker.

When the half-time whistle blew with the *Zebras* a goal in front, it was the least they deserved.

Die Roten emerged at the start of the second half with a greater sense of purpose and looked considerably better than they had done in the opening forty-five minutes, but even then they still struggled to make any sort of headway against a determined and energetic Duisburg team who looked to have got their tactics absolutely right.

The sprightly Giovane Élber was the one beacon of light for the Bavarians, but as the game approached the final twenty minutes it looked as though Trapattoni's dream of ending his second spell at Bayern with that precious piece of silverware was going to be left unfulfilled. It would take just one moment of controversy to change the momentum of the game completely.

For the best part of seventy minutes Duisburg had had the upper hand, with the irrepressible Salou continuing to run rings around the clueless Bayern defence. As the burly Togolose striker embarked on yet another bustling sprint towards the Bayern goal, a desperate Michael Tarnat swung out a dangerously high boot, sending his opponent crashing to the ground.

Salou's injury was clear for all to see, yet Tarnat remained on the field having received just a yellow card. The challenge had been more clumsy than malicious, but not even the biggest Bayern supporter would have complained had their side been reduced to ten men.

Within seconds of the restart, Bayern were on level terms and back in the match. After a desperate scramble inside the Duisburg penalty area the ball was swung back in towards the six-yard box, with 'keeper Thomas Gill unable to clear the danger. His weak attempted punch allowed Élber to nod the ball back into the danger zone, and with the flat-footed defence unable to clear it ended up at the feet of Markus Babbel out on the left of the penalty area.

With his back to goal the Bayern defender managed to pull off a fine impersonation of the great Gerd Müller, swivelling neatly on the spot before blasting a right-footed effort through a crowd of blue and white shirts and into the back of the net.

Tarnat's tackle on Salou and his being allowed to remain on the pitch had arguably been the game-turner, and when the Duisburg striker eventually gave in to the pain and limped off after seventy-three minutes, the momentum had swung completely towards Bayern. The burly Dane Stig Tøfting tested Oliver Kahn with a stinging long range effort with six minutes remaining, but the final quarter of the match belonged to the Bavarians.

With just over a minute of normal time remaining the tireless Élber was bundled over just outside the box by Dietmar Hirsch, and that heady combination of magic and just a little bit of luck – some would say a dollop of good old-fashioned *Bayern-Dusel* - saw the hitherto ineffective *enfant terrible* Mario Basler conjure up ultimate magic trick to complete the Munich side's comeback.

The Bayern winger struck the free-kick with his right boot, curling the ball over the wall and into the net on the bounce past the static Gill. Having been second best for most the game Trappatoni's side were in front when it mattered. There was no time for their stunned opponents to mount a comeback, and Basler's stunning effort proved to be enough as Bayern secured the richly-decorated golden trophy for a ninth time.

The dramatic last-minute victory in Berlin was the glistening final touch to what had otherwise been a turbulent two year spell in Munich for Giovanni Trapattoni, a period that had seen a number of moments that had resulted in FC Bayern hitting the headlines for all the wrong reasons.

With Bayern's disappointing league and European campaign it was always unlikely that Giovanni Trapattoni would see his contract in Munich being extended, but he had made it through to the end of his planned two-year spell in charge, something that a number of his predecessors had not managed to achieve. Victory in the cup final meant that he had at least been able to sign off on a decent note.

One of the most memorable – if one can call it that – Trapattoni moments would take place on 10th March 1998, two days after the 1-0 defeat in Gelsenkirchen against Schalke 04. With the club in something of a trough and unable to score a goal let alone win a match, the press had cast their eyes on the beleaguered coach – who then entertained the watching world with an infamous press conference outburst that has since become legendary.

Trapattoni's bad German certainly didn't help matters – the bellicose speech contained a number of grammatical howlers and bizarre non-sequiturs – and he openly criticised a number of players with no quarter given. Mario Basler, Didi Hamann, Christian Nerlinger and Mehmet Scholl were all name-dropped by the Italian, while the unfortunate Thomas Strunz ended up with his name all over the pages of the tabloids. The coach reserved most of his opprobrium for the midfielder, who was described as "always being injured".

This bizarrely theatrical and much-publicised rant from the coach helped justify Bayern's *FC Hollywood* label, and given the performance and attitude of some of the more senior players it was difficult not to sympathise with the Italian while at the same time acknowledge that his overly passionate approach suggested an impatience bordering on what could very easily have been passed off as borderline mental instability. The ranting, the crazy hand-waving, the table-thumping and the imperfectly-constructed German with an obvious Italian accent was reminiscent of the speech delivered – also in heavily-accented German – by Benito Mussolini during his visit to Berlin in September 1937.

The off-field drama continued with the lurid stories surrounding Mario Basler, a player who was for many fans a truly infuriating and complicated personality. On one day the mercurial midfielder would weave his magic on the pitch and leave everyone open-mouthed in awe, while on the next he would just do something completely petulant and brainless. I can remember moments when I would just smile as Basler effortlessly slithered past an opponent with the ball seemingly attached to his feet, but can recall just as many occasions when I found myself wanting to hurl a heavy object at the television.

Some Bayern supporters chose to love Basler unconditionally while others saw him as little more than a loudmouthed and unpredictable basket case, but I would eventually judge him on a match by match basis. He was always going to do *something*... You just had no idea what.

In true FC Hollywood style, there were stories of Basler spending the entire night before a match drinking and partying, turning up to morning training in a drunken stupor, and displaying that prima donna attitude that would make him the bane of coaches everywhere. Tabloid hacks spent their time following the controversial midfielder, and there were even tales of private detectives being tasked to follow his every move to ensure he kept on the straight and narrow. Unsurprisingly, Basler was one of those players who had continually got under the skin of Giovanni Trapattoni, but – one might say typically – he was the player who had produced that special moment of magic to win the cup final in the last minute.

Every time I watch the footage of Giovanni Trapattoni thumping the desk and hearing "Struuunz!" I can feel myself cringe. As a Bayern fan, these off-field moments were almost as nauseating as some of the performances on the field during much of the 1990s: Copenhagen, Norwich, Vestenbergsgrueth, Thomas Helmer's *Phantomtor* against Nürnberg and the fiasco involving the four amateur players against Frankfurt.

I am certainly not speaking for myself when I say that it had been a decade that most followers of the team would be happy to forget. Even so, nobody could have possibly imagined how painfully the decade would end.

SO CLOSE, AND YET SO FAR

Giovanni Trapattoni's departure at the end of the 1997/98 season led to a complete change in coaching style at the Säbenerstraße with the appointment of Ottmar Hitzfeld, the man who had guided rivals Borussia Dortmund to the European title the previous year. A quiet, thoughtful yet driven coach – the polar opposite of the loud, passionate and impulsive Trapattoni – Hitzfeld's first task following his arrival in Munich was to take the collective egos in the squad and turn them into a functioning unit. The determined but measured new coach was a welcome antidote to all the madness that had come before: slowly but surely, he gradually started to chip away at the mentality that had for much of the 1990s defined *FC Hollywood*.

Having left behind a Dortmund squad that had built its success on a solid and highly professional team ethic rather than on individual big names, the forty-nine year old coach found himself picking up the debris left behind by his predecessor – as well as having to manage the likes of Oliver Kahn, Mario Basler, Lothar Matthäus, Mehmet Scholl and the controversial midfielder Stefan Effenberg, who was back in Munich at a cost of just over DM8 million following a number of back-and-forth spells at Fiorentina and Borussia Mönchengladbach.

After the cooped-up madness of the "Era Il Trap", the more sedate Hitzfeld was seen by many as a breath of fresh air in Munich. The new coach's hard-nosed professionalism and calm demeanour brought a much-needed sense of stability to the squad, and even the "perpetually injured" Thomas Strunz managed to work his way back to full fitness and a place in the starting eleven.

For many, the healing process was mental as much as it was physical. Didi Hamann and Christian Nerlinger – along with bit-part Italian striker Ruggiero Rizzitelli and defender

Markus Münch – made their way out of the club, and joining Effenberg on the way in was TSV 1860 München's gritty defensive midfielder Jens Jeremies for DM1.5 million and Arminia Bielefeld's Iranian striker Ali Daei for DM5 million. The solidly reliable if unspectacular central defender Thomas Linke was signed from Schalke 04 on a free transfer, as was the skillfully versatile Bosnian midfielder Hasan "Brazzo" Salihamidžić, who headed to Munich from Hamburger SV.

The first trophy opportunity for the new coach was the pre-season DFB-Ligapokal, where the new-look Bayern side beat Bayer Leverkusen with a thirtieth-minute Mario Basler strike before a strolling to a far more convincing 4-0 win over VfB Stuttgart in the final, with Giovane Élber scoring a first-half hat-trick against his former side.

The 1998/99 Bundesliga season began with a hard-fought 1-0 win in Wolfsburg, but the following weeks saw Bayern stretch their winning start to six matches, propelling them to the top of the table by the end of September. A 6-1 thrashing of Hansa Rostock and a 5-3 win over HSV were the highlights of this impressive opening winning run, and by the beginning of October Bayern were a comfortable five points clear at the top ahead of local rivals TSV 1860 München.

Hitzfeld's side would not relinquish top spot for the remainder of the season, and would produce the best results of any side both home and on the road. At the Olympiastadion, *Die Roten* were unbeaten in their seventeen matches – winning fourteen and drawing three – and when they closed off the season with a 2-1 win against second-placed Bayer Leverkusen the gap between them and the *Werkself* was a staggering fifteen points. Bayern had in fact wrapped things up on match day thirty-one with one of their less spectacular results, a 1-1 draw against third-placed Hertha Berlin at the Olympiastadion.

Bayern's perfect six from six start had given them the perfect platform, but a decisive run of eight more straight wins either side of the *Winterpause* – part of an eighteen-match unbeaten streak – effectively clinched their fourteenth Bundesliga title. Of their thirty-four league matches they had won twenty-four, and led the league for the most goals scored (76) and least conceded (28).

While nobody stood out in the top scorer stakes with Giovane Élber and Carsten Jancker topping the charts with thirteen apiece, the seventy-six Bundesliga goals were distributed nicely across the squad: apart from the goalkeepers and defensive midfielder Thorsten Fink, every player who played more than two games would manage to find the back of the net at least once. It was in every sense a total team effort, and a complete contrast to the previous season.

	P	W	D	L	Goals	GD	Pts
FC Bayern München	34	24	6	4	76:28	+48	78
Bayer 04 Leverkusen	34	17	12	5	61:30	+31	63
Hertha BSC Berlin	34	18	8	8	59:32	+27	62

With the Bundesliga being won in such convincing fashion, many supporters finally started to believe that the gateway to football heaven had finally opened and that the perfect coach had arrived in Munich. After eight years of mediocrity, hyperbole and failed promises, Bayern finally had a squad that looked capable of taking on Europe's finest and challenging for major honours.

Bayern's dominant form saw them advance in both the DFB-Pokal and the Champions League, though in the latter things had only really begun to click after a scratchy start. A comfortably convincing 5-1 aggregate victory over Serbian side FK Obilić in the preliminary round placed the Bavarians in the group phase alongside Manchester United, FC Barcelona and Danish outfit Brøndby IF, and the opening match in Denmark saw Hitzfeld's side take a 76th-minute lead through Markus Babbel, only to see their unheralded opponents strike twice in the final three minutes to snatch a dramatic victory.

It was a grim portent of things to come.

Having salvaged a 2-2 draw and their first point at home to United courtesy of a last-minute own goal by striker Teddy Sheringham – whom Bayern would encounter again a little later in the season – Hitzfeld's side would get their campaign firmly back on track with home and away wins against FC Barcelona. The match at the Olympiastadion against the Catalans was settled just before half-time by Effenberg's slide in at the near post, but the return in front of an 85,000 crowd at the Camp Nou was far more dramatic.

Work commitments had taken me to the western Irish city of Shannon, and on the evening of the Barcelona match I found myself in a warm and cosy hotel lounge, just a stone's throw away from the small and rather nondescript airport famed for being a refuelling hub for transatlantic Soviet and Cuban air traffic during the Cold War. Apart from the odd guest shuffling in and out I was the only one sitting there in front of the fireplace on that chilly November evening, supping on a pint of Murphy's stout and scoffing the delicious home-made toasted cheese and ham sandwiches served at the bar. I had rushed back to the hotel after a busy day's work, and after the short taxi ride from the office had made it just in time for the kick-off.

Having to chase the game, the home side looked to put pressure on the Bayern goal from the start. The dangerous Brazilian Giovanni had the ball in the Bayern net as early as the tenth minute only to be penalised for a pull on Michael Tarnat's shirt, but just short of the half-hour mark when the same two players clashed again in the Bayern penalty area, it was Tarnat doing the tugging. The incident didn't escape the beady eyes of Italian referee Pierluigi Collina, and Giovanni was able to dust himself down before sending the resulting penalty low to Oliver Kahn's right to give his side the lead.

Barcelona were arguably the better of the two teams and one might have expected them to press on after taking the lead, but as half-time approached Bayern slowly started to establish a foothold. Just five minutes after going behind Ottmar Hitzfeld's side looked to have scored a crucial away goal as Élber nodded in from close range after a Markus Babbel effort had been clawed away by 'keeper Ruud Hesp, but it was correctly ruled out for offside. As the first half came to an end, everything rested on a knife edge.

Just two minutes into the second half, Bayern got the crucial breakthrough. The busy Élber was just a little too hot to handle for the Barcelona defence as he weaved into the box, and as four claret and blue shirts converged on him the Brazilian was able to tap the ball to his left towards Stefan Effenberg who in turn left it for the unmarked Alexander Zickler. The young striker made no mistake, tucking the ball neatly through the legs of Hesp.

Stung by Bayern's response, the Catalans started to open things up a bit as they looked to restore their advantage, and almost immediately Bayern started to find more space for the counterattack with Zickler and Élber looking particularly dangerous. Just after the hour mark *Die Roten* should have scored their second when Élber skimmed the outside of the post after the pacy Zickler had forced Hesp into a fine save, and not long afterwards the Brazilian was denied by the Dutch 'keeper after getting his head to a well-directed Effenberg cross.

Barcelona kept trying as Rivaldo gently warmed Kahn's gloves and Sonny Anderson sent a spectacular looking effort wide of the target, but the visitors would not be denied. With just three minutes remaining, man of the match Élber was at it again as he neatly nodded the ball forward to substitute Hasan Salihamidžić. The fleet-footed Bosnian then charged through two blue and claret shirts before coolly stabbing the ball past Hesp with the outside of his right foot. The 2-1 win secured a double over Barca, and the six points collected in the two fixtures against the Catalan giants would prove to be crucial in the tight three-way battle for the top two qualifying places.

I was very glad that no Manchester United supporters had decided to turn up that evening, as at the very same moment – on another television channel – their side were thrashing poor Brøndby 5-0 at Old Trafford having slaughtered the Danes 6-2 on their own ground a fortnight earlier. A defeat would have left Bayern in third place in the group table behind both United and Barça, but the win at the Camp Nou signalled a massive shift in momentum. With seven points from four games played – just one behind group leaders United and three ahead of Barça – Hitzfeld's side had hauled themselves back into contention. I can safely say that I slept well that night before the short flight back to London the following morning.

Two second-half goals from Cartsten Jancker and Mario Basler were enough to dispose of the group's bottom side Brøndby at the Olympiastadion, and with Barcelona and United sharing the points at the Camp Nou, Hitzfeld's side moved to the top of the group. One point ahead of the English side and five points clear of the Catalans, Bayern had one foot in the knock-out stage with a game to spare – a situation nobody would have thought possible after they had taken just a single point from their first two matches.

The final group match saw Bayern take on United at Old Trafford, with the Bavarians needing just a point to finish top of the group. Defeat would have left them on ten points – enough to secure second place but not necessarily enough to guarantee a slot in the last eight with only the top two group stage runners-up joining the six winners.

In what was a fast-paced and open match the home side took the lead two minutes before half-time through Irishman Roy Keane, but just eleven minutes into the second half Hasan Salihamidžić evened things up with a close range finish that was effective if not particularly pretty. The 1-1 draw ensured a first-place finish for Hitzfeld's side, with United claiming one of the two runners-up spots.

With teams from the same country not being kept apart by the draw process, the quarter-final pitted Bayern against Germany's other qualifier – reigning Bundesliga champions and bogey team Kaiserslautern. In what had been an encouraging first campaign in the rebranded competition, the Red Devils – coached by the much-unloved former Bayern *Trainer* Otto Rehhagel – had punched well above their weight, finishing top of a tough group that had contained Portuguese champions Benfica, 1988 tournament winners PSV Eindhoven and Finnish outfit HJK Helsinki.

Kaiserslautern had been handed out a four-goal thrashing earlier in the season at the Olympiastadion, but Hitzfeld's side could not afford to take any chances against a team that more often than not had managed to pull something out of nowhere when it mattered. As a result the first leg in Munich turned into something of a cagey affair, but the home side would get the basics right to put themselves into a decent position for the return. Giovane Élber and Stefan Effenberg put Bayern two goals up in the space of four frenetic first-half minutes, and the increasingly reliable defence kept a clean sheet – extending a flawless defensive record that stretched back to the group match against Manchester United before the winter break.

The second leg at a packed and noisy Fritz-Walter-Stadion saw Bayern take the lead through Effenberg inside the opening ten minutes, which quickly eased any remaining nerves they might have had. With the home side now needing to win by at least three goals to progress the Bavarians were finally able to relax, and they applied their foot firmly to the accelerator to run away with the match. Jancker doubled the lead on twenty-two minutes, and when striker Uwe Rösler put through his own net six minutes before half-time Bayern's place in the last four was already well beyond doubt. Hitzfeld's side eased off significantly as the match rolled towards its inevitable conclusion, though not before Basler had netted a fourth nine minutes into the second half to complete a four-goal rout for *Die Roten* and a resounding 6-0 win on aggregate.

Bayern's opponents in the last four were Ukrainians Dynamo Kyiv, perennial tournament dark horses that for many were highly fancied in the competition. Having topped a far from shabby first phase group containing Arsenal, Lens and Panathinaikos, the Eastern European side signalled their intent in disposing of defending champions Real Madrid in their quarter final, with striker Andriy Shevchenko scoring all of their goals in a convincing 3-1 aggregate victory. While Ottmar Hitzfeld would almost certainly have picked Kyiv over the other semi-finalists Manchester United and Juventus, nobody in the Bayern camp could afford to take them lightly.

On what was a grey, wet and soggy evening in the Ukrainian capital, Bayern fell behind to a Shevchenko strike with just over a quarter of an hour played as the in-form striker took advantage of a defensive lapse from Markus Babbel. Sammy Kuffour was denied by the upright as Bayern looked to get back into the contest, but two minutes from the break Shevchenko scored a freakish second from a left-sided free-kick that evaded everybody including the static Oliver Kahn to put the home side two goals in front. Suddenly, Bayern found themselves with their backs firmly against the wall.

While their second goal might have been slightly fortunate, the Ukrainians were more than good value for their two-goal advantage. Bayern were looking straight down the barrel, but completely against the run of play they managed to drag themselves back into the match. Right on the brink of half-time they won a free-kick some thirty yards out, and Kyiv 'keeper

Olexandr Shovkovskiy made a complete mess in dealing with Michael Tarnat's low skidding shot. Somewhat fortuitously, *Die Roten* managed to go into the break only 2-1 down.

Five minutes into the second half midfielder Vitaly Kosovsky restored Kyiv's two-goal cushion as he latched onto Kuffour's poor clearance, and as the rain continued to come down and the clock ticked by it surely looked as though Bayern's European campaign was coming to a sticky and soggy end. However with twelve minutes remaining Stefan Effenberg lined up a free-kick from out on the right, delivering a delicious right-footed strike that swerved around the wall of white shirts before skimming off the inside of Shovkovskiy's near post. Despite the opposition, the foul weather and the fanatical 75,000 crowd cheering on the home side, the Bavarians refused to give in.

The second away goal gave the visitors renewed hope of turning things around in Munich, but there was still plenty of work to do at the back. As the home side continued to press, there was another close call as Matthäus found himself swiping the ball off his own goal line.

The few visiting Bayern supporters in the crowd would have been willing for the final whistle to blow, but things got even better when a header into the Kyiv box by substitute Alexander Zickler found its way to Jancker. Despite not being known for his close control and skill on the ball, the bald and burly striker used his strength to hold off centre-back Olexandr Holovko before turning and sweeping the ball past Shovkovskiy to make it 3-3.

From almost nowhere and armed with three away goals, Hitzfeld's side had carved out a genuine advantage to take back to Munich. A creditable draw had been snatched from the jaws of what had looked like certain defeat, and with three away goals in the bag Bayern just needed to keep a clean sheet in the return leg. Having dominated the game for long spells, Kyiv knew that the onus would be on them to win the game in Bavaria.

Right from the kickoff in Munich, the Ukrainians came out fighting. Within the first quarter of an hour Olli Kahn in the Bayern goal was forced into producing a couple of world-class saves from Valentin Belkevich and Aleksandr Khatskevich, the first a stunning low turn around the right post and the second a spectacular tip over the crossbar. In fact Hitzfeld's men had to wait over twenty minutes until they created their first opportunity when Basler thrashed a long-range effort narrowly wide of the target.

Having blunted Kyiv's opening attack Bayern slowly started to assert themselves, and ten minutes before half-time the tie was settled with what can only be described as a moment of sublime magic – a truly special moment from a player that on his day was capable of producing football made in heaven. Even today just watching it still gives me goosebumps.

Ten minutes before half-time and roared on by a crowd of sixty thousand in the Olympiastadion, Bayern won a corner out on the right. The irrepressible Mario Basler swung it in with his right foot, but a white-shirted Kyiv defender got there first to clear. The ball almost immediately made its way back into the danger zone, with Basler collecting it on his way back from the corner flag. Cutting inside back towards the edge of the box and neatly side-stepping his marker with typical nonchalance, the Bayern number fourteen then unleashed a left-footed curling shot that pinged off the inside of the far post and into the back of the net, with Shovkovskiy left completely helpless as the ball whistled past him.

Kahn made his third fantastic stop to deny Serhiy Rebrov as Valeriy Lobanovskiy's side desperately looked for an opening, but there was no way back for the Ukrainians. With the visitors having to throw every man forward in the second half there were plenty of opportunities for Bayern to counter attack. Alexander Zickler should have really finished things off as he blazed a shot high over the bar with the goal at his mercy, and substitute Ali Daei's bullet header was brilliantly blocked by Shovkovskiy with a minute remaining. Then, the final whistle blew.

Bayern were through, and Basler's fantastic and almost otherworldly strike was one of those moments of magic that will forever be remembered by the Munich faithful. It completed an astonishing comeback over the course of the two legs, and after a hiatus of twelve years Bayern would once more grace the showpiece European final.

A return to the Camp Nou in Barcelona saw Bayern take on their earlier group stage opponents Manchester United, and coming into the match there was very little to choose between two closely-matched sides. While United were missing their skipper Roy Keane and influential midfielder Paul Scholes, Ottmar Hitzfeld was arguably more hindered by the absence of star striker Giovane Élber and French attacking left-back Bixente Lizarazu, a player that had made a massive difference to the Bayern back line. The space usually occupied by the dynamic Lizarazu was filled by the more workmanlike Michael Tarnat, while Élber was replaced by Alexander Zickler who joined Carsten Jancker in a two-pronged offensive line.

The earlier group phase encounters had produced two well-contested draws, and both teams were chasing domestic trebles: it was difficult for anyone to pick a favourite. In front of a crowd of just over ninety-thousand, ninety-three minutes of football would end with one of the most traumatic episodes in the history of FC Bayern München, and put the final seal on what had been a hugely disappointing decade.

It all began so well. With just over five minutes played, Bayern – playing in their silver and burgundy Champions League *Trikot* – were awarded a free-kick out on the left when Jancker's charge towards goal was clumsily ended by Norwegian defender Ronnie Johnsen. From just outside the eighteen-yard box semi-final hero "Super Mario" Basler sent in a low, right-footed curling shot that skidded off the turf and into the bottom right-hand corner of the United net with 'keeper Peter Schmeichel left rooted to the spot – possibly left unsighted with the sneaky Markus Babbel causing all sorts of confusion at the edge of the United wall.

As Basler charged off in celebration before sliding to a halt by the touchline on his knees, I punched the air. It was the perfect start: this time, surely, we were going to do it. After eighteen years as a Bayern fan and the bitter memories of Rotterdam in 1982 and Vienna in 1987, I felt that it was the right time to finally claim the coveted *Henkelpott*.

The English champions pressed hard for the equaliser and started to dominate possession as things started to settle down, but crucially they failed to create any chances of note. Bayern meanwhile had to be content to sit back and wait for the right moment to strike on the break, with both Basler and Zickler going close. As the game approached half-time the Bavarians continued to hold firm, and went into the break holding onto the lead.

United started the second half strongly, but as in the first half wouldn't really threaten Oliver Kahn in the Bayern goal. *Die Roten* meanwhile were beginning to look increasingly dangerous on the break, and as more gaps in the field opened up and time ticked by they were looking good for a second goal that would surely have wrapped things up.

On another evening Hitzfeld's side could very easily have killed off their opponents, but the combination of both Schmeichel and the frame of the goal would keep the English side in the game. Substitute Mehmet Scholl set up Stefan Effenberg whose rasping shot was acrobatically tipped over the bar by the Danish *Torhüter*, and just moments later a mazy run from the impressive Basler saw Scholl lift the ball beautifully over Schmeichel only to see it cannon off inside of the post and back into the 'keeper's grateful arms.

Bayern came even closer just past the eightieth minute, as Jancker's spectacular overhead kick clattered hard against the crossbar with Schmeichel completely beaten. The second killer goal just wouldn't come, and like me I could imagine millions of Bayern fans either biting their nails or sitting on their hands, praying for the final whistle to end the agony. The players out on the pitch meanwhile adopted a completely different attitude: with the match not yet over, they started to act as if they had won it already.

A grinning Lothar Matthäus saluted the Bayern crowd when replaced by Thorsten Fink in the eightieth minute, while goalscorer Basler also raised his fist in celebration as he made his way off the field at the end of the regulation ninety minutes. What followed was something that would haunt every Bayern fan for years: the moment when the infamous *Bayern-Dusel* was violently turned on its head in the space of ninety indescribable seconds.

Agony, horror, pain, anguish, frustration, despair and an inexplicable sense of profound shock all rolled into one.

As the clock ticked over into injury time, United won a corner out on the right, throwing everyone forward in what was surely going to be their last chance to save the game. Even Schmeichel, clad in a particularly toxic shade of bright green, ventured forward towards the Bayern penalty area. David Beckham swung the ball into the box and Dwight Yorke directed it towards the Bayern goal, but substitute Fink was on hand to clear. It was one of those moments that I would repeat in my head for long after this episode had reached its horrible conclusion: ninety-time times out of a hundred Fink would have leathered the ball back up the pitch and into the United half, but on this occasion he failed to connect cleanly, slicing his clearance straight back to the lurking Ryan Giggs.

The Welshman immediately whipped the ball back into the box, and on hand to meet it was the unmarked substitute Teddy Sheringham. The ball should really have been somewhere in the opposition half or high up in the stands, but instead it was swept past the helpless Oliver Kahn and into the back of the Bayern net. The Bavarians should really have been out of sight, but somehow the scores were all square at one apiece.

With Matthäus and Basler forced to endure this spectacle from the bench, the championship-winning smiles had been replaced with faces of open-jawed horror and shock. I cannot even begin to imagine what it must have been like for the Bayern fans at the ground; for me sitting at home it was like something from the Twilight Zone, something so surreal that it almost felt like an outer body experience.

We had won the trophy. Bayern were European champions. Well, not quite.

There was little opportunity to even discuss the matter of extra time, and United now had the smell of fresh Bavarian blood in their nostrils. Before the crowd even had time to draw breath and recover their composure, the Red Devils quickly won another corner. Beckham's kick was nodded down and across the goal by Sheringham, and fellow substitute Ole Gunnar Solskjær stabbed the ball from close range into the roof of the net. In a trice, it was all over: the pain of Rotterdam in 1987 and Vienna in 1987 were but flesh wounds compared to this.

While the United supporters were celebrating wildly and the infernal Clive Tyldesley was babbling like a madman in the ITV commentary box, the Bayern players were flat out in the pitch, unable to comprehend what had just happened. By far the most enduring moment for every Bayern fan was the sight of an inconsolable Sammy Kuffour beating the ground in sheer frustration and despair. Basler had won the man of the match award, but it was scant consolation.

In all my years as a Bayern fan – indeed, in all my years as a football fan – I had never witnessed anything quite like this. I immediately stopped the video recorder, deciding to tape over the evidence; I knew right at that moment I would never be able to watch this match again. Living in England I found myself unable to escape the constant repetition of those final dramatic moments, but over the years I slowly managed to make myself immune to it. Nevertheless, I have not been able to sit down and watch the entire match since; on those instances where I have stumbled across highlights of the match, I will always watch it until Basler's goal, and then change the channel. Even if Bayern were to win another dozen Champions League titles the memory of Barcelona 1999 will be impossible to wipe away.

The dramatic final moments have led some commentators to suggest that Manchester United's name had been on the trophy from the start; by the same token, it was probably written that Bayern's dismal run of form in the 1990s could have only ended like this. In winning the famous *Henkelpott* United would go on to complete a historic treble, and Bayern – who until the defeat in the Camp Nou had been seeking the same thing – returned back home to Germany completely deflated. United had looked dead and buried, yet had somehow managed to claw themselves out of the hole in the ground and drive the stake through Bavarian hearts.

Questions will continue to be asked about that horrible evening in Barcelona. How did it happen? Was it the coach's decision to make those late substitutions? Was it arrogance on the part of some of the Bayern players, who believed that the cup was already in the bag before the match was actually over? Was it the two shots that cannoned off the woodwork? Was it that unfortunate sliced clearance from Thorsten Fink?

Was it just a pure and simple case of bad luck? Or was it simply not meant to be?

Rather than throwing out theories and looking to find somebody or something to blame, I'd refer to the pithy comment made after the match by United manager Alex Ferguson: "Football. Bloody hell".

The final of the DFB-Pokal in Berlin against Werder Bremen ten days later should have been the final part of Bayern's own historic treble, but instead it turned into little more than a painful encore. An early strike by Bremen's Yuri Maximov was cancelled out by Carsten Jancker just before half-time, but that would be as good as it would get for Hitzfeld's side as they fell 5-4 in the resulting penalty shootout.

Oliver Kahn would keep out Jens Todt's effort to give Bayern the initial advantage, and after Hasan Salihamidžić, Ali Daei, Michael Tarnat and Jancker had found the back of the net it was left to the usually reliable Stefan Effenberg to finish things off. The script had long been written however, and there would be a sense of inevitability as the blond midfielder thrashed a right-footed shot high over the crossbar and into the crowd. Bremen 'keeper Frank Rost then stepped up to give his side the lead in the shootout, and just moments later dived brilliantly to his left to save from Lothar Matthäus.

Having dreamed about an historic treble, it had been a case of so near and so far for Hitzfeld's side. Football can be so wonderful, but in the space of ten days every Bayern supporter had found themselves brutally exposed to the game's ultimate cruelty.

TWO OUT OF THREE AIN'T BAD

Ottmar Hitzfeld's first season in Munich had certainly been a memorable one, and while many still found it hard to wipe out the memory of that late May evening in Catalonia, life would go on. The summer of 1999 saw the FC Bayern coach continue to fine-tune his squad: unsettled Iranian international Ali Daei headed north to Berlin to join Hertha Berlin and veteran Thomas Helmer moved to English club Sunderland, while Borussia Mönchengladbach's Swedish centre-back Patrik Andersson made his way to the Säbenerstraße for three million Euros alongside former Bayer Leverkusen winger Paulo Sérgio – signed from AS Roma for €6.6m – and exciting new Paraguyan prospect Roque Santa Cruz, snapped up from Asunción club Olimpia for €5m.

Both Andersson and Paulo Sérgio were more than familiar with life in the Bundesliga, and the only real gamble was teenager Santa Cruz, who had burst onto the scene with three goals in four games during the summertime Copa América tournament. Over the years Bayern had developed a habit of buying "promising" South American players, and the relatively unknown Paraguayan was one more prospect added to the list.

The summer saw a number of pre-season matches, culminating in the annual DFB-Ligapokal which saw the Bundesliga's top five sides and the DFB-Pokal winners come together for a week-long festival of football culminating with the final at Leverkusen's BayArena.

As reigning Bundesliga champions Bayern entered the competition at the semi-final stage, where they disposed of Borussia Dortmund at Augsburg's Rosenaustadion courtesy of a sixty-sixth minute own goal from defender Christian Wörns. The final saw *Die Roten* take on old foes Werder Bremen in front of a disappointing crowd of 13,000, with first-half goals from

Paulo Sérgio and Michael Tarnat proving to be enough to secure a 2-1 win – and with it a third DFB-Ligapokal in succession.

The 1999/2000 season saw Bayern continue to improve and come together as a unit, but with their being less dominant in the Bundesliga the campaign would develop into a particularly exciting and memorable one. Hitzfeld's side had got off to a sluggish start as they dropped two points at home to Hamburger SV – saved only by a last-minute equaliser from Giovane Élber – and in week two fell to a disappointing 2-0 defeat in Leverkusen; a scrappy 1-0 win over local new boys SpVgg Unterhaching was then followed by equally workmanlike wins in Duisburg and Frankfurt, but a home defeat at the hands of VfB Stuttgart would leave the Bavarians sitting in fourth place with six matches played.

A last-minute strike from Stefan Effenberg saw Bayern snatch a rather fortuitous 1-1 draw in Gelsenkirchen against sixth-placed Schalke 04, and with seven games played they had dropped back down to fifth place – five points behind early leaders Borussia Dortmund. However, the draw against Schalke was followed by five straight victories, enough to send them back to the top. In those five games the Bavarians scored nineteen goals, including five against Wolfsburg and half a dozen against mid-table SC Freiburg.

Bayern's high-scoring winning run would end with a scrappy 1-0 defeat at the hands of city rivals TSV 1860, but ten points from their next four matches saw them end the *Hinrunde* two points clear of Leverkusen. Off the pitch, an unhappy and unsettled Mario Basler decided to make his way back to his first club Kaiserslautern. Having been picked for only two Bundesliga matches all season, it was a sad final chapter at Bayern for the man who had come close to being the club's Champions League final hero less than six months earlier.

A goalless stalemate in the first match of the *Rückrunde* against HSV coupled with a Leverkusen win over Duisburg saw the *Werkself* pull themselves level on thirty-seven points, but just the following week Bayern turned on the style against their title rivals with a resounding 4-1 win at the Olympiastadion. An own goal from Torben Hoffmann with just two minutes gone would give Bayern the lead, and further strikes from Stefan Effenberg and Mehmet Scholl either side of half-time were enough to send the home side into the comfort zone. Leverkusen pulled a goal back through youngster Michael Ballack, but a last-minute Alexander "Zick-Zack" Zickler strike ensured that Bayern finished things off on a high note.

Bayern would keep on winning and stretched their lead to five points as Leverkusen slipped up in Gelsenkirchen, but a 2-0 defeat in Stuttgart and just a point in Berlin allowed the tenacious Rheinlanders to draw level once again as the season entered the home straight. The following weeks saw Hitzfeld's side drop points at home to Kaiserslautern and away to

Wolfsburg, and by the end of match day 27 they had slipped two points behind Leverkusen. With neither side hitting any sort of consistency, everything was perfectly set for what would be one of the most dramatic finishes to the Bundesliga season in years. It was a good old-fashioned slugfest, a fight that was always destined to go right to the final bell.

The *Rückrunde* continued with both Bayern and Leverkusen trading and taking punches in a topsy-turvy final struggle. The top two positions were swapped as Leverkusen dropped two points against relegation-threatened Hansa Rostock, and then again in match day thirty as Bayern suffered a shock 2-1 defeat in the Munich derby against TSV 1860 – with *die Löwen* completing a rare domestic double over their fierce city rivals.

With just four games remaining, the *Werkself* were three points clear of Bayern at the top, an advantage they continued to cling on to as the season reached its dramatic conclusion.

Bayern would win their next three games in a row as they found a rich vein of form just at the right time, but on the final day of the season the advantage was clearly with Leverkusen who also maintained their momentum to keep their noses in front. Since the 4-1 defeat in Munich in February, Christoph Daum's side had strung together an unbeaten run of fourteen league matches and had scored forty-one goals – including a club record of nine against relegation-threatened SSV Ulm 1846 – and as the final day of the season arrived they were clear favourites to win the coveted *Meisterschale* for the first time.

While Bayern entertained seventh-placed Werder Bremen in their final match at the Olympiastadion, Leverkusen would be just twelve kilometres down the road in the quiet suburb of Unterhaching – needing just a single point against SpVgg to claim their first Bundesliga title.

For Bayern, it was little more than a mission of play, win, put up a good final show for the Olympiastadion crowd and hope for the best. They needed to beat Bremen to have a chance of pipping Leverkusen on goal difference, but nobody in their right mind would have thought that the Rheinlanders – beaten only twice in their previous thirty-three Bundesliga matches – wouldn't pick up at least a point against tenth-placed Unterhaching. But over the years football has proved that even the most predictable fixture can often lead to the most unpredictable results; were this not the case, nobody would have had much to write about.

	P	W	D	L	Goals	GD	Pts
Bayer 04 Leverkusen	33	21	10	2	74:34	+40	73
FC Bayern München	33	21	7	5	70:27	+43	70

Bayern were quick off the blocks at the Olympiastadion, and had pretty much completed their part of the deal in just over a quarter of an hour against a poor Werder side. Bixente Lizarazu sent in a cross from the left for Carsten Jancker to nod in after just two minutes, and just ten minutes later the same man was on hand to double the lead in similar fashion after Paulo Sérgio's header had struck the crossbar. On sixteen minutes, the Brazilian winger scored a sublime third. Hasan Salihamidžić played a neat backheel inside to Mehmet Scholl, whose first-time pass was wonderfully met by Sérgio, who struck an even cuter backheel with his right foot past the static Frank Rost in the Bremen goal.

At that point however Bayern could have scored another dozen and it wouldn't have made a shred of difference: with Leverkusen and Unterhaching still locked at 0-0, the *Werkself* would still have the slight advantage.

Just five minutes later, things changed dramatically as news started to filter through that a Bayer Leverkusen player had got on the scoreboard – but at the wrong end of the pitch. His name: Michael Ballack. 'Haching winger Danny Schwarz had swung a harmless-looking right-wing cross into the Leverkusen box, and with nobody around him the unfortunate Ballack had slid in to execute the perfect textbook finish.

Bremen pulled a goal back in the Olympiastadion five minutes before half-time, but Bayern now held the advantage. Even then however, not even the biggest optimist in the Olympiastadion *Südkurve* would have been banking on Unterhaching to keep the door closed on the free-scoring Leverkusen side for another forty-five minutes.

There were no further goals at the Olympiastadion, but with eighteen minutes remaining there was one more in Unterhaching. Left-sided midfielder Jochen Seitz floated a cross into the Leverkusen penalty area, and there to meet it was the unmarked Markus Oberleitner, a player who had spent the 1996/97 season on the player roster at Bayern. Oberleitner timed his header perfectly, floating the ball in the top right corner of the net past the static Polish *Torhüter* Adam Matysek to double his side's advantage. There was no way back for Leverkusen, and the *Meisterschale* was on its way to Munich. With both teams finishing on seventy-three points from their thirty-four games, Bayern's superior goal difference meant that Leverkusen would have to keep waiting for their first Bundesliga title.

	P	W	D	L	Goals	GD	Pts
FC Bayern München	34	22	7	5	73:28	+45	73
Bayer 04 Leverkusen	34	21	10	3	74:36	+38	73

This had not been a case of *Bayern-Dusel*. Leverkusen – living up to their unfortunate nickname of "Vizekusen" or, among the English-speaking press, "Neverkusen" – would only have themselves to blame. Unterhaching's 2-0 win and Bayern's fifteenth Bundesliga title would see the entire city of Munich – save those from the light blue Löwenbräu-drinking corner of the city – join in the celebrations, and thanks to the wonders of satellite television I had been able to keep up with every twist and turn and ebb and flow in what was an amazing finale to an dramatic season.

Bayern's run in the Champions League meanwhile had seen the team overcome a slow start to work their way into the list of genuine contenders, only for disappointment to strike once more at the hands of an old foe. Making things even more frustrating was the fact that Bayern would meet this team on four occasions during the tournament, winning three games and losing only one.

With the Sky Sports network increasing their portfolio by the week, terrestrial television channel ITV made much of their Champions League coverage, with an increase in live matches – for the most part starring English teams – and comprehensive highlights packages. If I couldn't see Bayern live – in English on ITV or in German on one of the many available free to view channels – there were plenty of opportunities to see more than just the goals. The televised football revolution of the early 1990s had truly started to gather momentum, and the thirty-second highlights packages of the 1980s and much of the 1990s were long forgotten. It was getting a whole lot easier to be an FC Bayern fan in England.

The format for the ever-changing Champions League tournament had been adjusted to include more teams, and with this the introduction of an additional four-team group phase prior to quarter-final stage. Bayern were drawn alongside PSV Eindhoven, Glasgow Rangers and FC Valencia in their first phase group, and despite winning just two games from six would progress in second place behind Valencia. Having started with a 2-1 win over the Dutch champions at the Olympiastadion, Ottmar Hitzfeld's team had grabbed a point in Glasgow courtesy of a ninetieth-minute Michael Tarnat goal before sharing two 1-1 draws with Valencia.

A 2-1 defeat for Bayern in Eindhoven had left them teetering on the brink of elimination with a total of just six points from their five games played, three behind group leaders Valencia and one behind Rangers. The task was pretty clear for the Bavarians: nothing but a win in what was effectively a cup final against the Scottish champions would be good enough.

Given that they just needed a point to progress one might have thought Rangers would have simply piled everybody behind the ball, but instead they took on a refreshingly positive approach. Bayern had created some good chances early on through Élber, but most of the attacking play early on came from the visitors.

Time and again the Scottish champions swept forward, with Bayern left to rely on the woodwork and the reactions of 'keeper Oliver Kahn. While the upright denied Dutchman Michael Mols, it took some quick thinking from Kahn to charge out of his area to dispossess the pacy Rod Wallace.

Bayern were clearly playing on the edge, and were more than fortunate to be awarded a penalty just after the half-hour mark when Mehmet Scholl went down easily under a challenge from Giovanni van Bronckhorst. Thomas Strunz stepped up to take the kick, and almost succeeded in making a mess of it as Rangers ex-Dortmund 'keeper Stefan Klos got a right hand to the ball. Fortunately for Strunz and Bayern, it was able to make its way into the goal.

The tie had been turned on its head with Rangers now needing to score, but all Bayern had to do was keep playing the same way. Having taken the lead *Die Roten* switched to a more defensive mode, which only helped to give the opposition more space in midfield. Just five minutes after going behind Rangers again struck the woodwork, as Wallace saw his snapshot deflected against the underside of the crossbar by Kahn.

The second half saw more of the same, as the increasingly shaky red wall continued to resist the almost relentless flood of blue and white. Ex-Hamburger Jörg Albertz saw his firmly-struck shot well parried by the overworked Kahn, and van Bronckhorst sent in a thunderous long-range shot that cannoned off the right post with the Bayern 'keeper well beaten. In the fifty-fifth minute, Finnish substitute Jonatan Johansson – on for the unfortunate Mols – blazed a shot high over the bar with the goal at his mercy.

Bayern could very easily have been two or three goals behind, yet somehow they were still in front against a side that time and again had been cruelly denied. Even I as a diehard Bayern fan had started feel that there was something a little unjust about it all. Johansson forced Kahn into another flying save as the 'Gers continued to press, and substitute Gabriel Omar Amato found himself kicking at thin air with the Bayern defence all over the place.

When Bayern finally did get an opportunity on the break to settle the tie, substitute Paulo Sérgio could only shoot straight at the 'keeper with Élber screaming for the ball in space to his left. The missed opportunity to effectively settle the tie summed up what had been an ordinary performance from the home side, and when the final whistle blew the relief inside the ground was palpable. In front of the television screen on my sofa, I was finally able to stop sitting on my hands. Bayern were through.

Starting just three weeks later, the draw for the second group phase placed Bayern alongside Norwegian champions Rosenborg BK, their previous year's semi-final opponents Dynamo Kyiv, and the old enemy from Spain, Real Madrid. A turgid 1-1 draw in Trondheim against dark horses Rosenborg ensured that Bayern got the potential banana skin out of the way first, and a more exciting but equally hard-fought encounter at home to a dangerous Kyiv outfit saw Bayern claim all three points.

Carsten Jancker had pounced on an error by 'keeper Olexandr Shovkovskiy to give *Die Roten* the lead after just six minutes, but Serhij Rebrov brought the visitors level just five minutes into the second half. With just ten minutes remaining however, Hasan Salihamidžić's long throw-in was flicked on into the Kyiv six yard box by the dominant Jancker, with the sprightly Paulo Sérgio stabbing the ball home from close range.

The competition resumed in the spring of 2000, with Bayern suddenly finding a rich vein of form for the crucial double header against old foes Real Madrid. The first leg would result in the Munich side's first victory in their fourth attempt at the Santiago Bernabéu, with the Spanish champions truly being put to the sword as the visitors eased their way to an impressive 4-2 win. Bayern were 3-1 up by half-time with goals from Scholl, Effenberg and Fink, and even though *Los Merengues* reduced the deficit three minutes into the second half Paulo Sérgio wrapped things up with twenty-three minutes remaining.

The confident performance in Madrid was followed by an even more emphatic triumph the following week at the Olympiastadion, as Hitzfeld's side twisted the knife while turning on the style.

In front of a crowd of sixty-thousand on a cool March evening in the Bavarian capital, Bayern took the lead in controversial circumstances with just four minutes on the clock. Élber's ball into the box found Mehmet Scholl in a clearly offside position, but Dutch referee Dick Jol ignored the flag from his assistant on the touchline. The Bayern number seven calmly collected the ball and dinked it over the advancing Iker Casillas, and as Scholl ran off in celebration the referee found himself in the middle of a barrage of protests from the Madrid players. While it was true that the Spaniards had been hard done by, nobody except their own supporters cared. After all, it was Real Madrid.

This was just the break the home side needed, and from that point they were relentless. As the match approached the half-hour mark, the combination of the simple and the sublime doubled Bayern's lead. Oliver Kahn hoofed the ball deep into the Madrid half where Élber, allowed to drift into position by two white-shirted defenders, played some typically Brazilian keepy-uppy before lifting the ball over Casillas on the volley.

At half-time, Bayern were already looking good for another three points.

Iván Helguera pulled a goal back for the visitors midway through the second half as Bayern started to wind things down, but this was the perfect catalyst for a spectacular late burst inspired by substitute Alexander Zickler. Within five minutes of his arrival on the pitch, the twenty-five year old combined with both Matthäus and Effenberg before planting a perfectly-struck right-footed volley into the top-right hand corner of the Madrid net with eleven minutes remaining, and wrapped up a spectacular cameo display with a second two minutes into injury time. Bayern broke quickly through Paulo Sérgio, and Zickler collected the Brazilian's pass in his own half before sprinting towards the Madrid goal, rounding the stricken Casillas and finding the bottom left-hand corner.

Bayern's 4-1 triumph sent them clear at the top of the group table with ten points from their four matches, with the buzzing Olympiastadion also providing the perfect setting for what was Lothar Matthäus' final appearance in the famous red *Trikot*. Having spent two spells in Munich spanning a total of twelve seasons, Matthäus – German player of the year in 1999 at the age of thirty-eight – had long established his place in the pantheon of Bayern greats. As he walked around the pitch for the final time as an FC Bayern player, he was given a standing ovation by the crowd, his team-mates and a number of the Real Madrid team.

The result was more than fitting, for some thirteen years earlier Matthäus had played a central role in another memorable game at the Olympiastadion – where Madrid had been beaten by the same score. In that highly hard-fought and at times brutal semi-final match in 1987, Matthäus had not only scored twice from the penalty spot, but also ended up as the victim of one of the most hideous fouls - if one can call being stamped on the face a foul – in the history of the competition. Thankfully, this farewell encounter had finished far more peacefully.

Bayern went on to seal a deserved place in the quarter-finals with a somewhat less spectacular 2-1 win over Rosenborg with first-half goals from Mehmet Scholl and Paulo Sérgio, meaning that their final match against Dynamo Kyiv would provide the perfect opportunity for some of the fringe players to be given some valuable European competition experience. Promising young goalkeeper Stefan Wessels came in for Oliver Kahn, midfielder Michael Wiesinger made the starting eleven for the first time in European competition after two late substitute appearances, while Polish midfielder Sławomir Wojciechowski made his first start in only his third match for *Die Roten*.

Having won the group with a game to spare the final fixture in Kyiv had little meaning for Bayern, and in a rather drab encounter the home side scored two goals either side of half-time to take all three points. The win would take the Ukrainian champions level with Madrid on ten points and with a better goal difference, but the head to head record between the two sides saw the Spanish side squeeze into the quarter-finals, still lingering like a bad smell.

Striker Raúl's third-minute goal in Norway against Rosenborg was enough to see Real through to the last eight – and I had this nagging feeling about them crossing Bayern's path again before the competition was over. Bayern had effectively beaten the Spaniards 8-3 on aggregate over their two second phase group games, yet somehow Vicente del Bosque's side were still right in the mix – and as dangerous as ever. One sensed that it was only a matter of when rather than if the two teams would meet again.

The quarter-final draw pitted Hitzfeld's side against 1987 European Cup final opponents FC Porto, with the first leg being played at the atmospheric Estádio do Dragão. After a fairly quiet and even opening half the home side took the lead two minutes after the restart, but any immediate fears of a repeat of the 1987 final in Vienna were put aside ten minutes from time. Getting on the end of a well-directed Stefan Effenberg free-kick, Paulo Sérgio registered his sixth goal of the competition to level the scores, setting things up nicely for the return leg in Munich.

Having scored the crucial away goal Bayern started the second leg at the Olympiastadion with a slight advantage, and after just a quarter of an hour that man Paulo Sérgio was there again to give *Die Roten* the lead both on the night and on aggregate. Michael Tarnat's cross was swung expertly in from the left, with the Brazilian winger stretching out a leg and getting enough contact on the ball to lift it over Porto 'keeper Henrique Hilario.

Having taken the lead, Bayern then looked to lock down the defence to close out the match. Kahn made a fine save to deny Porto's Brazilian striker Mario Jardel, half-time came and went, and as what had been a rather dull match approached its final minute the 47,000 crowd could have been excused for believing that the job had been done. But one could not have a Champions League match involving Bayern without that little bit of last-minute drama – if just to keep the home supporters clinging on the edge of their seats.

As the clocked ticked into injury time, Porto hauled themselves back into the contest as Jardel took advantage of some slack marking from Thomas Linke to head his side level. Memories of Vienna in 1987 start flooding back again, as well as more recent nightmarish visions of the final in the Camp Nou less than a year earlier. At 1-1 and the aggregate score locked at 2-2, the game was surely heading towards extra time – or worse.

With part of me preparing myself for the inevitable Porto winner – let's say that past experiences had steeled me for such a moment – Bayern didn't allow the opposition to dictate matters. The Bavarians made their way up to the other end to win a free-kick, and Mehmet Scholl's well-flighted ball into the box was met by the most unexpected goalscoring hero: Thomas Linke. The tall central defender had scored only one goal all season, but made his presence felt in the crowded penalty area as he worked himself into position to head the ball through a pack of blue and white shirted defenders and into the back of the net, atoning for his error just moments earlier.

Almost a year after being physically and emotionally crushed by that horrific brace of injury time goals at the Camp Nou, Bayern would this time not only see things through without conceding a second – but make their way up the field to score the dramatic injury-time winner themselves. With the influential Effenberg out injured and without the recently retired Matthäus, Bayern had been sluggish and for the most part unimaginative, but were just a little too strong for what had been in truth a fairly ordinary Porto side.

Awaiting Bayern in the semi-final was the side they had demolished in the second group stages just a couple of months earlier: Real Madrid. Bayern had inflicted a comprehensive 4-2 defeat on the Spanish side in their second group phase meeting at the Santiago Bernabéu, but for the first leg of the semi-final there was a lot more at stake.

Real were out for revenge, the atmosphere in the ground was electric with a capacity crowd of over ninety-thousand, and the make-up of Hitzfeld's side was markedly different from the eleven that had torn Madrid to pieces in their previous encounter. The absence of both Effenberg and Matthäus had left a gaping hole in the Bayern midfield, and it was immediately apparent that things were going to be a lot tougher a second time around – and so it would prove.

With just four minutes on the clock, Bayern fell behind. Picking up possession in the middle of the pitch, the dangerous Raúl sent a diagonal through ball out to the left, beating the offside trap and finding Nicolas Anelka. The Frenchman had plenty of time and space, and made his way to the left corner of the six yard box before sending a curling shot over Oliver Kahn and into the roof of the net as a desperate Jens Jeremies slid in.

The early goal gave *Los Merengues* – and the noisy home crowd – just the spark they needed, and from that point on they were relentless. A Fernando Morientes effort was flagged for offside, the Bayern defence had been forced onto the back foot, and with just over half an hour gone Morientes, Raúl and Michel Salgado combined effectively to double the home side's advantage. Raúl's short pass into the box nutmegged Thorsten Fink and found Salgado, and having rounded Kahn the Madrid right-back saw the ball quite literally walked into the empty Bayern net by the unfortunate Jeremies.

It was a truly awful goal to concede, and pretty much summed up Bayern's entire evening. Chances were few and far between, Real could have had scored more than just their two goals, and while the likes of Jeremies, Fink and Michael Tarnat were solid and reliable enough, they just couldn't be compared to the absent Effenberg, Matthäus and Mehmet Scholl. It was always going to be difficult and nobody had expected a repeat of the 4-2 result in the second group phase, but the nature of the defeat was like a sharp punch in the gut for every Bayern fan.

In ninety disappointing minutes, all sense of expectation had been completely shattered.

Less than a week later the two teams would meet again in Munich, with Bayern needing a resounding victory by three goals or more to reach the final in Paris. Many fans would think back to the 4-1 win at the Olympiastadion earlier in the season, and having walked to a convincing cup final win over Bremen the previous weekend Hitzfeld's side were feeling fit and refreshed. Effenberg and Scholl were also back in the starting lineup, and there would be a sense of hope among the crowd of sixty-thousand people. We just needed an early goal to kick-start the recovery, and the deal would be back on again.

Right from the start the red wave streamed towards the Madrid goal, and with just three minutes gone Carsten Jancker beat 'keeper Iker Casillas in the air only to have his header cleared off the line by Iván Helguera. Nine minutes later, Bayern got that crucial early goal. Having won a free kick some thirty yards out, Effenberg rolled the ball forward to Jeremies out on the left, whose cross into the opposition box and out towards the byline was nodded back inside by Giovane Élber. Lurking just outside the six-yard box was the bald-headed Jancker, who outmanoeuvred the contrastingly big-haired Iván Campo before lashing the ball with a spectacular right-footed volley that flew past Casillas and slammed into the roof of the net.

The Olympiastadion crowd roared their approval and the passionate Jancker roared back at them, pumping his fists in acknowledgement. The game was back on. The flat performance of just six days earlier was now a distant memory; this was a completely different Bayern side. With the strutting Effenberg bossing the midfield, the busy Scholl buzzing down the wing, and the giant Jancker terrifying the Real defence, I felt a surge of confidence. At that moment, I truly believed that we could win it.

With twenty-six minutes gone, Bayern had the ball in the Real net for a second time. Paulo Sérgio had weaved some of his magic down the left before cutting the ball inside for Scholl, whose shot from just outside the box was fumbled by the nervy Casillas. There to meet the loose ball was Élber, who rolled it into the net before wheeling away in celebration.

The celebrations were short lived. As the players congratulated themselves, the linesman raised his flag.

When Scholl's initial shot had come in, Jancker had been marginally offside – but whether he was interfering with play was a matter of debate. Élber had clearly been onside when he collected the ball before dispatching it, but it wouldn't matter. The "goal" was quickly chalked off.

If the knife could not be twisted any deeper, just five minutes later Real had made it count at the other end, turning what was already a tough task into a almost herculean one. Brazilian Sávio was able to make his way down the left before swinging a cross into the Bayern penalty area, where Nicolas Anelka had ghosted like an assassin into the box. Positioning himself perfectly to rise above Sammy Kuffour, the Frenchman sent a glancing header past Oliver Kahn and into the top right-hand corner of the Bayern net. After having been one marginal decision away from levelling the tie just moments earlier, the Bavarians now needed an almost impossible three more goals to progress.

The second half started just like the first with the home side making most of the running, and it took just nine minutes for Hitzfeld's men to relight the dimly flickering flame of hope. Effenberg sent a looping ball into the Real penalty area, where it skimmed off Élber's head and into the net past Casillas. Bayern still needed two more goals and continued to press manfully, but as time started to run out you could see the tiredness start to take effect on the men in red. An Élber effort from close range was cleared off the line by Steve McManaman and Effenberg sent a shot over the bar, but there was no way back.

Bayern had won on the night with yet another heroic performance in an ultimately losing cause, and the Champions League dream was over for another year.

In winning 2-1 Bayern had registered their third victory in four matches against Real Madrid in the space of less than four months, but it was the Spanish side that would make their way into the final against compatriots Valencia CF. The long pattern of Bayern losing to the eventual champions would then continue, as *Los Merengues* claimed the trophy with a convincing 3-0 win over their *La Liga* rivals at the Stade de France in Paris.

Prior to their Champions League semi-final defeat Bayern had been eyeing the coveted treble, as had been the case in 1999. At the time of the first leg in Madrid they were just three points adrift of Bayer Leverkusen in the Bundesliga and had already secured a spot in the final of the DFB-Pokal, where they would meet Werder Bremen in a repeat of the previous year's showcase match in Berlin.

The final was played in the first week of May as opposed to June due to the scheduling of the Euro 2000 tournament finals in Belgium and the Netherlands, so the trip to the German capital would be the first chapter in the Bavarians' treble quest. It also landed slap-bang in the middle of the Madrid tie – not exactly the best piece of scheduling by the fixture planners at the DFB who for some absurdly daft reason hadn't considered the possibility of a German team reaching the last four of the Champions League.

With DFB-Pokal matches not being shown on the UK-based satellite sports channels I had happily followed Bayern's progress on both ARD and ZDF via my Sky analogue box, but impending changes to the system meant that the methods I used to keep up to date would change yet again. The old system was in the process of slowly being wound down: analogue set-top boxes all around the country were gradually being replaced by newer digital ones – and an updated service that promised a wider selection of new channels, features and functionality.

On the whole and for the vast majority of viewers in the UK the advent of Sky Digital at the turn of the millennium was a winning formula. No more scratchy images, a larger selection of channels, and the promise of Sky Sports' new interactive digital features, including their innovative "player cam". For a small number of viewers however the changes carried one massive negative: the majority of the foreign channels that had previously been free to view on the older analogue box would no longer be available.

For me, the new digital system meant no more DFB-Pokal matches, and my Bundesliga diet would be cut right back down to the highlights package on Sky Sports – which was at best inconsistent and not guaranteed.

No amount of being able to follow David Beckham or Alan Shearer around on "player cam" – a white elephant that would prove to be far less useful than its creators initially believed – could make up for my no longer being able to tune into the Bundesliga highlights on the late night football studio show where you would get to see special guests taking potshots at two small circular holes in a plastic "net".

The changes had been put into place in the late 1990s and the transition was set to be complete by 2002, but for me a house move saw things change in the summer of 2000. The last live match I would get to see on one of the German channels was the final of the DFB-Pokal in May that year.

Bayern's route to the 2000 DFB-Pokal final had been largely non-eventful, with a 4-1 win over Regionalliga Nord side SV Meppen followed by a workmanlike and rather flattering 3-0 victory over second division Waldhof Mannheim with two goals in the final ten minutes.

Hitzfeld's side would win their quarter-final by the same score against second division FSV Mainz 05, before overcoming Bundesliga strugglers Hansa Rostock in a match that saw five goals scored in less than twenty-five second half minutes.

After a goalless first half Roque Santa Cruz had put Bayern two goals in front with an eight-minute brace either side of the hour mark, and as soon as Rostock had clawed themselves back into the match on seventy-five minutes Sammy Kuffour restored the two-goal cushion. Swede Peter Wibran netted a second for the *Ostseestädter* with eight minutes left, but Bayern would do enough to prevent the shock equaliser and set up the chance for revenge in the final against Bremen.

Bayern had failed to score in the first half in both their quarter- and semi-final, and it would be the same story in the final in Berlin as both sides walked in at half-time with the score at 0-0. *Die Roten* had dominated the first forty-five minutes against a listless Bremen side and could easily have been two goals up in the opening twenty minutes, and if anything the star of the show had been referee Alfons Berg, who by half-time had collected more than half a dozen names in his notebook.

The second half saw things continue in much the same vein with Bayern making all of the running, and seconds after Aílton had headed a rare Bremen chance wide the Bavarians finally broke the deadlock. Stefan Effenberg played a perfectly weighted through-ball for Giovane Élber, who muscled past defender Mike Barten before sending a rasping left-footed shot past 'keeper Frank Rost from just outside the six-yard box.

With Bremen Trainer Thomas Schaaf showing little ambition by simply reassembling his midfield rather than trying to press for an equaliser, the final half an hour turned into something of a stroll for Bayern side that didn't need to chase the game. Hitzfeld was confident enough to take skipper Effenberg off with ten minutes remaining, and as the match trundled towards its conclusion the scoreline would eventually reflect the balance of the match.

With seven minutes remaining a pinpoint Michael Tarnat cross from the left corner found substitute Roque Santa Cruz in the Bremen penalty area, and the Peruvian's header across the box was collected by Paulo Sérgio. The Brazilian completed the move with consummate ease, taking the ball neatly on his chest before swaying smartly past his marker and slotting the ball home with the outside of his right foot to double Bayern's lead.

With the score at 2-0 with just minutes remaining, Hitzfeld and his team could afford to take their foot right off the pedal, with just the walk to collect the trophy between them and their encounter with Madrid. But there was more to come yet.

As the game entered the final minutes Santa Cruz nodded the ball forward to Hasan Salihamidžić out on the right, and with the Bremen defence caught cold yet again the Bosnian had plenty of time to play a neat reverse ball inside for substitute Mehmet Scholl. The Bayern number seven – on for the outstanding Élber – was easily able to settle himself before executing the perfect finish to put the final seal on what had been a dominant team performance. Advancing unthreatened into the box, Scholl took his time before smartly dinking the ball over Rost and into the left-hand corner of the net. The final whistle blew, and the first trophy of the season was safe and secure.

The easy 3-0 win in Berlin was Bayern's tenth cup triumph, and sweet revenge for the previous year's shootout defeat at the hands of the *Grün-Weißen*. Their clinching the Bundesliga title a fortnight later would secure a record third domestic league and cup double, but the big one – *der Henkelpott* – continue to elude them.

The following season, that long and painful wait would finally come to an end.

THE FOUR-MINUTE CHAMPIONSHIP

The start of the 2000/01 season would see things change massively for me as a UK-based FC Bayern supporter: after having access to German television to the point where I had started to take things for granted, I was suddenly transported back to the early 1990s. No more live Bundesliga matches, no more *Aktuelle Sport Studio*, no more DFB-Pokal drama. Yes, I'd have Sky Sports' potted Bundesliga highlights, Eurosport's somewhat manic *Eurogoals* compilation and ITV's ever-improving coverage of the Champions League – but it wasn't long before I would start having pangs at not being able to switch over to ARD, ZDF, Sat 1 or 3 Sat for some genuine German *Fußball*.

These changes also affected my watching matches involving the German national team: I had over the previous decade become used to seeing every single match live and hearing the dulcet tones of Waldemar Hartmann, Gerd Rubenbauer and Béla Réthy, but outside of the major tournament finals I found myself having to cobble together potted highlights with the occasional treat when Germany played a team from the home nations.

There were a few major changes to the Bayern squad with the only notable depature being that of defender Markus Babbel who joined Liverpool in the English Premier League on a free transfer, and among those coming in were AS Monaco's French international Willy Sagnol for DM 15 million and Swiss midfielder Ciriaco Sforza, who joined Bayern for a second time from Kaiserslautern for DM 4.5 million.

Joining Sagnol and Sforza in the first-team squad were a couple of youth team players – local boy Sebastian Backer, and a talented nineteen-year old born in Canada to British parents: Owen Hargreaves. Over time, with the help of the motor-mouthed ITV commentator Clive Tyldesley, Hargreaves would become known as "the boy born in Canada, to a father from Bolton and a mother from Rhyl".

The season rolled gently into action as usual with the DFB-Ligapokal in August, which was claimed by Bayern for the fourth time in a row. The mini-tournament saw two impressive performances from the Bavarians, with Kaiserslautern being brushed aside 4-1 and Hertha Berlin being subjected to a comprehensive 5-1 thrashing at the BayArena inspired by a second-half hat-trick from Alexander Zickler. While nobody could read too much into pre-season form, confidence was starting to build at the Säbenerstraße.

Bayern's Bundesliga campaign of 1999/2000 had seen events unfold dramatically on the final day of a highly competitive league season, and nobody could have believed that the following year would produce a finish that would serve up even more nail-biting, edge-of-the-seat, hair-pulling drama. The Bundesliga had long become a home for frenetic finishes and last-minute turnarounds, but the memories of 19th May 2001 – indeed, a few crazy minutes on the afternoon of 19th May 2001 – would surpass even those of the previous year and SpVgg Unterhaching's shock victory over Bayer Leverkusen that had seen Bayern snatch the title on goal difference right at the death from *Die Werkself*.

While Leverkusen had largely been responsible for their own undoing, the dramatic final twist at the end of the 2000/01 Bundesliga season would be witnessed on television screens across Germany and much of Europe – and with it another invocation of the infamous *Bayern-Dusel*. Unlike the previous season however there would be little sympathy for the victims, whose premature celebrations would quickly become part of German footballing folklore.

Bayern would never fall lower than fifth in the table, but it was a strange and rather inconsistent season for Hitzfeld's men – with the campaign being pockmarked by a number of curiously bad results. The Bavarians had started with three straight wins – scoring ten goals in the process – but a narrow 2-1 defeat in Stuttgart was first of nine defeats in what would turn out to be a very close competition.

Two more wins were followed by a dismal 1-0 home defeat at the hands of mid-table Hansa Rostock, and when this was followed by another single-goal reverse at the hands of bottom club Energie Cottbus, Bayern had dropped back into third place behind the two *Ruhrpott* sides Schalke 04 and Borussia Dortmund. A 3-1 win in the Munich derby against TSV 1860 saw them climb back to the top, and although they would only pick up a point in Bremen the following week to slip behind early pace-setters Hertha Berlin, an emphatic 6-2 demolition of Dortmund at the Olympiastadion appeared to suggest that Bayern had finally found their form.

After eleven matches the top of the table was very tight with just half a dozen points separating the top six positions, and the match against Dortmund was followed by the first of two pivotal matches against Schalke 04.

At the time Bayern were sitting in second place with Schalke back in fifth, and at half-time at the Parkstadion in Gelsenkirchen the visitors were well on course following a thirty-fourth minute strike from Giovane Élber. Andreas Möller brought a far more focussed Schalke side level thirteen minutes into the second half, but just a minute later Paulo Sérgio regained the advantage for Bayern.

The game looked to have taken a decisive swing towards Hitzfeld's side, but *Die Knappen* were far from finished. Roared on by a typically passionate home crowd of 62,100 in what was their last season at the massive grey bowl, two goals in the space of just three minutes either side of the seventieth minute mark from Gerald Asamoah and Danish international Ebbe Sand powered Schalke to a 3-2 victory, condemning Hitzfeld's side to their fourth defeat of the season.

Four losses in twelve matches became five in thirteen as Bayern fell to a second home defeat to mid-table Eintracht Frankfurt – a result that saw them drop into fourth place, just two ahead of Frankfurt who in turn leapt four places up the table. With just over a third of the season gone and just four games remaining before the *Winterpause*, the gap separating first-placed Bayer Leverkusen and Köln in tenth was just seven points – and when Bayern dropped another two points at the Dreisam-Stadion against strugglers SC Freiburg they found themselves five points adrift of the top spot.

Week fifteen saw Bayern take on Bayer Leverkusen in another crucial six-pointer at the Olympiastadion: while a win would take them within two points of the *Werkself*, defeat would see them fall eight points behind. Bayern were playing at home, but given their run of form they were not expecting an easy ride against a Leverkusen team that had been unbeaten in nine matches.

With the pressure truly on, Hitzfeld's men delivered. An early strike from Carsten Jancker helped calm the nerves of the 48,000-strong home crowd, and a second strike from Élber just three minutes into the second half more or less settled the matter. Leverkusen's cause wasn't helped by the dismissal of their Brazilian midfielder Robson Ponté after fifty-two minutes, and when the final whistle blew Bayern had secured all three valuable points. Leverkusen slipped into second place behind Hertha on goal difference, while Bayern remained in fourth place – though only two points behind the leaders.

As the first half of the season came to a close, Bayern laboured to a goalless draw in Kaiserslautern and fell back into fifth place – four behind Leverkusen who retook top spot – but a hard-earned come-from-behind 2-1 win over Hamburger SV and a 3-1 win in Berlin against fifth-placed Hertha saw *Die Roten* enter the *Winterpause* in third place, three points off the top in what was a highly congested top six where the constant shuffling and re-shuffling of the teams resembled a game of musical chairs. Meanwhile, Leverkusen fell to successive defeats at the hands of relegation-threatened VfL Bochum and high-flying VfL Wolfsburg, allowing the ever-improving Schalke to return to the top of the table and claim the title of *Herbstmeister*.

It had been a tough and frustratingly inconsistent first half of the season for Bayern and their supporters, and the winter break could not have come any sooner for Hitzfeld's men. The upside was that all of the top teams had been equally erratic and unable to stretch away from the pack, and as the league went into hibernation just six points separated the top six teams – with sixth-placed Hertha sitting on just twenty-eight points with nine wins, one draw and a staggering eight defeats.

The opening fixture of the New Year saw Bayern take on bottom side VfL Bochum at the Olympiastadion, and fans of the Munich side could have been forgiven for thinking that things had not improved since the end of the *Hinrunde*. In a disjointed performance against committed but limited opposition, Bayern had taken the lead twice only to be pegged back by Bochum's midfield playmaker Yıldıray Baştürk – and only a last-gasp winner from skipper Stefan Effenberg would save the home side's blushes.

The result might have been closer than desired, but the most important thing was the win. Three more points were secured in what was a tricky encounter in Wolfsburg, and with leaders Schalke collapsing to an inexplicable 4-1 defeat in Cottbus the *Münch'ner* returned back to the top of the table for the first time in nine weeks.

An early Élber strike against former side VfB Stuttgart saw Bayern secure their third *Rückrunde* win in three, and Bayern fans would have expected this winning run to be extended in their next game against local neighbours SpVgg Unterhaching – now struggling at the wrong end of the table.

Unterhaching might well have helped Bayern win the Bundesliga title the previous season, but with their own survival at stake there was little in the way of charity from Lorenz-Günther Köstner's side. Bayern coach Ottmar Hitzfeld had made a number of changes to his starting eleven with skipper Effenberg and star striker Élber being rested along with Bixente Lizarazu and Hasan Salihamidžić, but this plan very quickly unravelled against an Unterhaching team that made up for their limited talent and lack of top-class international stars with plenty of spirit, determination and no little luck.

After a listless first half Élber was sent on for the disappointing Alexander Zickler, but it was the home side that opened the scoring just short of the hour mark. Seizing on a mix-up in the Bayern defence, Polish under-21 international Mirosław Spiżak put 'Haching in front, and although Bayern suddenly woke up and upped the ante they couldn't find a way through the well-drilled home defence. Mehmet Scholl hit the upright and Sammy Kuffour forced 'keeper Gerhard Tremmel into a great reaction save, but the combination of Bayern's bad luck and some committed defending was enough to see Unterhaching chalk up a memorable and not wholly undeserved win against their more illustrious opponents.

The three points was enough to lift Unterhaching out of the relegation places, but Bayern would somehow manage to stay at the top of the table as their two main rivals both slipped up to away defeats. While Schalke went down 2-1 in Bremen, Leverkusen also fell by the odd goal in three against struggling Rostock. Meanwhile, Dortmund hauled themselves back into the mix with an emphatic 4-2 win at the Westfalenstadion against Hamburg. A mere two points separated the four teams at the top.

Two points clear of the chasing pack, Bayern would have an excellent chance to maintain and even extend the gap at the top against mid-table Köln at the Olympiastadion. With *Die Geißböcke* failing to pick up a point in their previous three matches Bayern were clear favourites, but despite fielding a strong side they once again failed to impress. Having fallen behind in the twenty-fifth minute *Die Roten* struggled to break down a highly obdurate opposition defence, though unlike the previous week were eventually able to draw level through a Carsten Jancker header with twenty-five minutes remaining.

Having collected just the single point from two games one might have expected Hitzfeld's side to fall off the top spot, but the continuation of what had clearly become a series of bizarre and unexpected results conspired to keep them two points clear of both Schalke and Dortmund.

With second placed Schalke and third-placed Dortmund up against in each other in the *Ruhrpott* Derby at least one of them was guaranteed to drop points, but the goalless draw that ensued was the best result possible for Bayern. Leverkusen meanwhile would throw away a golden opportunity to draw level on points at the top with the Bavarians as they fell to an inexplicable 3-1 home defeat at the hands of struggling Cottbus.

It was as if nobody even wanted to win the title.

Match day twenty-four saw Bayern take the long journey north to Mecklenburg-Vorpommern to play Hansa Rostock, another match they expected to win. One point from two matches however became one from three, as Hitzfeld's side once again hit the buffers in an ill-tempered match against a side that despite its obvious lack of star names was just willing to work that little bit harder.

Rostock would take the lead a minute shy of the half hour mark, and although Sammy Kuffour's equaliser saw the two teams walk in at half-time with the scores level a crazy ten minute spell in the second half pretty much put paid to any plans Bayern may have had of taking all three points back to Bavaria. Former Duisburg striker Bachirou Salou – he of the infamous Michael Tarnat DFB-Pokal tackle – would put the *Ostseestädter* in front on fifty-one minutes, and just after the hour mark Swedish defender Andreas Jakobsson doubled their lead.

Bayern pulled a goal back through Jens Jeremies five minutes later, but rather than seeing any sort of comeback the Munich side simply switched to self-destruct mode. Frustrated by their ongoing lack of form, the bloody-minded stubbornness of the opposition and the curious decision-making of referee Dr. Markus Merk, the Bavarians saw assistant coach Michael Henke banished to the stands with seventeen minutes remaining, and as the match boiled over at the end 'keeper Oliver Kahn would suffer from what could only be a mental lapse – well, either that or a bout of temporary stupidity – as he collected a second yellow card.

As Bayern pressed desperately for an equaliser, they won a corner – and Kahn, his eyes glazing over like a madman, sprinted all the way up the field and into the opposition penalty area to join in this last desperate attack on the Rostock goal. The ball was swung into the crowded penalty area, and the Bayern *Torhüter* was quite literally on hand to direct it towards the goal and past his opposite number Martin Pieckenhagen. Not with his boot or head, but in a fashion made famous by a certain Diego Armando Maradona. Unlike the diminutive Argentine's surreptitious paw into the net however, the giant blond Bayern *Torhüter's* blatant punch was comically obvious to almost everyone in the ground. It was like a scene from a bizarre comedy sketch.

As Herr Dr. Merk brandished the Bayern keeper's second yellow and then the inevitable *Rote Karte*, the now embarrassed Kahn – accompanied by loud hoots of derision from the home crowd – simply trotted back to his line looking like a naughty schoolboy who had just been caught pilfering a handful of Haribo goodies from his schoolmate's *Schultüte*.

Kahn had picked up his first booking just twelve minutes earlier for booting the ball off the pitch – narrowly missing a ball boy in the process – and there had been a sense of inevitability about his brainless charge into the Rostock penalty area. The man known as "Der Titan" had produced many great moments in a Bayern jersey in his long and illustrious career, but his rage-fuelled rants, gaffes and acts of general wild-eyed craziness would also feature highly on his record.

The defeat in Rostock saw Bayern drop back into second place behind new leaders Dortmund after the Westphalians had thrashed Eintracht Frankfurt 6-1, but both Leverkusen and Schalke again suffered defeats at the hands of mid-table opposition to keep things tight at the top. With Hertha edging closer to the top places and Kaiserslautern also joining in the fun, the gap between the leaders and the sixth-placed Red Devils was just four points.

	P	W	D	L	Goals	GD	Pts
BV 09 Borussia Dortmund	24	13	5	6	41:29	+12	44
FC Bayern München	24	13	4	7	47:28	+19	43
FC Schalke 04	24	12	5	7	43:26	+17	41
Bayer 04 Leverkusen	24	12	4	8	40:29	+11	40
Hertha BSC Berlin	24	13	1	10	46:41	+5	40
1.FC Kaiserslautern	24	12	4	8	34:30	+4	40

In keeping with the topsy-turvy season Bayern would beat local rivals TSV 1860 before collapsing to a 3-2 defeat at home to Werder Bremen, where Peruvian striker Claudio Pizarro scored an 88th-minute winner. The gap between first and sixth place was now just three points, and the following week the difference between the leading four clubs was just a single point.

Bayern would earn a crucial point in a typically hard-fought top-of-the-table clash in Dortmund with Roque Santa Cruz's sixth-minute effort being cancelled out by Fredi Bobic, but the league's form team were Schalke, who thumped sixth-placed Kaiserslautern 5-1 to claw within a point of Bayern and also increase their goal difference. Leverkusen meanwhile climbed one place into third, with Dortmund dropping back to fourth.

Slightly more worrying for Ottmar Hitzfeld's side would be the disciplinary fallout from the encounter at the Westfalenstadion: Frenchman Bixente Lizarazu was shown two yellow cards within the first thirty-five minutes, skipper Stefan Effenberg then followed the left-back for an early bath for a foul on Brazilian Evanilson five minutes short of the hour mark, and to cap things off striker Giovane Élber collected a yellow card that would take him over the limit and earn a one-match ban. In addition to Effenberg's straight red card and Lizarazu's *Gelb-Rot*, eight other Bayern players were also booked by referee Hartmut Strampe. Bayern were still right in the hunt for the *Meisterschale*, but seemed to be doing everything within their power to scupper their own title ambitions.

Dortmund had suffered slightly less with two yellow cards and a straight red for Evanilson right at the end, but the official from Handorf in Lower Saxony had succeeded in setting two new Bundesliga records – one for the total number of players carded in a single match (13) and another for the most cards shown to one team in a single match (10). Of the fourteen Bayern players that had taken to the field, only Patrik Andersson, Roque Santa Cruz, Paulo Sérgio and Alexander Zickler escaped making their way into Herr Strampe's notebook, and of these four, only one – Andersson – would actually play the full ninety minutes without attracting the official's attention.

The absence of Effenberg, Lizarazu and Élber was the last thing Ottmar Hitzfeld would have wanted before his team's next match, which pitted them against second-placed Schalke in what was widely seen as one of the most pivotal matches of the season up to that point. Victory for the Bavarians would take them four points clear of the *Königsblauen* and the rest of the chasing pack, while defeat would blow things right open again and send the Gelsenkirchen side back to the top. While the form book backed Schalke the records fell firmly in favour of the Bavarians: the Gelsenkirchen side had not registered a win at the Olympiastadion for more than eighteen years.

Despite the enforced personnel changes, Bayern made the perfect start to the match. With just three minutes gone, Jens Jeremies took advantage of a defensive blunder by Polish defender Tomasz Hajto to set up Carsten Jancker – whose left-footed effort set off what the home crowd hoped would be the final turn towards the run-in to another Bundesliga title.

They were seriously mistaken. The early goal proved to be little more than a false dawn as the blue-shirted Ruhr side responded in fine style. The Bayern defence was torn to shreds and reduced to jelly by the twin-pronged strike force of Belgian Émile Mpenza and Danish international Ebbe Sand, while a weak and tentative midfield allowed old hand Andreas Möller to take complete ownership of the pitch. Just nine minutes after falling behind, Schalke were level as Mpenza's shot was quickly followed up by Sand.

Jeremies would twice hit the woodwork in either half, but from that point on it was all Schalke. Bayern were arguably a little bit lucky to finish the first half on level terms after a Mike Büskens' effort had been disallowed for a dubious foul on Oliver Kahn, but there was no escape when the teams came out for the second half. Three minutes after the restart Mpenza set up Sand who outpaced Sammy Kuffour to give Schalke the lead, and fifteen minutes from time the deadly duo teamed up again as the lethal Danish striker completed a stunning hat-trick. *Der Spiegel* would throw out the (inevitably) memorable headline: *Sandsturm über München*.

The complete lack of a working midfield, a highly suspect defensive unit that was quite literally all over the place and a toothless attack had all come together in one ugly mix to send Bayern crashing to an embarrassing ninth defeat of the season – their fourth at the Olympiastadion. The result saw Schalke jump two points clear at the top of the table and Bayern slip down to second, with just a point separating them from Leverkusen, Dortmund, Hertha and Kaiserslautern, all locked together on forty-nine points.

	P	W	D	L	Goals	GD	Pts
FC Schalke 04	29	15	7	7	54:28	+26	52
FC Bayern München	29	15	5	9	55:35	+20	50
Bayer 04 Leverkusen	29	15	4	10	50:37	+13	49
BV 09 Borussia Dortmund	29	14	7	8	49:37	+12	49
Hertha BSC Berlin	29	16	1	12	52:47	+5	49
1. FC Kaiserslautern	29	15	4	10	45:44	+1	49

No statistician could have made it up: in the space of just four weeks, Huub Stevens' side had made up a six-point deficit and looked to have built up a final head of steam as the campaign entered its final straight. With Bayern slipping and stumbling, it was Schalke's title to lose.

Schalke maintained their momentum with a 3-1 win in another six-pointer against Hertha Berlin, but a hard-fought 2-0 win in Frankfurt against strugglers Eintracht kept Bayern within touching distance of the league leaders. Hot on their heels were Dortmund, who racked up a convincing 5-0 win over basement-dwellers and local *Ruhrpott* rivals VfL Bochum.

Bayern had built up a solid friendship with Bochum over the years – the two clubs had long established a *Fanfreundschaft* that remains in place to this day – and the bottom side did what any great friend would do in their next match against Schalke. A week after their five-goal thrashing in Dortmund, VfL somehow managed to pull the proverbial rabbit out of the hat to blunt Schalke's momentum with a hard-fought 1-1 draw at the Ruhrstadion.

Schalke's point coupled with Bayern's equally hard-fought single-goal triumph over Freiburg would see both sides locked on fifty-six points, with the *Königsblauen* ahead on goal difference.

It was like watching two boxing heavyweights slug it out, trading blows punch for punch. Schalke would quickly get back to winning ways with a 2-1 win over Wolfsburg, while Bayern grabbed the spoils three minute from time in a crucial six-pointer at the BayArena against Leverkusen. The win allowed them to stay level at the top, while at the same time effectively ending the *Werkself's* title ambitions. The win was typically dramatic, with substitute Roque Santa Cruz heading the Bavarians in front with just three minutes left on the clock.

Somehow, Bayern in the red corner were managing to stay in the fight, trading blows with the men in the blue corner. With each passing week, nerves on all sides were slowly being shredded. It was exciting to watch things slowly unfold, but part of me also wanted the season to come to an end. The agony was just too great, and at times almost unbearable.

The penultimate week of the season would really test my mettle. In a way, I was happy that I no longer had access to live footage, and instead would follow the updates on the Internet and watch the highlights after the dust had settled. Rather than being glued to the screen I could disappear to the kitchen for a drink, hit refresh and then, if necessary, disappear again for something that little bit stronger. I was thankful that I was not one of those people with a nail-biting compulsion, or else I might very well have bitten down right down to the quick.

The beginning of match day thirty-three saw Bayern and Schalke both locked together on fifty-nine points, with *Die Roten* taking on sixth-placed Kaiserslautern at the Olympiastadion and Schalke being entertained by fourteenth-placed VfB Stuttgart. *Die Königsblauen* were massive favourites against a struggling Stuttgart team that had been flirting with relegation for much of the season, while Bayern were up against a team that had for as long as I could remember been a constant thorn in their side.

There was something at stake for all four teams, so there were no easy points on offer. While Bayern and Schalke were both fighting for the Bundesliga title, strugglers Stuttgart were only two points above the drop zone and fighting to secure their survival in the top flight, while Kaiserslautern were looking to secure a prime European spot – with a top-four finish and a place in the Champions League qualifying round still up for grabs.

While the closing weeks of the season had always been guaranteed to provide plenty of tension and excitement, nobody could have possibly predicted how this day would turn out and how dramatic it would be – a crazy afternoon that not even a Hollywood writer could have scripted.

The day would start in the worst possible way for Bayern, and with just five minutes on the clock Kaiserslautern took the lead through Vratislav Lokvenc. The Czech international would beat centre-back Thomas Linke to the ball before sending a firm header past Oliver Kahn, and right from the off Bayern were up against it. The first forty-five minutes drew to a close with the visitors still on top, and ten minutes into the second half Bayern were still behind. The one bit of good news was that Schalke were still being held in Stuttgart.

Four minutes short of the hour mark the breakthrough finally came for Bayern. Hasan Salihamidžić made a characteristic burst down the right, muscling past Jeff Strasser before cutting the ball back inside for Carsten Jancker. The big centre-forward still had plenty of work to do, but beat Danish defender Michael Schjønberg on the slide to find the back of the Kaiserslautern net from close range. Bayern were right back in it, and with Schalke and Stuttgart still goalless, things were right back where they had started.

Bayern continued to make chances and press aggressively in search of the winning strike. A goal for Schalke in Stuttgart would have almost certainly ended any title hopes for the Bavarians, while even a draw would have been a good enough result for the Ruhr side who would take a significant goal-difference advantage into their final match at home to SpVgg Unterhaching.

Football is occasionally shaped on hopes and dreams, but as a realist I knew that a draw just wasn't going to be good enough.

With less than two minutes of normal time remaining, Ottmar Hitzfeld made his final gamble, throwing striker Alexander Zickler on for midfielder Salihamidžić. As the seconds ticked by with the ball still in the Bayern half, I had started to resign myself. Bayern would simply have to get a result in Hamburg the following week, and hope that relegation-threatened Unterhaching could pull off another end-of-season party trick in Gelsenkirchen.

As things stood at that very moment, both sides would be level on sixty points apiece, but with Schalke holding top spot on goal difference:

	P	W	D	L	Goals	GD	Pts
FC Schalke 04	33	17	9	7	60:31	+29	60
FC Bayern München	33	18	6	9	60:36	+24	60

As the clock ticked towards the end of the ninety minutes, Bayern made their way up the pitch quickly after a Kaiserslautern move broke down. Effenberg hoisted a hopeful long clearance up the field, and Élber rose above Schjønberg to nod the ball into space. There to pick things up was ex-*Lauterer* Ciriaco Sforza, whose perfectly floated ball out towards the left touchline found the fast-advancing Zickler.

The substitute would take control of the ball before cutting inside and unleashing a firm right-footed effort, but straight at a defender. The home crowd sighed; one long hoofed clearance, and it was surely all over. Instead, the ball looped up into the air where the man known as "Zick-Zack" was somehow able to line up a second opportunity. Taking the ball full on the volley, he gave it the full force of his right boot.

As straight as an arrow, the small leather sphere flew unerringly past 'keeper Georg Koch before crashing into the top right-hand corner of the Kaiserslauern net. *Wahnsinn! Wahnsinn!*

Zickler would hardly have any time to take in what he had done before being bundled over by Carsten Jancker and swamped in a seething mass of red-shirted team mates. Bayern had surely secured the three points, and would go into their last match two points in front.

But the drama was not yet over. As the Bayern players celebrated in Munich, news had started to filter through of a goal in Stuttgart, at almost the exact same time. When was this drama going to end?

Had Schalke scored? No, surely not. I feared the worst, but thankfully only for a few fleeting moments. Just as Zickler was settling matters at the Olympiastadion, Bulgarian Krassimir Balakov had scored a dramatic injury-time winner for VfB, seizing on a defensive blunder by Pole Tomasz Hajto before sending a rasping low drive past Schalke 'keeper Oliver Reck.

Just moments before Bayern had been looking at the impossible, but now they were three points in front – and would need only a draw in Hamburg the following week to secure the title.

Given that I had been following events on Sky Sports in the UK, I would have no idea of the sense of drama that had taken place in real time. When I finally got the opportunity to see the *Konferenz* footage from German television, the way how things had actually unfolded had been far more dramatic than I could ever have imagined. It is two minutes of football highlights that I can easily watch again and again. Right at the very moment Zickler was lining up his first shot at the Kaiserslautern goal, there had been a loud and distinctive shout in the background: *Tor in Stuttgart!*

If the events of the penultimate week of the season had not been dramatic enough, nobody could have prepared me and the rest of the Bundesliga-watching world for what would happen on the final day. Schalke were at home to Unterhaching in what would be the final match at the veritable old Parkstadion, while Bayern were further north at the Volksparkstadion in Hamburg, where they faced thirteenth-placed HSV needing only a draw to clinch the title.

	P	W	D	L	Goals	GD	Pts
FC Bayern München	33	19	5	9	61:36	+25	62
FC Schalke 04	33	17	8	8	60:32	+28	59

Even the final week had its own dramatic sub-plot, with Bayern's match in Hamburg kicking off four minutes later than scheduled on account of Oliver Kahn having to clear away a number of bananas kindly donated by the HSV faithful. With no love lost between the Bavarians and the side that had been their biggest rivals during the 1980s, it was clear that *Die Rothosen* were not there to simply roll over. Plenty of pride was at stake.

There was nothing at stake for mid-table HSV, save the desire to beat their old rivals. However in Gelsenkirchen Schalke found themselves up against an Unterhaching side that needed a victory to have even a hope of avoiding the drop into the second division. Could lightning strike twice? Could Unterhaching help deliver the *Meisterschale* to Munich for the second season in a row?

With half an hour gone, one could very easily have believed it. With Bayern and Hamburg still goalless, Schalke would already be two goals down and looking like a complete bag of nerves in front of sixty-five thousand loud and enthusiastic supporters in Gelsenkirchen. As news started to filter out of Schalke's predicament, large numbers of the travelling Bayern fans in Hamburg started to chant "Haching! Haching!"

While Bayern fans were ecstatic, neutrals could only marvel at this latest episode of what had been a truly bizarre season. Schalke had only lost one league match at home in their previous sixteen – coincidentally, against Bayern's opponents HSV – and were now two goals down against a team that had only managed to secure a single win on the road all season. Surely Huub Stevens' side were not going to do a Leverkusen and sink without trace?

Well, not quite. Two goals in the space of two minutes on the cusp of half-time from Nico Van Kerckhoven and Gerald Asamoah brought the Royal Blues back level at 2-2, but with Bayern and Hamburg still deadlocked the situation at the break would see the Bavarians retain their three point advantage at the top of the table. With just forty-five minutes remaining in the season – well, forty-nine given that the second half in Hamburg had begun four minutes later – everything was being set up for what was arguably the most heart-stopping and nerve-shredding finish in Bundesliga history.

To add just one more dash of spice to the slowly simmering drama a perfectly legitimate Carsten Jancker goal was scratched off for offside in the fifty-ninth minute, but Bayern still had their noses in front in the race for the title. For Hitzfeld and his team, all was going to plan irrespective of the result in the *Ruhrgebeit*: even if Schalke scored another dozen, as things stood the *Meisterschale* was heading back to the Bavarian capital.

With sixty-nine minutes gone in Gelsenkirchen, the Bayern fans were cheering again. Not for their own side who were still finding it difficult to break down the hard-working Hamburg defence, but for their last-season saviours who had once again taken the lead at the Parkstadion. A curling free-kick from Martin Čížek found Jan Seifert, whose header left Schalke needing a miracle. Not only would *Die Knappen* need HSV to beat Bayern, they now had to score at least two goals in the last twenty minutes.

Within just five minutes of going behind, Schalke woke up again. Once again they scored twice in the space of as many minutes, with midfielder Jörg Böhme taking centre stage with two exquisite finishes. The first, a glorious free-kick. The second, a wonderful delayed chip that made a complete fool out of 'Haching 'keeper Gerhard Tremmel. When news of Schalke's comeback started to filter through to the Volksparkstadion, the home crowd started to goad both the Bayern team and the visiting fans with cheers for their title rivals.

With a minute remaining at the Parkstadion Gerald Asamoah set up Ebbe Sand for Schalke's fifth to clinch the three points, and with what had been a pulsating 5-3 victory Huub Stevens' side had done all they could to fulfil their part of the bargain. Meanwhile, Unterhaching's brave fight to stay in the top flight had in the end been in vain: even if they had won the game they would have still been relegated following Energie Cottbus' 1-0 win in Munich against TSV 1860. It was a dramatic end to what had been a short but bittersweet spell in the top flight from the small team from the Munich suburbs.

After the final whistle had been blown in Gelsenkirchen, things were still happening in Hamburg. The game entered the final minute of the ninety, with Bayern still holding onto their precious point. They just had to keep things clean for a few more minutes.

There was nothing to fear. Hamburg weren't Manchester United.

Then, there were echoes of that infamous night in Barcelona. A poor Bayern clearance resulted in the home side launching an attack down the left, and a well-timed cross from Czech Marek Heinz was floated into the Bayern box. There to meet it was Bosnian journeyman Sergej Barbarez, who climbed above Patrik Andersson to break the deadlock and give Hamburg the lead. The Bayern players on the pitch were overcome with shock, and in an image that summed things up perfectly the suspended Hasan Salihamidžić simply slumped and slid back in his seat on the touchline.

The Hamburg fans roared their approval, a sound that was matched moments later in Gelsenkirchen as the news started to filter through via mobile phone and text message. Right at the death, the title looked as though it had gone to Gelsenkirchen, where the seething Parkstadion was a cheering, chanting, sea of blue and white. With both sides on sixty-two points, Schalke's superior goal difference would see them pinch the top spot.

The Schalke players were unsure about what was going on in Hamburg, but the thousands of supporters that had happily spilled onto the Parkstadion pitch appeared to be in no doubt. *Die Königsblauen* had sealed their first-ever Bundesliga title, and their first German championship since 1958. Bayern had been beaten, and Schalke were champions!

	P	W	D	L	Goals	GD	Pts
FC Schalke 04	34	18	8	8	65:35	+30	62
FC Bayern München	34	19	5	10	61:37	+24	62

But things were not quite over at the Volksparkstadion. Spurred on by a characteristically angry Oliver Kahn, a determined Bayern pulled together to charge forward for what was surely their last attack of the season. Deep into the third minute of additional time Stefan Effenberg looked to find Paulo Sérgio just outside the Hamburg penalty area, but there to intercept was Tomáš Ujfaluši who stabbed the ball back to 'keeper Mathias Schober.

Referee Dr. Markus Merk immediately put his whistle to his mouth. Not to blow for full-time, but for an indirect free-kick in the box for the back pass played by the Czech defender.

This was surely the last chance: an indirect free-kick in the Hamburg box some eight yards from the goal.

While the Hamburg defenders surrounded the referee to protest the decision, Paolo Sérgio calmly placed the ball on the ground. Oliver Kahn made his way up into the Hamburg box – no doubt to offer some small talk about the bananas that had littered his goal area earlier in the day – and perhaps the possibility of scoring the winning goal without using his hands. It was complete chaos, and the experienced official did well to get things back under control.

Swedish central defender Patrik Andersson had been beaten by Barbarez for Hamburg's goal, and had never scored his thirty-six appearances for Bayern. Yet he was the person skipper Effenberg would turn to for what was surely Bayern's last chance for a clear shot at the Hamburg goal. Whether it was last minute desperation or simply a moment of blind inspiration, nobody will ever really know. Effenberg tapped the ball inside to Andersson, who blasted it through the crowd of white shirts stationed in the six yard box – and into the back of the Hamburg net.

Dejection had turned into elation on the Bayern bench, goalscorer Andersson was mobbed by his ecstatic team mates, and in another memorable scene Oliver Kahn went crazy with a corner flag.

Back in Gelsenkirchen the tears of joy had quickly turned into tears of despair. The happy faces that filled the Parkstadion were now as blue as their shirts, and even I would feel a little bit sorry for Schalke's distraught cigar-chomping general manager Rudi Assauer. Well, for a few seconds anyway. Schalke had been Bundesliga champions – for just four minutes.

	P	W	D	L	Goals	GD	Pts
FC Bayern München	34	19	6	9	62:37	+25	63
FC Schalke 04	34	18	8	8	65:35	+30	62

In what was surely the craziest finish to the craziest Bundesliga season in recent memory, it was great to be a fan of FC Bayern München. But the season was not over yet: there was more excitement to come.

THE PAIN IS WASHED AWAY

After the previous season's painful Champions League semi-final defeat to Real Madrid coming hot on the heels of the 1999 final defeat in Barcelona, many Bayern fans must have started to feel that Champions League success was never going to happen. Bayern had last won Europe's most prestigious title in 1976, and in the twenty five years that had passed since then they had made the final on three occasions – losing every one. To make things worse, they would have to endure the likes of Hamburger SV and Borussia Dortmund getting their hands on the famous jug-eared trophy during that time.

Given Bayern's inconsistent form in the league not many would be predicting European success in 2001, and the first phase provided a pick and mix selection of performances in what was arguably a weak group. The Bavarians – wearing a wonderful version of the traditional red 1970s style *Trikot* with white round neck – had got off to a decent enough start with a 3-1 success in Sweden against Helsingborg IF and a win by the same score against Norwegian champions Rosenborg BK, but a last-minute defeat in France against Paris Saint Germain quickly put a spoke in the wheels of the campaign.

A far more encouraging performance at the Olympiastadion saw Bayern claim all three points against PSG with a 2-0 win, but they could only follow this with a grim goalless statemate at home to Helsingborg and a lucky 1-1 draw in Trondheim against Rosenborg, where they were saved by a Jens Jeremies goal two minutes from time. That crucial point in Norway was enough to see Hitzfeld's side top the group by a single point ahead of PSG, but it was clear that at this stage there was nothing to suggest that Hitzfeld's side were going to set the rest of the continent alight. Their form had been inconsistent at best, and could be thankful to have escaped from what was clearly a weak group. Bayern were through, but were hardly looking like a tournament-winning side.

The second group stage was slightly better, with Bayern being grouped with another French side in Ligue 1 champions Olympique Lyonnais, Russian champions Spartak Moscow and English Premiership side Arsenal.

Having picked up all three points against Lyon at the Olympiastadion courtesy of an early second-half strike from Jens Jeremies, Bayern were lucky to escape with a point in London after fighting back from two goals down against Arsenal. Thierry Henry's third-minute strike and Nwankwo Kanu's crisp finish ten minutes into the second half appeared to have given the Gunners a winning lead, but Michael Tarnat struck back immediately with a well-struck shot from outside the box to pull Bayern back into the tie.

On sixty-six minutes, winger and all-round schemer Mehmet Scholl rescued the Munich side with a sublime curling twenty-five yard free-kick that flew past the static Alex Manninger and into the top left corner of the Arsenal net. Scholl had slipped in the process of taking the shot and ended up flat on his backside, but a valuable point had been secured in what was on paper Bayern's toughest test in the second group phase.

Bayern's next opponents were the unpredictable Spartak at the Olympiastadion, who had started their campaign with highly contrasting results: a 4-1 thrashing of Arsenal followed by an equally comprehensive three-goal defeat in Lyon. It was always going to be a tough encounter that pitted Hitzfeld's side against determined opponents, and until deep into the second half it looked as though the Russians would hold firm and take a point back to Moscow. However with just eleven minutes remaining a long Bixente Lizarazu throw-in bounced nicely for Carsten Jancker, whose headed ball into the six-yard box was nodded in by the master poacher Élber. Having collected seven points from their first three matches, Bayern were sitting pretty at the top of the group table.

The return fixture at a chilly Luzhniki Stadium in Moscow would probably see Bayern's most convincing display of the second phase, as the Russian champions were put to the sword on what was a seriously rutted and nasty-looking surface. Bayern seized on a poor Spartak clearance after just seventeen minutes with the sprightly Élber setting up Mehmet Scholl, and the winger's crisp right-footed finish would set the perfect tone for the remainder of the evening.

A second for Scholl from the penalty spot after Dmitriy Ananko had hauled down Hasan Salihamidžić doubled the Bavarians' advantage, and with three minutes remaining Paulo Sérgio got on the end of the curling Stefan Effenberg free-kick – completing a comprehensive 3-0 win that took Bayern clear at the top of the group table with ten points from four games played.

However just as Hitzfeld's side finally looked to have turned the corner and started to gather some momentum, they'd throw in a yet another completely abject display to give further ammunition to the doubters and naysayers. This came a fortnight later at Lyon's Stade Gerland, where a flat, uninspired and at times unprofessional performance had none other than *Der Kaiser* Franz Beckenbauer shouting loudly from the sidelines.

Needing a win to secure their place in the last eight with a game to spare, a tired-looking Bayern were unceremoniously swept aside, with a Sidney Govou brace giving the French champions a two-goal lead inside the first twenty minutes. The game was pretty much over by half-time as the Bavarians seemed to be going through the motions, and it is fair to say that they looked nothing like potential European Champions.

Pierre Laigle scored Lyon's third some twenty minutes from full time to finish things off while at the same time reviving the French side's own faint hopes of making the last eight, and from being one step away from the knock-out round Bayern suddenly found themselves toying with possible elimination from the tournament altogether. *Die Roten* still headed the table with ten points ahead of Arsenal on eight and Lyon on seven, but a slip-up at home to the Gunners in their final fixture combined with a win for the French champions in Moscow would send them tumbling out of the competition.

Beckenbauer, a forthright man never known to hold back, had described Bayern's performance in France as a "disgrace" and a "disaster" – harsh words that would stick firmly in the minds of the players. Indeed, *Der Kaiser's* rant – in German, *Wutrede* – would later be seen by many at the Munich club as one of the defining moments of that year's Champions League campaign.

From that point on, the coach and the players were hell-bent on proving the legendary *Libero* wrong: nobody, not least *Trainer* Ottmar Hitzfeld, wanted to see Beckenbauer jump in to rescue the club for the third time. *Der Kaiser's* stinging comments would have the desired effect; it was the perfect catalyst, and from that point on the team never looked back.

The upturn would begin in the final group match against Arsenal, where an early goal combined with a solid rearguard effort was enough to secure a tight but ultimately easy 1-0 win against an opponent that had been woefully short of both energy and ideas. Giovane Élber would get on the end of a trademark pin-point Bixente Lizarazu cross to send a spectacular diving header past Gunners' 'keeper David Seaman to give Bayern the lead after just ten minutes, and despite missing both suspended skipper Effenberg and injured midfield dynamo Paulo Sérgio the Bavarians simply strangled their opponents as they dominated the contest.

The performance had been far from pretty, but Bayern had been clinical when it really mattered. Key to their success was a new-found sense of determination that would define the entire campaign.

The hard-fought win over Arsenal was the perfect antidote to Beckenbauer's critical wake-up call the week before, for next up for Bayern was a quarter-final tie against another English team – their 1999 conquerors, Manchester United. With everything back under control, Bayern were ready: the time had finally come to avenge the horror of Barcelona.

While many in the Bayern class of 2001 had been on the pitch in Barcelona two years earlier, the central nerve system of the team had changed completely. In place of the likes of Lothar Matthäus and Mario Basler the strings were now being firmly pulled by a man who was not just the captain but also the beating heart of the side – Stefan Effenberg.

The blond Hamburg-born midfielder had always brought with him a demeanour that for many bordered on arrogance, but the rather haughty and childish attitude that had defined his first spell in Munich – where, among other things, he had described the other clubs as being "too stupid" to win the championship – had over time been replaced by a sense of genuine self-belief and steely determination that would motivate, inspire and drive the team rather than divide it.

The departure of the old head Matthäus and the talented but temperamental Basler had clearly weakened the club initially, but the departure of these two big names allowed Effenberg to gradually make the "boss" role his own. He no longer had to compete with other big egos in the club dressing room, and as the team slowly started to develop around him it soon became clear that with the coach's support he had become *der Tiger* - a responsible, hard-working leader who would not only push himself to the limit on the pitch, but also harness the ability to get those around him to do the same.

The Effenberg of the early 1990s, with his peroxide-blond mullet and spoilt rock-star attitude, had often brought out the worst in opposition supporters; even during home matches for Germany he had found himself being loudly jeered by large sections of the crowd. The reinvented Effenberg of 2001 however was a completely different character. Although still shunned by the national team selectors for past misdemeanours, the Bayern skipper had turned into one of those players who would, if asked, have spilled blood for the team. There were no ifs and buts with Stefan Effenberg: you could see it on his face, on that distinctive furrowed brow.

The first leg of the 2001 Champions League quarter-final at Old Trafford would be a tight and cagey affair between two canny and experienced heavyweights, and pretty much followed the same pattern as the three encounters two seasons earlier – with Bayern in the same silver and burgundy *Trikots*. Sit back, and punch. Wait, wait, and counterpunch.

Both sides had their opportunities. Andy Cole for United, Carsten Jancker for Bayern. 1999 villain Ole Gunnar Solskjær was foiled by Patrik Andersson, and Effenberg sent a shot narrowly over the crossbar. As half-time and chances for the home side came and went, Bayern were looking good for the draw to take back to Munich – though Ottmar Hitzfeld had other ideas. With just over twenty minutes remaining, Carsten Jancker was replaced by the fleet-footed Alexander Zickler, and less than ten minutes later Mehmet Scholl made way for Paulo Sérgio.

Given that most of the visiting fans would have been happy just letting things run towards the inevitable goalless conclusion, the introduction of speedsters Zickler and Paulo Sérgio was a bold and positive move – the polar opposite from the late but not late enough withdrawal of both Matthäus and Basler in 1999. Perhaps the coach needed to make a point, if just to scour away the painful memories of that night in Barcelona once and for all.

Almost immediately Zickler made an impact, causing chaos in the United defence and then cracking a right-footed volley against the crossbar. Then, with just four minutes remaining, Effenberg swung in a free-kick, Thomas Linke nodded it on into the six-yard box, where the unmarked Paulo Sérgio stole in to stab it home from close range past Fabien Barthez.

In a curious parallel to the dramatic finish in 1999, United had been undone by what had been a master-stroke late substitution by the Bayern coach. It wasn't quite injury time, but was both late and sweet enough for the travelling Bayern supporters. The 1-0 win at Old Trafford was a far better result than anyone had hoped, and spirits would be sky-high ahead of the return fixture in Munich a week later. Just ninety minutes in front of their own home crowd separated Bayern from shedding the Barcelona baggage once and for all – or at least part of it.

The second leg at the Olympiastadion saw the home side back in their traditional all-red kit, spurred on by an enthusiastic capacity crowd of sixty-thousand bedecked in red and white. One might have expected the visitors to come out all with guns blazing, but Bayern were the fastest out of the blocks. The aggressive approach worked: within five minutes, *Die Roten* were in front.

Following yellow cards in the first leg both Bixente Lizarazu and Hasan Salihamidžić had been suspended, and it would be their replacements Willy Sagnol and Michael Tarnat who helped create and set up the opening goal. Picking up the ball in his own half, Frenchman

Sagnol cut inside from the right touchline before floating a lovely ball across the width of the pitch to find the fast-advancing Michael Tarnat. Tarnat's horizontal ball into the opposition six-yard box bypassed Carsten Jancker to find the unmarked Élber at the far post, and from just a yard out the Brazilian striker couldn't miss. With the goal at his mercy and Barthez unable to prevent the inevitable, Élber crashed the ball into the inside roof of the net to double Bayern's advantage on aggregate.

Having gone two goals up in the tie, Hitzfeld's side put their foot down. On seventeen minutes Jancker saw a shot deflected onto the crossbar – at this moment I would have flashbacks to his overhead effort that had clattered off the woodwork in Barcelona – and just minutes later the burly striker was denied by Barthez.

United still needed two goals to snatch the tie, but to do this they would have to puncture a Bayern defence that had not conceded at home in European competition since their first phase match the previous September against Rosenborg. Bayern for their part knew that a second goal would surely finish things off, and were determined not to be caught short again. On twenty-five minutes Mehmet Scholl cleared an Andy Cole effort off the line, but just under a quarter of an hour later the Bayern number seven – who like Jancker had also hit the woodwork at the Camp Nou two years previously – scored what would prove to be the crucial second goal.

The move was engineered by the energetic midfield dynamo Jens Jeremies, who burst down the right and danced past a number of white shirts – slicing through the United defence like a red hot knife through butter. His short pass inside found Élber, whose tap across the box was half-touched and half-dummied by Alexander Zickler to arrive at the feet of Scholl. With a smooth swing of his right foot the winger sent the ball hard and low between Barthez and the near post.

With their opponents now needing three goals the home crowd started to breathe more comfortably, but still nobody could take anything for granted. United had made a number of excellent comebacks before, and the memories of 1999 must have played heavily on the minds of the Bayern players. When Ryan Giggs pulled a goal back nine minutes into the second half there must have been a few butterflies on the Bayern bench, but as time continued to tick towards the end there was little else on offer from the English side.

United's goal proved to be nothing more than a consolation, and there would be no repeat of Barcelona 1999. When the final whistle blew Bayern had finally exorcised the ghost of the Camp Nou, but there was still plenty of work to do. In the semi-final, yet another nemesis awaited them.

In 1999/2000 Bayern had dominated Real Madrid in three of the four games the two teams had played, only to end up as losing semi-finalists while their Spanish conquerors marched on to another Champions League title. The spring of 2001 saw the Bavarians line up against *Los Merengues* in the last four yet again – their sixth encounter in the competition since Bayern's victorious semi-final of 1975/76.

As had been the case the previous year, the first leg was played at Madrid's Santiago Bernabéu, giving Bayern the advantage of playing the second in front of their own supporters in Munich. Having removed the Manchester United monkey from their backs in the quarter-final, Hitzfeld's men were determined to follow this up by settling the score with Real Madrid as well. The wounds created by the bitter defeat the year before were still raw, and the Bayern players were determined to make up for the previous season's failure.

Madrid had come into the game on the back of a seven-game winning streak at home, and with Bayern's patchy away form during the tournament – they had won just three of their six matches on the road on their path to the last four – the Spaniards started out as clear favourites. To pose any sort of challenge, Hitzfeld's side would have to play in much the same disciplined way as they had done in their quarter-final at Old Trafford.

In front of a crowd of over seventy-six thousand Bayern immediately found themselves under pressure, but managed to hold their form against an attack boasting the likes of Portguese star Luís Figo and the dangerous Raúl. Oliver Kahn was called into action five minutes short of the thirty-minute mark as he denied Figo, and in the second half Steve McManaman extracted the best out of the Bayern *Torhüter* as Real's pressure failed to turn into goals.

Five minutes short of the hour mark, Bayern broke fast down the left. Having made his way into the Madrid half, Thomas Linke's pass found the tireless Giovane Élber some twenty-five yards from the opposition goal. Élber swivelleled smartly past his marker to create space for a shot, and caught the ball perfectly on the volley with his left foot. The ball skidded low towards the Madrid goal, bouncing awkwardly before squeezing in between the diving 'keeper Iker Casillas and the near post. Bayern's goal had come completely against the run of play, and their biggest challenge was to hold onto the lead and take a significant advantage back home to Munich.

Within minutes of conceding the lead both McManaman and Iván Helguera fluffed further decent opportunities for the home side, but as the match rolled towards its conclusion it became a lot easier for *Die Roten* – or *La Bestia Negra* or "the black beast" as they had become known in Madrid. For all of their huff and puff, the challenge from the Spanish side slowly fizzled out as Bayern calmly saw things through to the final whistle. In what had been a solid and professional performance, the one negative point had been the yellow card shown to skipper Stefan Effenberg, who would have to sit out the second leg in Munich.

The second leg at the Olympiastadion saw Bayern in exactly the same situation as they had been in the quarter-final, holding a slender one-goal lead. It was a hard game to call, and although there would be the obvious temptation to just sit back in the knowledge that Real had to chase the game from the start I couldn't help but think back to all of those past encounters with *Los Merengues*. We needed an early goal, if just to settle the nerves.

With the inspirational skipper Effenberg having to take his seat in the stands, I cannot lie in saying that I was just a little bit nervous before the kick-off. In what was seen as a bold move by the Bayern coach, Effenberg's place in the starting lineup was taken by the nineteen year old Owen Hargreaves.

In front of a crowd of sixty thousand people at the Olympiastadion, those nerves were quickly settled by the perfect start from the home team. Far from going on the defensive and shutting up shop, *Die Roten* immediately laid siege to the Madrid goal – and within ten minutes they were rewarded. After Real had failed to deal with a corner Jens Jeremies nodded the ball against the crossbar, and when the defence failed to clear the dangerous and deadly Élber was on hand to head Bayern in front from less than two yards.

The pressure was really on the visitors now – but within ten minutes the visitors silenced the Munich crowd with a goal of their own. It was the perfect *Galactico* move, with Brazilian Roberto Carlos finding Raúl, who then squared it to Figo at the near post. Bayern were still in front in the tie, but with just the one goal separating Real from the lead on away goals things had once again swung to the precarious.

The nine-time European club champions had never won in Munich, but with the score sitting precariously at 1-1 with not even twenty minutes played my own nerves had started to jangle and fray just a little bit - more so when Roberto Carlos lined up a trademark long free-kick, which thankfully thudded harmlessly against the solid red wall.

Just over ten minutes from half-time, Bayern won a free-kick some twenty-five yards out. Mehmet Scholl played the ball for Jens Jeremies, whose perfect right-footed effort from just outside the penalty area skidded low and true to Casillas' right and into the back of the net. Bayern were back in front, and Real once again needed two goals. There was now more than a sliver of daylight between the two teams, but still nobody was taking anything for granted.

Bayern emerged at the start of the second half looking to maintain their lead, and managed to keep things together in the face of a determined but ultimatelty inadequate Madrid attack.

Although they looked to tighten things up at the back, Hitzfeld's side continued to attack swiftly on the break and create goal-scoring opportunities. The revelation of the evening was inexperienced teenager Hargreaves, whose stunning performance in midfield made me wonder why I had been so nervous about missing Effenberg. The Canadian-born youngster had taken to the task with gusto, bossing the field with a fine mix of defensive steel and offensive creativity.

In the end, just as it had been against Manchester United, Bayern would see things out comfortably to win 2-1 on the night and 3-1 on aggregate. They were through to their second Champions League final in three years, and awaiting them at Milan's famous San Siro would be another Spanish side in the form of Valencia CF – the team beaten by Real Madrid in the 2000 final.

The Champions League final of 2001 was arguably one of the most nerve-wracking matches in all my years as a fan of FC Bayern. While the 1987 final against FC Porto had provided a painful kick in the shins and the 1999 showpiece in Barcelona against Manchester United had felt like a sharp double blow to the solar plexus, most of the 2001 final was like Chinese water torture: an almost constant drip, drip, drip, never knowing what was coming next.

Bayern came into the 2001 final with a markedly different lineup from the 1999 team: while in Barcelona the starting eleven had included just one non-German player in Ghanaian international Sammy Kuffour, the team of 2001 would start with no fewer than seven non-Germans. One of these was the nineteen year old Owen Hargreaves, who started in the place of the injured midfield enforcer Jens Jeremies in what was otherwise a full-strength side.

Of the complete 1999 Champions League final squad only eight were among the eighteen named players in 2001 side: the aforementioned Kuffour, skipper Stefan Effenberg, goalkeepers Oliver Kahn and Bernd Dreher, defenders Thomas Linke and Michael Tarnat, Bosnian midfielder Hasan Salihamidžić and strikers Carsten Jancker and Alexander Zickler.

With Bayern *Trainer* Ottmar Hitzfeld playing a flexibly defensive 5-4-1/3-4-2-1 armed with French wingbacks Willy Sagnol and Bixente Lizarazu, 'keeper Kahn was protected by centre-backs Kuffour, Linke and Patrik Andersson, while the four-man midfield consisted of Hargreaves, Effenberg, Scholl and Salihamidžić. Up front, Brazilian marksman Giovane Élber led the line.

In front of a crowd of just under seventy-two thousand on what was a pleasant evening in northern Italy, things would get off to a suitably dramatic start. With just three minutes on the clock, last-minute Bundesliga hero Patrick Andersson was adjuged to have handled in the box. The penalty call by Dutch referee Dick Jol was incredibly harsh with the prostrate Andersson unable to do anything as the ball was pushed against his body by the boot of Gaizka Mendieta, and the Valencia skipper then beat the sprawling Kahn to put the ball into the left-hand side of the Bayern net from the penalty spot.

If there was one positive that could have been taken from this chaotic start, it would be that Bayern were not going to be in the position of taking an early lead themselves, only to have it snatched at the death – as had been the case in 1987 and 1999. With Valencia getting on the scoreboard first, there was going to be a different script – but one no less dramatic.

Mendieta's early penalty had set the theme for the remainder of the evening, and just minutes later a spot-kick was awarded at the other end when Effenberg's bold charge into the opposition box was ended by the flailing leg of Valencia's French defender Jocelyn Angloma. Mehmet Scholl stepped up to take the kick, but could only hit it straight at the legs of 'keeper Santiago Cañizares. Suddenly, I started to get the feeling that it was going to be one of those nights yet again, and another final where Bayern would flatter to deceive before falling at the final hurdle. It was typical of the rough justice often encountered in football: while Valencia's penalty had been extremely lucky and Bayern's pretty much clear-cut, the scoreboard would read 1-0 to the Spanish side.

As the first half ticked away the Bavarians were the better side, though without creating any genuine opportunities. Lizarazu and Salihamidžić terrorised the Spanish defence down the left flank, but overall it had been a frustrating forty-five minutes for the men in red.

As the teams headed off to the dressing rooms, the time had come for this Bayern side to prove itself once and for all. There had been too much heartbreak, pain and disappointment for too long, and it would take one man to drag the team back into the game. That man was Stefan Effenberg, who would finally come of age on this toughest of stages. As the two teams returned to the arena, the Bayern skipper was like a gladiator – eyes steeled, that famous blond brow furrowed. The *Henkelpott* was there to be won, and he wanted it.

The second half would start just like the first, with yet another penalty. This time it was Valencia's turn to be called for handball, with Italian defender Amedeo Carboni clearly striking the ball with a flailing arm under pressure from the lumbering Carsten Jancker. It was an easy decision for the referee.

There was only one man who could take the kick, and he stepped up without hesitation. With his bleached blond hair bristling and blue eyes burning, Effenberg thumped the ball home, sending Cañizares the wrong way. Finally, justice had been served as the scoreboard corrected itself. On the touchline, Ottmar Hitzfeld looked quietly determined with a firm yet calculated pump of both fists.

With the ball comfortably nestled in the back of the opposition net, the scowling Effenberg gestured to his team mates, in particular an ecstatic Sammy Kuffour, the man whose pain and suffering had been witnessed by everyone two years earlier in Barcelona. A massive banner in the Bayern crowd had read 23.5.2001. *Heute ist ein guter Tag, um Geschichte zu schreiben* – "23.5.2001 – today is a good day to write history". The fiercely determined Effenberg was the man to lead the team and make it happen.

Bayern were now level at 1-1 with just under forty minutes of the ninety remaining, but from that point on I just knew we were going to win. The look on Effenberg's face had said it all for me: it was not just a simple goal celebration, but a look of sheer bloody-minded determination that said "That's it boys. This trophy is ours".

The game was on now, and the gloves well and truly off. Suddenly both sides upped the ante, though *Die Roten* created the better opportunities. Jancker was foiled by Cañizares, Hargreaves spooned a shot over the bar, and with less than ten minutes remaining the Valencia 'keeper kept out Élber with a fine stop. With minutes remaining there was a fleeting flashback to the past, but Valencia substitute Zlatko Zahovič blew two excellent chances to turn himself into a hero and condemn Bayern to yet another last-gasp final defeat.

Unlike in 1999, things would at least go to extra time, and the "golden goal".

The thirty minutes of extra time saw both teams sit back a little more, but as had been the case in the regulation ninety minutes Bayern were the more positive of the two teams. There were a few half-chances, but both goalkeepers would have a relatively quiet time as the two hours of open play drew to its inevitable conclusion. The game had seen three penalties with each team scoring one, and it somehow seemed appropriate that the destination of the famous trophy would hinge on one crucial hit or miss from the *Elfmeterpunkt*.

The final act in this drama – rightly billed by the organisers on the official match programme as *L'Opera del Calcio* – would begin in the worst possible way for Bayern. Substitute Paulo Sérgio lined up to take the Bavarians' first spot-kick, only to send it flying high and not particularly handsomely into the crowd. With Mendieta then sending Oliver Kahn the wrong way to open Valencia's account, every Bayern supporter must have been wondering if they were ever going to see their team get their hands on that much-wanted trophy.

Thankfully, Bayern got on the scoresheet with their second effort as Hasan Salihamidžić planted the ball to Cañizares's left, but Norwegian John Carew calmly rolled his kick into the bottom right-hand corner to keep *Los Murciélagos* in front. Cañizares was then booked for trying to put off Alexander Zickler, but the Bayern striker – a 100th-minute replacement for Giovane Élber – held his nerve brilliantly to blast the ball into the top right-hand corner with the keeper going the wrong way.

The penalty count was 2-2, but with Bayern having taken one more the advantage was still with the Spanish side.

Up then stepped Zlatko Zahovič.

The Slovenian struck his penalty firmly, but not far enough away from Kahn who this time went the right way. The Bayern 'keeper flew to his right, beating the ball away firmly with both hands. We were now back in it, with last-minute Bundesliga hero Patrik Andersson up next with a kick to put the Bavarians back in front. Surely he was going to smash the ball into the back of the net, just as he had done four days earlier in Hamburg.

But it was not to be. Andersson's penalty was so weak one could have been excused for thinking that it was a back pass, as the ball ended up safely in the arms of Cañizares.

With the score still tied at 2-2 and Valencia having a kick in hand, the pressure was right back on Kahn in the Bayern goal to keep the Bavarians in the contest. With the chance to put his team one hit or miss away from the title, Amadeo Carboni struck the ball crisply, straight down the middle. Kahn dived the wrong way, but was able to instinctively throw up a firm right arm to direct the ball against the underside of the crossbar. Miraculously, it stayed out.

It was just too nerve-racking for words. With both sides having scored half of their four penalties, it now came down to sudden death. One save or one miss, and it was all over.

Bayern's fifth penalty was taken by a man who was never going to miss. Eyes steeled, a short run up, and bang. Cañizares dived the right way, but Stefan Effenberg's kick was just too good as it flew past the Valencia 'keeper and slammed into the left inside netting. A crazy-eyed glare and pump of the fists just showed how much Effenberg wanted this, and all that remained now was for those coming after him to follow his lead. It was hard to believe, but for the first time in more than two hours of breathless and nerve-jangling entertainment – if one could call it that – Bayern were finally in front.

Rubén Baraja stepped up to take Valencia's fifth kick, and he was more than up to the task as he kept his side in the game. Ten penalties had been taken with six successfully converted, with the score locked at 3-3. Now it was the turn of those players who hadn't signed up to take a penalty.

First for Bayern was Bizente Lizarazu, who made things look easy with an emphatic finish to send Cañizares the wrong way: 4-3. Then, under extreme pressure, Argentinian Kily González brought things back level at 4-4 with an equally well-taken spot-kick. It was pure drama for the neutral observer, but complete and utter torture for those involved on the pitch, in the stands and sitting nervously in front of television screens.

The seventh penalty for Bayern was taken by Thomas Linke, and to be honest I wouldn't have too much confidence. I had half expected Owen Hargreaves to step up, but the young and inexperienced teenager was spared – for the time being – as the tall central defender carefully placed the ball on the spot. With just Hargreaves, Sammy Kuffour, Willy Sagnol and 'keeper Kahn left, Bayern were fast running out of viable options. Linke just had to score to keep the pressure firmly on Valencia.

I need not have worried. With a measured sweep of his right foot, Linke calmly and clinically stroked the ball past the static Cañizares to maintain Bayern's lead and pile the pressure on their opponents' next kicker.

Argentinian Mauricio Pellegrino was next up for Valencia, and he struck the ball straight down the middle of the goal. Kahn dived to his right. I looked down, up, and down again. Kahn had made his third save of the shootout, and as the realisation slowly dawned on me the Bayern 'keeper was already charging towards the middle of the pitch in triumph. Just like that, it was all over. Bayern were champions of Europe.

The Bayern team piled up in a blur of red, though not before Kahn had walked over to console his beaten Spanish counterpart. The man known as the *Der Titan* was a fierce and at times fearsome character who had lived up to his billing by making three crucial saves to win the match, but his gesture in comforting the crestfallen Cañizares would show just how great a sportsman he was.

This was Bayern's triumph, but it was also a personal victory for *Der Titan*, King Kahn. Every one of Ottmar Hitzfeld's side was a hero, but that dramatic finale in Milan will always be remembered for the heroics of the Bayern 'keeper.

As Stefan Effenberg became the first Bayern player in a quarter of a century to receive the famous jug-eared trophy and hold it aloft, I found it hard to hold back the tears. After the dramatic finish to the league season, the team had put me through the emotional meat-grinder on the way to claiming Europe's biggest prize for the first time in my then twenty years as a fan.

I had seen the many photographs of Franz Beckenbauer lifting the European Cup in the 1970s, but to me these were little more than pictures from the historical archives, devoid of any deeper meaning or personal significance.

After witnessing the heart-breaking near misses of 1982, 1987 and 1999, I had finally got to see FC Bayern become champions of Europe.

The long wait had come to an end, and the pain washed away.

BACK DOWN WITH A BUMP

The victory in Milan and the dramatic Bundesliga title was always going to make the 2000/01 season a hard act to follow for FC Bayern, and so it would prove. In a season where they would never quite reach the same high standard, Ottmar Hitzfeld's team quickly came crashing back down to earth with a loud bump.

The start of the following 2001/02 season would see a number of personnel changes in Munich. Thomas Strunz announced his retirement from the game and title-winning hero Patrik Andersson joined FC Barcelona for just over DM15 million, while a number of fringe players also departed the Säbenerstraße. Among the new arrivals were Croatian brothers Niko and Robert Kovač who joined from Hamburger SV (DM10.7 million) and Bayer Leverkusen (DM16 million) respectively, Werder Bremen's Peruvian striker Claudio Pizarro (DM16 million) and VfB Stuttgart's Guinean defensive midfielder Pablo Thiam (free transfer). With the squad being significantly strengthened with these new signings, many commentators, pundits and fans were confident that Ottmar Hitzfeld's side would simply pick up where they had left off the season before.

Since the reintroduction of the pre-season DFB-Ligapokal in 1997 Bayern had won all four editions of the competitition, but July 2001 saw this run come to an end at the Rosenaustadion in nearby Augsburg. Their opening semi-final defeat at the hands of Hertha Berlin was settled by a thirty-ninth minute winner from Michael Preetz, and the defeat to the Berliners would pretty much set the standard for the remainder of the season.

The opening game of the 2001/02 season saw Bayern fall to a single-goal defeat against Borussia Mönchengladbach, but an eleven-game run that would garner ten victories – including nine in a row from the middle of August through to early November – would ultimately flatter to deceive.

Match day eleven would see one of the season's more bizarre moments, when Bayern took on Köln at the Müngersdorferstadion. Expecting the home side to be kitted out in their usual all-white ensemble, Bayern turned out in their wine-red *Trikots*, only to see their opponents ready to play in all red. It should have been a simple matter of going back to the kitbag and retrieving the set of away kits, but it turned out that they hadn't even been backed.

Evoking memories of France playing in the World Cup in 1978 in a green and white striped kit borrowed from a local club, Bayern opted for the creative solution of wearing their white Opel-sponsored training vests over their red shirts. The lack of numbers on the back must have caused nightmares for the match commentators, but the team simply took it in their stride. The Bavarians eased to a 2-0 win, with both goals scored by Claudio Pizarro either side of half-time.

Going into match day thirteen and their fixture against old rivals Werder Bremen, *Die Roten* were sitting on thirty-one points, one clear of unbeaten Bayer Leverkusen and six clear of third-placed Dortmund. A 1-0 reverse at the Weserstadion resulted in the top two swapping places, and after that point Ottmar Hitzfeld's side would never return to the summit.

The defeat in Bremen was the curtain raiser to a horrific run of poor results, which saw the Bavarians follow their eleven-game unbeaten run with a barren seven-match winless spell that straddled the *Winterpause*. Bayern maintained their unbeaten record at the Olympiastadion with draws against Nürnberg, Wolfsburg and Mönchengladbach, but four straight away defeats would send them spiraling back down the table into fifth place.

The season's nadir would come in the first match of 2002 at Schalke 04's new Arena auf Schalke, with Huub Stevens' side handing out a painful 5-1 hammering. Bayern were already two goals down when Michael Tarnat was shown the red card, and although Mehmet Scholl did halve the deficit three minutes into the second half there was no stopping the rampant *Königsblauen*.

Bayern's winless streak came to an end with a surprise 2-0 win over leaders Leverkusen, but an embarrassing 2-1 defeat at second-from-bottom St. Pauli would almost immediately send the clouds back over Bavaria. A rather lucky point at home to new leaders Dortmund saw Bayern drop back into sixth place, just about good enough to secure a place in the UEFA Cup.

It was at this point where the season mysteriously picked up again, and almost out of nowhere Hitzfeld's side managed to find their touch. A 2-0 win in Freiburg and a six-goal thrashing of strugglers Energie Cottbus had set things on their way, and the Bavarians would take themselves to the end of the season with a twelve-match unbeaten spell that saw them collect thirty points out of available thirty-six. Unfortunately this final charge had begun a game too late, with Dortmund just about holding their ground to clinch the title. *Die Schwarzgelben* would finish a point ahead of second-placed Leverkusen, with Bayern a further point adrift in third.

	P	W	D	L	Goals	GD	Pts
BV 09 Borussia Dortmund	34	21	7	6	62:33	+29	70
Bayer 04 Leverkusen	34	21	6	7	77:38	+39	69
FC Bayern München	34	20	8	6	65:25	+40	68

In contrast to their erratic domestic form Bayern's defence of their European title began solidly, and they suffered little damage in emerging from an opening group phase containing Feyenoord Rotterdam, Sparta Prague and Spartak Moscow. The campaign had started with an uneventful goalless draw at home to the Czech champions, but a far more convincing performance in Moscow saw the holders return home with a 3-1 win.

An evenly contested 2-2 draw in Rotterdam saw Bayern reach the half-way point in the group on five points – two behind early pace-setters Sparta – but three straight victories in their remaining matches saw them power into the second phase with plenty to spare. A 5-1 mauling of Spartak at the Olympiastadion was followed by a comprehensive 3-1 win over Feyenoord, and a hard-earned 1-0 win in Prague would put them top of the group with fourteen points.

Following on from the previous season's triumph, Bayern's unbeaten start also saw them stretch their unbeaten run in the competition to twelve games, their last defeat being the debacle in Lyon.

The second group phase in the new year saw Ottmar Hitzfeld's side drawn together again with old enemies Manchester United, along with Portuguese side Boavista and French outfit FC Nantes. A dramatic opening encounter at the Olympiastadion against United saw Paulo Sérgio maintain Bayern's unbeaten home record against the English champions with an equaliser three minutes from time, and the speedy Brazilian winger made his way onto the scoresheet again as Bayern secured all three points in France.

A goalless draw in Lisbon against Boavista followed, but with United scoring a late injury-time equaliser against Nantes they and Bayern would both top the table with five points at the half-way stage, with Alex Ferguson's side holding the edge on goal difference.

United increased their goal advantage by thrashing the French side 5-1 at Old Trafford, and while Bayern made heavy weather of the opposition they remained within touching distance of their adversaries. The match against Boavista in Munich was also settled late on, Roque Santa Cruz netting the winner with just nine minutes remaining.

The penultimate match saw Bayern visit Old Trafford, and with United needing a win to effectively secure top spot – and a quarter-final tie against one of the second-placed teams from the other groups – the pressure was on. Bayern would defend stoutly to shut out the English champions – taking their unbeaten run against them to four matches since the final defeat in 1999.

The point earned from the goalless draw meant that both Bayern and United would enter the final match day locked together on nine points, but with Alex Ferguson's side still holding a significant and in truth mathematically secure goal difference Bayern would need everything to go their way in order to snatch first place.

The final day saw United stroll to a 3-0 win in Portugal to confirm their position at the top of the group table, while Bayern extended their long unbeaten run in the competition to a staggering eighteen matches. *Die Roten* would fall behind just nine minutes into the second half of their match against Nantes but equalised almost immediately through Jens Jeremies, and it was left to Claudio Pizarro to secure the win three minutes from end after missing from the penalty spot fifteen minutes earlier. The final win in France took the Bavarians level on twelve points with United, but in second spot on goal difference.

With Bundesliga rivals Bayer Leverkusen winning one of the other groups and the draw not allowing ties between teams from the same country, Bayern were left with the worst possible scenario – a meeting with one of FC Barcelona or arch-enemies Real Madrid.

Over the years, matches against Manchester United had been high up on Bayern's list, but by far the biggest rivalry had been with Spanish giants Real Madrid. The first European encounter between the two sides had taken place in the mid-1970s, but the match that had really set things in motion was the infamously acrimonious semi-final in 1987. Bayern had the better overall record but matches had always been fiercely contested, and it was fair to say that there was little love lost between the two teams. Having beaten *Los Merengues* both home and away en route to claiming the title in 2001, Bayern were looking to do the same again. Only this time, the first leg would be played in Munich.

While the Olympiastadion had always been something of a fortress for Real, Bayern's home record against the Spanish champions would suggest that it was almost completely impregnable. In the six ties that had been played since their first encounter in 1975/76, the

Bavarians had won them all: 2-0, 4-1, 3-2, 4-1, 2-1 and 2-1. It was with good reason that the Bavarians were known in Madrid as *La Bestia Negra* – "the black beast".

Given that Ottmar Hitzfeld's side had also not been beaten in eighteen Champions League matches – a record that stretched well over a year – Bayern would start out as slight favourites against a Madrid team that in terms of personnel was at the peak of its powers. Perhaps the one significant difference between the Madrid team that had played Bayern in 2001 and the 2002 lineup was the presence of French midfielder Zinedine Zidane, considered by many to have been one of the greatest players of his generation.

To say that the tie was a mouth-watering one was an understatement, and the sixty-thousand people who made their way to the Olympiastadion would get to witness yet another pulsating, high-octane, dramatic encounter between two of the continent's finest teams.

Bayern would play with its now familiar 4-5-1 "wingback" system, but it was the visitors who had the better of the early exchanges. Worse was to come. Before the home side even had a chance to settle their nerves in front of an expectant capacity home crowd, Real took the lead.

It was a horrible goal. After collecting the ball just outside the Bayern penalty area, Cameroon international Geremi – who had never scored for *Los Merengues* – cut inside his marker before firing off a speculative shot with his left foot. The ball bounced in front of Oliver Kahn before beating him at his near post, with the Bayern *Torhüter* only able to get the slightest of touches to help it on its way into the back of the net. For the first time in seven matches played over twenty-five years, Real were in front at the Olympiastadion.

The shock of going behind shook Bayern out of their slumber, but for all of their efforts they couldn't find a way to threaten César in the Madrid goal. With their proud unbeaten record and with it a place in the last four under serious threat, half-time couldn't have come soon enough for Hitzfeld's side.

Bayern started the second half with far more purpose, but as in the first half found themselves unable to create any genuine clear-cut opportunities. The coach made his first move just past the hour mark in sending on Hasan Salihamidžić and Claudio Pizarro for Willy Sagnol and Paulo Sérgio, and with Real now looking at holding onto their lead Bayern gradually started to find more time and space in midfield. With sixty-nine minutes on the clock a Giovane Élber effort struck the crossbar, and two minutes later Salihamidžić was upended by Francisco Pavón in the box.

Bayern had finally got their break, and the home fans roared with approval as Scottish referee Hugh Dallas pointed to the penalty spot.

Without any hesitation Stefan Effenberg stepped up. Confident as ever, the Bayern skipper sent his kick firmly to César's right, but the 'keeper read it correctly to make the save. The crowd at the Olympiastadion suddenly found themselves in a state of shock and one could easily have forgiven the home side if they had collapsed under the pressure, but we had learned never to underestimate Effenberg. Rather than let things get to him and allow the team to wilt, the Bayern captain saw the missed penalty as the perfect opportunity to up the ante.

The team pressed ever harder, and with just eight minutes remaining finally got the equaliser. Roque Santa Cruz swung the ball into the Madrid box with Effenberg heading on to Élber, and the Brazilian shielded the ball expertly before leaving it for the fast arriving Bayern captain, who calmly stroked the ball past César with a sweep of his right boot. As the ball nestled at the back of the Real net, there was that furrowed brow, steely glare, and familiar, determined pump of the fists.

Suddenly, the tone of the match had changed completely. Roared on by the home crowd and seizing on the shift in momentum, the men in red swept forward with renewed purpose in search of the winner. Élber saw his header turned behind by César with six minutes remaining, and just four minutes later substitute Niko Kovač launched a ball long into the Madrid half. Pizarro nodded it into the box, Élber returned the favour, and the Peruvian drilled the ball into the net to send the bench and the crowd into paroxysms of unconfined joy. Even the usually calm and controlled Hitzfeld was going crazy on the touchline.

Die Roten had been behind for over seventy minutes and had missed a penalty, but had somehow been able to get back on their feet and deliver two hammer blows that had left the visitors completely deflated. Who knows what might have happened had there been a further five minutes? Who knows how things might have finished had Effenberg scored from the spot? For all their poor domestic league form, this was the Bayern we all knew and loved, the Bayern that never knew when to give up.

With their last-gasp 2-1 win the Bavarians had maintained their long unbeaten run in the Champions League and notched up their seventh home win from seven in European competition against Madrid, but the away goal would keep things delicately in the balance. In the end, it would prove to be decisive.

Bayern had secured a 1-0 win in Madrid on their way to winning the Champions League crown in 2001, and every supporter of the Munich side would have given their eye teeth for a similar result. While *Die Roten's* domestic form had been far from stellar for much of the season, they had managed to gather significant momentum in their quest to become the first team to retain the Champions League title since the competition's revamp in the early mid-1990s. Up to and including their win at the Olympiastadion against Real, they had strung together a club record nineteen games without defeat.

The return leg at the Santiago Bernabéu in Madrid saw the home side adopt a positive approach, and right from the beginning Bayern found themselves on the back foot. The first half hour was dominated by Vicente del Bosque's team, and while Bayern came back into the game slightly as the first half drew to a close, the crowd of just over 75,000 cranked up the noise.

At the half-way mark with the score still goalless Bayern still had one foot in the last four, but just watching wave after wave of white shirts streaming forward towards Oliver Kahn's goal was enough to turn me into a bag of nerves. One could only have imagined the levels of tension among the visiting Bayern supporters at the seething Bernabéu.

As with every match where one ends up clock-watching it was a case of when rather than if, and when Iván Helguera opened the scoring after sixty-nine minutes from close range there would be a sense of inevitability about it all. Having scored that crucial away goal in Munich, the eight-time champions were now ahead in the tie. Five minutes later first leg hero Pizarro came on for defender Sammy Kuffour as Hitzfeld decided to play his hand, but Bayern were now up against opponents that clearly had the bit between their teeth.

With five minutes remaining, the home side pretty much settled the issue. A long ball found Raúl, who benefited from a lucky rebound off Robert Kovač before finding substitute Guti just ouside the six-yard box. With 'keeper Kahn completely out of position, the Real midfielder was able to sneak in front of Owen Hargreaves before stabbing the ball into the empty net.

Bayern could still have taken the game into extra time with a second goal, but by now they were completely spent and desperately short of ideas. They ended up getting five minutes of additional time, but could offer very little as the game, and with it both their hold on the trophy and their long unbeaten record, came to an end at the twentieth time of asking.

To really put the seal on what had been a disappointing evening, Hasan Salihamidžić was shown a very harsh straight red card for a challenge on Santiago Solari that was clumsy at worst.

Having eliminated the defending champions, Real Madrid advanced to the semi-finals where they then overcame domestic rivals Barcelona. In the final at Glasgow's Hampden Park, they would go on to defeat first-timers Bayer Leverkusen in a closely-fought encounter that will always be remembered for Zinedine Zidane's spectacular goal.

Bayern's run of nineteen Champions League games unbeaten was a club record, just one behind the then overall record set by AFC Ajax between 1985/86 and 1995/96, and today sits in third place on the list – with Manchester United setting a new mark of twenty-five matches between 2007/08 and 2008/09.

A month before their Champions League quarter-final exit Bayern's domestic cup campaign had also fallen short, with a two-goal semi-final defeat in Gelsenkirchen at the hands of Schalke 04. Hitzfeld's side had been unconvincing throughout their entire DFB-Pokal campaign, with comfortable wins against lower league opposition before a come-from-behind 2-1 win over Wolfsburg and a penalty shootout victory over Kaiserslautern following a goalless draw. Their semi-final against Schalke 04 had also finished goalless after ninety minutes, but a goal in each half of extra time from Marco van Hoogdalem and Jörg Böhme would put paid to Bayern's domestic ambitions.

Bayern would actually win one trophy in 2001/02 – the one-off tie against South American champions Boca Juniors in the Intercontinental Cup at the end of November 2001. In front of a crowd of 51,360 at the National Stadium in Tokyo, the one-off showpiece between the European and South American champions saw things finish goalless after ninety minutes, with Bayern struggling to put away the Argentinians who had been reduced to ten men at the start of the second half following the dismissal of striker Marcelo Delgado.

As the game went to extra time and looked as though it would be heading towards a penalty shootout, it was ended with a scrappy goal four minutes into the second fifteen-minute period. A corner from Paulo Sérgio was headed towards the Boca goal by Thorsten Fink, with 'keeper Óscar Córdoba only managing to claw the ball away to the lurking Giovane Élber. The Brazilian's shot was cleared off the line by Clemente Rodríguez, and after the blue-shirted defenders failed numerous times to clear the ball finally fell to centre-back Sammy Kuffour, who swung a right boot to send it crashing into the net.

I had managed to catch brief highlights of this match on one of those compilation shows – something like FIFA Futbol Mundial – but having read the report was probably glad to have missed it. The fact that this round trip to the Far East had fallen slap-bang in the middle of two important Bundesliga fixtures was rather annoying, and while Bayern could rightfully claim to be world club champions, I had never really liked this fixture. It also didn't help that the match against Boca had fallen right in the middle of Bayern's worst spell of the season.

If 2001/02 had been a disappointing season, 2002/03 provided Bayern fans with a bizarre combination of domestic success and European disaster. While Ottmar Hitzfeld's side would overcome the previous season's domestic woes with an outstanding league and cup double, their form in Europe was arguably the worst in living memory, and certainly the worst since the early 1990s. Having won their preliminary round match to enter the first group phase, Bayern were eliminated without winning a single match.

On the transfer front, a number of established names made way for a selection of up and coming stars. The biggest departure was skipper Stefan Effenberg who headed north to VfL Wolfsburg on a free transfer, while unsettled Swiss midfielder Ciriaco Sforza returned for a third spell with Kaiserslautern. Paulo Sérgio moved to Emirati side Al-Wahda, while Carsten Jancker headed to Italy to join Udinese Calcio.

To make up for the loss of Effenberg and Paulo Sérgio, Bayern signed two of Germany's hottest young talents. The *Nationalmannschaft's* up and coming superstar Michael Ballack headed to the Säbenerstraße from Bayer Leverkusen for a bargain six million Euros, while twenty-two year old starlet Sebastian Deisler exchanged the blue of Hertha Berlin for the red of Bayern for nine million Euros.

Bayern's most expensive signing however was twelve-million Euro winger Zé Roberto, who having filled the space occupied by his countryman Paulo Sérgio at Leverkusen in 1998 would do exactly the same thing in joining Bayern. The snaring of the talented Brazilian was a major coup for Bayern, but one would not have blamed Leverkusen fans for being ever so slightly miffed: they must have felt as though their club was little more than a training ground for speedy Brazilian wingers.

2002/03 also saw a number of amateur second team players integrated into the first team squad in Munich, among them teenagers Philipp Lahm, Bastian Schweinsteiger and Piotr Trochowski – two of whom would go on to become legendary names for both club and country.

The season began as usual with the pre-season DFB-Ligapokal, but like the previous season Bayern would see their hopes ended early by Hertha Berlin. The two teams played out a 2-2 draw with two goals being exchanged in a frenetic final couple of minutes, but with extra-time failing to separate them it all came down to a penalty shootout. Having scored their first three spot-kicks to go 3-2 in front, Willy Sagnol, Michael Tarnat and Giovane Élber all failed to hit the target as the Berliners ran out 4-3 winners, en route to winning the trophy for the second year in a row.

Bayern's Bundesliga campaign would get off to a quiet start with a goalless draw in Mönchengladbach, but five wins on the bounce and a healthy return of sixteen goals helped propel the Munich side to the top spot – a position they would not relinquish. Defeats in Leverkusen and Bremen were not enough to upset or derail the campaign, and while Bayern continued to collect points their rivals would all take it in turns to dramatically drop off the pace.

At the half-way stage the Bavarians were six points clear of second-placed Borussia Dortmund with a record of thirteen wins, three draws and the two defeats, and from that point they would not look back. Bayern finished the *Hinrunde* on the back of a six-game unbeaten spell, extending this record to sixteen after the winter break.

A first home defeat of the season against seventh-placed Bremen saw the unbeaten run come to an end, but by this time *Die Roten* found themselves a massive eleven points clear of the chasing pack with just seven matches remaining. A 1-0 defeat in Dortmund followed, but with Stuttgart failing to capitalise after a 3-1 defeat to strugglers Bochum it was clear that the *Meisterschale* was surely on its way to Bavaria for the seventeenth time.

A two-goal triumph in Wolfsburg on match day thirty was enough secure the title, with Bayern a safe thirteen points clear of second-placed Stuttgart with four games remaining. Three further wins followed, and not even a defeat at the hands of seventh-placed Schalke in their final match could dampen the celebrations. With six more wins than Stuttgart and a staggering eight more than third-placed Dortmund, Bayern had won the title by a country mile – a massive sixteen points – sealing what had been a dominant campaign.

	P	W	D	L	Goals	GD	Pts
FC Bayern München	34	23	6	5	70:25	+45	75
VfB Stuttgart	34	17	8	9	53:39	+14	59
BV 09 Borussia Dortmund	34	15	13	6	51:27	+24	58

Having long lost my coverage of the DFB-Pokal I found myself unable to follow Bayern's progress – which was done the old-fashioned way through reading match reports and occasionally picking up the odd video report on the Internet. Hitzfeld's side had started their domestic cup campaign with a 3-0 win over Werder Bremen II before securing a 2-1 win over Hannover 96, and a win on penalties against Schalke 04 would secure a place in the last eight against Köln – at the time riding high at the top of the second division.

The second division side would come into their match in Munich with hopes of scoring an upset, but ended up being summarily swept aside by a clinical Bayern team that registered eight goals without reply – including a hat-trick from the in-form Élber. The Brazilian would then score twice in the space of a minute as the Bavarians surged ahead in what had for the most part been a tight semi-final encounter against Leverkusen, and the final in Berlin's Olympiastadion would see Bayern take on familiar opposition in the form of bogey team Kaiserslautern.

With it being a cup final and Kaiserslautern being Kaiserslautern many had expected a close contest, but with Bayern flying off the blocks the destiny of the golden trophy was effectively decided by half-time. Two goals inside the opening ten minutes from former 'Lautern man Michael Ballack effectively ended the game as a contest, and a strike from Claudio Pizarro five minutes into the second half helped take the Bavarians into the comfort zone.

Kaiserslautern's Bulgarian international Marian Hristov was shown a straight red card with twelve minutes remaining as Bayern looked to close things out, but despite being down to ten men the Red Devils managed to pull a goal back through Miroslav Klose just two minutes after Hristov's dismissal.

It was little more than a consolation, and Hitzfeld's side eased through to the final whistle. The victory in Berlin saw Bayern extend their record to eleven cup victories, and with it claim a fourth domestic double.

Unfortunately, Bayern's dominant domestic form would contrast markedly with their results in Europe, where they endured a Champions League campaign that was, frankly, humiliating. To find anything as embarrassing one had to go back to the early 1990s. Eliminated at the group stage without a single win, it was Bayern's earliest exit in continental competition since 1969/70, when French side AS Saint Étienne had inflicted a first round European Cup defeat.

Things had started well enough for *Die Roten* with a convincing 6-1 aggregate win over Serbian champions Partizan Belgrade in the final pre-group stage qualifying round. When Bayern were grouped alongside Italians AC Milan, Spanish side Deportivo de La Coruña and French league runners-up RC Lens nobody would have thought it too difficult a task to progress through to the knock-out stages.

While the dangerous Milan had always been a genuine threat at this level, both Deportivo and Lens were hardly European heavyweights – and Bayern's campaign seemed set fair with an opening fixture on home soil against the outfit from northern-western Spain.

With the Munich side unbeaten at the Olympiastadion for a record thirty-one matches stretching back six seasons, every Bayern supporter expected a positive start. Unfortunately, everybody was in for a very rude shock.

By half-time Bayern were already two goals down, with Depo's Dutch international Roy Makaay finding the net after twelve minutes and then on the cusp of the half-time. With their proud home record under threat Bayern rallied strongly after the break, with Hasan Salihamidžić and then Giovane Élber pulling them right back into the contest. One might have thought that the tide had turned and that the home side would see things through to the end, but Makaay completed his hat-trick with thirteen minutes remaining to bring the Bavarians' thirty-one match unbeaten home spell to an end.

Having dropped three points at home in their opening fixture the pressure was already on Ottmar Hitzfeld's team to get a good result in their next match, against group outsiders Lens. In front of forty thousand people at the compact Stade Félix-Bollaert the visitors made a confident start, and midway through the first half an inswinging free-kick found defender Thomas Linke, who rose above the opposition defence to give Bayern the lead.

Half-time arrived with the visitors unable to add to their lead as they struggled to create any further opportunities, but in truth neither team was particularly impressive. Bayern's inability to put additional daylight between themselves and their opponents would, of course, come back to haunt them in the second half.

Lens may not have been the most star-studded team in Bayern's group, but what they lacked in big names was more than made up by their spirit and determination. The second half saw the French side come out all guns blazing, and right from the whistle they started to apply some real pressure against an increasingly fraught Bayern defence. Having been the better team in the first half, Bayern found themselves firmly on the back foot. Antoine Sibierski went close twice and Nigerian John Utaka also had a decent opportunity as Lens continued to threaten the Bayern goal, but as the game entered the final quarter of an hour it looked as though Hitzfeld's men had just about done enough to hold on and take the three points back to Munich. However with fourteen minutes remaining a corner found Utaka, whose well-directed header flew into the Bayern net past Oliver Kahn.

Having had their lead pegged back Bayern were simply unable to gather any momentum, and a flat and at times insipid encounter came to an end with each team taking a share of the spoils. With just a single point from their two games against the group's two weaker opponents Bayern found themselves joint bottom of the four-team group, and their next task would be the most difficult of all: a double-header against European *bête noire* AC Milan.

With the Italians looking impressive with two wins from two including a four-goal demolition of Deportivo in Spain, Bayern clearly had their work cut out.

The first encounter between these two great European rivals would take place at the Olympiastadion, where Bayern looked to get their stuttering campaign back on track. Milan had never won in Munich, but with records continually being broken there was a nagging sense of inevitability about what was going to happen when the two teams stepped out onto the pitch.

Bayern would have the better of a somewhat cagey first half and managed to fashion a number of half-decent opportunities, but as in both of their previous matches they were unable to convert their possession and chances into goals. The opening exchanges of the second half saw Giovane Élber go close and a header from Michael Ballack flew narrowly wide of the target, and a familiar script would slowly begin to unravel. On fifty-two minutes, Milan created their first genuine opening – and duly scored.

With Ballack having just missed the target at one end, Rivaldo and Clarence Seedorf combined at the other, with the Dutchman's sharp low cross setting up Filippo Inzaghi. With Oliver Kahn left helpless on the ground after watching Seedorf's cross fizz past him, Inzaghi had the easy task of stabbing the ball into the empty net from all of four yards. It was typical Milan: having withstood what had been an almost relentless stream of Bayern attacks, they had somehow pieced together that one magical move to tear the Bavarian defence to shreds and take the lead against the run of play.

Having largely dominated the game Bayern were now staring right down the barrel, but from nowhere summoned the resolve to drag themselves back into the contest. The move that led to their equaliser was fashioned by the busy Hasan Salihamidžić, whose burst down the right saw him weave past Andrea Pirlo before delivering the perfect cross for Claudio Pizarro, who directed a firm header past 'keeper Dida. With the game back in the balance the home side continued to create opportunities, but with six minutes remaining Milan substitute Serghino blazed past Robert Kovač down the left, sending in a cross for Inzaghi to finish.

It was a crushing blow, and having been punched hard in the ribs right at the death there was no second chance for Hitzfeld's side as the Italians comfortably saw things through to the end. Milan had taken their record in the group to three wins from three, and with Deportivo beating Lens 3-1 Bayern found themselves joint bottom of the group with the French side.

The return three weeks later in Milan saw the Serie A champions turn the screw right from the start, and with just eleven minutes on the clock Serghino found the back of the

Bayern net. Michael Tarnat's equaliser just twelve minutes later would give Bayern some hope of taking something back home to Munich as they desperately tried to keep their tournament hopes alive, but midway through the second half the inevitable Inzaghi wrapped things up for Milan as the Italians completed the double over the hapless Bavarians.

With Lens beating Deportivo in France Bayern were now left on their own at the bottom of the group table with just a single point from their four matches, and their dreams of making the knockout stage were over, barring a number of next to impossible mathematical miracles. Having collected just the one point from an available twelve, they also found themselves off the pace for third place and a consolation place in the UEFA Cup third round.

Any remaining hopes of prolonging the European season would come to an end in La Coruña's compact Riazor stadium, where once again an inept Bayern were taken to the cleaners by their new tormentor Roy Makaay. With little more than pride to play for *Die Roten* fell behind nine minutes into the second half before drawing level through a seventy-seventh minute strike by Roque Santa Cruz, but the almost ubiquitous Dutchman popped up with just a minute remaining to snatch all three points for the Spaniards. With Lens pulling off an unexpected home win over runaway group leaders Milan to clinch third place, the end of the evening saw Bayern rooted to the foot of table.

With no hope of any further progress in Europe, Bayern's final dead rubber match with Lens at the Olympiastadion was little more than exercise in maintaining whatever pride was left – and the not so little matter of saving face in front of their own supporters. Only twenty-two thousand people had bothered to turn up, but at least for the opening twenty minutes it looked as though something might have been taken out of this miserable group campaign.

In all my years following the team I had never seen a Bayern side sitting in such a pitiful position in the Champions League group phase: with the exception of Spartak Moscow who had been beaten in all of their six matches, Bayern's record was the worst of all of the first phase groups.

While it would have been shocking for neutrals to see one of Europe's great footballing powers floundering at the bottom of their Champions League group with just two points from their six matches, for Bayern fans it had been nothing short of a disaster – the worst European campaign in living memory.

THE CHANGING OF THE GUARD

While 2002/03 had seen Bayern secure yet another domestic double, it was becoming increasingly apparent that this was never going to be good enough for many of Bayern's supporters, let alone club president Uli Hoeneß. European success had always been the benchmark of success, and the club's dismal showing in the Champions League would lead to a significant changing of the guard at the Säbenerstraße.

While Ottmar Hitzfeld remained at the helm, the squad would see a number of changes. Perhaps the most disappointing news was the departure of goalscoring hero Giovane Élber who headed to Olympique Lyonnais in France for €4.2 million just a few weeks into the new season, while Niko Kovač, Michael Tarnat, Bernd Dreher and Stefan Wessels also made their way to the exit door.

During the previous season, one player more than anyone else had helped define Bayern's poor season in Europe: Deportivo de La Coruña striker Roy Makaay. With four goals in two games including his stunning hat-trick at the Olympiastadion, the Dutch international had impressed the likes of Hoeneß and Karl-Heinz Rummenigge, and less than a year after he had almost single-handedly destroyed *Die Roten's* Champions League campaign he was making his way to Munich for the princely sum of 19.75 million Euros. Joining Makaay in Bavaria was the versatile Argentinian defensive midfielder Martín Demichelis, signed from Club Atlético River Plate for five million Euros, while the highly-rated young German left-sided defender Tobias Rau was picked up from VfL Wolfsburg for €2.25 million.

Despite over twenty-five million Euros being spent on new signings, I remained mildly sceptical. While Demichelis was something of an unknown quantity – Bayern had over the years invested in a number of dud buys from South America – and Rau was still pretty inexperienced and somewhat injury-prone, I initially saw Makaay as something of an impulse buy. For me, there was little or no difference between the Dutchman and the man he was replacing in Élber, a player who had consistently delivered for Bayern when it mattered. While close to twenty million Euros had been splashed out on the twenty-eight year old Makaay, Élber – just three years older – had almost been given away. It's not as though the Brazilian's form had fallen away either: twenty-one goals in thirty-three league matches was far from shabby.

The remainder of the new squad members for 2003/04 would come from the club's amateur ranks. Goalkeepers Michael Rensing and Jan Schlösser were both given their official shirt numbers, along with defender Christian Lell and promising young Peruvian striker Paolo Guerrero.

The season began with a disappointing showing in the pre-season Ligapokal in front of just under twelve thousand people at the Ernst-Abbe-Sportfeld in the eastern city of Jena, which saw Hitzfeld's side come back from 3-1 down against Hamburger SV to draw 3-3 before being beaten in a dire penalty shootout - with winger Hasan Salihamidžić the only Bayern player to find the back of the net.

This would pretty much set the tone for the rest of the season.

The 2003/04 Bundesliga campaign started well enough with a 3-1 win over Eintracht Frankfurt, and after week four and a two-goal victory in Hamburg *Die Roten* were in second place behind Werder Bremen on goal difference. The game in Hamburg saw Giovane Élber come on as a seventy-sixth minute substitute for Claudio Pizarro, and just two minutes later he scored Bayern's second. The Brazilian would never get what would have been a deserved home send-off, and his goal showed just how good a player he was in the Bayern *Trikot*. New man Makaay, meanwhile, had turned out two pretty disappointing displays in his first two games for *Die Roten*.

Perhaps happy with the weight being finally lifted from his shoulders following Élber's departure, the Dutch striker would finally open his goalscoring account the following week in Wolfsburg, but it would not be a happy ending for the Bavarians as the battling Wolves came back from 2-1 down to snatch a dramatic 3-2 win with two goals in the last eight minutes to see Bayern drop down to fifth place in the league table.

The defeat in Wolfsburg was followed by a 3-3 draw at home to Leverkusen, but Makaay was finally beginning to show that he was worth the money that had been paid for him. A goal against Bayer was followed by two more against Hansa Rostock and Hertha Berlin, but the striker was one of the few players to hit the right note in what was already turning out to be a very ordinary league season for Hitzfeld's side.

At the half-way point Bayern found themselves four points behind Bremen in second place, but would never be able to make up the ground. An inconsistent *Rückrunde* saw them continually take two steps forward and one step back, while Werder continued to keep their noses in front. A painful defeat in Bochum in mid-February saw Hitzfeld's side fall nine points behind their northern rivals, and as the season rolled towards its conclusion only a miracle could prevent the *Meisterschale* making its way to the Weserstadion.

Miracles had of course happened before, and Bayern would have a glimmer of hope with just three matches remaining when they faced the league leaders at the Olympiastadion. It was a must-win game, and every supporter knew that a victory would take the Bavarians to within three points of the summit and pile all of the pressure on Bremen. I too chose to hold tightly onto this last thread of hope: if we could beat them we might, just might, have a chance of snatching something out of nothing right at the death.

Unfortunately this time there was no miracle. Croatian striker Ivan Klasnić would give Bremen the lead after nineteen minutes, and just nine minutes later Frenchman Johan Micoud doubled the northerners' lead. When Brazilian Aílton made it three ten minutes before half-time, there was no way back. Not even Patrik Andersson could have pulled this one out of the fire.

Makaay would pull one goal back in the second half with his twenty-third league strike in what had been for him a successful debut season in Munich, but Bremen's 3-1 triumph had sealed the title for the *Green-Whites* with two games to spare.

A flat 3-1 defeat for Bayern in Stuttgart followed, and a final 2-0 win over SC Freiburg at the Olympiastadion would see them finish the campaign six points behind – perhaps a little flattering with Bremen taking their foot off the pedal and falling to successive defeats with the *Meisterschale* already safely in the locker. Until that point, the newly-crowned Bundesliga champions had gone twenty-three matches unbeaten.

	P	W	D	L	Goals	GD	Pts
SV Werder Bremen	34	22	8	4	79:38	+41	74
FC Bayern München	34	20	8	6	70:39	+31	68
Bayer 04 Leverkusen	34	19	8	7	73:39	+34	65

I hadn't got to see any of Bayern's DFB-Pokal campaign, where after victories over Borussia Neunkirchen, Nürnberg and HSV Hitzfeld's side had fallen in the quarter-finals to second division Alemannia Aachen – the winner being scored nine minutes from time by Dutchman Erik Meijer.

In stark contrast to the DFB-Pokal, television coverage of the UEFA Champions League in the United Kingdom would continue to get better and better. Prior to 2003, mainstream terrestrial channel ITV would have a firm hold of all the broadcasting rights to the competition; in winning shared broadcasting rights, the BSkyB satellite network changed the landscape completely. Suddenly, one could find extensive highlights of all of the big European matches, and while it would take a few more years to see every match being shown live I would never miss out on a Bayern match again. It was hard to imagine just how much things had advanced in as little as a decade.

Bayern found themselves in an opening group that included the champions of France, Scotland and Belgium – Olympique Lyonnais, Glasgow Celtic and RSC Anderlecht – and things looked far less testing on paper than the previous season. The reality, as is nearly always the case, was completely different. Bayern ended up being pushed all the way by all three of their group opponents, and every match would turn into a struggle as the Bavarians scrapped and scraped their way through to the knock-out stages.

The first of these struggles would come at the Olympiastadion against Celtic, where Alan Thompson headed the unfancied Scottish champions into a fifty-sixth minute lead. With the previous season's shock opening loss at the hands of Deportivo de La Coruña still fresh in the memory, the architect of that defeat took it upon himself to turn things around for the Munich side.

With seventeen minutes remaining Roy Makaay lashed in the equaliser from the edge of the Celtic box, and with four minutes left on the clock conjured up one of the most bizarre goals of the season. Cutting in from the right more than thirty yards out, the Dutchman had floated in a high left-footed cross towards the advancing Michael Ballack, but the ball evaded everyone, taking an awkward bounce before spinning into the net past 'keeper Magnus Hedman.

Finally, Bayern had managed to get a lucky break – and with three points in the bag were off to a winning start.

Bayern's visit to Brussels to take on Anderlecht would see them under pressure again. The Bavarians found themselves reduced to ten men nine minutes before half-time when striker Claudio Pizarro received two yellow cards in the space of a minute, and seven minutes into the second half Croatian Ivica Mornar rolled the ball into an empty net to give the Belgian champions the lead. Once again though Bayern would somehow work their way back in the game, with Pizarro's Peruvian colleague Roque Santa Cruz sending in a bullet header seventeen minutes from time to salvage a precious point – and crucially denying Anderlecht all three.

The toughest game however would come in Lyon, and in yet another closely fought encounter Bayern again managed to escape with what was a lucky point. Having taken the lead in the first half against the run of play through Makaay, the visitors were put under intense pressure from the home side. With just minutes remaining it looked as though Bayern's luck would hold, but a late equaliser from Péguy Luyindula meant that at the half-way point in the group stage Bayern would head a very tight group. With five points from their three matches, the Bavarians were a single point ahead of both Lyon and Anderlecht and two clear of Celtic.

The return fixture against the French champions at the Olympiastadion presented Hitzfeld's side with the chance to place one foot in the knock-out phase, but an off-colour display saw them spurn chance after chance. Brazilian Juninho had given the visitors an early lead which was quickly cancelled out by the inevitable Makaay, but with Bayern unable to make the most of their opportunities the momentum swung decisively towards the French side.

Eight minutes into the second half, Lyon scored the winning goal. It was one of those moments that could have almost been scripted in advance; as the ball nestled in the back of the Bayern net, the man wheeling away in celebration was none other than former Bayern hero Giovane Élber.

Try as they might, Hitzfeld's side couldn't bring themselves back into the game for a second time. As their frustration began to mount both on the pitch and in the stands among the home supporters, the remaining thirty-seven minutes saw Bayern collect no fewer than half a dozen yellow cards. Lyon's 2-1 victory saw them climb to the top of the table, while Bayern's dismal record in the competition continued: the defeat meant that *Die Roten* had won just one of their last eleven Champions League outings. With Celtic beating Anderlecht in the group's other fixture, the race for the two precious knock-out places was tighter than ever.

A dull goalless draw in Glasgow against Celtic saw Bayern inch to six points from five matches played, and with Anderlecht beating Lyon 1-0 all four sides would go into the final week with a chance of making the knock-out stage. Having looked a good bet at the halfway point, Hitzfeld's side were now bottom of the group – a point behind everyone else – but knew that nothing less than a victory in their final match at home to Anderlecht would be enough to take them through.

In a tough and at times nerve-racking encounter, the two sides would eventually be separated by a forty-second minute penalty from Makaay, awarded after Pizarro had been bundled over in the box by Pole Michał Żewłakow. In a typically nail-biting finale that had me turn away from the television many times, the Belgians would almost sneak an equaliser right at the death as Ukrainian substitute Oleh Yashchuk forced 'keeper Oliver Kahn into a stunning save.

Bayern had finally won their only second Champions League match in a round dozen attempts, and despite only being beaten just the once would sneak into the last sixteen by the skin of their teeth – a point behind group winners Lyon. Awaiting the Bavarians in the first knock-out round would be a familiar old foe – Real Madrid.

Following their poor group phase, Hitzfeld's side would save their best performance of the campaign for the home leg against Real - but once again they were plagued by missed chances and not being able to capitalise on their possession and domination. Iker Casillas in the Madrid goal was certainly made to earn his money, and the home side could have been away and clear before half-time.

Makaay, Bixente Lizarazu and Pizarro all spurned decent opportunities inside the first twenty minutes, and on twenty-four minutes Casillas denied Zé Roberto as Bayern continued to press. Nine minutes before Makaay set up Owen Hargreaves whose stunning drive was well parried by the Madrid 'keeper, who then punched away a Zé Roberto corner from under his own crossbar. Two minutes into added time, the unfortunate Makaay had yet another shot blocked.

On another evening Bayern could have been leading by three or four at half-time, and the opening period of the second forty-five minutes saw them pick up where they had left off. In the space of five minutes just short of the hour mark, Makaay missed a sitter from six yards, Pizarro sent in a low fizzing drive just wide of the post and Ballack blazed a shot over the goal, and on sixty-three minutes some wonderful interplay between Zé and Hasan Salihamidžić saw the Bosnian denied by the painfully ubiquitous Casillas, who just a minute later held onto a well-directed Ballack effort.

Still it went on. On sixty-seven minutes, Casillas got his hands to a curling Hargreaves free-kick only to see Ballack poke the rebound wide of the target, and just minutes later Willy Sagnol skipped down the right flank, skinning left-back Guti before finding the side netting. The red storm was relentless, but still the goal wouldn't come. It just looked as though it was going to be yet another one of those evenings.

Then, with just fifteen minutes remaining it came. Pizarro would send in the perfect cross from the left, and this time Makaay made no mistake as he nodded home from close range. There was a massive sense of relief among the crowd of fifty-nine thousand people, and given my own sense of pent-up frustration one could only have imagined how it must have felt in the stands.

Bayern should really have been out of sight, but given their early form in the competition many would have been happy with a one-goal lead to take back to Madrid. All the team had to do now was just play the same way and see out the remaining time, and maybe hope for a second.

If only things were so simple.

With eight minutes remaining, Real would win a free-kick well over thirty yards out, and there lining up was Brazilian Roberto Carlos – famed for his long-distance thunderbolts. This however was a good distance away from the Bayern goal – a distance that was surely even beyond the hard-hitting left-back. Or so we all thought. The shot came in – a low drive, skidding that lacked the usual fizz. All that remained was for Oliver Kahn to gather it up, and set up another red thrust forward.

Imagine then the horror as the Bayern 'keeper appeared to dive over the ball, which squirmed awkwardly underneath him before rolling into the back of the net. It was if the small sphere was itself offering a sad sigh of apology to every watching Bayern fan. Madrid had hardly threatened all evening in the face of a dominant Bayern side, yet here they were with the score standing at 1-1 with a crucial away goal. Even goalscorer Carlos couldn't quite believe his luck.

I cannot remember a game so one-sided that had produced such a result, and for all their dominance – some seventeen attempts on goal – Bayern would effectively be behind in the tie. It had truly been a tale of two 'keepers: while Casillas in the Real goal had been heroic in defying Bayern almost single-handedly, Oliver Kahn had made one of those mistakes that would be burned into the recurring nightmares of every Bayern fan.

The second leg at a packed Santiago Bernabéu saw Bayern having to chase the game almost right from the start, with Madrid already ahead in the tie on the away goals rule. Things began brightly enough as both Makaay and Ballack created early opportunities, but as the game wore on the home side would slowly slip into gear. Shortly after the half-hour mark Zinedine Zidane – who had been almost anonymous in the first leg – set up a move involving David Beckham, Raúl and Míchel Salgado, a move that ended with the Frenchman lashing the ball into the Bayern net.

Bayern still needed just the one goal to take the tie into extra time, and would fashion further chances as half-time approached. Bayern were having their best spell of the match as Real looked to sit back, but as in the first leg the men in red just couldn't get the ball over the line. Makaay had a shot blocked by Beckham. Zé Roberto then fired in a crisp shot that was parried by the immovable Casillas, who moments later dived low to keep out Makaay. Two minutes into injury time the Madrid 'keeper would finally make a mess of things as he missed an incoming corner, only for an incredulous Pizarro to see his goal-bound toe-poke shinned off the line by Salgado.

Over the course of one and half games of football, one could not have written a more horrific script – if you were a Bayern fan.

It was a case of more of the same in the second half. Makaay with a shot blocked, Casillas with another save, this time from the head of Ballack. With Bayern now throwing almost everything forward the field started to open up, and the visitors continued to be the more dangerous of the two teams. Fate continued to plague the Bavarians as Norwegian referee Terje Hauge failed to show the aggressive Salgado a second yellow card for a cynical foul on Zé Roberto, and eight minutes from time the infuriatingly omnipresent Casillas was on hand yet again to deny Makaay for the umpteenth time in the tie.

With the game now running from end to end Kahn made a fine save to keep out Guti's late effort, but that would be the end of the scoring. Bayern had played their hearts out over both legs and had thrown everything at their opponents in over three hours of football between two well-matched teams, but once again it had not been enough. One can forever talk about possession, dominance and opportunities, but the most important statistic will always be goals – and quite simply Bayern's inability to take their chances and breach the Madrid net had been their undoing.

Thus would be added yet another dramatic chapter to the long-running Champions League rivalry between the two sides – a rivalry that far surpasses all others among Bayern's European opponents. While Manchester United had provided the one big headline in 1999 and AC Milan would have the whip hand over the Bavarians during the 1990s, the rivalry with Real Madrid continued to produce a series of contests that would be both competitive, intense and spiced with just the right amount of needle. The hard-fought encounter in late 2003 would not be the last.

If the start of the season had seen a number of comings and goings in the squad, the conclusion to what had been an unsuccessful, trophyless season would result in the most significant change. Despite being the most successful coach in the long and successful history of FC Bayern München by a considerable distance, Ottmar Hitzfeld's time at the Säbenerstraße would come to an end a year before his agreed contract.

In six seasons, the Lörrach-born Hitzfeld had won eleven trophies: domestically, he had taken the club to four Bundesliga titles, two DFB-Pokal victories and three Ligapokal wins, and on the international stage he had guided the Bavarians to their first *Henkelpott* in twenty-five years before following that up with the FIFA Intercontinental Cup. Hitzfeld's time in charge – totaling 2,192 days –also made him Bayern's longest-serving coach, surpassing the previous mark of 1,756 days set by Udo Lattek between 1970 and 1975. It marked the end of an era.

While Hitzfeld's departure would have a sense of inevitability about it, there was a great deal of sadness at his departure. I for one thought that the club might have done better to keep him at the helm and give him the opportunity to see out his contract, but by the summer of 2004 he was old news. The Bayern board had clearly felt the need to strike while the iron was hot and seek out their next target.

That target was Felix Magath.

A FOND FAREWELL

Wolfgang-Felix Magath had made his name as a player for Hamburger SV, Bayern's biggest domestic rivals during the late 1970s and early 1980s. One of the most talented players of his generation, the stylish midfielder would become known for his habit of scoring important goals. Magath had scored the late winner in the 1977 European Cup Winners' Cup final against Belgians RSC Anderlecht as *Die Rothosen* captured their first European trophy, but would elevate himself to football's hall of fame with his spectacular long-distance strike against Juventus in the 1983 European Cup final in Athens.

In addition to becoming a legendary figure at the Volksparkstadion during what was arguably the best period in HSV's history, Magath also won forty-three international caps for the German national side; he had been a part of Jupp Derwall's winning team at Euro 1980 in Italy, and had also picked up runners-up medals at the 1982 and 1986 FIFA World Cup. Fittingly, the talented midfielder's final match in the *Nationaltrikot* would come in the final of the 1986 World Cup against Argentina in Mexico City.

Having ended his playing career Magath moved smoothly into coaching, first with HSV and then with Nürnberg, Werder Bremen and Eintracht Frankfurt – where he soon made a name for himself as a hard-working, no-nonsense coach who took great pride in getting results. Between 2001 and 2004 Magath had turned a struggling VfB Stuttgart back into a competitive unit, working with a number of young players to turn the Swabians into an exciting team capable of challenging for the Bundesliga title.

After guiding Stuttgart to second and fourth-place finishes in 2002/03 and 2003/04, Felix Magath was the man of the moment in Germany – and in seeking for a new *Trainer* to replace the departing Ottmar Hitzfeld FC Bayern immediately made a beeline for the Achaffenburgborn coach. Bayern got their man; at the beginning of July 2004, Magath signed a two-year contract that would see him take the short journey down the Autobahn A8 to Munich.

There were just four new signings at the start of the 2004/05 season. Brazilian international defender Lúcio was signed from Bayer Leverkusen for €12 million and Borussia Dortmund's German international Torsten Frings moved to Munich for a fraction under €10 million, while the promising twenty-two year old defender Andreas Görlitz was snapped up from local rivals TSV 1860 München for two and a half million Euros. Completing the quartet of new names was the experienced Iranian international striker Vahid Hashemian, a €2 million signing from VfL Bochum.

The departures were in comparison somewhat low-key: Midfielder Thorsten Fink retired from the first team to join FC Bayern II in a player-coach role, while second-string players Christian Lell and Zvjezdan Misimović moved to Köln and Bochum respectively.

Magath's first trophy in the Bayern hotseat would be the pre-season DFB-Ligapokal, where the Bavarians collected the trophy for the first time in four seasons with victories over Bayer Leverkusen and Werder Bremen. Leverkusen were easily dispatched 3-0 in the semi-final, and *Die Roten* would move into a simliar lead in the final against Bremen before seeing their opponents strike back with two late consolation goals. While the tournament continued to be seen as little more than a series of friendly warm-up matches and a prelude to the more serious stuff, it was nice to see the new coach start with two wins and get the first trophy of the season safely locked away.

The opening game of the new Bundesliga season saw Magath start with a well-earned 2-0 win against his former side HSV at the Volksparkstadion, but a disappointing 1-1 home draw with Hertha Berlin - which saw the eighty-sixth minute dismissal of new boy Görlitz - and a 4-1 thrashing in Leverkusen immediately pointed to signs of an early crisis in Munich. A four-game unbeaten spell with a draw in Dortmund and victories over Bielefeld, Freiburg and Bremen followed, but Bayern's unconvincing start to the season would continue with a scrappy 1-0 defeat at the Olympiastadion by Schalke 04.

With wins against Hansa Rostock and VfL Wolfsburg Bayern found themselves sitting in third place behind the Wolves and Magath's former side VfB Stuttgart, but just as it looked as though they had worked their way into a position to challenge for top spot another defeat would follow to undo all the good work.

A 2-0 reverse in Mönchengladbach pushed *Die Roten* down to fifth place in the standings, but an unbeaten spell saw them slowly climb back up the table as the end of the *Hinrunde* approached. Magath's side would then dispose of Hannover 96, VfL Bochum, Kaiserslautern and 1. FSV Mainz 05 as they put together a nine-match unbeaten spell, and by match day fifteen they were back at the summit – two points ahead of Schalke.

Bayern would close off the first half of the season with 2-2 draws against Nürnberg and Stuttgart; Schalke meanwhile missed out on the chance to claim the unofficial title of *Herbstmeister* following a late equaliser for opponents SC Freiburg at the Arena AufSchalke. In a somewhat less dramatic comparision to the last-day events of the 2000/01 season, *Die Knappen* had ended up as *Herbstmeister* for all of four minutes.

Schalke's slip-up meant that Magath's side would go into the winter break on thirty-four points from seventeen matches played – level with Schalke but with a far superior goal difference.

2005 would start well enough for Bayern with two wins and a draw from their first three games to see them edge away from the chasing pack, but a surprise 3-1 defeat against mid-table Bielefeld would blunt the momentum and see their three point advantage wiped out. A five-goal thumping of Dortmund was followed by gritty single-goal wins over Freiburg and Bremen, but Schalke would prove themselves equal to the challenge as they matched the Bavarians blow for blow. At the end of match day twenty-four the battle for the *Meisterschale* looked to have turned into a two-horse race, with Bayern and Schalke locked together on fifty points, seven clear of third-placed Bremen.

With little to choose between the leaders, the following week saw Bayern travel to Gelsenkirchen in what was billed as a pivotal encounter. The result was a cagey and unremarkable affair, with both sides choosing to sit back rather than attack. Brazilian Aílton would have two half-chances for the home side and Paolo Guerrero was foiled by Schalke 'keeper Frank Rost, and the half-time whistle brought an end to what had been an uninspiring forty-five minutes.

The second half would continue in much the same way. There were few if any genuine opportunities, with both sides cancelling each other out in a highly congested midfield. Bastian Schweinsteiger had managed to get a sight of the opposition goal before shooting wide and a Guerrero header was easily kept out by Rost, and with both sets of fans getting increasingly restless it looked as though both teams would go into the following week on fifty-one points – until the first and ultimately fatal blow finally came.

With just over twenty minutes remaining Schalke would win a free-kick just outside the Bayern box, and Brazilian midfielder Lincoln lifted the ball over the wall before sending it past Oliver Kahn and into the left-hand corner of the net. In a game that had been characterised by negative and sluggish play, it was always going to take a moment of brilliance to break the deadlock: unfortunately, that moment of brilliance had come from a man in a royal blue shirt.

The final quarter of the game would pass by without incident, and although Bayern cranked up the pressure in search of an equaliser they never really offered much of a threat to Rost in the opposition goal. It had been an uninspiring performance from Magath's side, and with Schalke now three points in front at the top of the table one must have wondered where the inspiration was going to come from. The only consolation was that there were still nine games remaining.

Felix Magath had built a reputation as a hard but inspiring coach, but the ninety minutes against Schalke had been dull, flat, and woefully short of ideas – anything but inspiring. With one more bad result, his time in Munich could very well have been under threat. However, a cursory examination of Magath's relatively short coaching career would reveal that he was a man who was at his very best under pressure – and from nowhere his team would produce a stunning series of results to first make up the lost ground and then power away from the rest of the chasing pack. It was as if the coach and players had been toying with everyone, only to flick the switch. Suddenly the Bayern engine clicked into gear, and the rest were left trailing in their wake.

The defeat in Gelsenkirchen would spark a nine-game winning streak, which not only saw Bayern charge to their nineteenth Bundesliga title, but win it by a massive fourteen points – an astonishing feat when one considers that with just nine weeks remaining they had been three points off the lead.

The last nine matches saw *Die Roten* score twenty-seven goals, racking up four against both Kaiserslautern and Mainz and a round half dozen in their final home game of the season against Bavarian rivals Nürnberg.

With the new high-tech Allianz Arena in the northern district of Fröttmaning set to open at the start of the following season, the 6-3 demolition of *Der Club* provided the perfect showcase finale for the veritable old Olympiastadion. Bayern were five goals ahead by half-time, and their final total would come courtesy of braces from Roy Makaay and Sebastian Deisler, with further strikes from Claudio Pizarro and Michael Ballack. Although FCN's Samuel Slovák blotted the Bayern copybook slightly with two consolation strikes in the final ten minutes, it had been an afternoon of celebration for the crowd of sixty-three thousand.

The title had long been won, but a 3-1 victory against third-placed Stuttgart was the perfect way to round off Bayern's fine finish to the season. In the end, it had been something of a breeze. *Crisis? What crisis?*

	P	W	D	L	Goals	GD	Pts
FC Bayern München	34	24	5	5	75:33	+42	77
FC Schalke 04	34	20	3	11	56:46	+10	63
SV Werder Bremen	34	18	5	11	68:37	+31	59

After the shaky beginning, Bayern's spectacular sprint to the title had been the ultimate vindication for the new coach. Despite the talk of an overly harsh training ground regime, the outstanding run in to the title offered clear proof that Magath's methods worked. With the *Meisterschale* back in its rightful place in the display cabinet at the Säbenerstraße, both the Bayern board and the fans were happy again.

Having led Bayern to the title in his first season in charge, Felix Magath would make it a domestic double with victory in the DFB-Pokal – with Schalke 04 once again the victims. The run to the final had started against non-league TSV Völpke who were subjected to a six-goal thrashing, and a tight 3-2 win against VfL Osnabrück would be the last time Bayern were tested en route to the final in Berlin. A 3-0 win over VfB Stuttgart was followed by a glorious seven goals against a hapless SC Freiburg, with Claudio Pizarro finding the net four times, and a semi-final in Bielefeld against Arminia saw *Die Roten* score a goal in either half to book their place in Berlin.

I once again missed out on Bayern's cup run, finding myself "watching" the final on Kicker Online and constantly refreshing the live page for updates. While this would never come close to actually watching a match, it was a whole lot better than waiting until afterwards for the post-match report. Bayern had taken the lead three minutes before half-time through Roy Makaay, but their opponents managed to get the equaliser just before half-time. After Aílton had been felled in the box by Willy Sagnol, Lincoln slotted the ball past Kahn to level things up.

Matches between Bayern and Schalke had produced a number of memorable encounters, many of which had included more than a little controversy, and the 2005 final was no different. With just fourteen minutes left Makaay set up Salihamidžić, whose shot beat Frank Rost to give Bayern the lead. The Schalke players raised their arms in protest, only to see referee Florian Meyer point to the centre circle. The Bosnian had been well offside, but the goal would prove to be decisive.

Having achieved home and away victories over Bayern during the Bundesliga campaign, Schalke had clearly fancied their chances of wresting the Pokal from the Bavarians – only for the infamous *Bayern-Dusel* to strike again. Makaay's disputed winning goal was just one more kick in the guts for the men from Gelsenkirchen, and yet another chapter in the ongoing rivalry between the two sides.

Bayern had secured their twelfth cup win and with it their fifth domestic double, and as far as domestic results were concerned Magath's first year in charge had been a triumph. Together with the pre-season *Ligapokal*, the new coach had three domestic trophies safely locked away.

Bayern had cleaned up all available trophies at home, but in Europe things were a little more testing. While the team may have been dominant domestically, they would once again show that they were not quite up there with Europe's élite. Magath's side had in the end done well to reach the last eight, but at no time did they really threaten to set the tournament alight.

Drawn alongside Juventus, Ajax and Israeli champions Maccabi Tel Aviv in the group stage, Bayern would start the campaign with a hard-earned 1-0 win in Israel, with a Roy Makaay penalty separating the two sides. A more impressive display against Ajax then followed, with the Dutch side being put to the sword by their countryman Makaay who effectively settled the match himself with a hat-trick twenty-three minutes either side of half-time. Zé Roberto then added a fourth to cap off an impressive evening at the Olympiastadion.

For a fleeting moment one might have thought that things had really taken off, but the truth was that Bayern were not as good as Ajax were dreadfully bad – as the rest of the group fixtures would prove.

The first real test for Magath's men came in the double-header against two-time European Champions Juventus, and the first of the two meetings in Turin had been encouraging enough, with Bayern looking just as good as the home side in front of a paltry crowd of just under twenty thousand. Curiously, this was the first meeting between the two teams in the long history of the tournament.

The Bavarians had been looking good for at least a point to take back to Germany, but with fifteen minutes remaining a long punt forward by Frenchman Lilian Thuram caught the red-shirted defence off their guard. Czech midfielder Pavel Nedvěd calmly collected Zlatan Ibrahimović's well-weighted pass, before slotting the ball past Oliver Kahn to break the deadlock.

Juve's opener provided the spark for a rousing riposte from the visitors, but for all their efforts Bayern were unable to get back into the game. Bastian Schweinsteiger saw a well-struck effort brilliantly saved by Gianluigi Buffon in the Juve goal, while Makaay shot straight at the 'keeper, substitute Vahid Hashemian mis-timed a headed effort and an unmarked Hasan Salihamidžić headed wide of the target. When yet another Makaay effort was blocked with just minutes remaining, it was always going to be Juve's night.

The return at the Olympiastadion two weeks later saw Bayern show the same symptoms that had plagued previous European campaigns – their inability to convert possession and chances into goals. In what was a frustrating November evening in the Bavarian capital, Magath's side had dominated proceedings for the entire match, only to fall to the ultimate sucker punch right at the death.

Everything had conspired to deny Bayern. Schweinsteiger had rattled the crossbar with less than a quarter of an hour gone, and numerous opportunities went begging as Buffon found himself working overtime to keep the Bavarian attack at bay. Meanwhile, strikers Pizarro and Makaay had done everything but put the ball in the back of the Juventus net. When Makaay saw his header tipped over the bar by Buffon with just over a minute of normal time remaining, I would start to get that all too familiar feeling.

As the match approached the end of the ninety minutes, Ibrahimović squeezed in a rare shot on the Bayern goal, and with Kahn only managing to parry the Swede's effort Alessandro del Piero was on hand to stab the ball into the unguarded net from less than five yards. Juve's winner was not a fatal blow in the context of the tournament as a whole, but had been a real confidence-shatterer.

The unlucky Makaay would almost carve out an equaliser in stoppage time, but once again Bayern had ended up with nothing to show for all their efforts. *Die Roten* had managed to fire eighteen shots at the Juventus goal against their opponents' eight, but it was the Italians who had snatched the points, to storm to the top of the table with four wins from four. Bayern meanwhile were left sitting back on six points, three ahead of both Ajax and Maccabi.

A crowd of forty-five thousand at the Olympiastadion would see Bayern entertain the Israeli champions, and having gone more than three hours without scoring they took just twelve minutes to get on the scoresheet through Pizarro. A seven-minute burst saw Salihamidžić and Frings effectively settle the match before half-time, and although Maccabi pulled a goal back from the penalty spot, a late brace from Makaay rounded off the scoring to secure a crushing 5-1 win. Bayern were now on nine points from their five games, and with Ajax losing in Turin the Bavarians were safely through to the knock-out phase with just the game in Amsterdam to come.

With a place in the last sixteen assured, Bayern could afford to relax a little against the Dutch champions, who themselves would be chasing third place and a berth in the UEFA Cup. In an exciting and open encounter, Makaay opened the scoring on nine minutes, only for Czech Tomáš Galásek to level the scores with a deflected shot seven minutes from half-time. Romanian winger Nicolae Mitae would put *de Godenzonen* in front four minutes after the hour mark with a well-taken effort, but Michael Ballack rose unchallenged twelve minutes from time to get on the end of Zé Roberto cross to give the *Die Roten* a share of the spoils. In the end the result mattered little to either side: Bayern were already secure in second spot behind Juventus with ten points from their six matches, and Ajax would pip Maccabi for third place.

In the first knockout round Bayern were drawn against Arsenal, who had topped their group ahead of PSV Eindhoven, Panathinaikos and Rosenborg BK. The Premier League side had been favourites going into the match, but at the Olympiastadion Magath's side produced one of their better performances of the season to carve out a dominant 3-1 win.

The teams had emerged from the tunnel at the Olympiastadion with Arsenal looking more like the home side in their famous red and white strip, while Bayern were kitted out in their special Champions League *Trikot* – all black with dark red trim. There was an additional twist to the encounter, with Bayern 'keeper Oliver Kahn up against his rival for the number one spot in the German national side, Jens Lehmann.

It was the Bayern 'keeper who would have the first laugh, with not even five minutes on the clock. Having collected the ball after an Arsenal attack had broken down, Kahn launched the ball deep into the opposition half. Defender Kolo Touré managed to get his head to it, but only succeeded in knocking it towards his own goal as Claudio Pizarro accelerated outside him. With Lehmann in no-man's land and the red-shirted defence completely helpless, the Peruvian nonchalantly swept the ball into the net on the volley with his left foot.

Arsenal would have a couple of half-chances to level things up before half-time, but Bayern were more than good value for their lead at the break. Having failed to impress during the group phase of the competition, there was more than a glimmer of hope that Magath's side might be able offer a little bit more on the bigger European stage.

Despite Bayern's narrow advantage I had a good feeling about this game, and was proved correct thirteen minutes into the second half when *Die Roten* scored their second. Two minutes after Lehmann had tipped a Makaay effort over the crossbar and Salihamidžić had found the side netting, Pizarro escaped his marker – again, the unfortunate Touré – and found the back of the net with a close-range header. The gloves were well and truly off now, and just six minutes later Torsten Frings charged down the left, sending in a cross that floated over the helpless Lehmann towards Salihamidžić at the far post. This time the Bosnian made no mistake, sweeping the ball into the net with his left foot to make it three.

Six minutes later Bayern should have been four in front, but Frings would scuff his shot wide with the goal at his mercy.

All that remained now was for Magath's side to close out the game to take a clean sheet to Highbury for the second leg, but once again a lapse right at the end saw the Gunners grab the smallest of lifelines. It was like a game of pinball in the Bayern box: Vieira hit the far post after neatly collecting a ball looped over the Bayern defence, and when the men in black would fail to clear, none other than Touré was on hand to find the back of the net with a well-struck shot.

Arsenal's late goal in Munich had left the tie perfectly balanced. With the home side needing to win 2-0 to claim the tie on away goals, the plan for Bayern was simple: avoid conceding an early goal, and look to strike on the counterattack. An injury to leading scorer Makaay saw Peruvian Paolo Guerrero brought into the starting lineup, and Sebastian Deisler was brough in to replace the injured Torsten Frings.

Bayern would start well enough with both sides playing carefully, but had to endure their first torrid spell in the last five minutes before half-time. Arsenal captain Vieira had a shot blocked, and not long afterwards Thierry Henry, and ever-present danger, was foiled by Oliver Kahn. Bayern started the second half well and had managed to make it past the hour mark with the score still goalless, but on sixty-six minutes the door was finally prised open by Henry, who collected a long ball from Ashley Cole with nonchalant ease before slotting it past Kahn with perfect precision from the tightest of angles. Suddenly, the game was on and everything was back in the balance again.

Arsenal would have just over twenty minutes to score the vital second and Bayern could not afford any more mistakes, but they looked solid. With the game starting to open up, captain Ballack engineered Bayern's best chance of the match. Jinking towards the edge of the box, the Bayern number thirteen steadied himself before launching the ball towards the Arsenal goal, only to see Lehmann pull off a stunning save to deny him.

As a result of Bayern's solid defensive play and ball retention, the pressure from the home side would never really come: in all, Arsenal would have only three shots on target in the entire ninety minutes. Despite missing the firepower of Makaay and the midfield strength of Frings, Magath's side had made it through to the last eight for the first time in three years.

Awaiting *Die Roten* in the quarter-finals would be another English club, Chelsea.

The first leg in the first week of April 2005 would see the two sides meet at Stamford Bridge, with the Bavarians having to field a weakened starting eleven without striker Makaay and Pizarro. Right up against it from the start, Bayern suffered a vicious slice of bad luck with not even five minutes on the clock, as Joe Cole's speculative long-range effort took a nasty deflection off Lúcio before spinning past the helpless Oliver Kahn to give the home side the lead.

Both sides created opportunities before half-time, and despite falling behind early on Bayern continued to press in the opposition half. Owen Hargreaves had a shot blocked by John Terry, and Zé Roberto took advantage of a defensive lapse by Glen Johnson before pulling a shot wide of the post from seven yards out. With the game being played in a congested midfield, the play was littered with mistimed tackles and free-kicks.

Chelsea started the second half strongly, but the replacement of Hasan Salihamidžić with youngster Bastian Schweinsteiger would prove to be the perfect move by the coach. Within seven minutes of his arrival, the twenty year old Schweinsteiger was on hand to tuck the ball smartly under 'keeper Petr Čech after the Czech international had done well to parry Zé's stinging shot from the edge of the box. With the game closing in on the hour mark with the score at 1-1, Magath's side found themselves in pole position.

Unfortunately for Bayern, the equaliser proved to be the catalyst for José Mourinho's side to slip into second gear. Right on the hour Frank Lampard restored the Blues' lead with a low drive from the edge of the penalty area after another long punt forward had caught out the static black-shirted defence, and roared on by the Stamford Bridge faithful Chelsea kept one foot on Bayern's throat and the other firmly on the accelerator. Chances came aplenty: Damien Duff shot wide before forcing Kahn into a fine diving save, and moments later substitute Robert Huth headed narrowly wide of the target.

Chelsea were looking good for a third goal, and it was a matter of when rather than if. When it finally came, it was a beauty: that man Lampard again, this time collecting a right-wing cross from Claude Makélélé on his chest before turning on a sixpence and striking a fantastic left-footed volley past Kahn.

Magath responded by sending on Mehmet Scholl for the tiring Zé, but there was little Bayern could do to stem the flow of one-way traffic. As *Die Roten* continued to flounder, the Blues created more opportunities. It was now a simple matter of shutting up shop to prevent a complete meltdown, but there was no stopping the relentless blue wave. Chelsea's fourth goal came with nine minutes remaining, as Didier Drogba slammed the ball into the Bayern net after Kahn had barely managed to keep out Icelandic striker Eiður Guðjohnsen's goalbound effort.

With the score at 4-1 Bayern were staring elimination straight in the face, but from quite literally nowhere managed to grasp a potential lifeline. Three minutes into added time, Ballack went down easily in the box to a Ricardo Carvalho challenge, and perhaps more out of sympathy that anything else Dutch referee René Temmink pointed to the penalty spot. Ballack would get up and dust himself down before drilling the *Elfmeter* low inside the right upright – and at 4-2 Magath's side had given themselves more than an outside chance of turning things around at the Olympiastadion.

With Chelsea having dominated the second half the scoreline clearly had flattered the visitors, and while I could imagine Chelsea fans fuming at the soft penalty I was able to look forward to the second leg with at least a small morsel of hope.

The teams would meet again six days later at a packed Olympiastadion, with a crowd of fifty-nine thousand roaring the Bavarians on. With the strike force of Makaay and Pizarro both fit again Bayern would have a lot more firepower up front, and with the home crowd behind them they started confidently.

In the opening twenty minutes the home side were well on top, but try as they might they were unable to get that crucial early goal to put the pressure right back on their opponents. Ballack had a shot blocked by John Terry, Pizarro shot across the 'keeper and wide of the target, Schweinsteiger sent the ball wide from the edge of the box, and Makaay also saw a goalbound effort blocked by a man in a blue shirt.

The frustration and not being able to get the breakthrough was compounded on the half-hour mark, as the combination of bad luck and Lúcio's foot conspired to give the visitors an undeserved lead. Bayern's first leg tormentor Frank Lampard collected the ball from Joe Cole at the edge of the area before firing in a shot that was expertly backheeled past Kahn by the unfortunate Brazilian centre-half. Bayern now needed three goals to progress.

The visitors would take their lead into the half-time break, but not before Schweinsteiger had forced Čech into a fine diving save and Ballack had fluffed two excellent opportunities to drag his team back into the tie. The first saw him play a pass across goal when a shot at goal would have been the better option, and the second saw him send the ball harmlessly over the crossbar.

It just looked as though it was going to turn into yet another one of those evenings – though this time with added poignancy with it potentially being the last European match to be played at the Olympistadion.

The opening minutes of the second half saw Kahn deny Drogba with a fine save, and with Bayern now having to chase the game there were more opportunities for both sides. Twenty minutes into the second half, Ballack saw his well-time effort strike the post – and miracle of miracles Pizarro was right on hand to bundle the rebound into the Chelsea net.

At 1-1 Bayern still needed two more goals, but that small flickering flame of home had been reignited once more. Another quick goal, and there was everything to play for.

Energised by their equaliser, Bayern were suddenly all over Chelsea like a black rash. Bixente Lizarazu's cross was deflected by Robert Huth onto the crossbar, and just moments later it was all hands to the pumps for the Blues as striker Guðjohnsen cleared Lúcio's well-directed header off the line. Determined to make up for his part in two of Chelsea's goals, the Brazilian had another effort, only to see the uniquitous Lampard get his body in the way to make the block.

The clearly unfit Makaay was replaced by Paolo Guerrero and left back Lizarazu made way for Hasan Salihamidžić as Magath looked to play his last hand, and with ten minutes remaining the busy Čech was called into action again to keep out a Schweinsteiger effort.

Bayern's high-risk focus on getting back into the game had left gaping holes in the defence however, and inevitably they were caught out by a real sucker punch. Joe Cole had chased the ball down the left and made his way towards the corner flag, and with the Bayern players expecting him to play for time the Chelsea midfielder unexpectedly clipped the ball back into the box. With the Bayern defence at sixes and sevens, the dangerous Drogba timed his arrival perfectly to send a well directed header into the bottom of the right side of the Bayern net to restore Chelsea's advantage.

In a stroke the tie was effectively over, leaving Bayern 2-1 down and just ten minutes away from making a sad and ignominious farewell to the old stadium. They had to score three more times to take the tie into extra time, but at that moment just the one goal to spare the crowd a final defeat at the Olympiastadion was enough to motivate the team. The tie had surely been lost, but there was still plenty of time to give the Olympiastadion the farewell it deserved.

Bastian Schweinsteiger's energy and youthful enthusiasm provided the impteus for the Bavarians' desperate final push, and with just seconds remaining the youngster collected a pass from Zé Roberto before sending it fizzing towards the Chelsea goal – where the fast-arriving Guerrero stabbed the ball past Petr Čech to level the scores at 2-2.

Every Bayern fan knew that two more goals in added time would have been touching the boundaries of the impossible, but the team tried all the same. In what would prove to be the last attacking move on a European football night at the Olympiastadion, Pizarro burst into the opposition box and all the way to the byline before cutting the ball back to substitute Mehmet Scholl, who made no mistake with his right foot.

Five minutes of additional time after the regulation ninety had already been played. Was there still time for a miracle?

Bayern now needed just one more goal to take the tie into extra time, but it was just too much to hope for. When Spanish referee Manuel Mejuto González blew the final whistle not long after the players had retrieved the ball from the Chelsea net and sprinted back to the centre circle for the restart, it brought to an end to what had been yet another story of heroic midweek failure at the Olympiastadion.

Magath's side had dominated the game and had created plenty of chances to win the tie, but their spurt had come just a little too late to deny their opponents a place in the last four. Bayern had racked up an astonishing twenty-two shots at goal compared to their opponents' seven, but would be left regretting the catalogue of missed opportunities.

The Bayern revival had come way too late to extend the tie, but the late goal at least meant that the final Champions League night at the Olympistadion had finished with a Bayern victory. Fittingly the winner was scored by Scholl, a long-established crowd favourite and one of the most successful players to play for the Munich club.

In all, 2004-2005 had been a successful season for FC Bayern München. Three domestic trophies and a battling quarter-final exit in the Champions League was a return that most coaches would have given their eyeteeth for, but the pressure remained firmly on Felix Magath to deliver the big one. In turn, the coach continued to turn the screw on the training ground.

QUALITÄT KOMMT VON QUÄLEN

Felix Magath had made his way to Munich from VfB Stuttgart in the summer of 2004 with a fast-growing reputation as a coach, but casting an almost constant shadow was the somewhat darker accusation of his being an excessive and even cruel taskmaster with his players – particularly on the training ground. At Bayern, Magath's methods were never going to be an issue so long as he was getting results; while there was the occasional media gossip, most of what was said about his training regime could best be described as background noise.

The former European Cup winner had turned around an ailing Werder Bremen and had taken VfB Stuttgart back to the right end of the Bundesliga table, and his first season in Munich had seen him take Bayern to a domestic treble; there was plenty of optimism at the Säbenerstraße ahead of the 2005-06 season, which would also see the team move to their new high-tech home in Fröttmaning with Munich's other side, TSV 1860.

Built with the 2006 World Cup in mind, the 66,000-seater Allianz Arena was truly unique. Designed by the Swiss firm Herzog and de Meuron, it was the first stadium in the world that could change colour outside – the result of an unique design feature consisting of nearly three thousand individually-lit ethylene tetrafluoroethylene foil panels inflated with dry air. From a distance, the stadium would look like a spectacular bowl of light made out of neatly-arranged padded bags; with each panel being individually lit a number of different patterns could be created, including the Bavarian lozenge flag using white and blue light. When the German national team were playing the stadium would be lit in bright white, when TSV 1860 were hosting matches the ground would be bathed in blue, and when FC Bayern were at home visitors would be greeted by what looked like a large red spaceship.

Located in the north of the city between the centre and the airport, the Allianz Arena was equipped with its own underground car park, a convenient exit off the Autobahn A9 and the dedicated Fröttmaning U-Bahn station on the U6 line connecting it to the city centre – just a fifteen-minute journey from the historic Marienplatz in the centre of the city. Unlike the old Olympiastadion with its 1970s-era facilities and wide athletics track that separated the crowd from the action on the pitch, the new ultra-modern stadium was designed to be a genuine temple of football.

As much as the old stadium might have been loved by many and provided a number of great moments in the history of FC Bayern München, the new ground was set to be the perfect home as the club looked towards a new era. The Allianz quickly became one of the best places to watch football in Germany, and all of the available season tickets were quickly snapped up.

There would be no big-name signings in Munich at the start of the 2005/06 season, as Magath looked to fill in weak areas and tighten up the squad. Veteran goalkeeper Bernd Dreher was re-drafted into the squad along with youth player Andreas Ottl, and promising defender Philipp Lahm returned to Munich after a loan spell at Stuttgart, where he had first come to prominence under the guidance of Magath.

The most significant signing ahead of the new season was Werder Bremen's French defender Valérien Ismaël who made his way south to Bavaria for €8.5 million, while the attack was bolstered with the acquisition of experienced Iranian international Ali Karimi from UAE outfit Al-Ahli for €4.8 million.

Meanwhile, a number of players headed for the exit. After a disappointing season in Bavaria Torsten Frings returned to Bremen for five million Euros – a €4.25 drop on the price Bayern had paid Borussia Dortmund a year earlier – while Vahid Hashemian, like Frings another single-season failure, headed north to Hannover 96 for just over half of the two million Euros it has cost to bring him to Munich from VfL Bochum. The clearout would also see Tobias Rau, signed in 2003 as a promising left-back from VfL Wolfsburg for €2.5 million, head to Arminia Bielefeld for a mere €750,000.

It was not just a matter of jettisoning the failures, however. Experienced duo Thomas Linke and Alexander Zickler – both Champions League winners in 2001 – would start to wind down their careers with a move across the border to Austrian side Red Bull Salzburg, while Robert Kovač and Sammy Kuffour, both out of contract, moved to Juventus and AS Roma respectively on free transfers. A larger than life figure who had spent a year short of a decade in Munich, the passionate Kuffour – who will always be remembered for his heart-rending emotional outburst after the 1999 Champions League final defeat – would be sorely missed by the Bayern faithful.

Bayern had won their last nine matches to storm to the title in 2004/05, and they continued in exactly the same vein at the start of 2005/06. Six wins on the trot would take them to a record fifteen wins on the bounce, and by the end of September Magath's side were four points clear of second placed Hamburger SV. The opening half a dozen victories included a stunning 5-2 win in Leverkusen where the fit-again Roy Makaay had helped himself to a stuning hat-trick, as well as three-goal triumphs over Borussia Mönchengladbach and Hertha Berlin.

The match against Borussia Mönchengladbach would be the team's first competitive encounter at the new Allianz Arena, with the opening goal being scored by Owen Hargreaves in the twenty-eighth minute. With two goals in four minutes at the end, the clinically lethal Makaay provided some additional gloss to the opening day celebrations.

The first big six-pointer of the season would take place on match day seven when Bayern headed north to unbeaten Hamburg, where the long winning streak finally came to an end. Dutchman Rafael van der Vaart had given *Die Rothosen* the lead after ten minutes, and former Bayern youth Piotr Trochowski would put things beyond doubt with Hamburg's second goal two minutes after the hour mark. HSV's 2-0 win would pull them up to within a single point of the Munich side, and with third-placed Werder Bremen also making ground on the leaders it was suddenly a little bit tighter at the top.

Things were quickly put back on track with a 2-0 win over Wolfsburg, but two dropped points in Gelsenkirchen against a battling Schalke 04 resulted in Bremen leapfrogging everybody to assume top spot ahead of Bayern on goal difference. With Wolfsburg winning in Hamburg the following week and ending the Hansestadt's unbeaten start, Schalke were the only unbeaten side in the league after match day nine.

Having been dislodged from the top Bayern responded in the best way possible, with a welcome run of five straight victories. In the middle of this run Magath's men notched up a crucial win against Bremen, recovering from the shock of going down with just thirty seconds on the clock to register a convincing 3-1 win that lifted them five points clear of *Die Grün-Weißen*.

2-1 wins in Bielefeld and at home to FSV Mainz were followed by a goalless encounter with mid-table draw specialists Stuttgart, where Bayern would spend more than half of the game with ten men following the dismissal of Sebastian Deisler for a roughhouse foul on Swiss defender Ludovic Magnin. The meeting at the Gottlieb-Daimler-Stadion would also see

Bayern meet old coach Giovanni Trapattoni, now in charge of the Swabians in his third stint as a Bundesliga coach.

With the end of the *Hinrunde* in sight after fifteen matches, Bayern were six points clear of Hamburg, with Bremen a further two points adrift in third place. Bayern's first seven matches at the Allianz had seen them stroll to a flawless hundred percent record with eighteen goals scored and just two conceded, and the final home game of 2005 would see *Die Roten* take on strugglers Kaiserslautern, then sitting right at the foot of the table with a miserable five points.

On form alone, one should have expected an easy win for Bayern. Magath's men had been beaten just once in two dozen Bundesliga games and the Red Devils' only win had come way back on match day two. However, Kaiserslautern were not just any other opponent; every time the two sides met one might as well have thrown the form book straight out of the window. FCK had over the years become a real bugbear for the Bavarians, and the meeting at the Allianz on a chilly early December afternoon was typical of the tough challenge always posed by the men from the Betzenberg.

Michael Ballack would get his head on the end of an Ali Karimi corner to give Bayern the lead after twenty-six minutes, but six minutes before half-time a battling Kaiserslautern had somehow worked their way back into the contest through Ivorian Boubacar Sanogo.

Nine minutes into the second half referee Manuel Gräfe pointed to the penalty spot after FCK defender Marco Engelhardt had felled Zé Roberto, and with Makaay making no mistake one might have thought that would have been the end of that. But like the proverbial scuttling bug that refuses to die after being treated with half a can of insect repellent, Kaiserslautern just kept on coming. Just four minutes after falling behind, Wolfgang Wolf's side would win a penalty of their own after a foul by Philipp Lahm on Halil Altıntop.

Albanian Ervin Skela stepped up to take the spot-kick, but his shot was weak and easily gathered by Oliver Kahn. The last half an hour was less than pretty as Bayern knuckled down to keep their lead against a stubborn opponent, and Magath was forced to tighten up the midfield to see things through to the final whistle. Kaiserslautern had shown plenty of spirit, but it was not enough to stop Bayern from extending their winning start at the Allianz to eight matches.

A comfortable 2-1 win in Dortmund saw *Die Roten* go into the *Winterpause* on forty-four points from their seventeen matches, a comfortable six points clear of Hamburg in second place. The football had not been particularly spectacular with an average of just over two goals a game, but once again Magath had produced results.

The resumption of the Bundesliga campaign in the last week of January 2006 saw Bayern pick up where they had left off before the break, with a Roy Makaay brace inspiring a 3-1 win over a flaccid Mönchengladbach side, and with Hamburg falling to only their second defeat in Nürnberg Magath's side would extend their lead at the top of the table to eight points.

A tight 1-0 win over mid-table Bayer Leverkusen extended Bayern's winning start at the Allianz to nine matches, and despite being held to a goalless draw in Berlin by Hertha, results elsewhere would see things remain the same with twenty matches played. Bavarian rivals Nürnberg had provided stiff resistance on their visit to Munich's new fortress in Fröttmaning, but once again the home side would do just about enough to claim all three points with a 2-1 win and move ten points clear at the top.

Matchday 22 saw Bayern travel to sixth-placed Hannover 96, a solid and well-drilled unit that came into the match on the back of a ten-game unbeaten run – albeit one that had included no fewer than six draws. Peter Neurerer's unfashionable team had been slowly but surely working their way up the table, and unsurprisingly the match quickly turned into a tactical affair. *Die Roten* had concentrated on attacking on the break and had created more opportunites in a goalless first half with goalkeeper Robert Enke the standout player for the home side, but just ten minutes into the second half Thomas Brdaric would give the team from Lower Saxony a surprise but not wholly undeserved lead.

Sparked into upping another gear, Bayern launched themselves at their opponents and created plenty of chances to equalise. A Claudio Pizarro header. What looked like a clear handball by Polish defender Dariusz Żuraw. A shot from substitute Mehmet Scholl that crashed against the post. Felix Magath was far more animated than usual, and there was a growing sense of frustration in the visitors' dugout.

As the clock ticked by a shock defeat was looking increasingly likely, but right at the death *Die Roten* deservedly levelled the scores. With what was surely their last attack, a right-wing cross from Willy Sagnol was met perfectly by Michael Ballack, who beat both Żuraw and Brazilian Vinícius Bergantin to head in the long-overdue equaliser. The hard-fought 1-1 draw also ensured that both Bayern and Hannover extended their unbeaten runs.

An emphatic 5-2 win over Eintracht Frankfurt inspired by braces from Ballack and Paolo Guerrero extended Bayern's winning run at the Allianz to eleven matches, but the Bavarian express would finally hit the buffers the following week against third-placed Hamburg.

Bayern were eleven points clear of Hamburg before the match at the Allianz, and not many commentators would have predicted that the gap wouldn't have been extended to fourteen by the end of the afternoon. *Die Rothosen*, however, had other ideas. In a snow-laden Munich, Thomas Doll's side played the perfect last-minute trick to bring an end to Bayern's spotless home record.

Die Roten were sluggish from the start, and it took just sixteen minutes for HSV to establish an early foothold through Guy Demel. It was a bizarre goal, with the Ivorian left-back finding plenty of space on the right inside the Bayern penalty area before sending the ball almost straight through Oliver Kahn at his near post. Whether it was a mishit cross or an audacious attempt to catch *Der Titan* off guard, it mattered little as the ball crashed into the back of the net. With the home side clearly struggling with the conditions and the falling snow, the crowd became increasingly impatient. Just before half-time, Hamburg almost doubled their advantage when a firm and low shot from Japanese international Naohiro Takahara narrowly skidded past the upright.

With Doll's side chasing and fighting hard for every ball, Bayern for the first time started to look genuinely vulnerable on their home turf – and the visitors' overly aggressive approach made matters even worse. Having replaced the disappointing Sebastian Deisler at the start of the second half, substitute Ali Karimi lasted just fifteen minutes until he himself was replaced by Mehmet Scholl, and Hamburg racked up a series of yellow cards as they continued to resort to the worst tactics to keep *Die Roten* at bay.

With seven minutes remaining, it was that man Scholl who hauled Bayern back into the contest. Straight from a quick throw-in from Michael Ballack, the number seven made perfect contact on the half-volley to send the ball low into the left-hand side of the Hamburg net. Goalkeeper Stefan Wächter had no chance, and having been a distant second best for most of the afternoon Magath's side looked to have rescued a face-saving draw out of nothing.

Rather than settle for what would have been a hard-earned and arguably undeserved point, Magath's side went all out for all three. The momentum should have been with the home side, but as the game turned its final corner it was the visitors looking far more dangerous.

The warning signs were already there when the dangerous Takahara headed straight at Kahn when he should have done better, and there was a grim sense of foreboding when Iranian Mehdi Mahdavikia stepped up to take what looked like an innocuous looking free-kick from out on the right touchline with just over a minute remaining. The ball was floated into the Bayern penalty area and over Willy Sagnol to find Dutchman Nigel de Jong, who rose above a static Valérien Ismaël to head the ball past Kahn and secure Hamburg's first win in Munich for twenty-four years. De Jong's late winner also secured a season double over Bayern for Doll's men, who closed the gap between the two teams to eight points.

Bayern's advantage at the top was trimmed further to six points as they were held to a goalless draw at the Volkswagen-Arena by a typically gritty Wolfsburg, but a 3-0 win over Schalke would get things back on track at the Allianz. *Die Knappen* had managed to keep things clean until half-time, but an early second-half header from Hasan Salihamidžić helped settle the nerves of the home crowd. Claudio Pizarro doubled the lead just eight minutes later, and Roy Makaay – on as a second half substitute – provided some additional gloss a minute from the end.

A 3-1 win against relegation-threatened MSV Duisburg coupled with a surprise home defeat for Hamburg at the hands of Borussia Dortmund saw Bayern stretch their lead at the top to a massive nine points, and the Bavarians would be thankful for the gap as they staggered towards the finish line. Two points dropped at home against Köln and a resounding three-goal beating at the hands of Werder Bremen at the Weserstadion saw Bayern's advantage dramatically cut to just four points.

With four matches remaining everything was back in the balance, but a bizarre end to the season would see Bayern stumble rather than saunter to the title. Magath's side would win only one of their remaining four games and collect six of the available twelve points on offer, but their rivals would fail to take advantage.

While Bayern were coming from two goals behind to scrape a 2-2 draw against struggling Mainz, Hamburg blew their chance to narrow the gap with a two-goal defeat at home to Bayer Leverkusen. A victory would have seen HSV close to within two points of Bayern's lead, but their second defeat in three games at the Volksparkstadion only served to widen the gap even further. A 3-1 win for Bayern against Stuttgart at the Allianz would more or less settle matters as they maintained their five-point lead with just two fixtures remaining, and from that point on it was always going to be a matter of when Bayern would claim the *Meisterschale* rather than if.

The game that clinched the title wasn't exactly one to note in the memory, an otherwise forgettable encounter in Kaiserslautern that once again saw *Die Roten* come from behind to grab another draw. With Bayern a goal down and Hamburg leading 2-1 in Berlin against Hertha Berlin at half-time things had been looking more than a little shaky, but Andreas Ottl's sixty-eighth minute equaliser together with a spectacular three-goal Hertha comeback put an end to Hamburg's chances.

Hamburg had done their level best to hand the title to a stuttering Bayern side, and the season would end on a particularly miserable note for *Die Rothosen* with a 2-1 home defeat at the hands of Werder Bremen, who slipped past the northern rivals into second place.

In the end, Bayern had clinched their twentieth Bundesliga title – and a fourth star on their shirt – by finishing five points ahead of Bremen. *Die Roten* had only suffered three defeats all season, but as a supporter there had been nothing there to fire my enthusiasm. The stark truth was that a fairly ordinary Bayern team had managed to finish top dogs in what had been a poor competition.

Magath would make it two domestic doubles in his first two seasons with victory in the DFB-Pokal, where a solid if not necessarily memorable path to the final in Berlin was finished off with Claudio Pizarro's fifty-ninth minute header in an uninspiring 1-0 win over Eintracht Frankfurt.

The cup campaign had got off to a perfunctory start with a four-goal thrashing of non-league MSV 1919 Neuruppin, but a scrappy 1-0 win against second-tier outfit Erzgebirge Aue – settled only by a Ballack goal ten minutes from time – preceded uncomfortably tight extra-time wins over Hamburg and Mainz where Magath's men were just about able to scrape past their opponents.

While the third round match at the Allianz against HSV was a dour and frankly forgettable affair, settled seven minutes before the end of extra time by Owen Hargreaves, the quarter-final against Mainz showed just how close Bayern had flirted with disaster.

Having taken the lead with a Mohamed Zidan penalty after twenty-one minutes, Mainz managed to keep out everything that Bayern threw at them off until nine minutes from time, when Claudio Pizarro finally gave the home crowd something to cheer about. Bayern would then take the lead through Paolo Guerrero only to be pegged back again, and with a penalty shootout looming Pizarro popped up three minutes before the end of extra time to seal a dramatic 3-2 victory, once again eliciting mentions of the *Bayern-Dusel*.

Perhaps Bayern's most impressive showing – on the scoreboard at least - would come in the semi-final against second division St. Pauli at a packed Millerntor, but even then the result was at best flattering. Having taken the lead after a quarter of an hour Bayern absorbed plenty of pressure from the home side before finishing things off in the last six minutes with two clinical Pizarro strikes.

With the opposition not being particularly testing and the performances largely uninspiring, not many people will remember the 2005-06 season. To every other club in the Bundesliga a domestic double would have been something to write about in the history books, but for Bayern supporters the almost blind stumble to the Bundesliga title had been far easier than it should have been.

Clearly, a bigger challenge was needed. Thirty-three league and cup titles were all well and good, but what we all really wanted was the big one – the Champions League.

Sadly here, once again, Bayern would be found wanting.

The opening group phase of the 2005-06 Champions League pitted Bayern in a winnable group alongside Italians Juventus, Austrian champions Rapid Wien and Belgians Club Brügge.

The opening fixture in Vienna was a typically solid performance from Magath's men: *Die Roten* offered nothing special at the Praterstadion, with a Paolo Guerrero goal on the hour mark enough to secure all three points. The first European contest at the Allianz Arena a fortnight later saw another workmanlike performance and the same scoreline, with Martin Demichelis's strike enough to dispose of the Belgian champions and maintain Bayern's one-hundred percent record in the competition.

Juventus had given Bayern nightmares during their previous Champions League meetings, but this time things were little more balanced. Magath's side had looked ordinary during their opening two games against arguably lesser opposition, but would save their most impressive display for the first of what was hard-fought double header against the old lady from Turin. Two first-half goals in the space of seven minutes from Sebastian Deisler and Demichelis would put Bayern comfortably in front, and although Zlatan Ibrahimović blotted Oliver Kahn's copybook right at the end the home side did enough to move clear at the top of the group with a maximum nine points.

Juventus would turn the tables on the Bavarians in Turin, but unlike the game at the Allianz Bayern were unlucky not to make their way back to Germany with at least a point. After a cagey first hour Frenchman David Trezeguet had opened the scoring for the Italians, but just four minutes later the impressive Sebastian Deisler evened things up. Juve would once again wait until the end before landing the killer blow to take all three points and sneak to the top of the table on goal difference, with Trezeguet finishing things off in the eighty-fifth minute.

Match day five saw Bayern really click into gear, as Rapid were put the sword at the Allianz. The in-form Deisler opened the scoring just past the twenty-minute mark, and an early second half strike from Karimi allowed Magath's side to relax. With the hapless Austrians starting to fall apart, a two-goal salvo from Makaay completed a wholly satisfactory 4-0 rout. With Juve beating Brügge 1-0 with a late goal, Bayern edged back to the top - securing a spot in the knock-out stage.

Bayern made the journey to the Belgian capital on match day six knowing that a win would almost certainly see them top the group and avoid a tough second-round draw, and they got off to the perfect start after just twenty-one minutes. Pizarro would put Magath's side on front and set them on their way at the Jean Breydel Stadium after getting on the end of a free-kick floated into the box by Deisler, but a determined home side playing for little more than pride quickly established a foothold as they clawed themselves back into the contest. Bayern's lead lasted only eleven minutes, with Spaniard Javier Portillo levelling the scores.

Juventus meanwhile had strolled to an easy 3-1 win in Vienna, leaving Bayern in second place in the group table. The draw for the first knockout round saw Bayern thrown together with a familiar foe: AC Milan.

Milan had for a long time held the whip hand over the Bavarians, and when the two teams met in the early spring of 2006 things wouldn't change that much. Once again, it would be a case of Bayern flattering to deceive at home before collapsing in a dazed and confused heap in northern Italy; in other words, just one more chapter in what had become a miserable long-running story.

Bayern had got off to the perfect start in their new stadium with three wins out of three in the group phase, and this winning run looked set to continue against their illustrious Italian visitors with an inspired first half performance in front of a capacity 66,000 crowd. Kitted out in a traditional-looking all-red ensemble, the hosts shot straight out of the traps, and for the first quarter of an hour Milan were firmly on the back foot. Pizarro had a shot blocked, Ballack headed a hard chance over the crossbar, and both Willy Sagnol and Lúcio created half-chances before Milan had even offered a threat in front of the Bayern goal – staffed by youngster Michael Rensing in place of the injured Olli Kahn.

With twenty-three minutes played, Bayern's relentless pressure on the Milan goal paid off with a moment of pure brilliance – the sort of moment that could only be produced by Michael Ballack. A long and high looping ball was played up the field towards the Milan box, and when Alberto Gilardino failed to clear Ballack, in plenty of space and with more than enough time, brought the ball under control with his left foot. Turning towards goal, the Bayern number thirteen lashed it on the half volley, his perfectly-timed shot curling deliciously past the desperate outstretched left arm of 'keeper Dida and into the right-hand side of the net.

It was one of those sublime moments you could watch again and again without ever getting tired of it.

The Allianz was really rocking following Ballack's spectacular strike, and Bayern continued to press as the enthusiastic sea of red and white upped the ante. Just two minutes later Makaay got on the end of another perfect long pass to stab the ball just inside the left post, but this time Dida was more than equal to it, diving low to his right to make an excellent save. With their opponents finding it difficult to even get a foothold in the contest, Magath knew that his team had to take advantage and score a second.

The visitors would start the second half with more confidence than they had finished the first, but it was a typical moment of misfortune for *Die Roten* that allowed the Italian side to get themselves back into the contest. Serghino's low cross from the left struck Valérien Ismaël full on the arm, leaving the Belgian referee with no option but to award the penalty. Ukrainian Andriy Shevchenko calmly rolled the ball to Rensing's left, sending him the wrong way. It was yet another tale of European woe for Bayern: once again they had dominated the game, once again they had failed to capitalise on their dominance, and not for the first time they had let their opponents back into the contest. In truth, it could and arguably should have been over long before half-time.

The remainder of the second half saw things dramatically turned on their head, as Milan – with a crucial away goal safely in the bag – started to play with a lot more confidence. The style and swagger that had defined Bayern's approach in the first half had long disappeared, and when Gilardino threatened to give his side the lead the tension in the Allianz Arena was palpable.

Even the impressive Dida being carried off injured in the sixty-ninth minute couldn't swing the momentum back to the *Münch'ner*. For all Bayern's huffing and puffing, substitute 'keeper Zeljko Kalac didn't even need to make a save.

After the brilliant start and Ballack's even more brilliant goal, Bayern had once again failed to deliver when it really mattered. They were simply unable to kill off an opponent that had looked like a bag of nerves for most of the first half, and would pay the price as soon as they took their foot off the pedal. What made things even more annoying was that the opponent was AC Milan – a team that over the years had been the cause of so much grief to every FC Bayern supporter. For some curious reason, there had always been some mental block when playing them.

Oliver Kahn was back between the sticks for the second leg at the San Siro, and Bayern went into the game knowing that they simply had to score to keep their hopes alive. They couldn't have got off to a worse start however, as with just eight minutes gone Serghino's left-wing cross was met at the far post by Filippo Inzaghi, who sneaked in front of the ball-watching Bayern defence to send an angled header across Kahn and into the left-hand corner of the net.

Despite going a goal behind even before they had a chance to settle, the overall equation hadn't changed. Magath's side could no longer win the tie with just the one goal, but could take things into extra time. Unlike in the first leg however, Milan were the team upping the ante – and looking more than dangerous with it. Kaká had a shot blocked, Austrian Johann Vogel sent a well-struck volley just past the post, and it took the gold-shirted Bavarians over a quarter of an hour just to put together their first attack.

However just as Bayern thought they might be starting to get a foothold, the unfortunate Ismaël was again punished in the box by the referee. This time the Frenchman was penalised for a foul on the ubiquitous Inzaghi, and as in the first leg Shevchenko stepped up to take the kick. Kahn dived to his right but was unable to get a hand on the ball, but to every Bayern supporter's relief the Ukrainian's skiddy effort rolled narrowly wide of the upright.

One might have thought that Bayern had finally got a break, but any such enthusiasm was dampened just moments later as Shevchenko made almost immediate amends for his missed penalty. A swift break down the right, a perfect cross from Dutchman Jaap Stam, and a well directed near-post header that seemed to surprise Kahn before finding its way into the bottom left-hand corner of the net. Two goals adrift, it was surely beyond Bayern now.

Milan were moving like a well-oiled machine, Bayern coach Felix Magath was standing expressionless on the touchline, and on my sofa at home I was already resigned to witnessing yet another disappointing European exit.

Bayern had already dodged a bullet with Shevchenko's penalty miss, and ten minutes from half-time were given an unexpected lifeline. Having done next to nothing for most of the opening period, a foul on Willy Sagnol by Vogel resulted in a free-kick to the Bavarians.

Bastian Schweinsteiger's effort was low and on target but not massively testing, yet Dida managed to make a complete hash of it, clumsily palming the ball into the path of the fast advancing Ismaël. Making up for his earlier mistake, the central defender easily stroked the ball home to bring Bayern back into the contest.

At 2-1 Bayern needed a second away goal to progress, but the feeling seemed to be one of desperate hope rather than expectation. Ismaël's goal had come completely against the run of play, and there was no real indication that it was going act as a springboard to turn the game around.

The first half finished more positively for the visitors and the start of the second saw the disappointing Makaay replaced by Paolo Guerrero, but almost immediately another defensive calamity resulted in the Italians restoring their two-goal cushion. Serghino's low left-wing cross should have been easily dealt with, but between them Ismaël and Bixente Lizarazu conspired to lay things on a plate for Inzaghi who gleefully nodded in his second from right on the goal line.

It was all Milan now, and to rub salt into the already gaping Bavarian wound a fast break just before the hour mark saw the *Rossoneri* sweep up the length of the pitch. The move was finished emphatically by Brazilian star Kaká, who charged in on the Bayern goal before launching a thunderous right-footed shot that flew over Kahn and into the roof of the Bayern net.

4-1, game over.

Magath's men continued to throw themselves forward in search of what would have been a miracle, but there was to be no consolation. Pizarro had a shot blocked from point-blank range by Dida and further half-chances would fall to Lúcio, Guerrero and Ballack, but the door had been well and trult bolted shut. The 4-1 defeat closed the book on yet another failed Champions League campaign, but perhaps more pointedly the nature of the loss had shown the real gulf in quality between the Bundesliga and the rest of Europe. There could be no complaints about the result.

Bayern would of course go on achieve the domestic double; their conquerors from Milan would advance to the semi-finals, where they were beaten 1-0 on aggregate by eventual champions Barcelona.

Felix Magath had taken FC Bayern to back to back domestic doubles – the first time this feat had been achieved in the long history of German football – yet the feeling in Munich was far from happy. The club had failed to impress in their two Champions League campaigns, and many supporters had been left unimpressed at the gulf between a Bayern team that was head and shoulders above the rest of the pack in Germany while remaining a considerable distance behind their rivals in the rest of Europe. Yet, this was just part of what was a growing sense of discontent in the Bavarian capital.

Magath had clearly delivered in his promise to bring trophies to the Säbenerstraße, but with it he also brought an atmosphere that had quickly started to descend like a dark cloud coming out of the Bavarian Alps. While previous Bayern coaches had cultivated good relationships with the press Magath often remained tight-lipped, and stories would soon begin to emerge about training group exercises, regimented calisthenics and gruelling runs up steep mountain trails.

The coach's almost militaristic attitude to training and condition was no great secret: Norwegian striker Jan Åge Fjørtoft had made his infamous remark to describe Magath's regime at Eintracht Frankfurt, suggesting that the coach might not have been able to save the Titanic, "but at least all the survivors would have been fit". Elsewhere, he was known as "Saddam", *der letzte Diktator in Europa* – "the last dictator in Europe" – and "Quälix", a portmanteau of his christian name and *quälen*, the German word for torture. Magath had never said it himself, but a phrase often used to describe his methods was *Qualität kommt von quälen* ("Quality comes from torture").

Magath's no-nonsense and somewhat attritional style was more than sufficient to ensure domestic success, but would prove to be extremely limited against more sophisticated continental opposition – something that was never lost on the club's supporters, many of whom had been sceptical about his appointment in the first place. With nothing to say about the team's domestic form, the press spent much of the time digging around in search of juicy morsels – a situation that was not helped by the coach's generally uncooperative approach. Simply, Magath wanted to get on with the business of coaching; the press could be managed by somebody else.

With little much else to go on, the coach's methods again became a subject of interest for the press. Nobody had actually come out and said anything – that would come later in a series of revelations made by defender Philipp Lahm – but it soon became apparent that Magath's methods of motivating his players on the training ground were anything but orthodox. His approach stood in stark contrast to that practiced by *Nationaltrainer* Jürgen Klinsmann, and it must have been something of a training ground culture shock for many of the younger players. One day they would be invited to group therapy sessions and training routines that incorporated Klinsmann's holistic, new age techniques, only to return back to Munich and a wet field full of medicine balls.

In July 2006 Magath signed an extension to his original contract that would see him in Munich until the end of the 2007/08 season, and despite the discontented rumblings in the background nobody could have forseen him not seeing things through. However, when results started to go against him everything would slowly start to unravel.

THE RETURN OF DER GENERAL

The months before the start of Felix Magath's third season in Munich would see a number of significant changes to the squad, with a number of high-profile moves in and out of the Säbenerstraße. By far the biggest story would be the departure of Michael Ballack, who after four successful seasons at Bayern left Germany for Chelsea in the English Premier League on a free transfer. Accompanying Ballack on the way out was Paolo Guerrero (HSV, €2.5 million), Zé Roberto (Nacional Montevideo, free) and the retiring Jens Jeremies and Bixente Lizarazu.

There were three high-profile signings in the summer of 2006: World Cup hero and young player of the tournament Lukas Podolski made his way to Bavaria from Köln for €10 million, while Dutch midfield enforcer Mark van Bommel – the perfect replacement for the hard-working and gritty Jeremies – was signed from Barcelona for €6 million and Belgian central defender Daniel van Buyen was snared from northern rivals Hamburger SV for €8 million. Also joining the first-team squad were a number of youngsters from the FC Bayern II squad including Stephan Fürstner, Christian Lell and Stefan Maierhofer.

While the departure of Ballack would be a major blow, the promise offered by the young Podolski helped to soften the impact: the twenty-one year old had been one of the stars of the World Cup, and for many it was just a matter of time before he settled in and made a name for himself in Bavaria. Having secured back to back domestic doubles, Bayern fans were looking at Magath to deliver the big one: expectations once again were high - perhaps too high.

The first action of the season in the DFB-Ligapokal semi-final would see the Bavarians defeat Schalke 04 4-1 in a penalty shoot-out at the Allianz Arena after a 0-0 draw, but the final in Leipzig's Zentralstadion against Werder Bremen saw the northerners stroll to an easy win with goals either side of half-time from Ivan Klasnić. It would pretty much set the tone for the rest of the season.

The opening two Bundesliga matches against Borussia Dortmund at the Allianz and away at Bochum saw Magath's team collect all six points on offer, but a disappointing goalless draw at home to Nürnberg and 2-1 a defeat in Bielefeld would signal the beginning of a long and frustratingly inconsistent spell. Top flight new boys Alemannia Aachen put up a decent fight before losing 2-1, and although Bayern would return to winning ways with a 4-2 win over Hertha Berlin, they conceded three more goals and more crucial points against early pace-setters Werder Bremen. Yet despite losing three of their opening eight games Bayern would still only be four points off top spot: no one team had started particularly well.

The league table would have a strange look to it: All of the top six teams had lost at least twice, and the two unbeaten teams, Nürnberg and Eintracht Frankfurt, had only been able to fashion three wins between them. Bayern would move into second place by inflicting Eintracht's first defeat of the season at the Allianz and a comeback from two goals down rescued a point a week later at Schalke, but the gap of three points between Magath's side and leaders Bremen would stretch to six following a shocking home defeat at the hands of bottom side Hannover 96.

Bayern responded positively with three wins on the bounce, but even then results were deceptive and masked the nature of the performances. Magath's men would be 2-1 down in Leverkusen with just seven minutes remaining before scoring two late goals to grab all three points, and would also come from behind to claim 2-1 wins over VfB Stuttgart and HSV. This was then followed by a 1-1 draw – and two more dropped points – against strugglers Borussia Mönchengladbach. It was becoming increasingly difficult to predict what was going to happen next.

A 2-1 win over Energie Cottbus at the Allianz Arena in the penultimate game of the *Hinrunde* would take Magath's side back to within three points of the lead, and a resounding 4-0 thumping of basement side FSV Mainz 05 ensured that the first half of the season ended on a positive note. Having collected thirty-three points, Bayern would go into the *Winterpause* in third place, just three adrift of Bremen and a resurgent Schalke 04.

The second half of the season would start off with a ding-dong battle against mid-table Dortmund, with Bayern leading at half-time having gone behind, only to be undone by two Dortmund strikes in the space of two minutes just short of the hour mark. With Bremen and Schalke both winning the gap at the top opened up to six points, but little did we know that things in Munich would come to a head the following week against VfL Bochum – the game that would see the end of Felix Magath.

The goalless draw against the relegation-threatened Ruhr team coupled with wins for the top two resulted in Bayern dropping back down into fourth place, with eight points separating them from the summit. There was a clear sense of disappointment that rung around the ground, and both the team and the coach trudged off the pitch in the face of a barrage of jeers from the home supporters. The story would unfold in such a way as to bring back horrible memories of *FC Hollywood*: according to many reports, the tabloid *Bild* were quick to post the news of the coach's imminent demise, having been tipped off by none other than Franz Beckenbauer.

It was just a matter of time before the announcement was made officially, and Magath coolly went about his duties like a man preparing for the last rites. Having taken the team for Sunday morning training, he departed briefly for a haircut before returning to face the Bayern board for the final time. Magath was far from the only one to blame for the team's inconsistency, but the board would decide that he simply had to go.

German football had found itself in extremely good shape during the summer of 2006. The unexpected success of the national team during the World Cup on home soil had created a new-found enthusiasm for what was a young, dynamic and highly promising squad, and after years in the doldrums there was a definite feeling of optimism. The semi-final exit at the hands of old rivals Italy was a heartbreaking case of so near yet so far, but it was clear that a corner had been turned.

Despite initial reservations about his modern coaching techniques, airy-fairy views and transatlantic lifestyle, the team's success had generated massive support for *Nationaltrainer* Jürgen Klinsmann, who with his assistant Joachim Löw had almost single-handedly altered the perception of the *Nationalmannschaft* both in and ouside Germany.

During what would become known as the *Sommermärchen* ("A Summer's Tale"), German football was no longer seen as arrogant, stilted and brutish, but fast-paced, exciting, pleasant to watch and even fashionable. Suddenly, the German team was "cool", even in less receptive countries like England where old stereotypes had always been difficult to break down.

The success of Germany's third-place finish and what was in effect a vindication of Klinsmann's new-fangled methods would arguably be the worst possible outcome for more traditional coaches like Felix Magath. In the space of a couple of hazy and exciting summer months, the FC Bayern coach's old-school techniques had suddenly become outmoded; it is difficult to determine what might have been going through peoples' minds at the start of the 2006/07 season, but the sudden enthusiasm for Klinsmann's more exciting approach may well have dampened any of the lingering enthusiasm for the Magath regime in Munich. Having seen the national team play with total freedom, the last thing some supporters may have wanted to see was yet another unspectacular league and cup double. Magath may have collected trophies, but he was *boring*.

Magath's contract in Munich had been extended by a year to the end of the 2007/08 season, but one could feel that this had been little more than just the expected reward for what had been a successful first two years where he had ticked all the right boxes. There was no real enthusiasm or fanfare, and Karl-Heinz Rummenigge's official statement on the club website would say it all: "Both parties agree that one year is enough".

Despite his contract being extended there was a distinct feeling that Magath was little more than a dead man walking in Munich. While results went his way there would be no reason to dump him, but as soon as things started to get just a little unstuck the knives were quickly unsheathed and sharpened. Despite the success of the two previous seasons, the sense of discontent accelerated.

I was more than a little shocked on hearing the news of Felix Magath's dismissal, but on reflection there was a sense of inevitability about it all. Nevertheless, there appeared to be no obvious logic behind the decision: while things had not exactly been running to form Bayern were not completely out of the title race, and they had also made it through to the last sixteen of the Champions League unbeaten for the first time in five seasons. If anything, despite their inconsistent form in the Bundesliga the team had finally started to look more capable of taking on the best of the rest of the continent.

Of course, all of this doesn't take into account what could best be described as the *Klinsmann-Sommermärchen-Effekt*. Magath's old-fashioned training ground drill techniques were being scrutinised more closely than ever, and when results started to go against him his being jettisoned was effectively a *fait d'accompli*. Quite simply, the Bayern board had taken the first and arguably easiest opportunity to get rid of the coach. Magath was quickly ushered out of the door with the minimum of fuss, and denied the opportunity to set things right and get the league campaign back on course.

While one could accuse the board of being far too hasty in raising the axe, one also needs to look at the personality of the coach as well. Magath had never really been close to the team; as far as he was concerned they were professionals playing a professional sport, and it was not his job to be a parent as well as a coach. This remoteness would undoubtedly have a negative effect on some of the younger players, and one could look for example at Lukas Podolski, who had left his home city of Köln and what would have been a massive support network to move to a new club in an unfamiliar city.

Magath had proved to be an excellent coach when results were going his way, but as soon as things started to go awry it had become obvious to many at Bayern that he lacked the softer touch to encourage and work with the team in a manner that was geared to maintaining and building collective morale. Not that he would have tried anyway – it just wasn't his way of doing things.

Rather than take a young player under his wing, Magath would simply expect him to straighten his back, dust himself down and get on with things. For Magath, exercising tact and stretching his patience was tantamount to mollycoddling, and it was easy to see how some players could have taken things the wrong way.

The majority of the articles about Felix Magath paint a picture of a horrible little man, the "Quälix" of popular legend, German football's coaching folk demon. In fact, nothing can be further from the truth. Well read, intelligent and with an unappreciated sense of humour, Magath is the footballing equivalent of Marmite. If you "get" him, he'll get you, while if you choose not to understand him, he'll choose not to care. In the end, all of this theatre would just get too much for the players and, more crucially, the board.

With potential first-choice Klinsmann unavailable, the club immediately turned to a familiar face: Ottmar Hitzfeld, *Der General*, would leave a comfortable life of semi-retirement to return to the Säbenerstraße.

Magath's sudden departure at the end of February 2007 had seriously upset whatever stability had remained in Munich, and not even Hitzfeld could engineer an immediate solution to the club's poor form. *Der General's* first match in charge was a visit to mid-table Nürnberg, who would just pile on the misery with a convincing 3-0 win – Bayern's sixth and biggest defeat of the season.

With *Die Roten* languishing a distant eleven points behind league leaders Schalke in fourth place, it was clear that Hitzfeld would have his work cut out just securing a place in the following season's Champions League.

A narrow 1-0 win at the Allianz Arena against Bielefeld earned Bayern their first three-point haul in four attempts, but a defeat by the same score against strugglers Aachen immediately dampened any hopes of an assault on the top three places. The change of coach had not affected Bayern's inconsistency, and while narrow successes over Wolfsburg and

Hertha Berlin saw them finally put together successive wins for the first time in the *Rückrunde*, a 1-1 draw in Bremen and a disappointing 1-0 reverse against sixteenth-placed Eintracht Frankfurt ensured that the Bavarians remained in fourth place, two points off the last Champions League slot occupied by Stuttgart.

With eight matches remaining any hopes of a third successive Bundesliga title were all but lost, and all of the focus was turned towards chasing down that crucial third spot.

The defeat in Frankfurt was followed by an encouraging 2-0 win over leaders Schalke, two results that provided the perfect summary of Bayern's imbalanced, inconsistent season. An early strike from Roy Makaay had set the Bavarians on their way, and they would have run away with the match were it not for the post and Schalke's promising young 'keeper Manuel Neuer. Twelve minutes from the end Hasan Salihamidžić would cap off a superb team performance to clinch the three points, and hopes were raised once more.

2-1 wins over mid-table Hannover 96 and fifth-placed Bayer Leverkusen would give Bayern their first three-game winning run since November 2006, and with just five matches remaining they were just two points behind third-placed Stuttgart.

Things would be set up perfectly for what was a crucial six-pointer on matchday thirty, with Bayern making the short journey west to take on Stuttgart at the Gottlieb-Daimler-Stadion. While a Bayern victory would lift them into the top three for the first time since the start of the *Rückrunde*, defeat would put them five points adrift of the Swabians – and needing nothing short of a miracle to grab that precious and highly lucrative Champions League place.

It was never going to happen. In what was yet another slack and disjointed display, Hitzfeld's side were undone in the space of two minutes by VfB's Brazilian-born German international Cacau, whose twenty-third minute header and right-footed strike two minutes later settled the issue. Cacau could very easily have destroyed Bayern by himself before half-time, sending a shot wide in the twenty-eighth minute before being denied by the post just four minutes later. The Swabians created further opportunities to extend their lead in the second half, and it is fair to say that the eventual 2-0 defeat was more than a little flattering for the Munich side.

If things couldn't get any worse, a tenth defeat of the season at home to tenth-placed Hamburger SV would finally put the nail in the Bavarian coffin. Claudio Pizzaro's thirty-sixth minute goal had seen Bayern take a 1-0 lead into the break, but two goals in five minutes from Rafael van der Vaart and ex-Münch'ner Paolo Guerrero were enough to see the northerners snatch all three points. The defeat left the Bavarians seven points behind third-placed Bremen with just three matches remaining, and the ill-fated quest for a place in the Champions League was over.

A 1-1 draw in Mönchengladbach saw Bayern drop nine points behind the top three, but with the pressure now completely off they would finish the season on a relative high with eight goals in their final two games. A three-goal triumph in Cottbus against Energie was followed by a too-little-too-late 5-2 gala display against mathematically-relegated Mainz, with five different players getting on the score sheet.

Bayern would finish the season on a poor sixty points from their thirty-four matches, six adrift of third-placed Bremen and ten behind champions Stuttgart, who had built on their 2-0 win against the Bavarians to storm to the title. In winning their final eight matches, Armin Veh's side had pulled off a stunning feat to snatch the title from poor Schalke 04, who would miss out yet again despite topping the standings for thirteen weeks right up to match day thirty-two.

	P	W	D	L	Goals	GD	Pts
VfB Stuttgart	34	21	7	6	61:37	+24	70
FC Schalke 04	34	21	5	8	53:32	+21	68
SV Werder Bremen	34	20	6	8	76:40	+36	66
FC Bayern München	34	18	6	10	55:40	+15	60

The disappointing performance in the league would leave me wondering if Felix Magath had been truly to blame, or if the rest of the league had just managed to catch up. The change of coach in the early spring had made little difference, and Bayern's up and down season had simply picked up under Ottmar Hitzfeld where it had been left off under Magath. The fourth-place finish and elimination from the Champions League at the quarter-final stage also ensured that Bayern would miss out on Champions League football for the first time since 1997/98.

Bayern's run in the Champions League in 2006/07 would actually start very well, with Magath leading the team unbeaten through the group phase for the first time in five years. Grouped together with Italians Internazionale Milano, Portuguese side Sporting Clube de Portugal and Russian champions Spartak Moscow, Bayern's group would be slightly tougher than in 2005/06, but by no means impossible.

Bayern's start in the Bundesliga may have been patchy, but they would get off to the perfect start in Europe. Spartak were crushed 4-0 at the Allianz following a sublime second-half display from the home side, and Magath's men followed this emphatic start with a hard-earned 2-0 win at the San Siro against group rivals Internazionale. In what was an even contest the two sides had been firmly locked at 0-0 until just short of the hour mark, but the dismissal of star man Zlatan Ibrahimović for a second bookable offence allowed the Bavarians to up a gear and stamp their authority on the game.

Up against the ten men Bayern started to choke their opponents, and with just nine minutes left on the clock a chip in the box from Mehmet Scholl was collected by Claudio Pizarro, who bundled the ball into the net from five yards. A straight red card for Inter defender Fabio Grosso saw the Italians reduced to nine men, and a minute into added time Lukas Podolski scored his first European goal after seizing upon on an error by Iván Córdoba. The win took Bayern to the top of the group on six points, two clear of Sporting.

Two wins from two became three from three following the trip to the Portuguese capital, where after another hard-fought encounter Bayern returned to Munich with the three points. The decisive goal was scored by Bastian Schweinsteiger after eighteen minutes, but the young midfielder quickly turned from hero to villain just two minutes into the second half with his second yellow card for a silly foul on Yannick Djaló. Having largely dominated the game Bayern suddenly found themselves forced onto the back foot, but despite being a man down they managed to keep the Sporting attack at bay.

At the half-way point, the Bavarians were clear of the rest with a maximum nine points from their opening three matches, followed by Sporting on four points, Inter on three and Spartak on one. With their three excellent clean-sheet performances, Bayern would already have one foot in the second round.

A victory in the return fixture against the Lisbon side at the Allianz Arena would have secured Bayern's berth in the knockout phase with two matches to spare, but this time Sporting managed to keep a clean sheet to earn a hard-fought and ultimately deserved goalless draw. Bayern had dominated the possession from the start and had created more opportunities over the ninety minutes, but their Portuguese opponents had battled hard to maintain their chances of making the last sixteen. Meanwhile, an improving Inter snatched all three points in Moscow to move ahead of Sporting into second place.

Bayern's penultimate group game against Spartak in Moscow would see a tighter encounter than had been the case at the Allianz, with the Russian side taking the lead through Maxym Kalynychenko after sixteen minutes – the first goal Bayern had conceded in over 375 minutes of their Champions League campaign. Spartak's lead would only last six minutes as Claudio Pizarro's glancing header squeezed into the corner of the net, and the

Peruvian would score his second in a more spectacular fashion to give Bayern the lead, drilling a powerful right-footed effort from all of twenty-five yards.

The home side would put up a decent showing in the second half, and grabbed a not wholly undeserved equaliser through Czech defensive midfielder Radoslav Kováč. It was a scrappy goal scored at the second attempt, but Bayern could have no complaints about the 2-2 scoreline, which reflected a game that had been competitive and well-balanced. Daniel van Buyten would have a half-chance to snatch all three points late on, but the draw was enough to see Bayern through to the knockout stages.

With Inter winning their third game on the trot in Lisbon, Bayern headed the group table with eleven points, two ahead of the Italians. Sitting back on fve points, Sporting would be left facing Spartak for a place in the UEFA Cup.

The group could not have developed in a stranger way. After three games Bayern had been clear at the top with a maximum nine points and Inter had been struggling with just the one win, but when the two teams met in Munich on match day six the Italians were right back in the battle to finish top of the group. Bayern would just need a draw in front of their own supporters to secure top spot and a favourable draw in the knockout phase, but a fourth win in four games from Inter would see them pip the Bavarians by a point.

With both sides sure of their place in the last sixteen there was a relaxed atmosphere at the Allianz Arena, and after a goalless first half Bayern – kitted out in an all-Burgundy *Trikot* – would open the scoring two minutes past the hour. Taking possession in his own half, Hasan Salihamidžić sent a well-aimed ball forward – with the clinical Roy Makaay doing the rest. After neatly bringing the ball under control with his left foot, the Dutchman coolly stabbed a low shot into the bottom left-hand corner and past 'keeper Francesco Toldo with his right.

Magath's side looked to have all but secured top spot with their third home win and another clean sheet, but right at the death Inter would create a chance from nothing to grab a party-pooping equaliser. A minute into injury time, a shot from Fabio Grosso was only parried by the hitherto untested Oliver Kahn, and French international Patrick Vieira was on hand to roll the ball into the empty Bayern net.

It was a slightly flat end to what had been an otherwise decent performance, but Bayern had done enough to top the group with a total of twelve points from their six matches. With three wins and three draws and just three goals conceded, Magath's men had taken a convincing step into the last sixteen.

Nobody would know it at the time, but the 1-1 draw against Inter would be Magath's last Champions League game as Bayern coach. When the draw for the last sixteen was made, it pitted *Die Roten* against a familiar foe: Real Madrid.

I had witnessed a number of classic encounters between Bayern and Real over the years, and when the two teams were thrown together yet again there was that familiar sense of fear and trepidation mixed with an almost dizzy excitement. Yes, it was "them" again, but then there would be the opportunity to get one on Real and build on the myth of Bayern's reputation in the Spanish capital as *La Bestia Negra*, "the black beast" – a monicker I always considered somewhat strange, given that Bayern usually played in red. On the other hand, the name may well have been the inspiration for the succession of dark *Trikots* the *Münch'ner* had sported in recent European tournaments.

Of course, this would all make no sense with Bayern playing in an all-burgundy outfit, which made them look more like walking adverts for a fine Bordeaux than some scary black beast from the eerie lagoon at the foot of the Bavarian Alps.

Having won their first phase group Bayern would have the advantage of playing at home in the second leg, and the first meeting at the famous Estadio Santiago Bernabéu provided an atmosphere that had become all too familiar: a raucous, baying crowd of over eighty thousand, and opponents featuring names such as Brazilian defender Roberto Carlos, Dutch striker Ruud van Nistelrooy, local legend Raúl and England superstar David Beckham. On paper Real had far bigger names than Bayern, and despite sitting in second place behind Barcelona in the Spanish league *Los Merengues* had shown far better form than their opponents, who would come into the match off the back of a dismal 1-0 defeat against Alemannia Aachen in the Bundesliga.

On a damp evening in Madrid, the opening ten minutes would run true to form, with the home side applying most of the early pressure. Daniel van Buyten would present van Nistelrooy with an opportunity that the Dutchman scooped over the bat with five minutes gone, but as the game reached double figures the opening goal would come. Beckham seized the ball after the Bayern attack had broken down, finding van Nistelrooy in the middle of the pitch. A defence-splitting pass from the Dutchman sent Raúl in pursuit, and Oliver Kahn could not get quite enough of a hand on the ball to prevent the prolific Spanish striker from executing a cool left-footed finish from close range.

With the crowd firmly behind Fabio Capello's team one might have seen Bayern fold under the pressure, but this was clearly not the same insipid group that had found themselves sleepwalking in Aachen. Going a goal behind seemed to wake them up, and within thirteen minutes the men in burgundy were level. Having won a free-kick out on the right just inside the opposition half, Willy Sagnol sent the ball into the penalty area. There to meet it was the unmarked Lúcio, who drilled a perfectly directed header past Iker Casillas.

Bayern were back in the game with a crucial away goal, but before they could even settle down Real scored their second. An outswinging corner was met by Iván Helguera, who appeared to clamber all over Lúcio before sending a looping header over Kahn towards the far post. Lying in wait was the prolific Raúl, who forced himself in front of Philipp Lahm to nod the ball in from right on the line. Kahn made his protest, but the Belgian referee just waved play on. With twenty-eight minutes gone, Bayern were behind again.

2-1 would become 3-1 just four minutes later, as the men in white threatened to take the visitors apart. A left-sided free-kick from inside the Bayern half was swept into the box by Beckham, and with the ball having been missed completely by the entire burgundy-shirted defence van Nistelrooy ghosted in at the far post ahead of the static van Buyten and Lahm to stab the ball past Kahn. Bayern were 3-1 down but had not played badly: in fact, they had had little time to play at all.

Casillas would do well to deny Makaay as half-time approached, but at the break Real were looking more than comfortable. One more goal would surely have killed the tie, but at 3-1 Hitzfeld's team were not quite out of the contest. Just one more goal would give them at least something to take back to the Allianz Arena for the decisive second leg, and the coach showed his intent by replacing defensive midfielder Martín Demichelis with the more dynamic Hasan Salihamidžić.

To win the Champions League it takes a combination of both skill and luck, and Bayern would have plenty of the latter as the early stages of the second half progressed. With the home side looking to close out the game Kahn made a good save to keep out Argentinian Gonzalo Higuaín, and the veteran 'keeper was called into action soon afterwards to tip a well-struck Beckham free-kick up and onto the crossbar.

Bayern could very easily have been 4-1 down, but would ride their luck to get back into the contest as the game entered the final quarter. From nowhere, they began to apply pressure on an increasingly vulnerable Madrid back line. Owen Hargreaves had a shot blocked. Bastian Schweinsteiger shot wide. Skipper Mark van Bommel forced Casillas into making another excellent save. Then substitute Claudio Pizarro, on for Lukas Podolski, hit the outside of the post with a sharply-angled header.

As time ticked by, hopes of a second away goal started to grow.

Still they came, in waves of burgundy, a fine claret poured smoothly into a well-polished glass. Bayern now seemed to be winning every fifty-fifty ball, and continued to launch wave after wave of attacks on the Madrid goal. The busy Schweinsteiger created another opportunity, and the nimble Salihamidžić's run down the right found the nimble Pizarro, who showed great skill and close control to create a shooting chance – only to see the diving Casillas pull off another stunning save with his left hand.

Sensing the clear change in momentum Hitzfeld threw on veteran winger Mehmet Scholl for the tiring Schweinsteiger, and the chances continued to come. With just over two minutes of normal time remaining, Scholl's cross into the penalty area was only half cleared by the desperate white-shirted defence where it was collected just outside the box by van Bommel.

What happened next was simply magical. With little time to get a good sight of the target, the Bayern skipper lashed a majestic and unstoppable half-volley past the diving Casillas and into the left-hand corner of the net.

It was no less than Bayern deserved for all their efforts, and in what was a particularly emotional celebration, former Barcelona man van Bommel twice served up a cheeky *bras d'honneur* – also known as the "Kozakiewicz" after Poland's 1980 Olympic pole vault champion Władysław Kozakiewicz – to the noisy and hostile home crowd. The Bayern skipper quickly apologised for his offensive gesture after the match and was later fined €6,200 by UEFA, but at the time I would pretty much be doing the same thing in front of the television.

The reaction was arguably over the top and not at all in the spirit of fair play, but the pressure of the match, the unbridled relief at scoring a well-deserved goal, and in van Bommel's case the fact that he once played for Real's *La Liga* rivals Barcelona made it understandable. While I would never support or condone players making offensive gestures on the field of play, given that the recipients were Madrid's loud and obnoxious supporters the fine was probably worth it. The truth was that most Bayern supporters would have happily chipped in to cover the cost.

This was FC Bayern München. This was *La Bestia Negra*.

The match would finish in a flurry of petty fouls, but in pegging the score back to 3-2 Bayern had shown just how much fighting spirit they had, and how good they could be if they steeled themselves to the task. The woes of the patchy domestic campaign were momentarily forgotten: with two away goals, Bayern were right back in the contest.

Everything had been set up perfectly for the return leg in Munich in early March, a city where Real Madrid had never won. It would be the first meeting between the two sides at the new Allianz Arena, but in the eight games played at the Olympiastadion since 1975/76 Bayern had won seven, with just the one draw in 2003/04 when the Bavarians would be denied by a late and lucky Roberto Carlos strike.

Bayern would play essentially the same side that had started in Madrid, with Salihamidžić coming in for Demichelis to offer a slightly more attacking edge. Bayern had to win to progress, but with the advantage of having two away goals Hitzfeld's side could afford to be patient.

With everybody expecting the home side to settle in and slowly exert pressure, nobody expected such a stunning start. Real got the game under way, and with his very first touch Roberto Carlos would give the ball away to Hasan Salihamidžić, who skipped past the hapless Brazilian before rolling the ball into the Real box for Roy Makaay - who finished the move with a clinical right-footed shot past Iker Casillas and into the bottom left-hand corner of the Madrid net. Timed at just over ten seconds – 10.12 to be exact – it would be the fastest goal in the history of the competition.

It was the perfect start, and having been almost down and out at half-time in the first leg in Madrid *Die Roten* were ahead in the tie for the first time. Rather than sit back and defend the early lead, they look to clinch it. With the overall situation having been turned on its head Madrid now had to score, increasing Bayern's chances of scoring on the break. The stage had been set perfectly for yet another classic encounter between these two great European rivals.

With the Spaniards on the back foot, *Die Roten* continued to create opportunities. Casillias blocked a Podolski effort, and pushed aside another shot from Makaay. The imbalance between the two sides forced Madrid coach Capello into replacing Emerson with the more attacking Guti, and this would have the desired effect as the visitors slowly started to establish a foothold.

The second half would follow much the same pattern as the first, with Bayern creating yet more chances to extend their narrow lead. The pressure would finally tell however in the sixty-sixth minute, as a right-sided corner from Willy Sagnol was finished by Lúcio. Rising majestically above the white-shirted defence, the Brazilian headed the Bavarians into a deserved two-goal lead.

With Madrid now needing two goals to progress, the game opened up completely. Capello threw on Brazilian Robinho, and Raúl forced Kahn into a save. Meanwhile, both Pizarro and Podolski had chances to score Bayern's third goal finish things off once and for all.

One could not expect a match between Bayern and Real to simply peter out to its natural conclusion, and things would hot up dramatically as the game entered the final ten minutes. Real's Mahamadou Diarra was shown a second yellow card as the Spaniards were reduced to ten men, and skipper van Bommel would soon be making his own way off the field for an early bath after bringing down Robinho in the box. Real Madrid were once again living up to their reputation as a side that would not go down quietly, and when van Nistelrooy pulled a goal back things were right back in the balance again.

Ottmar Hitzfeld would try to tighten things up at back in sending on Andreas Görlitz for Sagnol, and despite a flurry of activity in the Bayern penalty area the home side were able to see things through to the final whistle. The final act of a dramatic five minutes of additional time saw Real 'keeper Casillas join in the attack, and in the process be penalised for a foul on his opposite number Oliver Kahn.

With the score finishing 2-1 on the night and 4-4 on aggregate, Bayern had seen off the Spanish champions to book their place in the last eight on away goals. Awaiting them would be yet another old foe, AC Milan.

If Bayern had been Madrid's *Bestia Negra*, AC Milan had by the same token been the Bavarians' *schwarzer Pest*. In all my time as a Bayern fan the Italians had always come out on top, and had been responsible for a series of particularly painful episodes in European competition.

With the first leg being played at the San Siro Bayern would have the slight advantage, but this would count for nothing without a decent result. *Die Roten's* away record in European competition against the *Rossoneri* was far from promising: in four games going back to a semi-final meeting in the European Cup Winners' Cup in 1968, they had failed to register even a draw; in those four games Milan had scored a total of nine goals to Bayern's two.

To make matters worse for Ottmar Hitzfeld's side, they would be without two of the most influential players. An accumulation of yellow cards saw 'keeper Oliver Kahn replaced by his twenty-two year old understudy Michael Rensing, while skipper Mark van Bommel would be serving a one-match ban following his dismissal against Madrid.

The omens were far from good.

Despite their weakened line-up Bayern would start brightly and would be on top for much of the early exchanges, but Milan soon started to assert themselves. As the home team started to get into their stride, the chances started to come. Rensing would pull off a great reflex save to deny Massimo Ambrosini after fifteen minutes, and just over twenty minutes later would do even better to keep out Alberto Gilardino's close-range header. With Lúcio lucky not to concede a penalty with his challenge on Brazilian team mate Kaká, it is fair to say that Bayern were riding their luck.

This luck would run out five minutes from half-time. Milan streamed forward, attacking right-back Massimo Oddo chipped the ball into the box, and Andrea Pirlo burst forward to calmly send a looping header over Rensing. There might have been a shout for offside against one of a number of Milan players, but there would be no doubt about the goalscorer's positioning as the Bayern defence went to sleep. Rensing had no chance, and Milan had the lead.

The second half would continue in much the same vein, but as soon as the visiting supporters might have been resigning themselves to going back to Munich with a defeat, a goal came out of almost nowhere. A high, looping cross from Hasan Salihamidžić found Claudio Pizarro, and the Peruvian would do enough to beat Oddo with a downward header to keep up the pressure. Milan 'keeper Dida scrambled to grab the loose ball, but not before Daniel van Buyten had swept it into the back of the net to score what looked to be a precious equaliser. Having barely threatened the Milan goal up to that point, Hitzfeld's team were back in with a shout.

The joy wouldn't last for long however, as once again the curse of Milan returned with a vengeance. Chasing the ball as it rolled to the byline, Kaká was brilliantly challenged by Lúcio; with the Bayern players preparing to set things up for the resulting corner, they would instead see Russian referee Yuri Baslakov pointing to the penalty spot. Kaká would get up and dust himself down, and after sending Rensing the wrong way Milan were in front again.

One might have expected such things to happen against an opponent where there appeared to be some sort of ancient curse always hanging in the air, but this was just too much to bear.

I would start to resign myself to yet another bitter defeat against this red and black pestilence, but the Bayern team had other ideas. The last five minutes saw the Bavarians finally apply some concerted pressure deep in the opposition half, and van Buyten collected a long, high and hopeful pass three minutes into injury time. Taking the ball on his chest inside the six-yard box, the Belgian defender rifled an angled shot into the low right side of the net, beating Dida at his near post. The net bulged emphatically, and Bayern were level.

The miracle had happened. When the final whistle blew with the score at 2-2, Bayern would just need to keep a clean sheet to reach the semi-finals. Finally, it seemed that the curse had been broken.

Bayern would be strengthened for the second leg with the return of Oliver Kahn and Mark van Bommel, and while they had not beaten Milan at home in two attempts – the last win coming in the dramatic European Cup semi-final of 1989/90 – the Bavarians were quietly confident as the two teams lined up at a sold-out Allianz Arena. Bayern would boast an unbeaten record in the Champions League at their new ground, and one would also have to look back to November 2004 for their last home defeat in the competition, a 1-0 loss to Juventus at the group stage at the Olympiastadion.

Hitzfeld's side would start well enough and control much of what was a static early period, but it would be yet another false dawn. The *Münch'ner* would create more opportunities and have more shots at the Milan goal over the course of the ninety minutes, but two clinical strikes from their opponents in the space of four frantic first-half minutes would settle the issue and call time on their European ambitions for yet another year.

It was as if Bayern's poor form in the Bundesliga had finally caught up with them.

With twenty-seven minutes gone Dutch midfielder Clarence Seedorf created space for himself at the edge of the Bayern box, skipping past Lúcio to drill a low shot into the bottom left-hand corner past Kahn – and before Hitzfeld's side would have time to recover a marginally offside Filippo Inzaghi collected a cute Kaká backheel before blasting the ball emphatically over the advancing Kahn from the edge of the penalty area to double the visitors' lead.

The second half saw Hitzfeld's side throw themselves at the Milan goal, but they were both predictable and profligate. Amidst the miscued shots and scuffed half-chances, Milan 'keeper Dida also conjured up a decent performance to shut out the misfiring Bayern attack in what was overall a poor quality match. The solid but unspectacular *Rossoneri* once again marched through to the last four, and would inevitably go on to win the trophy – beating Liverpool 2-1 in what was a rematch of the 2005 final.

With Bayern way off the pace in the Bundesliga and already eliminated from the DFB-Pokal following a disappointing 4-2 defeat in Aachen against lowly Alemannia, the hunt for silverware was over. After the back to back domestic doubles in 2005 and 2006, the Säbenerstraße would be a depressing place at the end of the 2006/07 season: not only had Bayern failed to win a trophy, their fourth-place finish in the Bundesliga would result in them missing out on the Champions League for the first time in over a decade.

THE GREEN SHOOTS OF RECOVERY

The recall of Ottmar Hitzfeld following the dismissal of Felix Magath had failed to make any significant difference to Bayern's fortunes in 2007. The team's most successful coach had not been able to lift the club to any higher than a barely satisfactory fourth place in the Bundesliga, and the disappointingly flat exit from the Champions League against an equally ordinary AC Milan had been more to do with a lack of confidence and collective self-belief than anything else. Morale was low, and new energy clearly needed to be injected into the team.

Hitzfeld could very easily have taken the easy option and made his own way out of Munich, but there was a job to do. *Der General's* first glorious spell at Bayern had come to an unsatisfactory end in 2004, and there was no way the proud man from Lörrach was going to let this happen again. He had one year remaining on his contract in Bavaria, and determined to try and make the most of it.

Hitzfeld was ably assisted by the board, who would give him the green light to undertake what was a complete changing of the guard. Long-established names made way for a number of incomers, and at the beginning of the 2007/08 season the squad had taken on a completely different look.

Among those leaving Munich were a number of stars from the 2001 Champions League winning side. By far the most poignant departure would be that of crowd favourite Mehmet Scholl, who announced his retirement after fifteen seasons with *Die Roten*, finishing his career as one of the club's most decorated players. After signing for Bayern as a twenty-one year old from Karlsruhe SC in 1992, Scholl had won a total of eight Bundesliga championships, five DFB-Pokals, five DFB-Ligapokals, the UEFA Cup in 1996 and the most coveted one of all, the UEFA Champions League in 2001.

One of my favourite players for more than a decade, Scholl would remain with the club, taking on the role as coach to the Under-13s.

The other 2001 winners on the departure list were Owen Hargreaves and Hasan "Brazzo" Salihamidžić; having forged his youth career in Bavaria, Canadian-born Hargreaves would move to Manchester United for a new challenge in the Premier League for €25 million, while Bosnian stalwart Salihamidžić – one of the penalty scorers on that memorable night in the San Siro in 2001 – headed to Italy to join Serie A giants Juventus on a free transfer.

More big names would join the exodus. Striker Roy Makaay ended a successful four-year spell at Bayern to return home to the Netherlands with Feyenoord, Peruvians Claudio Pizarro and Roque Santa Cruz headed across the North Sea to join Chelsea and Blackburn Rovers in the English Premier League, Iranian star Ali Karimi would take his first step to retirement with a move to Qatari outfit Qatar Sports Club, and the promising but ultimately disappointing Andreas Görlitz made the move down a division to join second division Karlsruher SC.

The massive squad clearout in Munich was matched by a number of high-profile imports, with rising French star Franck Ribéry, established German goalscorer Miroslav Klose and Italian striker Luca Toni just three of the names making their way to Bavaria.

The signing of the twenty-four year old Ribéry from Olympique Marseille was a major coup, and would prove to be a bargain at €25 million – the same amount Bayern had received for Hargreaves. The Frenchman had impressed many during the 2006 World Cup in Germany and had been highly sought after by a number of top European clubs, and his arrival in Munich was clearly part of a mission to inject more pace and trickery into a Bayern side that had become staid, stodgy and far too predictable.

The departure of Makaay and Pizzaro had left a gaping hole in Bayern's firepower up front, and Klose was the perfect man to fill the breech. A relative snip at €15 million, the SV Werder Bremen man had been an established goalscorer at the highest level for the best part of a decade; his arrival not only added much-needed firepower, but top-level experience. Experience was also the key factor in signing Italian marksman Toni from ACF Fiorentina for €11 million, and making up Bayern's new-look strike force was the €1.2 million youngster Jan Schlaudraff, who had certainly made an impression in Munich for second division Alemannia Aachen.

The emphasis on bolstering the attack was illustrated by the other signings: twenty-two year old midfielder José Ernesto Sosa was signed from Argentinian side Estudiantes for nine million Euros, Gelsenkirchen-born Turkish international playmaker Hamit Altıntop joined from Schalke 04 on a free transfer, while attacking left-back Marcell Jansen made his way to Bavaria from Borussia Mönchengladbach for €14 million.

The list of new names would not end there. The relatively unknown Paraguyan midfieder Julio dos Santos arrived from Club Cerro Porteño for €2.7 million, promising youngsters Sandro Wagner and Toni Kroos graduated from FC Bayern II, and a name from the past would return to the Säbenerstraße to complete what had been an astonishing transfer-fest. For the bargain sum of just a million Euros, flying Brazilian winger Zé Roberto returned for a second spell at Bayern from Uruguayan side Nacional Montevideo.

With just short of eighty million Euros being spent on new players, the coach would have everything he wanted; the pressure was now on him to take these players and turn them into a trophy-winning outfit. As the new season approached, there was a new-found feeling of optimism in Munich.

Bayern's season would begin in July with the pre-season DFB-Ligapokal, and Hitzfeld's new-look side immediately impressed with three straight wins to take them to the title in Leipzig's Zentralstadion. The new signings were quick to get off the mark: Ribéry would score a brace and Altıntop also found the back of the net in a 4-1 thumping of Werder Bremen, young Sandro Wagner joined the Frenchman on the scoresheet in a 2-0 semi-final defeat of VfB Stuttgart, and the final against Schalke was settled by a twenty-ninth minute strike from Klose. It was the perfect preparation for the upcoming challenges ahead.

With the finals of the European Championships being held in June in neighbouring Austria and Switzerland, the 2007/08 edition of the DFB-Pokal was played with an accelerated schedule, meaning that it was brought forward to the end of April before the end of the Bundesliga season rather than its usual slot in the first week of June.

Bayern's quest to regain the bejewelled golden *Pott* would begin shakily against local *Regionalliga-Süd* side Wacker Burghausen, and shadows of 1994 and TSV Vestenbergsgreuth would loom large at the 11,600 Wacker-Arena with the amateurs taking the lead in the sixty-second minute.

Miroslav Klose would save Bayern's blushes with an equaliser eleven minutes before full time, and with extra time yielding no further goals the game would go to a dramatic penalty shootout. Both the crossbar and Wacker 'keeper Manuel Riemann played their part in keeping the amateurs in the contest, and both sides would need their seventh penalty taker before the result was finally decided. After Christian Lell had put *Die Roten* 4-3 up, Oliver Kahn kept out Thomas Mayer's kick as Bayern squeezed into the second round.

A second round meeting with Borussia Mönchengladbach would prove less testing as Hitzfeld's side strolled to an easy 3-1 win, and although Regionalliga outfit Wuppertaler SV more than held their own in their third round encounter until half-time at 2-2, three unanswered second half strikes saw Bayern ease through to the last eight and a meeting with city rivals TSV 1860 München, then sitting in seventh place in the second division.

The meeting at the Allianz Arena – with Bayern the designated "home" team – would prove to be suitably dramatic and worthy of any Munich city derby. From the start, Bayern created chances: Toni Kroos sent a shot narrowly over the bar, and Luca Toni looked to have given *Die Roten* the lead late in the first half only to see his effort disallowed for the gentlest of gentle pushes on 1860 defender Torben Hoffman.

The start of the second half would see the arrival of Franck Ribéry in place of Hamit Altıntop, and the Frenchman almost immediately started to cause panic in the 1860 defence. A typically swashbuckling run down the left from the Bayern number seven resulted in Mark van Bommel's snapshot being well parried by substitute 'keeper Philipp Tschauner – on for the injured Michael Hofmann – and Ribéry then spooned another opportunity into the crowd after a robust run down the right by Christian Lell.

Despite the opportunities there were no goals, but as the game went on the undoubted star of the show would be everybody's favourite man in black, Peter Gagelmann from Bremen.

With six minutes remaining in normal time Gagelmann waved a second yellow card at Toni for a harmless arm-waving challenge on 1860's central defender Markus Thorandt, yet moments later would inexplicably keep his hands away from his pocket when Lúcio was clearly shoved in the face in the 1860 penalty area by Benjamin Schwarz.

The Bayern players must have been seething at the decision, but the ten men in red and white were able to maintain their composure and keep their shape to take the game into extra time.

Nine minutes before the end of the additional half an hour, the numbers were levelled out on the pitch when the volatile Schwarz was rightly dismissed for what could be described as a physical assault on Ribéry. With both sides now down to ten, the game was heading inexorably towards a penalty shoot-out.

With seconds remaining however, 1860's German-Cambodian substitute Chhunly Pagenburg – on loan from Nürnberg – brought down Miroslav Klose right at the very edge of the penalty area, though the 1860 players loudly protested that the incident had taken place just outside. Ribéry stepped up to give *Die Roten* to take the kick, and a firm sweep of the Frenchman's right boot would send the ball into the bottom right-hand corner past the outstretched fingertips of Tschauner. In what had been a truly dramatic finish to a pulsating and hard-fought contest, Bayern were on their way to the last four.

Or were they?

The referee had spotted an infringement with two red and white striped players encroaching into the area. The decision was ultimately the correct one, but it just added amother layer to the already volatile atmosphere as Herr Gagelmann became the centre of attention.

With both sets of supporters among the capacity 69,000 crowd going ballistic, the kick would have to be retaken. Tschauner again dived to his left, but this time Ribéry coolly chipped a "Panenka" into the centre of the goal. As the Bayern number seven charged off to the touchline for a second time I immediately looked at Herr Gagelmann: yes, now it was finally over.

Bayern had won the game right at the death and *Die Löwen* would have nothing left in the tank, but that was not the end of the entertainment from Herr Gagelmann: four minutes into additional time Thorandt, his brain clearly addled by the red mist, slid viciously on the fast-moving Ribéry, and the *Schiri* unhesitatingly issued his third *Gelb-Rot*.

The dramatic quarter final was followed by a less testing semi-final against VfL Wolfsburg as Ribéry and Klose settled matters in the space of six second-half minutes, but the final in Berlin against Dortmund would prove to be yet another close affair – somewhat surprising given that just six days earlier the visit by the *Schwarz-Gelben* to the Allianz Arena had resulted in an emphatic 5-0 thrashing at the hand of a rampant Bayern side.

There were no obvious signs that things would be any different in Berlin, when as early as the eleventh minute Ribéry stormed down the left flank before delivering the perfect cross for Toni to stab home from from four yards. The early opening goal didn't open the floodgates however, and Dortmund had clearly taken plenty of lessons from their earlier beating. Knowing they had nothing to lose, they threw themselves in to the contest.

Klose headed wide and then had another header cleared off the line by Jakub Błaszczykowski within three minutes early in the second half, while at the other end Florian Kringe spurned two good opportunities to bring Dortmund level. Seven minutes from the end Ribéry forced 'keeper Marc Ziegler into a fine parry, and Luca Toni's shot on the rebound was on target, but somehow stayed out after hitting a blur of yellow and black bodies.

In the dying minutes coach Ottmar Hitzeld would look to tighten things up with Lukas Podolski and Willy Sagnol coming on for Klose and Bastian Schweinsteiger, but with the Bavarians unable to finish off their stubborn opponents, I could sense a twist in this tale.

Thomas Doll's side continued to press and Błaszczykowski would earn a booking for a desperate dive in the Bayern box, but two minutes into injury time a goalmouth scramble resulted in Mladen Petrić's effort spinning off the legs of Lúcio before dribbling over the line, with a desperately unlucky Philipp Lahm unable to hack the ball away. The whistle blew with the score locked at one goal apiece.

The first chance in extra time would fall to Kringe whose full-blooded strike was brilliantly turned around the post by Kahn, but moments later a Ribéry ball picked out Podolski, whose shot found a way past the helplessly wrongfooted Ziegler by Toni. The replay suggested that the Italian had no idea where the ball had been when he made contact, but with it happily nestling in the back of the Dortmund net Toni charged off with his familiar hand cupped over ear celebration. Bayern had taken plenty of firm punches from their brave opponents, but looked to have delivered the final knockout blow.

The unfortunate Błaszczykowski would earn a second yellow card for a late lunge on Christian Lell three minutes into the second period of extra time, and against ten men Hitzfeld's side would have no problem shutting up shop to secure a fourteenth cup triumph. It was Oliver Kahn's sixth DFB-Pokal winner's medal, taking him one clear of Mehmet Scholl.

Bayern's Bundesliga campaign kicked off in fine style with a 3-0 demolition of Hansa Rostock at the Allianz, and they would never look back from there. The new strike force of Luca Toni and Miroslav Klose was already ticking, with the Italian opening the scoring in the first half and the German marksman adding a second half brace. The result saw Bayern fly to the top of the league – the first time they had occupied the spot since the previous September.

The positive start continued with a 4-0 rout of old rivals Bremen at the Weserstadion with the goals being spread around, and two wins from two games would become three from three following an equally impressive dismantling of Hannover 96. With a record of three wins from three matches and ten goals scored with none conceded *Die Roten* edged two points clear at the top, a position they would not relinquish.

The perfect one hundred percent start would come to an end in Hamburg with a 1-1 draw, and despite dropping two more points the following week against Schalke, the Bavarians were able to switch into second gear. Five wins on the bounce – and a total of fifteen goals – saw Hitzfeld's side stretch their lead at the top to six points, and although they would suffer a slight drop in form with two successive goalless draws and their first defeat of the season against eleventh-placed defending champions Stuttgart they were able to keep enough distance between themselves and the chasing pack led by Bremen. The defeat in Stuttgart would actually be the worst thing for Bayern's opponents, as Hitzfeld's side once again turned on the afterburners.

A ten-game unbeaten spell either side of the *Winterpause* saw the Bavarians extend their advantage to seven points, and while a shock 2-0 defeat against relegation-threatened Energie Cottbus made the headlines there was nothing much for Bayern fans to be concerned about.

Bayern's second league defeat simply jolted them into life once again, and they would finish the season with an even more impressive unbeaten run that saw them win eight of their remaining ten games. Borussia Dortmund were emphatically dispatched 5-0 with Toni scoring a brace, revenge was meted out on Stuttgart with Ribéry scoring twice as Bayern romped to a 4-1 win, and the celebration of the return of the *Meisterschale* to Munich was completed with a 4-1 demolition of Hertha Berlin with Toni netting an imperious hat-trick.

	P	W	D	L	Goals	GD	Pts
FC Bayern München	34	22	10	2	68:21	+47	76
SV Werder Bremen	34	20	6	8	75:45	+30	66
FC Schalke 04	34	18	10	6	55:32	+23	64

After the disappointment of 2006/07 the new-look Bayern side had returned to their rightful place at the top of German football, finishing an impressive ten points clear of *Vizemeister* Bremen.

Significantly, there had been a massive improvement in Bayern's form away from home: in 2006/07 they had put together a dismal 7-2-8 record, but 2007/08 this had this improved dramatically to a dominant 10-5-2. Meanwhile, the Allianz Arena had returned once more to being a fortress: Hitzfeld's side would finish undefeated over their seventeen home fixtures, dropping just ten points from the available fifty-one and scoring forty-one goals and conceding just eight.

Having finished out of the Champions League qualifying places in 2006/07, Bayern found themselves among the also-rans in the UEFA Cup, a tournament they had last won in 1995/96. The first round had seen the Bavarians take on Portuguese side C.F. Os Belenenses, and following a surprisingly tight 1-0 win at the Allianz Bayern would ease through to the group phase with a 2-0 victory in Portugal.

The group phase draw saw Bayern placed alongside Premier League side Bolton Wanderers, Greek outfit Aris Thessaloniki, 1991 European Champions Red Star Belgrade and another Portuguese opponent in SC Braga. Miroslav Klose would cancel out Red Star's early lead in the opening match in Belgrade, but when the Serbian side retook the lead with just over a quarter of an hour remaining things would start to look ominous for Ottmar Hitzfeld's side. Five minutes from time Klose score his second to secure a valuable point, and four minutes into injury time teenage substitute Toni Kroos would ensure Bayern took all three points back to Munich with a sublime free-kick.

The meeting at the Allianz Arena against Bolton produced a similar game, with the visitors taking an eighth-minute lead only for Lukas Podolski to score a brace nineteen minutes either side of half-time. Bayern looked set to take all three points, but with just eight minutes left on the clock Kevin Davies would grab a crucial point for the Trotters. Klose was on target in Portugal as *Die Roten* earned another point against Braga, and with one match remaining Hitzfeld's men were sitting rather precariously in third place behind Bolton and Aris, with the Portuguese team two points further adrift. Bolton had completed their fixtures to finish on six points, Aris and Bayern were both locked on five, and despite being two points further adrift Braga were still not out of the contest for the top two positions.

With the Portuguese side favourites to pick up all three points at home against winless Belgrade, Bayern's meeting with the men from Thessaloniki was essentially a cup final. While a win would see the Bavarians safely through to the knock-out rounds, a draw or defeat would almost certainly see them tumble embarrassingly out of the competition.

In the end, Bayern fans need not have worried about the outcome or the possible permutations. The Greek side had only conceded two goals in their previous three group games, but they were no match for the Bavarians – and an inspired Luca Toni. The Italian would strike in the twenty-fifth and thirty-eighth minutes to send put *Die Roten* two goals ahead at half-time, and two further strikes in the space of two minutes midway through the second half closed the door completely. Defenders Christian Lell and Philipp Lahm also found the back of the Aris net to complete a stunning 6-0 triumph, turning what had been a potential banana skin into a complete rout.

At the final whistle Bayern had climbed smoothly to the top of the group table, two points clear of both Bolton and Braga. Aris meanwhile were eliminated after slipping from first down to fourth place.

The first knock-out round would pit Hitzfeld's side against Aberdeen, the first meeting of the two sides since the infamous 3-2 defeat in the Cup Winners' Cup in 1983. The 2008 Pittodrie vintage was never going to be as threatening as the team that had gone on to claim the silverware twenty-five years earlier, but they still managed to put up a decent fight on their home ground against a Bayern side that looked sluggish and out of sorts. After falling behind in the twenty-fourth minute Klose equalised with a typical poacher's finish, but the home side restored their advantange four minutes before half-time when Michael Rensing in the Bayern goal was beaten by a brilliant curling shot from teenager Josh Walker.

The second half display was considerably better for the visitors, and just ten minutes after the restart they were awarded a penalty for handball. Hamit Altıntop's spot-kick was well saved by Aberdeen keeper Jamie Langfield, but the Turkish international was able to get to the rebound first to net the equaliser. Both Lukas Podolski and Luca Toni would come close to snatching a late winner for the visitors, but the 2-2 draw was probably a fair result. Despite the poor performance Bayern fans could be happy; with two away goals in the bag, the Bavarians were firm favourites to complete the job in the return leg in Munich.

Any lingering fears of a shock result at the Allianz were allayed after just twelve minutes, with Lúcio scoring the opening goal to set Bayern on their way. A Daniel van Buyten header doubled the advantage nine minutes before half-time, and although the 66,000 crowd had to wait until the seventy-first minute for the next goal, Podolski made it worth their while with a six-minute brace – first with his left foot, then with his head.

Aberdeen would score a late consolation seven minutes from time, only for skipper Mark van Bommel to net the Bavarians' fifth just two minutes later to cap off a comfortably emphatic 5-1 win.

Another old European foe in the form of Belgian champions RSC Anderlecht were Bayern's opponents in the last sixteen, and what had been assumed to be a tough meeting in Brussels would turn into yet another free-scoring display from the in-form Bavarians. Altıntop would open the scoring after only nine minutes, the in-form Toni added a second a minute into stoppage time, and second half strikes from Podolski, Miroslav Klose and Franck Ribéry provided the gloss on what was a perfect team performance.

Anderlecht had been a major force in the European game during the 1970s and 1980s and had often presented a serious obstacle to Bayern teams in the past, and the 5-0 triumph in Brussels was the first away win for *Die Roten* at their fifth attempt. Unfortunately, Anderlecht would return the favour in the second leg in Munich, restoring some of their battered pride with a surprise 2-1 win. Lúcio had given the home side the lead after nine minutes, but first-half replies from German-born Turkish international Akin Serhat and Ukrainian Oleksandr Yakovenko condemned Bayern to what would be their only home defeat of the season.

If the ties against Aberdeen and Anderlecht had been fairly straightforward, the same could not be said of the quarter-final against underrated Spanish side Getafe CF, which would provide Bayern fans with one of the most dramatic evenings of the entire season. The first leg in Munich had seen *Die Roten* take the lead through the free-scoring Toni in the twenty-sixth minute, but a last-minute equaliser from Romanian Cosmin Contra would suddenly shift the advantage back to the team from the Madrid suburbs.

Bayern headed to the Spanish capital for the second leg knowing that they had to chase the game from the start, and they were given a massive boost with the dismissal of Getafe central defender Ruben de la Red for a professional foul after just six minutes. One might have expected the vastly superior Bayern side to use their numerical advantage to take complete control of the game, but de la Red's red card seemed to galvanise the home side. They were down to ten ten, but playing as if they had twelve.

When Contra struck for the second time in the tie a minute before half-time after a fantastic counter-attack, the crowd of just over fourteen thousand in the compact Coliseum Alfonso Pérez must have thought that they were dreaming. Founded only in 1983 and with no European pedigree whatsoever, Getafe were somehow beating the mighty FC Bayern München. Not just that. They were beating the mighty FC Bayern München with just ten men.

With time ticking by it looked as though Bayern's campaign was dribbling to a sorry end in front of a crowd of just over fourteen thousand, but with the Getafe supporters gearing up for what would have been the biggest victory in their history Bayern would from nowhere grab a lifeline. With just over a minute remaining the awkward Toni was creating all sorts of havoc in the opposition penalty area, and with the defence unable to clear the ball it fell to Ribéry, who thrashed home a stunning volley to level the scores both on the night and on aggregate. The French winger had been largely disappointing all evening, but right when it mattered he had produced a moment of sublime magic.

With their dramatic last-gasp equaliser taking the game into extra time, Bayern had to be clear favourites to push on and finish the job. The ten men of Getafe had fought their hearts out, but surely they were finished now? Having fought tooth and nail for the best part of the ninety minutes with a man short only to have their hopes ripped away right at the end, nobody would have blamed the Spanish side if they just folded completely. Yet somehow they dragged themselves up from the canvas, dusted themselves down and from somewhere found the energy and sheer will to throw everything at the Bavarians in one last desperate charge.

What followed would be thirty minutes of the most heart-stopping – and for one side, heart-breaking – football.

Michael Laudrup's side threw everything forward as if their lives depended on it, and it took less than a minute for them to score their second. Once again, the ten men pulled a rabbit out of the hat to stun the visiting Bayern supporters and send their own into raptures.

Collecting a throw-in from the left, substitute Braulio cut back inside and found Francisco Casquero, who launched a ferocious right-footed shot from just outside the box. Kahn's dive was futile, and the ball cannoned off the inside of the left upright before flying into the back of the net.

On the touchline, a visibly concerned Ottmar Hitzfeld had started to prowl around like a nervous cat.

The visitors hardly had time to draw breath before they found themselves 3-1 down, and barring a miracle on their way out of the tournament. With Bayern desperately pressing for an equaliser Getafe broke fast down the right and the finish from the impressive Braulio was suitably emphatic, but the defending from Bayern was just as suitably shambolic. Catching every single white shirt off guard as he swept down the right flank, Mario Cotelo's cross should have been cleared by Lúcio, only for the sleepy-looking Brazilian to make complete a pig's ear of the clearance. Braulio was never going to refuse the open invitation, blasting his shot from close range between Kahn and the near post. It was scarcely credible.

The Spanish side would make it through to the end of the first period of extra time unscathed, and to make matters worse for Bayern Toni picked up a yellow card that ruled him out of semi-final – though any hopes of Bayern actually making it that far were fading rapidly. The clocked ticked by, and with Bayern still trailing by two goals with five minutes remaining the tie was surely done and dusted.

Getafe were surely on their way to pulling off one of the biggest surprises of the season, but one man begged to differ. When Mark van Bommel's speculative looping free-kick into the opposition penalty area was inexplicably spilled by 'keeper Pato Abbondanzieri, Luca Toni was on the spot to tap the ball into the empty net. Out of nothing, Bayern had been gifted with an unexpected lifeline.

As the game entered the final minute of extra-time, the visitors made one last desperate thrust. Picking the ball up on the left, substitute José Ernesto Sosa floated a left-footed cross into the box towards the lurking Toni, and a firm downward header from the big Italian striker bounced over and past the poorly-positioned Abbondanzieri. With just seconds remaining, Bayern had levelled the score on the night and put themselves ahead on away goals. As the stunned Getafe players struggled to comprehend what had just happened, the beaming Toni celebrated his tenth goal of the tournament by embarking on that wonderfully familiar run towards the touchline.

There would be no time left for Getafe to respond. Just moments later after Bayern's equaliser, the three welcome peeps from referee Massimo Bussaca'a whistle brought an end to what had been a nail-biting, heart-stopping evening of European midweek footballing madness.

The home crowd had been stunned into silence, and the Bayern players could scarely believe their luck. Toni had been on hand to conduct one of the most improbable escapes in the history of the competition, but Abbondanzieri had done his best to gift-wrap both chances. Getafe and their supporters had every right to be proud of their performance, but the Argentinian 'keeper must have wanted the ground to swallow him up.

As a Bayern fan, my own sense of celebration was tempered by the feeling that we genuinely didn't deserve to win, and had got away with murder. That feeling would last for just a few fleeting moments, however.

If the quarter-final against Getafe had provided one of the more memorably dramatic moments of the 2007/08 season, the semi-final against Russian outsiders Zenit St. Petersburg would serve almost every Bayern supporter a bitter dose of reality. Like many others, being up against unfashionable "second class" opposition in the UEFA Cup had given me a somewhat slanted perspective, and before the first leg in Munich I had pretty much treated an appearance in the final as a given.

All set to get hold of a couple of tickets from a Spurs supporter whose team had been knocked out in the second round, I had started to look forward to the relatively short journey to Manchester's Etihad Stadium the following month.

When following and supporting a football team, faith and belief are fundamental when expressing that support – but sometimes this can lead to a most embarrassing underestimation of your opponent. So it would prove with Zenit, a team that had sat comfortably out of focus.

Coached by Dutchman Dick Advocaat, Zenit had barely managed to make it past the group stage, finishing in third place with five points from their four games – behind a dominant Everton and Bayern's Bavarian rivals Nürnberg.

Remaining well under the radar, Advocaat's team had squeezed past Spaniards Villarreal CF and French side Olympique de Marseille on away goals to make the last eight, before bursting into life in the quarter-finals against Bayer Leverkusen. Bayern's Bundesliga rivals had been massive favourites to make the last four at the expense of the Russian side, but a thumping 4-1 defeat at the BayArena showed that Advocaat's side meant business. A 1-0 defeat in the return leg was not enough to derail Zenit, and their 4-2 aggregate victory had made the rest of Europe sit up and take notice – including semi-final opponents FC Bayern München.

Ahead of the first leg of the semi-final at the Allianz Arena, the onus was on Ottmar Hitzfeld's side to put themselves into a strong position ahead of the return leg at Zenit's Petrovsky Stadium. Having just claimed the DFB-Pokal, confidence was high both on the pitch and in the stands. Zenit were clearly not to be underestimated, but the Bavarians were massive favourites to progress through to their second UEFA Cup final.

With the game just short of the twenty minute mark Bayern's positive approach was duly rewarded. Dutch defender Fernando Ricksen's tussle with Zé Roberto in the Zenit box resulted in Slovakian referee Ľuboš Micheľ pointing to the penalty spot, and although Franck Ribéry's kick was directed straight at 'keeper Vyacheslav Malafeev the Frenchman was sharp enough to slot in the rebound with his left foot. The crowd roared their approval, and Bayern were surely on their way.

Ribéry's early goal was met with an increase in volume from the capacity home crowd, but for all the pressure from Bayern the half-time whistle blew with no further addition to the score. Zenit had clearly come to Munich to park the bus and hit *Die Roten* on the break, and at only one goal down their plan seemed to be working.

The second half would start as the first had ended with the home side continuing to dominate possession and create opportunities, but with no second goal there was a growing sense of foreboding among the home support. Zenit had offered little in the way of an offensive threat, but just as the stadium scoreboard struck sixty minutes a hopeful cross from Viktor Fayzulin was glanced into the net by the unfortunate Lúcio, with Oliver Kahn left helpless. Out of nowhere, the Russian side didn't just have an undeserved equaliser – but a crucial away goal.

To make matters worse for *Die Roten*, Kahn had to limp off seven minutes later with youngster Michael Rensing taking his place.

Bayern continued to press, but their opponents – buoyed by their surprise goal – would come close to adding a second. Lukas Podolski had a shot blocked and the unfortunate Lúcio had a stinging effort well parried by Malafeev, but the final whistle brought an end to what had been a truly disappointing evening. As far as the statistics were concerned Bayern had been well on top, but their having four times as many shots on target and a corner count of ten to one had counted for nothing. As with the quarter-final against Getafe, the Bavarians had to chase the game away from home.

Despite the disappointing result at the Allianz Bayern fans were confident ahead of the second leg in Russia, but by the end of the evening they had witnessed the blackest moment in what had otherwise been a satisfactory season. Few positives could be taken from a performance that had bordered on the embarrassing, as Bayern's more talented line-up fell to pieces against a solid Zenit side whose sharpness in front of goal proved decisive.

The initial direction of the match had hinged on one short sequence of events with less than three minutes on the clock: at one end Miroslav Klose would have a shot cleared off the line by Roman Shirokov with Malafeev beaten, but just seconds later the highly-rated Pavel Pogrebnyak had the ball in the back of the Bayern net with a twenty-five yard free-kick.

From that point on, even the return of suspended quarter-final hero Luca Toni to the starting lineup couldn't save Hitzfeld's beleaguered side. As in the first leg there was plenty of huff and puff, but with no result. As the Bavarians pressed harder for an equaliser there was more room for their opponents to play their well-drilled counterattacking game, and it was no great surprise when Konstantin Zyryanov doubled Zenit's lead six minutes before half-time. Bayern now needed to score at least two goals to progress, but the stark reality was that they never really looked like threatening Malafeev's goal.

The second half was almost identical to the first: more Bayern pressure that came to nothing, and two more well-crafted goals for the home team. The 4-0 scoreline was perhaps a little flattering to Zenit, but nobody could deny that the better team had won the contest. There would be some whispers in the press about the result and that Bayern had been offered millions of Euros by the Russian mafia to throw the match, but later investigations would prove all of these allegations to be false, with two UEFA officials being fired after being convicted of slander.

The simple truth was that while Bayern had been slightly unlucky at various points during the tie, they had been well beaten over the two legs by a team that had understood its limits and played to their potential.

Apart from the nature of the defeat and the shocking scoreline, perhaps the biggest shame was that the debacle in Saint Petersburg would be 'keeper Oliver Kahn's final appearance in European club competition for FC Bayern. A winner's medal in Manchester for *Der Titan* would have been a fitting send-off, but it was not to be.

In the final, Bayern's Russian conquerors stuck to their plan. In a largely one-sided contest, they eased to a 2-0 victory over Scottish side Glasgow Rangers.

There was no plan to extend Ottmar Hitzfeld's contract at Bayern; the coach had already signed an agreement to take charge of the Swiss national side with the aim of qualifying for the 2010 World Cup finals in South Africa, and the hunt for a new coach in Munich would begin as early as the winter of 2007.

Despite the disappointing end to the UEFA Cup campaign in St. Petersburg, the completion of yet another domestic league and cup double was the perfect sign-off for the departing coach, whose collection of trophies enhanced his already impressive record as FC Bayern's greatest ever *Trainer*. In his two spells in Munich, Hitzfeld had won a total of eleven trophies: four Bundesliga titles, two DFB-Pokals, three DFB-Ligapokals, and both the Champions League and Intercontinental Cup in 2001.

Bayern meanwhile were looking at another coach with the right international credentials to take the helm in Munich. Former Bayern striker and German *Nationaltrainer* Jürgen Klinsmann had become hot property after leading the revived *Nationalmannschaft* to third place at the 2006 World Cup, and after plenty of negotiations Uli Hoeneß and Karl-Heinz Rummenigge would get their man.

Klinsmann was officially unveiled as the next coach of FC Bayern in the second week of January 2008, to much media hype and fanfare – and more than a few discordant voices from the club's fanbase.

At the start of July, a new era in Munich was all set to begin.

HYPE, HYSTERIA AND HUBRIS

The arrival of former goalscoring hero Jürgen Klinsmann at the Säbenerstraße was one of the biggest talking points in European football at the start of the 2008/09 season. After a number of years where FC Bayern München had not quite reached a level good enough to threaten the continent's other established footballing powers, Klinsmann was promoted by the media as the breath of fresh air who would turn domestic into continental success, and propel the team into a new and bountiful era.

With a management style that was in complete contrast to his predecessors Ottmar Hitzfeld and Felix Magath, Klinsmann brought with him an army of off-field experts and gurus – psychologists, nutritionists and modern fitness trainers were all part of the new coach's transatlantic ideology.

While the coaching regime would undergo a significant facelift, there were very few changes to the squad. The biggest departure by far would be the retirement of goalkeeping stalwart Oliver Kahn, while Marcell Jansen and Jan Schlaudraff – two players who had failed to make the grade at Bayern – made their way to Hamburger SV and Hannover 96 respectively. Promising youngster and European Under-21 champion Sandro Wagner departed for second division side MSV Duisburg, while veteran 'keeper Bernd Dreher also called time on his professional career.

One might have expected Klinsmann's appointment to be backed up by a raft of new and glamourously expensive signings, but the grand total spent on the new additions to the squad would be one appreciated by accountants everywhere: the grand sum of zero.

With the retirement of goalkeepers Kahn and Dreher Bayern fans found themselves scanning the rest of Europe for replacements, but the two men who came into the squad could best be described as unheralded representatives of the old and the new. Former Bayer

Leverkusen and HSV *Torwart* Hans-Jörg Butt made his way back to Germany after a torrid season in Portugal for Benfica, and youth player Thomas Kraft also made his way into the first team. While the twenty year old Kraft was touted as a man for the future and a possible long-term replacement for *Der Titan* Kahn, Butt was the insurance cover, bringing with him a wealth of top-level experience – including a long-established reputation as a reliable penalty taker.

Probably the biggest addition to the squad was the Werder Bremen and Germany international midfielder Tim Borowski, who made his way from the Weserstadion to Bavaria on a free transfer, while veteran Italian defender Massimo Oddo made a similar cost-free move from European rivals AC Milan.

Without the pre-season DFB-Ligapokal which had been wound down – Bayern being the holders – Klinsmann's first meaningful game in charge was the Bundesliga opener against Hamburger SV at an expectant Allianz Arena. After all of the media hype and glorious fanfare, Munich expected.

Things would start off in fine fashion for the new coach, with two players who had been an integral part of his 2006 World Cup success putting *Die Roten* two goals up in the space of four minutes. Bastian Schweinsteiger opened the scoring after twelve minutes, and a Lukas Podolski penalty doubled the lead a minute after the quarter of an hour mark. However that was as good as it got, as the visitors fought back with a goal either side of half-time to grab a point. Interestingly, *Die Rothosen's* two scorers were Paolo Guerrero and Piotr Trochowski – both former Bayern players.

A seventy-fifth minute equaliser from new signing Borowski saw Bayern pick up a point in Dortmund, and the first win of the campaign finally came in match day three at home to Hertha Berlin, with the team finally clicking into gear with goals from Luca Toni, Philipp Lahm, Bastian Schweinsteiger and Miroslav Klose. This was followed by a hard-fought but ultimately convicing 3-0 win in Köln with a second-half brace from Toni and a ninetieth-minute third from hometown boy Lukas Podolski.

The doubters had seemingly been put in their place. Just two points behind early leaders Hamburg, Bayern looked to have finally settled down with the new coach.

20th September 2008 saw a Klose-less Bayern entertain long-time foes Werder Bremen, with everybody expecting a three-point return against the slow-starting *Werderaner* who had won just one of their opening four matches. It had been billed as a day for celebration, with the match coinciding with the beginning of the famous Munich *Oktoberfest*.

The visitors would start well – so well in fact that one might have wondered which of the two teams were playing at home. The men in green had an early shot hit the woodwork, but on the half-hour mark nineteen year old playmaker Mesut Özil threaded the perfect pass straight through the middle of the Bayern defence for Swede Markus Rosenberg. Beating the offside trap, Rosenberg deftly flicked the ball past the advancing Michael Rensing, rolling it low into the bottom right-hand corner of the net.

It would get worse. Werder now started to turn the screw, and right on the brink of half-time the busy Özil sent in a curling left-footed free-kick that Rensing could only parry. The ball fell straight to the feet of the big Brazilian defender Naldo, who made no mistake.

Bayern and Klinsmann would no doubt spend the half-time break looking for an answer and the coach looked to change the game's course by bringing on new boys Oddo and Borowski for the shaken Christian Lell and Daniel van Buyten, but just nine minutes into the second half the impressive Özil would get on the scoresheet himself. Dancing down the left and bursting into the Bayern box, the Gelsenkirchen-born midfielder unleashed a left-footed rocket that flew past Rensing and into the top of the net.

Still Bremen kept going. Five minutes after Özil's goal, the visitors swept up the entire length of the pitch, with Rosenberg setting up former Bayern hero Claudio Pizarro who executed the perfect poacher's finish to make it 4-0.

The misery didn't end there. With twenty-three minutes still remaining the excellent Rosenberg took advantage of more panic in the shellshocked Bayern defence to score his second and Werder's fifth. With the jeers and whistles ringing around the Allianz Arena, there was no escape for poor Klinsmann, who must have been wishing that the ground could just swallow him up.

With a record home defeat looming large, Bayern were able to take advantage of their opponents releasing their foot from the pedal – and the departure of their tormentors Özil and Rosenberg – to avoid further embarrassment. Two consolation goals in thirteen minutes from substitute and ex-*Bremer* Borowski arguably flattered the home side, who had been made to look like amateurs by Bremen's energy and positive, fast-paced play.

Having seemingly worked his way into everybody's good books with back to back wins, the eyes were back on Klinsmann again.

Not content to play their role as perennial party-poopers, Thomas Schaaf's side had also inflicted Bayern's biggest defeat at their new ground. The *Oktoberfest* celebrations had been well and truly dampened, and the visitors headed back north with a well-deserved three points.

The defeat against Bremen saw Klinsmann's side drop into eighth place in the Bundesliga table, and a flat single-goal defeat against fourth-from-bottom Hannover 96 at the AWD-Arena would lead many to conclude even at this early stage was that the "Klinsi Revolution" was not all it was cracked up to be.

Things would go from bad to worse the following week at the Allianz against lowly VfL Bochum, with Klinsmann's side throwing away a two-goal lead in the final ten minutes of the match. *Die Roten* had looked more than comfortable against the sixteenth-placed team with a 3-1 lead and should have closed things out, but two goals for the visitors in the space of as many minutes resulted in two more crucial points being dropped.

With a paltry nine points from seven games played, the Bavarians found themselves languishing down the table in eleventh place – just three above the drop zone.

Bayern's next match with Karlsruher SC had begun with both teams on nine points, and despite creating a number of decent opportunities early on the Bavarians continued to look toothless and short of ideas. KSC could even have snatched the lead in the second half, but the luck that had seemingly deserted Klinsmann's side for the previous three matches made a welcome return with just four minutes remaining.

A tiring home defence was unlocked by full-back Massimo Oddo, whose well-timed cross found master poacher Miroslav Klose. It was the break both Klinsmann and Bayern needed, but it could also have been described as the perfect smash and grab in a game where Bayern had been second best for long spells.

Five points adrift of top spot, the win in Karlsruhe provided the much-needed spark for a mini revival – and with it the guarantee of Klinsmann's survival until at least the winter break. Three second-half goals including a brace from Franck Ribéry saw Bayern come back from a 2-1 half-time deficit against mid-table VfL Wolfsburg to secure their first win in three matches at the Allianz, and another two-goal comeback against Eintracht Frankfurt reduced the gap with surprise early pace-setters Hoffenheim to just four points.

Two goals in the final quarter of an hour helped secure a 3-1 win over strugglers Arminia Bielefeld, and a far more solid performance in Gelsenkirchen against fifth-place Schalke 04 resulted in a hard-earned 2-1 win. The three points took Bayern to within a point of joint leaders Hoffenheim and Bayer Leverkusen.

A sixth win on the bounce at an icy-cold Borussia-Park against relegation candidates Mönchengladbach would have kept *Die Roten* right on the tail of the leaders, but not for the first time Bayern proved to be their own worst enemies as they threw away a decent advantage.

Having opened up a comfortable two-goal lead courtesy of a first-half strike from Luca Toni and a Ribéry penalty twenty minutes into the second half, Bayern's defence simply switched off before imploding completely in the face of the late pressure exerted by an energetic home side. Despite the successful return to the starting lineup for Philipp Lahm after a month-long injury break, the Bayern back line buckled under the pressure as a brace of unchallenged headed goals from Canadian Rob Friend and American Michael Bradley in the space of three minutes levelled up the scores at two apiece.

It looked another case of same again at the Allianz the following week, as Bayern fell behind to bottom side Energie Cottbus after twenty-five minutes. However before the capacity crowd could turn again on the beleaguered Klinsmann, Franck Ribéry sparked an almost immediate recovery for *Die Roten*.

Energie's lead lasted just four minutes, and when Martín Demichelis added a second seven minutes before half-time things were looking slightly better for both Bayern and the beleaguered coach. The second half saw Klinsmann's men run away with things in the end, as Klose and Toni completed the scoring in a five-minute second half burst.

A high-quality display at third-placed Bayer Leverkusen was settled in the exact same way – second-half strikes from Toni and Klose – and Bayern would have leaders Hoffenheim clearly in their sights.

The win in Leverkusen was the perfect prelude for a top of the table clash against Hoffenheim, the newly-promoted side from Baden-Württemberg that had taken the Bundesliga by storm. Ralf Rangnick's side knew that a win in Munich would take them six points clear at the top and with it the unofficial title of *Herbstmeister*, while for Bayern it presented a chance to draw level with the leaders and give them an opportunity to finish 2008 on a positive note.

After an opening forty-five minutes that saw few genuine opportunities for either side, the game ignited four minutes into the second half. With a league-leading forty goals in their fifteen games, the odds were always going to be good on Hoffenheim finding the net at least once; with his eighteenth goal of the season, TSG's top scorer Vedad Ibišević gave his side the lead.

Having looked initially offside, the Bosnian international had taken advantage of a panicked Bayern defence to turn on the spot and slot the ball low past Michael Rensing from close range. Rensing kept Bayern in the game with a fine save from Brazilian Carlos Eduardo as the confident visitors threatened to double their advantage, but on the hour mark it would take a moment of magic to bring the home side level.

That moment came courtesy of the tireless Philipp Lahm, whose bustling solo run from just inside the opposition half was finished with a shot from the edge of the box. Taking a slight deflection off defender Marvin Compper, the ball looped viciously before ending up in the back of the Hoffenheim net, with 'keeper Daniel Haas left completely helpless.

It was the moment of luck Klinsmann's side so desperately needed, and after that they were relentless in their pursuit of the three points. Chance after chance came and went, and between them Toni and Klose must have had half a dozen decent opportunities to snatch the winner.

It was like an unstoppable red and white waves crashing against a blue wall.

As the game ticked into the final minute the scene was perfectly set for the inevitable cries of "Bayern-Dusel": a long punt forward from Rensing was met in the air by Toni, whose header in turn found Klose. Getting the better of defender Andreas Ibertsberger, Klose smartly collected and then worked the ball back inside for his strike partner, and the big Italian made no mistake as he swept in a dramatic last-minute winner past Haas.

The emotional Klinsmann was leaping on the bench, a crucial three points were safely in the bank, and with just one game left before the *Winterpause*, Bayern had finally managed to get themselves level with the league leaders.

In all my years as a Bayern fan I have never understood how the idea of the "Bayern-Dusel" has managed to stick. For every last-minute winner, I can remember at least one that had gone the other way. This would be the case in the final game of 2008 in Stuttgart, where just a week after scoring their dramatic late winner against Hoffenheim, Bayern fell victim to exactly the same trick.

Defensive midfielder Sami Khedira had given VfB the lead on the stroke of half-time, but in the second half Bayern took command with goals from Tim Borowski and the prolific Toni. As the clock hit the ninety-minute mark it looked as though Bayern had at the very least guaranteed a winning finish, but Khedira would complement his late first-half strike with a dramatic injury time equaliser.

It was typical of what had been an inconsistent and at times unconvincing first half of the season under the new coach, but with Hoffenheim dropping two points at home to Schalke later that afternoon, Klinsmann's side were still able to finish level on points at the top. Just three points would separate the top five teams.

The first league game of 2009 saw Bayern travel up north to Hamburg, against a resurgent HSV side sitting just two points behind in fourth place. The home side would put in a disciplined display with 'keeper Frank Rost in fine form, and a Mladen Petrić strike a minute from half-time saw *Die Rothosen* collect all three points and hand Bayern their third defeat of the season.

HSV leapfrogged the Bavarians into third place, and with Hertha Berlin also winning Bayern dropped back into fourth – three points behind Hoffenheim, who started 2009 as they had ended 2008.

A 3-1 win over mid-table Dortmund coupled with Hoffenheim's 1-1 draw in Mönchengladbach helped close the gap at the top to just a point, and after the leaders had slipped to a shock 4-1 home defeat – their first of the season – against fifth-place Leverkusen, Klinsmann's side finally had an opportunity to get themselves into top spot for the first time. Their opponents on match day twenty were another one of the title challengers, third-placed Hertha.

On the Saturday afternoon just two points separated the top three teams. Hoffenheim led the way with thirty-nine points, but with a game in hand, both Bayern and Hertha had the opportunity to leap above the early pacesetters. In front of a capacity 74,200 crowd at the Olympiastadion, Hertha had the better form: since a shock 1-0 home defeat against Cottbus in late September, Lucien Favre's side had put together a run of seven straight home wins.

The confident Berliners were quickly into their stride, and a Bayern side lacking offensive spark were quickly stifled by a well-drilled blue and white-shirted defence. With Lukas Podolski left out of the match day squad, Klinsmann's woes increased even further ten minutes shy of half-time, when Luca Toni was forced off through injury. The Italian was replaced by US international Landon Donovan, on short-term loan from Major League Soccer side LA Galaxy.

Things had started to look just a little desperate for the under-pressure coach, and it would get worse just three minutes later when a mistake from Christian Lell presented Ukrainian Andriy Voronin with Hertha's opener. Unable to deal with Patrick Ebert's speculative long ball into the penalty area, the Bayern right-back ended up standing like a statue as the pony-tailed Voronin almost nonchalantly stepped in front of him to nod a looping header into the right hand corner of the net and past the helpless Michael Rensing.

Nine minutes into the second half Donovan forced Hertha's Czech 'keeper Jaroslav Drobný into a fine save, and having been bossed around for most of the first half, the Bavarians finally started to look like a team battling for top spot. Two minutes after the hour mark a long-range effort from Lúcio forced Drobný into another excellent stop, and the Czech pulled off an almost superhuman effort to parry Bastian Schweinsteiger's effort from the rebound before finally being beaten by arch-poacher Klose. The goal was far from pretty as Klose quite literally bundled the ball into the back of the Hertha net, but Bayern were back in the contest.

Stung into action, the men in the red and white hoops finally started to break the shackles. Ribéry was able to find a lot more freedom on the left, and the Frenchman's slick move to find Donovan ended with another fine save from Drobný, who stuck out a leg to deny the American. However just as Bayern had appeared to have gained a foothold, Hertha broke effectively to catch the red defence cold with thirteen minutes left on the clock. A bustling run from Raffael found Lúcio horribly out of position, and the Brazilian's simple pass found the unmarked Vorinin who swept the ball unerringly past Rensing into the bottom left hand corner of the goal.

Bayern would have the better of the closing stages, but the Hertha defence and the impressive Drobný held firm. With their eighth home win on the bounce the Berliner edged past Hoffenheim to claim top spot, while Bayern slipped back down to fourth. Bayern had been out-thought and out-muscled by a determined opponent, and the pressure was back on Klinsmann.

While losing in Berlin to an impressive and in-form Hertha was one thing, the following week's meeting with mid-table Köln at the Allianz would have the *Südkurve* baying for Klinsmann's blood. Football is often a game of luck, and the coach's critics could very well have been singing a different tune had Bayern had more luck early on.

Within the space of two minutes *Die Roten* would have a good shout for a penalty ignored and a header from Miroslav Klose ruled out, and when defender Martín Demichelis became the latest Bayern defender to suffer an inexplicable brain scramble, Klinsmann's side suddenly found themselves a goal down against the run of play.

The move was engineered by Serbian midfielder Nemanja Vučićević midway through the first half, whose run towards the Bayern box from inside his own half set up Frenchman Fabrice Ehret, who strolled past the statuesque Demichelis before slotting the ball past Rensing. Vučićević was also the architect of Köln's second goal just twelve minutes later, ghosting down the right and jinking past left-back Philipp Lahm before cutting the ball back into space for the unmarked Daniel Brosinski.

While Bayern had been a little unlucky up front, a combination of defensive frailty and complete tactical brainlessness resulted in the dropping of three points that had largely been taken for granted. A late consolation from Daniel van Buyten provided a flattering finish for the home side, but the defeat gave Köln coach Christoph Daum his first win in nine attempts in Munich. Given the dislike for the arrogant and outspoken Daum among the Bayern fans, the defeat was twice as bitter. It was clear that from this point on that Klinsmann was living on borrowed time.

The last week of February and a flat goalless draw against mid-table Bremen saw Bayern drop four points behind league leaders Hertha into fifth place, with an in-form VfL Wolfsburg – coached by former Bayern coach Felix Magath – continuing their gradual climb up the table into fourth spot. Klinsmann knew that there could be no room for any slip-ups against Hannover 96 at the Allianz, and from almost nowhere the team provided the coach with what many saw as a stay of execution with a stunning 5-1 win.

Czech striker Jiří Štajner had given the visitors the lead after a quarter of an hour to once again put the home supporters on edge, but following van Buyten's equaliser five minutes later Bayern did not look back. Klose and Hamit Altıntop extended the Bavarians' advantage before half-time, and two futher strikes from Podolski and Demichelis were enough to keep the knives in the *Südkurve* sheathed – for the time being, at least. The win took Bayern into second place: four points behind Hertha, and part of a group of four teams locked on forty-two points. Things couldn't have been any tighter, with Bayern, early leaders Hoffenheim and in-form Wolfsburg all on the same goal difference of +18.

	P	W	D	L	Goals	GD	Pts
Hertha BSC Berlin	23	14	4	5	38:27	+11	46
FC Bayern München	23	12	6	5	49:31	+18	42
TSG 1899 Hoffenheim	23	12	6	5	49:31	+18	42
VfL Wolfsburg	23	12	6	5	46:28	+18	42
Hamburger SV	23	13	3	7	35:35	+0	42

A 3-0 win at relegation-threatened Bochum kept Bayern in second place behind Hertha on matchday 22, and a tight encounter at the Allianz against Karlsruhe settled by Argentinian José Ernesto Sosa coupled with a defeat for the leaders in Stuttgart helped close the gap back to a single point. By now the top four were separated by a single point, with Hoffenheim dropping off the pace four points further behind in fifth.

Since the defeat against Köln Bayern had picked up ten points from four games and looked to have found form just at the right time. Match day 26 would see Klinsmann's side take on the Bundesliga's form team, VfL Wolfsburg.

Having had a slow start to the season, the unheralded Wolves had slowly but surely started to creep up the table - tapping a rich vein of form that had seen them put together an eight-match unbeaten run, with the last seven yielding seven wins. This was a genuine top of the table clash, one that was given extra spice with the presence of former Bayern coach Felix Magath.

The Magath-inspired Big Bad Wolf was always a beast to be feared, and a somewhat cagey first half suddenly opened up with an exchange of goals right at the end. Yet another defensive lapse from *Die Roten* saw the unmarked Christian Gentner drill in a near post header from a Zvjezdan Misimović corner to give the home side the lead, but an almost immediate response saw Bastian Schweinsteiger send a free-kick into the Wolfsburg box which was well met at the far post by Lúcio. The Brazilian centre-back's header was well kept out by Diego Benaglio, but the Wolves' 'keeper, now having fallen behind his goal line, could do nothing to prevent Luca Toni's sliding effort from crossing the threshold. Just seconds after their team had taken the lead, the noisy crowd at the Volkswagen-Arena had been silenced.

Having finished the first half on a positive note the men in red and white walked out for the start of the second half, completely unprepared for the storm that was about to hit them. With the game having meandered past the hour mark with the score still 1-1, the Big Bad Wolf suddenly snarled into life. There would be no happy fairytale ending for Klinsmann's side; in the space of twelve frenetic minutes, they found themselves living through Red Riding Hood's worst nightmare.

With sixty-five minutes played, a slow build up in midfield from the men in green was finished with an injection of pace from Marcel Schäfer, whose pinpoint cross into the Bayern box zipped past a line of red and white shorts before finding Edin Džeko. The dangerous Bosnian striker looked marginally offside as the cross came in, but the linesman's flag stayed down. The ball flashed past Rensing and into the Bayern net, and the Wolves were back in front again.

The moments that followed provided the perfect summary of Bayern's season, particularly the chaotic management from the touchline. Bayern immediately looked to get back into the contest and win a corner, and in the process Lúcio received what looked like a particularly painful knock. Rather than use the break in play to assess the fitness of the Brazilian, the coach stood back as the corner was sent harmlessly into the Wolfsburg box, where it was easily collected by Benaglio.

With the Bayern defence completely out of position and the injured Lúcio unable to keep up with the play, Benaglio rolled the ball smartly out to Džeko, who found Misimović to his right while continuing his charge towards the Bayern goal. Misimović's beautifully floated return ball was perfectly collected on the run by the Bosnian, who finished the move with an even more perfect left-footed finish that fizzed low into the bottom right-hand corner of the net with Rensing left completely flat-footed.

Just moments after the Wolfsburg goal, the limping Lúcio slowly made his way off the pitch to be replaced by Andreas Ottl.

The usually animated Klinsmann was left staring into space with his arms folded on the Bayern bench, as things went from bad to worse. Just eight minutes after the third goal, a looping ball into the danger zone from the impressive Gentner found Brazilian striker Grafite, who took the ball expertly on his chest and held off countryman Breno before swiveling back towards goal and sending a firm low strike into the bottom right corner.

The Wolves were now in complete control, and just three minutes later Magath's men inflicted further humiliation on a Bayern side where the wheels had well and truly come off. Following another failed Bayern attack and another fast counter, Grafite picked up the ball deep inside the Bayern half. After two-stepping between a flat-footed Lell and Ottl (two names Bayern fans never mention in the same breath without the slightest chuckle) and waltzing past a desperate Rensing, the Brazilian could have turned to shoot with his right foot, but instead chose to send the cheekiest of back-heels into the bottom left-hand corner.

Klinsmann was left dumbstruck, Uli Hoeneß chose to focus his gaze elsewhere, and even as the most fervent Bayern fan I found myself applauding not just the skill and control but the sheer audacity of the opposition.

It was like walking in a heavy rain shower. At first you just want to find any sort of shelter, but once you have been soaked to the skin and know that it cannot possibly get any worse, it is a lot easier to just stand still and enjoy the experience. By this time I found myself laughing along with the Wolfsburg bench; there was nothing I wanted more than to see Klinsmann turfed out as quickly as possible.

Having stumbled through the season deluding myself into thinking that things had not been so bad, those dramatic twelve minutes at the VW-Arena had proved once and for all that Klinsmann's side were simply not good enough to win the title. They had not just been beaten; they had been completely mauled by the rampant Wolves.

Wolfsburg assumed top spot with Bayern only three points behind in fourth, but any remaining desire to win the title was tempered by the equally strong wish to see Klinsmann sent on his way. It was, for me, a Catch-22: if Klinsmann turned things around and managed to drag the team to another title, he was almost guaranteed to stay. A couple more bad results, he was out. The perfect scenario of course was to see him given his marching orders with enough time for his replacement to turn things around.

Klinsmann was playing for his position on a weekly basis by now, and as had been the case when coach of the national team in 2006 he was always just one game away from being fired. Defeat against twelfth-placed Eintracht Frankfurt would surely have sealed his fate, but just a week after the mauling in Wolfsburg the team produced a solid display to stroll to a comfortable 4-0 win. A 1-0 win at struggling Bielefeld kept *Die Roten* within spitting distance of leaders Wolfsburg with six match days remaining, but a return to bad ways at home to sixth-placed Schalke 04 would finally bring the guillotine down.

Any sort of win against the *Königsblauen* would have taken Bayern level with Wolfsburg at the top of the table after the leaders' shock defeat at the hands of relegation-threatened Energie Cottbus, but there was little point doing the calculations. A completely insipid performance culminating in a one-goal defeat, decided by yet another collection of defensive blunders and the dismissal of a brainlessly petulant Franck Ribéry, signalled an appropriately bitter end for the Klinsmann experiment.

In the face of loud demands by the fans for the beleaguered coach's departure, the club finally decided to part ways with the former striker who had remained optimistic to the last.

While older Bayern fans could find ways of balancing Klinsmann's abject failure as a coach with his success as a goalscorer in the club's colours during the previous decade, younger supporters would always associate the much-fêted golden hope as one of the worst coaching appointments of the modern era.

Whether Jürgen Klinsmann was actually worse than the likes of Søren Lerby or Erich Ribbeck is a matter of opinion, and his time at Bayern will continue to be the subject of much debate. In the eyes of many of the club's supporters, Klinsmann's high-profile reputation – first as a player, then as the coach of the German national team - had been permanently tarnished during his turbulent nine months in Munich. For those too young to remember Wattenschied, Norwich and Copenhagen, the Klinsmann era was the ultimate nadir.

In fairness, Klinsmann had never been provided with the suitable ammunition to see through his radical plans at Bayern. With just one recognised world class player in Ribéry, the team had become far too reliant on the Frenchman as the hapless coach continued to blunder his way through the season with a squad that could best be described as ordinary.

The retirement of goalkeeping legend Oliver Kahn and his replacement with the spirited but ultimately inadequate Michael Rensing was just one example, while a terrifyingly error-prone defensive backline was arguably the most consistent feature of Klinsmann's frustratingly inconsistent tenure. Klinsmann was by no measure a great coach, but even the likes of Lattek, Hitzfeld or Heynckes would have struggled with the same resources.

Then there were the unorthodox and ultra-modern coaching techniques and sports psychology – fine so long as the results were right, but a soft-targeted source of ridicule once things had started to go awry. When Klinsmann arrived in Munich, his ideas had been seen my many as a breath of fresh air; by the time of his departure, it was simply transatlantic hot air.

Lest we then forget the completely pointless signing of Landon Donovan, who would join the likes of Adolfo Valencia, Michael Sternkopf and Tobias Rau on the list of the most useless players to ever pull on a FC Bayern *Trikot*.

With just five games remaining and the club precariously positioned in fifth place in the league table, the Bayern board would turn to a tried and tested figure to fulfil the minimum requirement of Champions League football the following season: Jupp Heynckes.

In contrast to the team's inconsistent domestic form, Jürgen Klinsmann's side would perform more than adequately in the Champions League, putting together an impressive unbeaten run before becoming unstuck in the last eight against a star-studded Barcelona team that had rightly been described as one of the greatest of its generation.

En route to the quarter-final Bayern had emerged unbeaten in what had been seen as a testing first phase group, before setting a new tournament record in their second round meeting with Portuguese side Sporting Clube de Portugal – arguably the one positive and memorable thing that Klinsmann could take away from his nine months in charge of *Die Roten*.

The group phase had seen Bayern drawn alongside Italians AC Fiorentina, familiar foes Olympique Lyonnaise and Romanian champions FC Steaua București, and the campaign would get off to a solid start with a hard-earned 1-0 in Bucharest courtesy of an early header from Daniel van Buyten. A second half effort from Miroslav Klose gave Bayern a share of the points at the Allianz in what was a disappointing game against Lyon, but a resounding 3-0 victory over Fiorentina was enough to put the Bavarians on top at the half-way point with seven points, two clear of the French champions.

The return meeting in Florence against Fiorentina saw Bayern snatch another point courtesy of a Tim Borowski strike twelve minutes from time, and three second half goals at the Allianz against Steaua were enough to guarantee a spot in the last sixteen for Klinsmann's side. Ahead of Lyon on goal difference with eleven points from their five games, the final game in France would decide top spot.

This final game at the Stade Gerland would arguably produce Bayern's best performance of the group phase, at least in the first half where they overcame a shaky start to storm into a three goal lead. Two Miroslav Klose strikes sandwiched a goal from Franck Ribéry, and Bayern were excellent value for their lead. The second half was a slightly different story as the home side pegged the score back to 3-2, but having just needed a draw to top the group Bayern safely saw things out to finish on an impressive fourteen points – four wins and two draws – from their six group matches.

The second round draw set up an encounter with Portuguese side Sporting Clube de Portugal, who had finished second in a tough group behind Barcelona and ahead of Ukrainians Shakhtar Donetsk and Swiss champions FC Basel.

Bayern's previous meetings with Sporting at the group stage in 2006/07 had produced two well-contested draws, and following defeats against Hertha Berlin and Köln expectations were mixed ahead of the first leg at the Estádio José Alvalade. Sporting may not have been on the same level as Barcelona, Manchester United or Juventus, but they were more than capable of getting a result against a defensively suspect Bayern side that had shown itself to be weak at the seams. In the end, the Bavarians pulled out a performance as surprising as it was stunning.

The opening forty minutes provided little indication of what was to follow with Philipp Lahm having to hack the ball off his own line early on, but just three minutes before half-time Franck Ribéry would weave straight through the green and white defence before drilling a low shot into the bottom left corner of the net past 'keeper Tiago to give Bayern the lead.

Playing in an all white *Trikot*, there was a suitably ethereal flow to Bayern's play as they slipped into a higher gear in the second half. The smooth build-up and approach play from Klinsmann's side was something alien to those who had seen them struggling to break down less heralded defences in the Bundesliga, with Ribéry in particular producing moments of magic whenever he touched the ball. Three minutes short of the hour mark, a cross from full-back Massimo Oddo found Miroslav Klose via the head of Luca Toni, and the striker was left with a simple tap-in to double *Die Roten's* advantage.

There was the slightest whiff of offside about the goal, but on days like this that little bit of luck can make all the difference. Just days before Klose had been denied an early goal against Köln in a game that would eventually go against Bayern, but this time luck was on his side. Two goals down, the *Sportinguistas* simply folded in the face of a Bayern attack that had suddenly found its touch and confidence.

Just six minutes later Ribéry scored his second from the penalty spot after Lahm was brought down by Sporting substitute Pereirinha, and with the result no longer in doubt it was just a matter of how many goals Bayern would score. Another jinking run down the left from the effervescent Ribéry set up Toni to score Bayern's fourth, and the same duo combined right at the death with the Italian tucking the ball past Tiago from close range at the second attempt.

The stunning win in Portugal appeared to have kicked Bayern's season back into life, and on the weekend ahead of the second leg at the Allianz they had trounced Hannover 96 5-1. With their place in the last eight guaranteed barring a complete catastrophe, it was now a simple matter of maintaining their rhythm and form and delivering a good performance in front of their own supporters. The Bayern team clearly fulfilled their part of the bargain, and with the tie already over as a contest before a ball had even been kicked in the second leg, their traumatised opponents offered little in the way of resistance. What happened afterwards could best be described as a massacre.

Even without first-leg hero Franck Ribéry, the Bavarians served up a footballing display – and with it a new tournament record. Jürgen Klinsmann's short spell in charge at Bayern had produced very few memorable moments, but that evening against Sporting, the capacity crowd at the Allianz Arena was treated to ninety minutes of attacking football many would remember for a long time.

With just eight minutes gone Lukas Podolski made the most of a rare start to set things on their way, and the underused winger doubled Bayern's lead eleven minutes before half-time. That second goal precipitated a quick glut before the break: defender Ânderson Polga put the ball past his own keeper after thirty-nine minutes under pressure from Bastian Schweinsteiger, and although João Moutinho pulled a goal back for the visitors just three minutes later, an almost immediate response from the impressive Schweinsteiger saw the free-flowing Bavarians march into the dressing room 4-1 up on the night and 9-1 in front on aggregate.

For once, I found myself watching a match with no nervous tension whatsoever, and enjoying every minute of it. With the opposition defence looking ragged and forlorn, there would surely be more goals to come in the second half. Seeing the opportunity to try something a little different, the Bayern coach sent on youngsters Breno and José Sosa for Brazilian duo Lúcio and Zé Roberto, and with eighteen minutes remaining Schweinsteiger made way for one of the latest products from the Bayern academy: a tall and slightly spindly winger by the name of Thomas Müller.

The men in the famous green and white hoops would try their best to stem the tide, and for the opening half hour of the second half managed to keep Bayern out. But spurred on by the capacity 65,000 crowd, Klinsmann's side finally scored their fifth with just over a quarter of an hour left on the clock. Following some neat approach play from Miroslav Klose, Skipper Mark van Bommel thundered the ball into the net with a typical long-range effort. The floodgates had been opened again, and with eight minutes remaining Klose deservedly added his name to the scoreboard.

Teenage prospect Müller completed the rout, extending the score to a scarcely credible 7-1. The 12-1 aggregate victory would set a new mark in the Champions League, breaking the record for a winning margin in the knock-out rounds of the competition.

In the end, the record-setting second round would prove to be a false dawn for the Klinsmann era, the sort of event that takes fans to cloud nine, only to leave them plummeting back down to earth without a parachute.

The quarter-final matchup against Spanish giants FC Barcelona at the Camp Nou could not have come at a worse time for Bayern and their beleaguered coach. It had been just four days since the horrible 5-1 thrashing at the hands of Wolfsburg, and a Champions League quarter-final against an in-form, star-studded *Blaugrana* was the last thing everybody wanted to see.

Any hopes of making the semi-finals had been well and truly crushed as Pep Guardiola's side found the back of Hans-Jörg Butt's goal no fewer than four times before half-time. Argentinian star Lionel Messi netted a brace, with Samuel Eto'o and Thierry Henry also contributing. The second half was no more than an exercise in self-preservation for the home side, and to their credit Bayern wouldn't ship any further goals as the home side switched into their relaxed *tiki-taka*.

With the tie as good as over ahead of the second leg at the Allianz, the biggest mission for *Die Roten* was to restore their badly battered pride. A goal two minutes into the second half from Franck Ribéry would give the home supporters something to shout about, but Malian Seydou Keita's equaliser seventeen minutes from time levelled the scores on the night as Barcelona eased to a 5-1 aggregate victory.

Bayern's dismal Bundesliga season and the Champions League thrashing by Barcelona were perfectly complemented by an inconsistent run in the DFB-Pokal. A topsy-turvy 4-3 struggle against third division Rot-Weiß Erfurt was followed by a more sedate 2-0 win over local rivals Nürnberg, but in the third round Bayern rediscovered their elusive form against VfB Stuttgart, subjecting the *Schwaben* to a 5-1 demolition at the Gottlieb-Daimler-Stadion to set up an intriguing quarter-final against Bayer Leverkusen.

After a goalless first half at the BayArena, a stunning sixteen-minute spell saw the *Werkself* storm into a three-goal lead. Bayern did respond, and two goals in as many minutes from Lúcio and Miroslav Klose gave Klinsmann's side a sniff of a chance, but the Bavarian-born Stefan Kießling settled the matter in the final minute as Bayer marched into the last four.

Within a fortnight of the Champions League defeat against Barcelona, Jürgen Klinsmann was making his way out of the Säbenerstraße. For all the pre-season promise and media hype, the former striker's short spell in charge would constitute one of the poorest spells in FC Bayern's history since Søren Lerby and Erich Ribbeck in the early 1990s.

It was one of those great ironies that the man who arrived to rescue Bayern's season at the end of April 2009 was Jupp Heynckes – whose dismissal in 1991 had resulted in the appointment of the unfortunate Lerby. Bayern supremo Uli Hoeneß had come to regret his treatment of Heynckes all those years before – describing it as his greatest error – but seventeen years later the former coach was back at the helm in Munich, part of an emergency plan to rescue and make the best of what had been a desperately disappointing season for *Die Roten*.

Having spent more than two years out of the game following his resignation from Borussia Mönchengladbach in January 2007, Heynckes arrived with Bayern sitting in third place in the Bundesliga table, just three points behind leaders Wolfsburg with five games remaining. With the Wolves in dominant form, the title was still something of a long shot; the most immediate task for the new coach was a finish in the top two, and with it an automatic berth into the following seasons' Champions League. Just a point behind second-placed Hertha and ahead of both Stuttgart and HSV on goal difference, a tight run in towards the finishing line was pretty much guaranteed.

Heynckes' first game of his caretaker spell in Munich – interestingly, against former club Borussia Mönchengladbach – saw Bayern scrape a tight 2-1 win, which combined with Hertha's draw in Hamburg pushed the Bavarians into second place behind Wolfsburg. A 3-1 win at relegation-threateded Cottbus coupled with a 4-1 defeat for the leaders at the hands of fourth-placed Stuttgart the week after saw the Bavarians pull themselves level at the top, separated by just two goals' difference.

Hopes of salvaging what had been a miserable season with the *Meisterschale* had been suddenly rekindled for every Bayern fan, and a three-goal second-half display against mid-table Bayer Leverkusen maintained the pressure on the leaders. Wolfsburg for their part bounced back impressively from their beating in Stuttgart with a resounding 3-0 win over fifth-placed Dortmund, while a resurgent Hertha Berlin closed to within one point of the leaders, with Stuttgart a further point adrift.

Fifth-placed Hamburger SV would have a remote mathematical chance of snatching the title, but with two game days remaining it was all about the top four.

	P	W	D	L	Goals	GD	Pts
VfL Wolfsburg	32	19	6	7	70:40	+20	63
FC Bayern München	32	19	6	7	67:39	+18	63
Hertha BSC Berlin	32	19	5	8	48:37	+11	62
VfB Stuttgart	32	18	7	7	60:41	+19	61

A topsy-turvy encounter at the Dietmar-Hopp-Stadion against Hoffenheim saw Heynckes drop his first points in four matches, with the Bundesliga new boys making Bayern work for what was a hard-earned point. Franck Ribéry had given Bayern an early lead, but two strikes in the space of eight minutes from Demba Ba and Carlos Eduardo would turn things on their head just short of the hour mark. An equaliser a minute from half-time from Luca Toni helped breathe some life back into the visiting Bayern supporters, but neither side could make the crucial breakthrough in the second half.

Wolfsburg meanwhile had truly slipped into another gear altogether. While Bayern were heading into the dressing room at half-time in Hoffenheim with the score locked at 2-2, the Wolves were already three goals to the good against mid-table Hannover 96 at the AWD-Arena. Driven by their men of the season Edin Džeko and Grafite – Bayern's tormentors in that infamous 5-1 beating – the 96ers were simply blown away as Magath's side strolled to a stunning 5-0 win.

The margin of Wolfsburg's victory in their penultimate fixture would put the ball firmly in their court heading into the final weekend of the season. Up against tenth-placed Werder Bremen, the Wolves needed just a point at the VW-Arena to clinch their maiden Bundesliga title.

Bayern meanwhile were hoping for a shock defeat for the Wolves against Bremen and a win against third-placed Stuttgart, who were themselves still in with an outside chance of claiming the coveted "salad bowl". Like Bayern, the Swabians needed a win at the Allianz-Arena coupled with a Wolfsburg defeat to leapfrog into to top spot. The day was set to take one of two paths: either Wolfsburg would wrap things up with minimum fuss, or there would be yet another nail-biting finish.

Fourth-placed Hertha Berlin would also have a theoretical chance of winning the title, but for them it was more about claiming one of the three coveted places in the Champions League, with just three points separating the top four teams. A defeat for Bayern combined with a win for Hertha at home against already relegated Karlsruher SC would have sent them down to fourth – and a season of second-tier European football in the UEFA Cup – soon to be renamed the UEFA Europa League.

	P	W	D	L	Goals	GD	Pts
VfL Wolfsburg	33	20	6	7	75:40	+35	66
FC Bayern München	33	19	7	7	69:41	+28	64
VfB Stuttgart	33	19	7	7	62:41	+21	64
Hertha BSC Berlin	33	19	6	8	48:37	+11	63

Ahead of the kickoff, some Bayern fans must have been dreaming of past titles snatched right at the death, stories that had gone down in the annals of footballing folklore in Munich and condemned as *Bayern-Dusel* elsewhere. Bayer Leverkusen had thrown away the title having needed just a draw in 2000. The following year, Schalke 04 would have their hands on the *Meisterschale* for four minutes. Would the same fate befall VfL Wolfsburg?

For one of the very few times in my life I found myself sitting down to watch the final weekend of a Bundesliga season cheering on Werder Bremen. If they were to pull off the impossible, I would have happily eaten undercooked boiled fish for a week while singing their fan song *Lebenslang Grün-Weiß*.

With seven minutes on the clock, bad news would come from Lower Saxony with Wolfsburg taking the lead. To make matters worse, the man at the centre of it was former Bayern midfielder Zvjezdan Misimović. Just eight minutes later, the prolific Grafite had more or less drawn a line under things with a second. A Khalid Boulahrouz own goal just moments later in Munich put Bayern in front at the Allianz, but from this point on it would be all about securing second spot and that automatic place in the following season's Champions League.

A third Wolfsburg goal courtesy of Bremen's Austrian defender Sebastian Prödl effectively sealed the deal for Magath's side, and although Diego pulled one back for Werder, Grafite restored his side's three-goal cushion just short of the hour mark.

The Wolves had surely won their first title, with perhaps the biggest, baddest one of all at the helm. Having been shunted out of the Säbenerstraße just two years earlier, revenge must have tasted sweet for Wolfsburg coach Felix Magath. By this time his team were thumping in goals for fun, and even the biggest and most unobjective Bayern fan could not deny that the team from Lower Saxony had been the better side over the closing weeks of the season.

Mark van Bommel scored a second goal on the hour mark for Bayern to put a bit of daylight between them and Stuttgart, and with Hertha being hammered by a Karlsruhe side determined to say goodbye to the top flight with a smile on their faces, second place was pretty much in the bag for the men from Munich. A Mario Gómez strike after sixty-four minutes for VfB proved to be little more than a minor annoyance as Bayern chalked up their fourth league win in five games.

As the dust began to settle, the only real regret was not getting rid of the hapless Jürgen Klinsmann a lot earlier.

Jupp Heynckes had done all he could in the short time he had been given, but not even he could stem the green tide that saw Wolfsburg sweep to the title. Just to rub it in just a little further, Džeko rounded off the Wolves' final home show with a fifth goal.

His thirty-five day task complete, the caretaker coach was on his way again having signed a new contract with Bayer Leverkusen. The hunt for a permanent replacement was already well under way, with a new name set to arrive at the Säbenerstraße. After the failure of the Klinsmann experiment, the Bayern board made a sharp turn back to more experienced candidates.

	P	W	D	L	Goals	GD	Pts
VfL Wolfsburg	34	21	6	7	80:41	+39	69
FC Bayern München	34	20	7	7	71:42	+29	67
VfB Stuttgart	34	19	7	8	63:43	+20	64
Hertha BSC Berlin	34	19	6	9	48:41	+7	63

Unlike Klinsmann, the man who arrived in Munich at the beginning of July 2009 did not come with a resident army of psychologists, technological tacticians, nutrition specialists and American fitness gurus. Instead, he brought with him a sterling coaching record, and a reputation as an established, tried and tested master and commander.

GOING DUTCH

When Aloysius Paulus Maria van Gaal walked into the Säbenerstraße as coach for the first time on 1st July 2009, yet another new era would begin in Munich. In contrast to the previous grandiose project that had elevated the inexperienced Jürgen Klinsmann as the man to take Bayern into the new era, Uli Hoeneß and the board decided on employing a coach with considerably more experience.

Louis van Gaal arrived in Munich with a reputation and a solid CV, which had started with a six-year spell in his home city of Amsterdam where he coached Ajax to three successive domestic titles between 1994 and 1996, a UEFA Cup title in 1992 and the coveted Champions League in 1995. Bringing back memories of the powerful side of the early 1970s, van Gaal had also led Ajax to the Champions League final in 1996, only for them to fall short against Juventus on penalties.

Van Gaal's domestic success with Ajax resulted in him signing a three year contract with Catalan giants Barcelona, but two domestic titles and one *Copa del Rey* was not enough to satisfy the faithful at the Camp Nou. An acrimonious departure was followed by a dreadful spell in charge of the Netherlands national team, which saw the *Oranje* fail to qualify for the tournament for the first time in sixteen years. Yet despite this lack of success Barcelona once again turned to the Dutchman for the start of the 2002/03 season; this time, he wouldn't even last six months in the post before he was on his way again.

A failed year as technical director at Ajax would look like the beginning of the end of van Gaal's high-flying coaching career, and with the successes of the mid-1990s slowly fading he returned home to the Netherlands to take the helm at former UEFA Cup finalists AZ Alkmaar, at the time one of the unfashionable also-rans in the *Eredivisie*.

Van Gaal's results at AZ were solid rather than spectacular, and up against the duopoly of Ajax and PSV Eindhoven three successive top-three finishes between 2005 and 2007 were seen as a good result for a side that had won its only previous title back in 1981. However, an eleventh-place finish in 2007/08 looked to have condemned van Gaal to the ranks of the once-greats. With the Alkmaar club once again sinking into the depths of mid-table mediocrity, van Gaal offered his resignation.

Football is a game of twists and turns however, and the decision by the AZ players to persuade the coach to stay on would not only change the fortunes of the club, but also provide van Gaal with a springboard back into the big time. Twenty-eight years after they had claimed their last domestic championship, AZ finally did enough to stay ahead of their more illustrious and decorated rivals to take the crown. Louis van Gaal was once again the miracle man of Dutch football.

The second coming of Louis van Gaal would come just at the right time for him and FC Bayern. While it might have been a wrench leaving AZ after five seasons, *Die Roten's* first-ever Dutch coach would have been entitled to believe that his mission in Alkmaar had been achieved and that a new challenge awaited him in Bavaria.

The arrival of Louis van Gaal in Munich coincided with a wholesale series of personnel changes, with a number of well-known players heading to Bavaria and plenty of established faces heading out the other way. Perhaps the most talked about new name was the highly-rated VfB Stuttgart striker Mario Gómez, who arrived in Munich for a hefty €30 million, while hard-working Croatian striker Ivica Olić headed south to join *Die Roten* on a free transfer from Hamburger SV.

The gritty and versatile Ukrainian defensive midfielder Anatoliy Tymoshchuk was signed from Zenit St. Petersburg for €11 million and Croatian winger Danijel Pranjić made the move from Dutch side SC Heerenveen for a snip under €8 million, while one-time German international Andreas Görlitz returned to Munich following a two-year loan spell in the second division with Karlsruhe SC. Promising attacking midfielder Alexander Baumjohann arrived from Borussia Mönchengladbach on a free transfer, along with unknown Dutch defender Edson Braafheid (FC Twente Enschede, €2 million).

A number of players from Bayern's amateur ranks were also elevated to the senior squad during the course of the season, including the highly-rated Austrian midfielder-cum-wingback David Alaba, centre-back Holger Badstuber, left-back Diego Contento and attacking midfielder Mehmet Ekici. In fact, one of the biggest features of what would turn into the *Ära van Gaal* was the integration of younger players from the club's youth development programme.

There had been plenty of changes to the squad, but the biggest new face at Bayern would make his first appearance at the Säbenerstraße just before the closing of the transfer window: the temperamental but highly talented Dutch winger Arjen Robben. A long-time favourite of the new coach, Robben made the move to Munich from Spanish giants Real Madrid for what was clearly a bargain sum of just €24 million. It would be the beginning of a beautiful partnership.

Among those leaving Munich included Brazilian duo Lúcio and Zé Roberto who departed for Internazionale and HSV respectively, while a number of players who had proved to be a disappointment also made their way out. Both Lukas Podolski and Tim Borowski headed back to their previous clubs Köln and Werder Bremen after unproductive spells in Bavaria, loanee Massimo Oddo returned to AC Milan, while former youth prospect Stephan Fürstner dropped down a division with a move up the road to second division outfit SpVgg Greuther Fürth.

Meanwhile Argentinian José Sosa, signed as a relative unknown in 2007 for €9 million, ended up in Serie A with Napoli after spending a year on loan with his former club Estudiantes. Having been little more than a ghost for the best part of three seasons in Munich, the midfielder departed at a loss to the club of €6 million.

The nature of the challenge facing Louis van Gaal in Munich became apparent very quickly, and not even a month into the campaign some of the Bayern faithful would already be wondering whether the decision to appoint the Dutchman had been a wise one after all. Here was a man who had won nothing of note for over a decade, a coach who might have continued on his journey into obscurity were it not for his winning the Dutch first division – which was, by all accounts, something of a Mickey Mouse league.

Having disposed of the spluttering VW Beetle that was Jürgen Klinsmann, Bayern fans were left wondering if they had been left with a lemon: an old Bentley or Rolls-Royce that still had the hand-stitched leather seats and crafted wooden fascia, but underneath the expensive veneer an uninsurable monster that needed constant visits to the garage; the sort of vehicle that looked great sitting in the driveway, resting solely on its reputation and the swift and rather flattering polish of its chrome bumpers provided by an *Eredivisie* title.

Bayern would get their season underway with a 1-1 draw in Hoffenheim, and were lucky to get a point at home against Werder Bremen with new signing Mario Gómez levelling the scores with just eighteen minutes remaining. However, the biggest shock would come in the third week against newly-promoted 1. FSV Mainz 05, which saw the Bavarians fall two goals behind before the break. An own goal from Macedonian Nikolče Noveski halved the deficit, but with three games played Bayern found themselves sitting in fourteenth place on a paltry two points, five adrift of early pace-setters Leverkusen, HSV and Schalke 04.

Van Gaal's side would have to wait until the last week of August for their first three-point haul at the Allianz against Wolfsburg, when the new signings finally clicked. Picking up from where he had left off at Stuttgart, Gómez opened the scoring, but the star of the show was the mercurial Arjen Robben, who drove Bayern to their first league win of the season after coming on for Hamit Altıntop at the start of the second half. Two goals in twelve minutes from the Dutchman were enough to finish off the stubborn Wolves.

If Bayern had been abject in their opening three matches, they would be absolutely sublime on match day five against Dortmund at the Signal Iduna Park. With both teams floating in mid-table on five points there was plenty to play for, and with no love lost between *Die Roten* and their rivals from the *Ruhrpott*, a capacity crowd of over eighty-thousand settled down for what promised to be another closely-fought encounter.

Former Bayern youth talent Mats Hummels would put the home side in front with a close-range header after just eleven minutes, but after a somewhat rocky and error-strewn start the Bavarians gradually weathered the storm with the prolific Gómez netting the equaliser with a header from right on the goal line nine minutes before the break.

When the two teams emerged for the second half, a game that had gently simmered over the first forty-five minutes exploded into life. The Bayern coach was largely responsible for the change in momentum, with Franck Ribéry and Thomas Müller coming on for Gómez and Altıntop at the restart. Immediately the two substitutes had an impact, carving open the Dortmund defence to set up Robben, whose short pass inside to Bastian Schweinsteiger was returned in the direction of the Dortmund goal with considerable interest to give van Gaal's side the lead.

Having played more than a considerable part in creating Schweinsteiger's goal, the two substitutes now took over to turn what was already an encouraging scoreline into a massacre. The first act was an unerring free-kick from Ribéry after sixty-five minutes, with the Frenchman leaving Dortmund 'keeper Roman Weidenfeller rooted to the spot as the ball swerved around the yellow-shirted wall before crashing into the top-right hand corner of the net.

After that it was the Thomas Müller show, with the fresh-faced, gangly and awkward-looking nineteen year-old lashing in his first Bundesliga goal from thirteen yards before capping things off with a spectacular twenty-yard strike two minutes from time to complete a stunning 5-1 rout.

Bayern had clearly found a new young star in Müller, and the van Gaal show finally looked to be underway.

With eight goals in two games spirits were high ahead of the journey north to Hamburg to take on unbeaten HSV, but the spark of the previous two weeks was extinguished by a solid home side who took all three points through Croat Mladen Petrić just eighteen minutes from time – with the assist provided by former Bayern crowd favourite Zé Roberto.

With seven matches played Bayern found themselves in seventh place on eleven points – six behing the high-flying Hamburgers – and the following week things would get even worse as van Gaal's side drew an uninspiring blank at home to struggling Köln.

A 2-1 win in the Black Forest over SC Freiburg inspired by the ever-improving Thomas Müller lifted *Die Roten* into sixth place, but the team still looked far from championship material. Another tight 2-1 win at home to Eintract Frankfurt – with matters decided only two minutes from time – saw Bayern sneak into the top five, but any momentum was almost immediately lost the following week with a flat goalless draw against a Stuttgart side hovering just above the relegation zone.

Louis van Gaal demanded more time in reworking the team to get things right, but with just under a third of the season gone some fans were already starting to get a little impatient with the Dutch *Trainer*. This feeling would intensify the following week with two more dropped points at home to Schalke 04, a result that saw Bayern slip back down into eighth spot, six points behind new league leaders Bayer Leverkusen.

The *Topspiel* meeting with the league leaders at the Allianz in week thirteen would see Gómez' early goal quickly cancelled out by Stefan Kießling's strike, and despite a purple patch for Leverkusen that saw Kießling have a second goal ruled out for offside and force Bayern 'keeper and former Leverkusener Hans-Jörg Butt into a fine reflex save, the *Werkself* would be more than content with a scoreline that saw them maintain their unbeaten start to the season, while also keeping Bayern at a safe distance in seventh place.

With only four games remaining before the *Winterpause* – cut down to less than a month due to the World Cup later in the year – van Gaal was still looking to find the right formula. A poor result against tenth-placed Hannover 96 would have surely put the coach on the brink, but it was here where things finally started to come together. A resounding 3-0 win at the AWD-Arena with Müller, Olić and Gómez sharing the goals secured Bayern's first three-point haul in more than a month, and a well-contested 2-1 win over Borussia Mönchengladbach the following week would see the emergence of another talented youngster in left-sided centre back Holger Badstuber. The twenty year old would help Bayern take the points with his first competitive goal, a stunning free-kick that would be a certain goal of the season candidate.

Van Gaal had certainly taken his time in tweaking the team, but the emergence of both Müller and Badstuber – both of whom would make a break into the German national team in the following months – was crucial in the development of a new core of young players in Munich.

As things finally started to fall into place Bayern started to gather some serious momentum, and first to fall into the path of the juggernaut were VfL Bochum, a team struggling just above the danger zone. Bayern's friendship with VfL and the friendly relationship between the two sets of fans would not be reflected on the pitch, with *Die Roten* storming into a five-goal lead with less than an hour gone, including two from Croat Ivica Olić. Bochum would pull a goal back as *Die Roten* eased off late on in the second half, but with one game remaining before the winter break Bayern had worked their way up into third place, just two points behind leaders Leverkusen.

Van Gaal's side had clearly found their goalscoring boots, and five more goals against a hapless Hertha Berlin secured a fourth win on the bounce as they consolidated their position in the top three.

Rather than halt the momentum, the *Winterpause* would simply provide a healthy break. When the terms returned to action in January, Bayern just picked up where they had left off. A 2-0 defeat of Hoffenheim kept the pressure on the top two, and a dramatic 3-2 win in Bremen clinched with an audaciously beautiful free-kick twelve minutes from time by Arjen Robben saw Bayern edge ahead of Schalke into second place – just two points behind still unbeaten leaders Leverkusen.

Six wins on the bounce became seven with a three-goal second half show against Mainz at the Allianz, and an easy 3-1 win in Wolfsburg extended the winning run to eight – part of an unbeaten sequence stretching back to September and the 1-0 defeat in Hamburg. Meanwhile, leaders Leverkusen were held to a 1-1 draw by Bochum – and with twenty-one games played a goal difference of just two separated Bayern from top spot.

Week twenty-two saw the top two both win – but with Bayern beating Dortmund 3-1 and Leverkusen edging out Wolfsburg 2-1 things tightened up just a little further. As if to heighten the sense of slow-burning drama the following week, Leverkusen would blow a 2-1 lead in Bremen right at the death, only for Bayern to see their nine-game winning streak come to an end in Nürnberg with a 1-1 draw.

On match day twenty-four, Bayern finally made it to the top of the Bundesliga – ending a wait of 652 days stretching back almost two seasons. With Leverkusen only managing a goalless draw at home to local rivals Köln on the Saturday, the onus was on Bayern to nudge in front the following day at home to fourth-placed Hamburg.

Fittingly, the classic north-south derby would mark the 110th anniversary of the foundation of the Munich club – with a suitably tense encounter being settled with a touch of pure genius from Franck Ribéry. With just over twelve minutes remaining, the Frenchman collected Bastian Schweinsteiger's well-weighted pass midway inside the opposition half – but still had plenty of work to do. Cutting inside and evading defender Guy Demel, Ribéry sent a perfectly-struck shot that fizzed almost through the hands of the unfortunate Wolfgang Hesl – who was only on the pitch following an injury to regular number one Frank Rost. It was the perfect birthday present as Bayern consolidated their position.

The following week saw things take another interesting turn at the top of the table. Bayern were perfectly positioned to increase their advantage with a visit to lowly Köln, but just as in their game the previous week against Leverkusen, *Die Geißböcke* would resort to herding all eleven men behind the ball in their desperate struggle to keep clear of the relegation zone.

Köln would take a shock lead in the thirty-second minute, and in looking for a goalscorer one could not have written a more appropriate script. When Lukas Podolski lined up a free-kick in the thirty-second minute, there was a sense of inevitability about it all; he had done next to nothing in his three years in Munich, but back here in front of the *Effzeh* faithful it was if nothing had changed.

Bastian Schweinsteiger levelled the scores just before the hour as Bayern started to find their rhythm, but when the final whistle blew it was a pure and simple case of two more crucial points being dropped.

Just a point behind Bayern with a game in hand, Leverkusen had the perfect opportunity to reclaim top spot the following day in Nürnberg. Hanging precariously onto the play-off spot at the bottom end of the table, *Der Club* had not registered a win in over month, and nobody expected anything out of the ordinary against the unbeaten *Werkself*. Yet by half-time Nürnberg were two goals up, and when two became three ten minutes into the second half a shock was clearly on the cards.

Leverkusen ensured a dramatic finale with two goals of their own, but couldn't force an equaliser to maintain their unbeaten run. It wasn't quite a case of *Bayern-Dusel* as Leverkusen only had themselves to blame, but all of a sudden *Die Roten* were two points clear at the top.

To make matters worse for Leverkusen, in-form Schalke 04 had also squeezed above them into second spot.

The top three teams would all win at home the following week, but this time it was Bayern's turn to be involved in a hard struggle against a team from the other end of the table. Firmly entrenched in the relegation zone, SC Freiburg took a thirty-first minute lead at the Allianz Arena, and in front of a frustrated home crowd van Gaal's side had to wait until fourteen minutes from time for the equaliser – another special free-kick from Arjen Robben. Just seven minutes later Thomas Müller was upended in the Freiburg penalty area, and Robben smashed home the spot-kick to turn things on their head completely and claim the three points.

Despite sitting at the top of the table Bayern were not having an easy ride, and might have found themselves in second or third were it not for their opponents continually slipping up. At times it looked as if they simply wanted to hand the *Meisterschale* away, and a chastening defeat at the hands of mid-table Eintracht Frankfurt provided the perfect example.

In a game that ran a similar but inverted course to the previous week's win against Freiburg, Bayern took the lead after just six minutes through Miroslav Klose – a lead they would successfully protect until three minutes from time. Then, for no reason whatsoever, the defence went into a full scale meltdown. When David Alaba collected the ball at the edge of his own penalty area, all he had to do was clear the danger; a simple matter of hoofing it up the pitch and away. Instead, the young Austrian's botched attempted backpass provided the perfect gift for Congo-born German Under-19 international Juvhel Tsoumou, who edged in front of Hans-Jörg Butt to send the ball into the back of the Bayern net.

Now smelling blood, Frankfurt continued to press the punch-drunk Bayern back line, with the unfortunate Alaba suddenly looking like a mass of jelly. Facing Czech international Martin Fenin, the young Austrian again looked all at sea as the Frankfurt man junked inside him before sending a low shot across Butt to complete a dramatic turnaround.

Despite the defeat, Bayern had somehow managed to stay on top. Leverkusen would slump to a second defeat in three matches with a 3-0 defeat against a resurgent Dortmund, while Schalke missed an opportunity to draw level with a 2-2 draw in Hamburg.

As the season moved towards its conclusion, things remained unpredictable at the top. Needing a win against mid-table Stuttgart to stay in pole position, Bayern once again dropped all three points after taking the lead. Ivica Olić's thirty-second minute goal was quickly cancelled out by Christian Träsch just nine minutes later, and five minutes into the second half Romanian Cirian Marica struck what would be the winner for the Swabians.

Bayern were not the only team suffering at home. Second-placed Leverkusen, who less than a month before had been sitting pretty at the top, would fall to a third defeat in four against third-placed Schalke, a result that saw the improving *Königsblauen* leapfrog both *Die Werkself* and Bayern into top spot.

The situation was setup beautifully for matchday twenty-nine which would see a potentially pivotal clash between the top two at the Veltins-Arena in Gelsenkirchen. With Leverkusen continuing to slip off the pace, it came down once again to a meeting of red against blue. Adding further spice to the encounter was the spectre of Schalke coach Felix Magath, who only the previous year had humiliated the Bavarians in taking VfL Wolfsburg to their maiden Bundesliga title.

The equation was simple: while a win for *Die Knappen* would see them stretch their lead to five points, a result against the run of form for van Gaal's side would keep things in the balance as the season turned into the home straight. With just one defeat in their previous fourteen league matches, Magath's side were clearly the team in form – with Bayern coming into the match on the back of two successive defeats. However, just over a week before a dramatic DFB-Pokal semi-final at the same stadium had seen a wonder goal from Arjen Robben settle a hard-fought encounter in extra time.

Bayern arguably held the slight psychological advantage, but this in turn would be offset by the absence of the injured Robben. Nobody was making any predictions, least of all me. It was the sort of fixture that fans all long for, but when the day finally comes they find hard to watch. Contests between Bayern and Schalke had always provided that heady mix of tension and entertainment.

Fittingly, the game would see plenty of drama. No last minute shocks or surprises, but a typically tense encounter that included two dismissals – one for each side – and three goals all packed into a crazy six first half minutes. The initial skirmishes suggested that it would be an open game; Schalke had a half-decent shout with eleven minutes on the clock when Peruvian winger Jefferson Farfán went down under a robust challenge from Daniel van Buyten, and just minutes later Bayern skipper Mark van Bommel sent a firm shot skidding just wide of the target.

With twenty-five minutes on the clock, the visitors would break the deadlock. Collecting the ball inside the opposition box Bastian Schweinsteiger saw Franck Ribéry lurking just inside the area. The Frenchman executed the perfect finish, collecting the well-timed pass before calmly sweeping the ball with his right foot past Schalke 'keeper Manuel Neuer and into the back of the net.

Less than a minute later Bayern doubled their advantage. Seizing on a moment of indecision or simple carelessness by the Brazilian Rafinha, Hamit Altıntop took possession and stormed forward, finding Ivica Olić with a perfectly weighted pass. After drawing the advancing Neuer with a smart step outside and then back in, the Croat's neat square ball was bundled in by Thomas Müller.

Louis van Gaal was all smiles on the Bayern bench, but within five minutes the familiar frown quickly reappeared. As if to make up for his earlier gaffe Rafinha sent in a teasing left-wing cross, with the unmarked Kevin Kuranyi sending a well-timed looping header past Butt and into the top right-hand corner of the Bayern goal. As the home side streamed forward, it was game on again. Schalke were up for the fight again, and their supporters suddenly rediscovered their voice as they sensed a turn in momentum.

Four minutes before the break Bayern suffered another blow. Having been booked earlier in the game Altıntop was shown a second yellow for a clumsy challenge on the ubiquitous Rafinha, and despite being behind all of the momentum swung firmly towards Magath's side.

The visitors would make it into the dressing room at half-time still in possession of their slender lead, but when the two teams reemerged for the start of the second half the challenge was well and truly on for van Gaal's ten men to batten down the hatches and take the precious three points back to Bavaria.

To nobody's great surprise it was all Schalke for the majority of the second half. Magath's side streamed forward in what seemed like a continuous series of royal blue and white waves, but a combination of poor passing in the final third, profligate finishing and some stoic defending by the Bayern defence would keep the red wall intact and the door firmly shut. While the home side were relentless in the determination to find an equaliser, ten-man Bayern were nothing short of heroic. For anybody watching, this was what the Bundesliga was all about.

Bayern's inconsistent form, the absence of Arjen Robben and having to play in front of a packed and hostile Gelsenkirchen crowd meant that Bayern had started the game as marginal second favourites, but their managing to survive with a man down for almost an hour was nothing short of a miracle. A tiring Schalke were themselves reduced to ten men when Brazilian Marcelo Bordon was shown a second yellow for a reckless challenge on Mario Gómez, effectively killing off their challenge. The final whistle sounded, and once again Bayern had ground out a result when it really mattered.

Apart from the bizarre six-minute three-goal spell it had been a fractured and at times frustrating game to watch, but Bayern had torn up the form book to not just avoid defeat but take all three points back to Munich. With five games remaining, van Gaal's side stood a point ahead of Schalke, with Leverkusen a further five points behind in third spot.

A 1-1 draw at the BayArena against third-placed Leverkusen coupled with a surprise defeat for Schalke at relegation-threatened Hannover saw Bayern extend their slender lead at the top to two points, a result that also effectively eliminated Leverkusen from the title contest.

Having led the way for so long *Die Werkself* had fallen away dramatically, not for the first time threatening to deceive. Bayern had undoubtedly been helped by the inconsistency of their opponents, but after the dreadful start to the season Louis van Gaal found himself within four games of turning things around completely. Although nothing could be taken for granted, the Bavarians would have a relatively easy run towards the finish line with all four of their final opponents languishing in the bottom eight: Hannover 96, Borussia Mönchengladbach, VfL Bochum and bottom side Hertha Berlin.

	P	W	D	L	Goals	GD	Pts
FC Bayern München	30	17	9	4	58:28	+30	60
FC Schalke 04	30	17	7	6	49:28	+21	58
Bayer 04 Leverkusen	30	14	12	4	59:34	+25	54
BV 09 Borussia Dortmund	30	15	7	8	48:35	+13	52

The epic struggle in Gelsenkirchen and the scrappy draw in Leverkusen were followed by an altogether more comfortable Saturday evening at a packed Allianz against Hannover, with the charge led by an inspired Arjen Robben. After storming out of the blocks *Die Roten* would take the lead through Ivica Olić's close-range header midway through the first half, with Robben doubling the advantage on the half-hour mark with a delightful dinked effort. Not content to just put himself on the scoresheet, the Dutch winger then set up Thomas Müller for Bayern's third a minute before half-time.

The break provided only a brief respite for poor Hannover, with Bayern simply upping a gear in the second half. Four minutes in Müller turned provider in setting up Olić's second after Robben's chip into the opposition box, and just a minute later the Dutchman was able to dance past a number of static defenders before stroking the ball calmly into the bottom right-hand corner, giving 'keeper Florian Fromlowitz no chance.

Robben was in his element now. The familiar charges down the right flank were accompanied with some deft flicks and tricks, and a well-timed pass to almost set up Müller was quickly followed by a firmly-struck shot that tested the busy Fromlowitz. The sixth goal came courtesy of Müller's crisp left-footed strike on sixty-two minutes, and with thirty minutes remaining all three Bayern goalscorers were all looking for a hat-trick. The home fans had to wait until the final minute for that moment to arrive, and naturally it was that man Robben. After a series of sidesteps past a number of flat-footed defenders and poor Fromlowitz, a neat stab into the back of the net capped off a magnificent display from the Bayern number ten.

Hannover were never going to be the most testing opposition, but Bayern had found their mojo just at the right time. Schalke's 3-1 win over Mönchengladbach would keep them in the hunt, but with just three games remaining hopes were high in Munich for the return of the *Meisterschale*. It was now theirs to lose.

Within twenty-four hours however, the bouyant mood in Munich had darkened dramatically. Rumours had emerged on French television about four members of their national team being investigated as clients of a Paris prostitution ring – and the involvement of a minor. As the news started to unfold, the names started to hit the headlines – among them Franck Ribéry.

With the story breaking around him and the inevitable rumour mill whirring into action on the Internet, the Frenchman was looking at a trial and with it a possible prison sentence – in spite of his protestations at not knowing one of the prostitutes involved was a minor. With the scandal threatening to spill over in Munich, the club quickly took action. Uli Hoeneß immediately took Ribéry under his wing, providing much needed support while at the time making his position perfectly clear about the situation and the player's responsibility to the club. Hoeneß had over the years been a father figure to many players at Bayern, and things were no different with the talented but at times tempestuous Ribéry.

Ribéry had clearly crossed the line, but would remain forever grateful to Bayern and in particular Hoeneß for sticking by him. The scandal continued to rumble on throughout the summer, overlapping a particularly torrid World Cup campaign for Ribéry and the French national team in South Africa. But while the vultures were out in force in his home country, the player had really started to appreciate what it meant to be a Bayern player. Being in Munich was not just about football, but being part of a large family, one that included the board, coaching staff and supporters.

I for one saw Ribéry's actions as foolish in the extreme, but as a player he continued to wear his heart on his sleeve. He was, after all, *unser Franck*.

More was demanded from Ribéry on the pitch as the club continued to help him work his way through the media storm, and in return the player's gratitude and visible loyalty towards the club and the fans that had also supported him quickly became evident.

Ribéry was in the starting lineup against Mönchengladbach the following week, but Bayern found it surprisingly tough against a side with little to play for mid-table. *Die Fohlen* took the lead with a goal from young starlet Marco Reus on the hour mark, but thirteen minutes later Miroslav Klose – on as a substitute for Thomas Müller – ensured that Bayern headed back to Munich with a share of the points. A winner three minutes from time in Berlin against Hertha was enough for Schalke to draw back level with Bayern at the top of the table, and with both Werder Bremen and Bayer Leverkusen seven points adrift, it was a two-horse race going into the final two matches.

	P	W	D	L	Goals	GD	Pts
FC Bayern München	32	18	10	4	66:29	+37	64
FC Schalke 04	32	19	7	6	53:29	+24	64
SV Werder Bremen	32	16	9	7	68:39	+29	57
Bayer 04 Leverkusen	32	15	12	5	63:36	+27	57

The penultimate week of the league campaign saw Bayern facing sixteenth-placed VfL Bochum at the Allianz, while Schalke faced a far stiffer challenge at home against a Bremen side that had started to find some decent form. While the destination of the title would not technically be decided until the following week, a win for Bayern and a defeat for *Die Knappen* would surely be enough to send the "salad bowl" back to Munich.

Bayern were well on the way inside twenty minutes, with two Thomas Müller headers easing the nerves in Munich. While the Bavarians went into the half-time break looking comfortable, it was still goalless in Gelsenkirchen.

Things would change quickly in the second half. Mesut Özil scored for Bremen against his former youth side to put the visitors ahead ten minutes in, and nine minutes later Portuguese international Hugo Almeida doubled the visitors' lead. The news had only started to filter in when Müller completed his hat-trick on sixty-nine minutes, and although a consolation from Christian Fuchs six minutes from the end saw Bochum get on the scoreboard, the mood was one of celebration among the Bayern players and fans.

Mathematically the title race was not quite over, but by Saturday evening the *Meisterschale* would have been given a final polish before making its way to Berlin ahead of Bayern's final match against table-proppers Hertha. Three points ahead of Schalke with a massive goal advantage of +17, it would take little short of a miracle to deny the Bavarians a twenty-second league triumph.

The end was fairly predictable. With Hertha already doomed to playing second division football the following season there was little but pride to play for, and Ivica Olić set Bayern on their way in the twentieth minute. Adrian Ramos brought the brave Berliners level a minute just short of the hour mark, but that brief show of resistance only served to set things up for the final act by Bayern's player of the season, Arjen Robben.

Two goals from the flying Dutch winger would give Bayern a 3-1 win and provide the perfect finish to the campaign. Schalke meanwhile had concentrated on earning a point in Mainz to make sure of securing second place, while Bremen finished their season with a 1-1 draw in the *Nordderby* with HSV. Having been at the top of the pile for so long, Leverkusen finished the season in a distant fourth – eleven points behind Bayern.

	P	W	D	L	Goals	GD	Pts
FC Bayern München	34	20	10	4	72:31	+41	70
FC Schalke 04	34	19	8	7	53:31	+22	65
SV Werder Bremen	34	17	10	7	71:40	+31	61
Bayer 04 Leverkusen	34	15	14	5	65:38	+27	59

With the Bundesliga shield safely in Munich Louis van Gaal's side headed back to Berlin for the final of the DFB-Pokal against Werder Bremen, and it was hard to believe that after such a wobbly start to the season the Dutch coach would be looking at securing a domestic double.

Bayern's path to Berlin was a fairly smooth one, with the only real resistance provided by a tenacious Schalke 04 in the semi-finals and, for a few bothersome moments, second division side SpVgg Greuther Fürth in the last eight. Other than that, it was pretty much business as usual for *Die Roten*, who played out a solid cup campaign without ever really needing to find a second gear.

The journey to Berlin started with a tougher than expected 3-1 win against SpVgg Neckarelz, with the amateur team from the sixth-tier Verbandsliga Baden being roared on by a capacity 30,000 crowd at Hoffenheim's home ground in Sinsheim.

With the game not being shown in the United Kingdom I had naturally sought out a source on the internet – a shared stream, where one's enjoyment of the game in a small video window is often interrupted by screen hangs, dropped connections and irritating popup boxes advertising shifty Russian mobile phone companies.

While it is very easy to complain about such minor annoyances, I often think back to the 1990s where my "watching" a match consisted of refreshing teletext pages – or worse still the 1980s where I would have to wait days for newspaper reports or the hope of finding the result in a small corner of specialist football magazines like *Shoot* and *Match*. The advance of modern technology has been so widespread and rapid that we have all pretty much taken it for granted; had I been offered the chance to watch a DFB-Pokal first round game twenty years ago, I would have probably put up with a popup every ten seconds – complete with adverts for mobile telecommunications services in Cyrillic.

My enjoyment of the Neckarelz game was peppered with popup adverts and a ten minute black hole that resulted in my missing Mario Gómez's opening goal that would break a frustrating deadlock six minutes into the second half, but when the striker doubled the lead from the spot soon afterwards the whole experience was somehow less annoying. I was soon clicking the little crosses at the top right-hand corner of every popup with an almost mechanical efficiency.

The non-league side would make their fans' day ten minutes from time with a goal of their own, but Hamit Altıntop wrapped things up at two minutes later to make sure of Bayern's berth in the second round against second division Rot-Weiß Oberhausen. The game at the Allianz against the *Kleeblätter* ("clover leaves") from the north was a much easier affair, with *Die Roten* strolling to a comfortable 5-0 win.

It was much the same in the round of sixteen against Bundesliga rivals Eintracht Frankfurt at the Commerzbank-Arena, where the game would effectively be over inside the first thirty minutes. Two goals in the space of five minutes from Miro Klose and a third from Thomas Müller effectively ended the contest, and van Gaal's men were already in wind-down mode when Luca Toni added a fourth seven minutes into the second half. There was clearly a stark difference between Bayern's league and cup form: just four days earlier against the same opposition at the Allianz, they had come from a goal behind – clinching the points only two minutes from time.

Having played the *Kleeblätter* from the north in the third round, Bayern would next meet the *Kleeblätter* from the south in the quarter-finals – SpVgg Greuther Fürth.

For some Bayern supporters the meeting with Fürth stirred memories of the infamous encounter with non-league TSV Vestenbergsgreuth in August 1994, a 1-0 defeat that had since become part of German cup folklore. Since that meeting in Nürnberg sixteen years earlier where Bavaria's David had defeated its Goliath, Vestenbergsgreuth had merged with neighbours SpVgg Fürth to form the new club, which had since climbed through the ranks into the second division.

On a chilly February evening in Munich, Thomas Müller would put the home side on the scoreboard with just five minutes gone, but just five minutes later Fürth were level when a defensive blunder from Martín Demichelis allowed Christopher Nöthe to charge into the Bayern box before stroking the ball calmly past Michael Rensing.

Inspired by their moment of good fortune, the visitors switched up a gear, and fashioned a number of excellent opportunities. Midfielder Bernd Nehrig danced into the penalty area before hitting the ball straight at Rensing, and Tunisian Sami Allagui saw one effort deflected over for a corner and another fly over the target when he arguably should have done better.

With Bayern looking increasingly sluggish and careless at the back, Fürth should have aready been in front. They would get their reward five minutes from half-time, when a completely unmarked Allagui was allowed to stroll into the penalty area to nod home Nicolai Müller's nicely weighted left-wing cross. 2-1 down at the break, I again had visions of that game in 1994. After opening the scoring, Bayern had offered little in the way of a threat to Fürth 'keeper Stephan Loboué, and the scoreline hardly flattered the visitors.

There was a growing sense of frustration amongst the crowd of just over fifty-three thousand as the hour mark approached with no change to the score, but then Bayern got their lucky break when Robben's shot struck the arm of a lunging Stephan Fürstner. The Dutchman stepped up to take the kick, and although Loboué would get a hand to the ball it finished up in the back of the net.

Suddenly it looked as if all of the life had been sucked out of the visitors, and from that point on *Die Roten* did not look back as they finally found their form and pressed hard on the accelerator pedal.

Just two minutes after the equaliser Franck Ribéry put the Munich side in front, and four minutes after the hour Philipp Lahm made it four with a vicious shot that curled in front and away from the Fürth 'keeper before nesting inside the far left corner.

Having looked so poor for so long, Bayern were now able to turn what might have been a potential banana skin into a goalscoring procession. Eight minutes from time Müller made it five after a picking up a defence-splitting pass from Robben, and right at the death the unlucky Allagui – who could so very easily have had a first-half hat-trick – glanced a corner from Bayern sub Hamit Altıntop into his own net.

The emphatic-looking 6-2 scoreline clearly flattered van Gaal's side, but once again they were in the last four. There they would face Bundesliga rivals Schalke 04 at a packed Veltins-Arena, with a place in the final against old rivals Werder Bremen at stake.

The game was far from a classic, a typical attritional encounter between two well-matched teams genuinely in with a chance of claiming the silverware. While Bayern looked to set the tempo, their opponents were prepared to bide their time.

Bayern had created the better opportunities in the first half with both Ivica Olić and Miroslav Klose going close while Robben was brilliantly denied by Schalke 'keeper Manuel Neuer, and in a more evenly balanced second half Bastian Schweinsteiger was denied by the excellent Schalke *Torhüter*.

Like so many intense cup ties, it was settled by a moment of supreme individual brilliance – deep into extra time with just eight minutes left on the clock.

It all began inside the Bayern half, with Robben collecting Butt's throw just inside the right touchline. Sprinting down the right flank and just keeping the ball in play, the Dutchman burst past the first two royal blue shirts, but looked to have been chasing a lost cause as two more attempted to close him down.

A sudden burst of pace saw Robben charge away from Heiko Westermann's sprawling challenge, taking him towards the byline right at the edge of the penalty area. Outfoxing the desperate Christoph Moritz and cutting back inside towards the penalty spot, Robben created enough space to swing that lethal left foot from some eleven yards.

The curling shot was unerring, leaving Neuer no chance as it slammed into the top left-hand corner. The 'keeper would actually get the slightest of touches as he desperately leapt to his right, but the shot was just too good.

Bayern headed to Berlin in search of yet another domestic league and cup double, against a Bremen team that had finished strongly in third place in the Bundesliga. A decent contest was expected, but sadly for the neutrals it was anything but that. Once Bayern had made the initial breakthrough, it turned into a procession.

Thomas Schaaf's side had just about managed to hold their own for the first half an hour of the contest, but after Arjen Robben had opened the scoring from the penalty spot it was all downhill from there for the men in green. The penalty decision was an easy one for referee Thorsten Kinhöfer, with Ivica Olić's attempted dink into the box clearly handled by centre-back Per Mertesacker. Robben's well-struck *Elfmeter* was calmly stroked into the bottom corner of the net, leaving 'keeper Tim Wiese no chance.

Wearing their newly-released red and white striped *Trikot*, Bayern went into the half-time break holding their slim one goal advantage, but after the resumption they hit the afterburners. The busy Olić stabbed in the second from close range as the Bremen defence made a complete mess of a Robben corner after fifty-two minutes, and just twelve minutes later the Bremen defence was split wide open by Mark van Bommel, whose perfectly timed pass was collected by Franck Ribéry and finished with equal aplomb.

Bremen's day went from bad to worse with skipper Torsten Frings' lunging challenge on Schweinsteiger resulted in a second yellow card, and just moments later Schweinsteiger himself delivered the *coup de grace*. Collecting Lahm's beautifully floated pass, *der Fussballgott* calmly chested the ball down before calmly rolling it past the helpless Wiese.

The final whistle signalled yet another cup triumph for the *Münch'ner* – their fifteenth in all. Having also made their way into the final of the Champions League against Italian giants Internazionale, Bayern were now just one match away from a historic treble.

After the disappointing quarter-final exit in 2009 Bayern were desperate to do better in the Champions League, and much like the Bundesliga campaign their route to the showcase final at the Bernabéu in Madrid would take a number of at times excruciating twists and turns. It was an exciting time to be a fan of FC Bayern, but not if you happened to value your sanity and fingernails.

Bayern's four-team group had looked competitive without being massively threatening, with the opposition being provided by Italian giants Juventus, French side Girondins de Bordeaux and Israeli champions Maccabi Haifa. Confident of earning a place in the knock-out stage, van Gaal's side made a solid start to the campaign with three points from their journey to Israel. The 3-0 result was slightly flattering for *Die Roten*, with Thomas Müller scoring twice in the last five minutes after Daniel van Buyten had given them the lead shortly after the hour mark.

The next three games however would see a dramatic slump in form. A goalless draw at the Allianz Arena saw two points dropped against Juventus, and despite taking an early lead in Bordeaux courtesy of a Michael Ciani own goal Bayern contrived to throw the points away. Ciani made amends for his earlier error with a cheeky backheel just before the half-hour mark, and either side of the equaliser Müller picked up two yellow cards for a couple of badly-timed tackles.

From that point it was all about survival, but four minutes from the break Bordeaux snatched a lead they would not relinquish. Hamit Altıntop failed to pick up roving midfielder Marc Planus, who slipped the ball past Hans-Jörg Butt to complete the comeback for the home side.

The second half was little more than a series of moments that could best be described as comical. The first culprit was Luca Toni, who made a complete hash of a chance following Bastian Schweinsteiger's cute chip into the opposition penalty area. Then a horrendous backpass from Holger Badstuber would put Butt into all sorts of trouble, and as the keeper desperately tried to get into position to clear, Moroccan Marouane Chamakh dispossessed him before being chopped down just inside the box.

The resulting penalty would have given the home side the opportunity to effectively close out the match, but Yoann Gourcuff provided a comedy moment of his own as his audacious attempt to chip the ball over Butt resulted in a save by the Bayern 'keeper, followed by an awful scuff wide of the target as the French youngster followed up.

Despite being a man down Bayern continued to create chances, but when Toni hit the base of the post with a towering header it surely wasn't going to be their night. The drama continued right until the closing minutes, as Bordeaux received their second penalty and Bayern their second red card. Daniel van Buyten was shown a straight red for his attempted bearhug on Chamakh, but once again Butt kept the scoreline at 2-1, flying to his right to deny Brazilian substitute Jussie.

It had been a bizarre match and Bayern would have their moments, but without van Buyten and Müller there were going to be some serious changes before the return fixture in Munich.

The game at the Allianz two weeks later was even worse, and once again Bayern were starved of luck. They started well enough as Bordeaux 'keeper Cédric Carasso turned the ball onto his own crossbar before turning away a well-struck free-kick from Schweinsteiger, and a clear handball on the line was casually waved away by the referee. As if to rub salt into the wound, a floated free-kick from Brazilian Wendel found Gourcuff, whose header squirmed past Butt and into the back of the Bayern net. You really couldn't have written a more bizarre script, with the hitherto untested Bayern defence caught completely cold as Gourcuff ghosted in at the far post.

It was much the same story in the second half. As in the first game Toni proved to be one of the arch villains when he sent a gilt-edged chance over the crossbar, and substitute Arjen Robben turned brilliantly inside the box before seeing his low effort skid narrowly wide of the far post.

The final act right at the death saw Chamakh charge past a sluggish Badstuber and roll the ball calmly into the net, with Butt flying out like a madman before kicking and flapping at thin air. Bayern had dominated the game and had produced the better chances, but the two shocking moments were enough to see Bordeaux laughing all the way back home to France with the three points.

With just two match days remaining, van Gaal's side were left standing right on the brink of elimination from the competition. Surprise leaders Bordeaux headed the table on ten points followed by Juventus on eight, with Bayern a further four points adrift of the Italian side.

At this stage, even the most optimistic of Bayern fans had largely dismissed the team's chances of progressing into the knockout stages. Not only did they have to beat bottom side Maccabi Haifa in Munich, van Gaal's men were also reliant on Juventus dropping points in Bordeaux. Then they would have to get a result in their final game in Turin, a touch challenge in any circumstance. When all of the calculations were put together, it was close to a mathematical miracle.

With Maccabi dead last in the standings with no points, Bayern's penultimate game at home against the Israeli champions was effectively a play-off game to ensure their place in the Europa League. A place in the top two may have been a long shot, but the immediate priority was securing at least third place.

With their Israeli opponents needing at least a draw to keep their hopes of staying in European competition alive, it was a tough and at times frustrating match in front of a crowd of just under sixty thousand in a chilly Allianz Arena.

A barren first half was followed by a frustrating opening to the second, but just after the hour mark the shackles were finally broken. A through-ball from Mark van Bommel found Mario Gómez in space, and a fine run inside set things up perfectly for a shot at goal. Gómez's right-footed effort was well-struck, but Maccabi 'keeper Nir Davidovitch dived well to his right to keep it out. As the 'keeper desperately tried to regain his footing, the ever-reliable Ivica Olić arrived to calmly roll the ball home. To warm the crowd further, news had filtered in that Bordeaux had taken the lead against Juventus.

Maccabi were now forced to change their approach as they looked for an equaliser, but the Bayern defence stood firm to secure the crucial three points. The performance had been far from spectacular, but when the final whistle blew they knew they had secured at the very least a stay of execution.

With a place in the Europa League now secure, *Die Roten* were in with a chance of having a decent crack at Juventus, who conceded a second in Bordeaux in injury time. The French side were away and clear at the top of the table, and the equation was very simple for van Gaal's team. To overhaul Juventus and progress into the knockout phase, only a win in Turin's Stadio Olimpico would do.

With the Italian side needing only a draw to progress, the onus was on Bayern to chase the game. The Bavarians made a bright start and created an excellent chance early on that saw Olić hit the post, but with just under twenty minutes gone yet another defensive blunder would gift the home side with the lead against the run of play. Martín Demichelis charged out of defence with the ball, only to be dispossessed by Diego inside his own half. With a gaping hole in the Bayern back line Claudio Marchisio lifted the ball back into the danger area for David Trezeguet, whose spectacular first-time shot fizzed low to Butt's outstretched right hand. Suddenly, Bayern's task had doubled in size.

The tournament had seen plenty of poor football from the Bavarians, but things had not been helped by their having no luck whatsoever with either the bounce of the ball or the officials. This changed after half an hour, when Josè Martin Cáceres' rather soft challenge on Olić saw the Croatian stumble in the box and Swiss referee Massimo Busacca point to the penalty spot.

Bayern turned to 'keeper Hans-Jörg Butt, who not for the first time lined up to take a spot kick in the Champions League against Juventus. The first had come for Hamburger SV in a 4-4 draw at the group stage in 2000, and the second for Bayer Leverkusen in a 3-1 second phase win in 2002. With a subtle step towards the ball and smooth sweep of his right foot, Butt struck his shot firmly past Gianluigi Buffon to net a record-setting third. There was still plenty of work to do, and the Bayern 'keeper jogged back down to the other side of the pitch with little ceremony. The comeback had begun.

With the score at 1-1 at the break the equation was exactly the same as it had been at the start, with just forty-five minutes separating the home side from a place in the round of sixteen.

Bayern started the second half as they had done the first, but this time would get the rub of the green seven minutes in. Van Bommel's swerving right-wing cross was well met by van Buyten, and although Buffon got down well to parry the Belgian's firm header the ball fell straight into the path of Olić at the far post. The Croat calmly slotted it home to give Bayern the lead.

Trezeguet had an excellent opportunity for a second goal to bring the home side level, but Olić's strike had clearly sucked the life out of the Old Lady. As the Italians slowly turned to jelly, van Gaal's side upped the ante. With seven minutes remaining a Badstuber corner set up another van Buyten header, only for the usually reliable Buffon to make a complete mess of it. The Juve 'keeper fumbled and squirmed like a beached squid as he attempted to grab the ball, which escaped his clutches before rolling temptingly along the goal line. With the black and white shirted defenders at sixes and sevens, Mario Gómez made his way towards the far post to thump it in.

As the clocked ticked down the miracle had been achieved, and substitute Anatoliy Tymoschuk would put the final gloss on one of Bayern's most memorable European evenings with a thumping shot from the edge of the area after a neat assist from Thomas Müller.

Four weeks earlier a place in the knockout stage had been little more than a distant hope, but somehow Bayern had managed to achieve the near impossible. After a number of ordinary displays, they had done what they needed to do when it really mattered. Awaiting them in the second round would be another Italian opponent, ACF Fiorentina.

With five wins and one defeat in a group containing Olympique Lyonnais, former champions Liverpool and Hungarian side Debreceni VSC, Fiorentina had easily finished top of their group, ensuring home advantage for the second leg against Bayern. It was a well-balanced tie, where once again Bayern would battle their way back from the brink.

With Fiorentina prepared to bide their time and attack on the break, the first leg in Florence developed into a slightly one-sided affair with Bayern making most of the running.

Despite the presence of both Arjen Robben and the fit-again Franck Ribéry, Bayern found it difficult to break down the purple Florentine wall and 'keeper Sebastién Frey. Robben and Ribéry both featured heavily in Bayern's attacks, and a minute into injury time Robben and Gómez played a lovely one-two, leaving the Dutchman to set up Ribéry. The Frenchman was bundled over by Danish defender Per Krøldrup, but with Frey scrabbling around on the turf Gómez collected the loose ball and finished the job.

Gómez immediately wheeled away towards the Bayern supporters in the stands, but back in the penalty area other things were happening. Having signalled for the foul on Ribéry just moments earlier, Norwegian referee Tom Henning Øvrebø would have no choice but to disallow the goal. Robben – looking a little like Casper the Friendly Ghost in the all-white *Trikot* accompanied by matching white leggings – stepped up to take the kick, and what might have been a contentious moment was avoided as the Dutchman drilled the ball low into the bottom right-hand corner with Frey diving the wrong way.

The start of the second half saw Daniel van Buyten replaced by Diego Contento, and the unfortunate youngster would be more than partly responsible for yet another defensive mess just six minutes later. A testing right-sided corner from Montenigrin Stevan Jovetić was floated into the Bayern box, and Contento's indecision allowed Krøldrup to make up for his earlier lapse from close range to give his side an unlikely lifeline. Having been dominated for most of the preceding fifty minutes, Fiorentina were back level in the tie with a potentially crucial away goal.

Bayern continued to press, and their cause was helped by Fiorentina's Massimo Gobbi, whose late and unnecessary shoulder barge on Robben with seventeen minutes remaining resulted in a straight red card. The decision was arguably a little harsh, but it was the perfect catalyst for Bayern to up the ante.

In keeping with the dramatic course of Bayern's entire Champions League campaign, the 66,000-strong crowd at the Allianz were kept on the edge of their seats right until the end. Moments after Olić had spooned a golden opportunity high over the bar, a long-distance effort from Robben was only parried by Frey. Seizing the loose ball Olić found substitute Miroslav Klose, who stooped and nodded it into the empty net. Klose looked a good couple of yards offside, but the flag and whistle didn't come.

After not getting the rub of the green in the group stage, Bayern had finally got a crucial break.

The second leg in Florence was no less dramatic, with Bayern fans again taken through the mangle. Not for the first time in the competition, the team threatened to throw the match away with a number of careless defensive mistakes.

With twenty-eight minutes gone, a badly directed defensive header from Holger Badstuber conceded possession. Hans-Jörg Butt could only parry Riccardo Montolivo's long-range effort, and a static Daniel van Buyten was caught cold by Peruvian Juan Vargas, whose left-footed shot at the near post was both firm and accurate. The aggregate score was now 2-2, but with Fiorentina's goal in Munich the Serie A side had grasped the advantage on away goals. Striker Mario Gómez then hobbled off the field, and all of a sudden things were not looking promising at all for van Gaal's men.

Needing to score to edge back in front in the tie, things only got worse for *Die Roten* just nine minutes into the second half. Once again, it all started with a moment of carelessness. Butt had been able to get his body in the way of a shot from Alberto Gilardino after both Badstuber and van Buyten had failed to intercept a low cross across the penalty area, but a quickly taken free-kick in the Fiorentina half turned into yet another assault on the Bayern goal. The men in violet moved quickly down the right as Franck Ribéry was quite literally left tying up his bootlaces, and Gilardino's short layoff found Stevan Jovetić who blasted the ball past Butt.

There was a slight whiff of offside about Gilardino's final pass, but Bayern fans could hardly complain after Klose's controversial winner in the first leg. The situation had not changed much for Bayern; they still needed the one goal to bring the tie level, but the momentum was clearly with the home side.

Just six minutes later right on the hour mark things turned around again. After winning the ball just inside his own half, Schweinsteiger found Ribéry out on the left. The Frenchman charged forward with purpose, sending in a low pass that took a gentle arc into the space just beyond the D. There skipper Mark van Bommel arrived to drill a low right-footed shot that skidded past 'keeper Frey and into the bottom left-hand corner.

The tie now stood with the two teams locked at 3-3 on aggregate. Less than half an hour was left on the clock, which was ticking towards extra time and a possible penalty shootout.

The home side were not bothered about that however. Four minutes later Gilardino and Jovetić combined again to score Fiorentina's third, once again edging them in front. Once again van Buyten was found wanting, allowing Jovetić to muscle past him before watching the diminutive Montenegrin almost stuff the ball under the advancing Butt.

After the slow and cagey start, the game had suddenly been transformed into a frenzy of goals. Bayern were left chasing the game again, but the visiting supporters had to wait less than a minute before *Die Roten* re-established their advantage. The crucial away goal was a goal for the ages, one that would forever live in the memory of every Bayern fan.

Arjen Robben had already scored his fair share of spectacular goals, but the scene was set for the mercurial Dutchman to pull another rabbit out of his bag of tricks. Picking up a pass from van Bommel on the touchline midway inside the Fiorentina half, Robben cut inside and danced past a number of violet shirts before sending an unstoppable left-footed shot into the top left-hand corner of the net from all of twenty-five yards. Bayern had been on the ropes throughout, but having stared elimination in the face they once again had their noses in front.

This time there would be no reply from the home side, and substitute Miroslav Klose came close to scoring a fourth as he desperately tried to get a foot on yet another killer ball from the magnificent Robben. Defensively Bayern had been a complete shambles, yet somehow they had been able to put everything to matter when it mattered. After the miraculous escape from the group stage and the memorable win in Turin, it had been yet another glorious Italian night in Florence.

Watching a football match can be an intensely emotional experience, but this was starting to get a little too much for me. Bayern had come back from the dead so often that they were starting to resemble Lazarus, and that oft-used phrase "name on the trophy" – made infamous by ITV commentator Clive Tyldesley during the horror show against Manchester United in 1999, came to mind. Bayern's defence had throughout the entire season resembled Swiss cheese, yet they were somehow still in the competition. When van Gaal's side were drawn in the quarter-finals against their 1999 conquerors, I could only laugh at what might happen next.

The first leg at the Allianz Arena against United would finish the same way as it had done against Fiorentina, with van Gaal's side edging out their opponents by the odd goal in three. However the route they had taken to get there was far more dramatic, with the visitors taking an early lead through Wayne Rooney before the home crowd had even settled into their seats.

Once again, the Bayern defence was all over the place. Nani's free-kick from close to the right corner flag found the unmarked Wayne Rooney, who broke free from both Ivica Olić and Martín Demichelis to give the Red Devils the lead. Looking like the Man in the Iron Mask in his black face protector, Demichelis would suffer the ultimate indignity, ending up flat out on the turf as the England striker's shot powered past Hans-Jörg Butt.

Both sides would create changes in what was a fairly even first half, but after the break Bayern pressed hard for an equaliser only to be denied by excellent Edwin van der Sar in the opposition goal.

It looked as though it was going to be one of those evenings with the Dutchman looking very much like Peter Schmeichel had done in 1999, but with just thirteen minutes remaining *Die Roten* would benefit from first a moment of madness and then a moment of good luck. A brainless handball by United captain Gary Neville saw Bayern awarded a free-kick just outside the penalty area, and van der Sar was finally be beaten by Franck Ribéry's effort, taking a nasty deflection off the unfortunate Rooney who had positioned himself at the edge of the six-man defensive wall.

The visitors would come close to retaking the lead when Nemanja Vidić hit the crossbar seven minutes from time, but two minutes into injury time the ground erupted as the Bavarians made the final thrust into the opposition half and dispensed some last-minute medicine on their own.

A goalward charge by Mario Gómez saw the big striker go down just outside the penalty area, and the referee's decision not to award the free-kick appeared to confuse the United defenders. With most of the opposition eyes on the official, the ever-alert Olić was quickly on the scene to steal the ball from a disorientated Patrice Evra. The Croatian still had plenty of work to do, but cut inside smartly before drilling the ball with his left foot past the helpless van der Sar.

While nothing could ever scrub away the memories of that horrible May evening in Barcelona just over a decade earlier, Olić's dramatic injury-time winner had helped to lift some of the load. Right at the death, the pressure from the home side would finally count.

Bayern had snatched victory from the jaws of defeat, and had something to take back to Manchester for the return leg.

The slim advantage Bayern had taken to Old Trafford would evaporate completely inside the first seven minutes. As in the first leg in Munich, Alex Ferguson's team were quickly into their stride before the Bavarians could even draw breath.

It would take only three minutes for Darron Gibson to put the Red Devils ahead with a stunning right-footed effort that fizzed past Butt, and just four minutes later Bayern's hopes of making the last four were looking as black as their shirts as Nani knocked in an outrageous backheel to double United's lead. In the space of seven minutes, the tie had been turned completely on its head.

But there was yet more drama to come. This was FC Bayern München versus Manchester United, after all.

Bayern were wobbling like a jelly, and with twelve minutes gone could very well have gone three down as a poor pass from Butt wasn't punished by Michael Carrick, and Brazilian Rafael sent a shot skidding just wide of the far post with the Bavarian defence all at sea. It seemed to be a matter of when rather than if United would score their third.

When Ecuadorian Antonio Valencia turned the Bayern defence inside out to find Nani in space inside the Bayern penalty area, I was already staring to look forward to 2011. The Portuguese sent his shot unerringly into the net, and at 3-0 that was surely that.

Or so we all thought.

From almost out of nowhere, Bayern grabbed a crucial goal against the run of play to stay in the contest. Just two minutes after falling three behind, Olić did well to beat his marker Carrick before sending a low shot across 'keeper Edwin van der Sar and into the low right-hand corner of the United net. Just moments later, Robben forced his Dutch compatriot into a fine diving save. It was as if someone had suddenly hit the "on" switch; half-time arrived, and Bayern had established a foothold.

Bayern should really have been finished off by the home side long before, but with the away goals rule in play they needed just one more strike to nudge themselves ahead in the tie. Even so, United fans would have backed their team to score at least one more against Bayern's porous defence to put things beyond all doubt.

Five minutes after the restart, Bayern were given an additional boost. Rafael was shown a second yellow card for a silly foul, and the visitors felt there was a clear opportunity to turn things around. Two goals behind against ten men, the game looked far more balanced as the field started to open up.

Chances would come at both ends: van der Sar did well to parry a firm Ribéry effort, Butt's solid outstretched hand denied the dangerous Nani a hat-trick, and with just over twenty minutes remaining a far-post header from Bayern substitute Mario Gómez skimmed the top of the crossbar.

Then it happened.

With just over a quarter of an hour remaining, *Die Roten* won a corner out on the left, and the usual tall target men - Gómez and Daniel van Buyten - assumed their positions inside the opposition penalty area. With United piling seven men inside the danger zone, Ribéry swung the corner out towards the edge of the box, where the lurking Robben delivered the perfect first-time strike with his magical left boot. An audacious training ground move, executed to perfection.

It had everything: timing, precision, power and accuracy. Robben lined himself up beautifully to stroke the ball into the net, sending it low into the bottom corner with a beautiful gentle arc that took it away from the desperate van der Sar before creeping inside the far post.

Unerring, unstoppable. *Unfassbar, unhaltbar*. It was just sublime, the perfect dream goal in the so-called "Theatre of Dreams". There was still enough time for the home side to turn things back around again, but I was confident that Bayern had done enough.

Robben charged away with his arms outstretched, and in front of the stunned home crowd signalled that his ears were burning at the sudden silence. It was a celebration far more subtle than Mark van Bommel's aggressive "Kozakiewicz" against Madrid, but just as memorable. Bayern's second goal had pulled the score back to 3-2 on the night, but ahead in the tie on away goals with the aggregate score at 4-4. Like Rocky Balboa, Bayern had quite literally hauled themselves off the canvas before delivering a telling blow on the chin of an opponent that just half an hour earlier had threatened to take them apart completely. It was the sort of story you just couldn't make up.

Rather than accept the defeat gracefully, Alex Ferguson chose to engage in his own war of words that would make him look even more ridiculous. Fulminating at the dismissal of Rafael and referring to "typical Germans" – whatever that meant – in his post-match interview, the United manager was left talking to the wall.

Louis van Gaal offered a measured and polite response, but in truth nobody cared about the mealy-mouthed Manchester United coach and what he had to say. Old "Red Nose" could moan and complain as much as he liked; his team were out, and Bayern were through to the last four. Oh how I celebrated.

The last three journeys away from home had produced what could best be described as three miracles, and in spite of their topsy-turvy season Bayern were in the semi-finals.

In stark contrast to the previous three matches, the semi-final against French outfit Olympique Lyonnais was considerably less fraught – though it wouldn't be without its moments of drama. Having made a bright start at the Allianz Arena Bayern found themselves down to ten men after the dismissal of Franck Ribéry for a late challenge on Lisandro López – a straight red card that would have serious implications later on. While there was little doubt about the correctness of the referee's decision, the three-match ban that was meted out to the Frenchman by UEFA after the match would effectively rule him out of the final.

Two silly yellow cards in the space of three frantic minutes for Lyon midfielder Jérémy Toulalan evened things out, and in spite of all the pressure and opportunities for the home side it would take yet another spectacular long-distance strike from the irrepressible Arjen Robben to break the deadlock. Even then there was a tiny slice of luck involved, with Robben's shot taking a deflection off Thomas Müller's head to wrong-foot Lyon 'keeper Hugo Lloris.

It was enough to secure the slimmest of advantages for the second leg in France.

After the previous three away journeys, a close match was expected at the Stade de Gerland. In the end however, it would be an easy ride for Bayern against a subdued and surprisingly one-dimensional Lyon side. While Robben had dominated the headlines in the previous rounds, this time Ivica Olić stole the show.

Long seen as the provider of vital if unspectacular team goals, the Croatian delivered the crucial opening blow with a nicely-taken goal after twenty-six minutes. Robben's ball into the Lyon box had found Müller, whose bustling run and sharp cutback was finished in style as Olić collected the ball with his back to goal before swivelling through 180 degrees and slamming a firm right-footed shot past Lloris.

Needing at least three goals to progress, things would get worse for the home side a minute short of the hour mark with the sending off of Brazilian Cris. The French resistance faded after that, and Bayern simply overpowered their opponents to book their place in the final with ease. Olić's second arrived on sixty-seven minutes as he got on the end of a neatly-threaded pass from Hamit Altıntop to beat Lloris with a nicely-struck left-footed shot that fizzed in front of the keeper and into the bottom right-hand corner, and twelve minutes from time the Bayern number eleven completed his first hat-trick for the Bavarians with a regulation header from Philipp Lahm's right-sided cross to round off an unexpected but not at all flattering 4-0 aggregate victory.

In stark contrast to Bayern's dramatic route to the final, the showpiece in Madrid's Santiago Bernabéu was something of a damp squib. Playing their eighth European Cup or Champions League final this was the first time Bayern would come into the game as underdogs, and against an Internazionale side that had strangled and suffocated tournament favourites Barcelona in their semi-final, the mood in Munich was one of hope rather than expectation.

As I sat down to watch the final I was expecting one of two things: either Jose Mourinho's side would turn the screw and see out a regulation win for the Serie A side, or Bayern would pull yet another trick out of their hat to complete what would surely have been one of the most unlikely trophy trebles. In the end, everything would go with the form book as the tournament's kings of the spectacular comeback were subdued by the masters of the clinical counterattack.

Bayern had not missed Franck Ribéry in the second leg of the semi-final, but against an Inter side with a defence that required careful unlocking rather than brute force the Frenchman was sorely missed. The men from Munich would start the game brightly and keep the ball well, but the front line was never allowed to get into any sort of rhythm as Inter gradually settled and started to exercise control in almost every vital area of the pitch. When Argentinian Diego Milito opened the scoring for *I Nerazzurri* ten minutes before half-time, there was no coming back for *Die Roten*, sporting new red and white vertically-striped *Trikots*.

Despite dominating the possession Bayern would go into half-time a goal down, and as in the first half they were the more energetic side after the break. However when Thomas Müller missed an excellent chance to level the scores less than a minute after the restart, one could feel that it was not going to be Bayern's night.

Inter were more than happy to let Bayern keep hold of the ball, only to snuff out the threat in the final third as Mourinho's suffocating tactics were executed to perfection. Not surprisingly, the Bavarians started to fade. Robben would test Inter 'keeper Júlio César with a typically well-struck left-footed effort, but that was as good as it got for the Bavarians on an evening that had turned rather flat.

Unlike Aston Villa in 1982, FC Porto in 1987 or Manchester United in 1999 there would be no complaint or any sense of injustice at the result. Louis van Gaal had been comprehensively outthought and outwitted by his former assistant, and when the impressive Milito scored a second to effectively wrap things up twenty minutes from time it was a simple case of going through the motions.

As Bayern continued in their struggle to work their way through the solid and well-organised black and blue wall, another swift break engineered by Cameroon star Samuel Eto'o sent Milito through on goal. Leaving the lumbering Daniel van Buyten trailing in his wake, the Argentinian's confident finish left Hans-Jörg Butt with no chance.

After the torrid start to the competition, it was hard to believe that Louis van Gaal had taken Bayern within one win of achieving the coveted "Triple". In doing so, he had almost singlehandedly transformed the team's style and approach. The awkward and at times abrasive Dutchman may not have been everybody's cup of tea, but he had changed Bayern for the better, setting them on a path that had once again taken them to the very pinnacle of the European game. Perhaps more crucially, he had successfully integrated a number of the younger players into the first team, creating a core of talented individuals who would quickly establish themselves in the German national team.

A league and cup double was not a bad way to start as coach, and despite the defeat in Madrid many Bayern fans would be looking ahead to the following season with much anticipation.

DAS FEIERBIEST

Louis van Gaal's first season in charge in Munich had been a success with another domestic double and an appearance in the Champions League final, and spirits were high ahead of the 2010/11 season. There was little activity on the transfer market, but with the influx of talented players from club's youth ranks nobody was overly worried that Bayern had not turned to their cheque book.

A number of the summer incomers were returning from loan periods elsewhere: Dutch left-back Edson Braafheid returned to Bavaria following a spell in Scotland with Glasgow Celtic, Brazilian Breno and Andreas Ottl rejoined *Die Roten* from Nürnberg, while youth prodigy Toni Kroos headed back to Munich after eighteen productive months on loan with Bundesliga rivals Bayer Leverkusen.

Few waves were made in the other direction, with a number of fringe players making the move away. Youngster Mehmet Ekici headed up the road to Nürnberg on loan, while fading stars Andreas Görlitz and Christian Lell made their way to FC Ingolstadt 04 and Hertha Berlin on free transfers. Having briefly challenged for the number one spot, goalkeeper Michael Rensing also joined this small exodus with a move to Köln.

Bayern's first competitive encounter of the new season would come in early August with the return of the revamped DFL-Supercup, which threw together the league and cup winners. As double winners Bayern played league runners-up Schalke 04 in front of a packed Impuls Arena in nearby Augsburg, and in a well-contested match van Gaal's side scored two unanswered second-half goals to claim their first silverware of the new season.

Thomas Müller would score the opening goal with fifteen minutes remaining, with Miroslav Klose wrapping things up just six minutes later.

Just under a fortnight later the Bundesliga campaign would start in equally positive fashion with a 2-1 win over VfL Wolfsburg, but the following week a dismal display against newly-promoted Kaiserslautern marked the start of a very ordinary spell of form that almost mirrored that of the previous season.

Bayern conceded two goals in a minute as they fell to the resurgent Red Devils, and their barren spell in front of goal was extended further with two disappointing goalless draws at the Allianz Arena against Werder Bremen and Köln. Daniel van Buyten's ninetieth-minute goal was enough to secure the points in Hoffenheim to cap a second-half comeback, but even the return of the infamous *Bayern-Dusel* would come at a cost with an injury to Franck Ribéry.

With five matches played *Die Roten* were sitting in eighth place with just eight points from an available fifteen, and just a paltry four goals scored – the joint fewest in the league.

Things would go from bad to worse the following week against high-flying 1. FSV Mainz 05, who left the Allianz Arena with all three points to extend their 100% record and increase the gap between them and Bayern to a staggering ten points. One could hear the knives slowly being withdrawn from their sheaths, and another lifeless performance in Dortmund the following week saw van Gaal's men fall back into twelfth place, thirteen points adrift of the league leaders. A first win at the Allianz over third-placed Hannover 96 temporarily arrested the slump, but another goalless draw in Hamburg left Bayern on fifteen points after nine matches – ten points behind new league leaders Dortmund.

Bayern would show a marked improvement in their home form with an emphatic 4-2 against mid-table SC Freiburg, but a rather fortunate 3-3 draw at bottom side Borussia Mönchengladbach once again put things back into perspective. Goals from Mario Gómez and Bastian Schweinsteiger had given Bayern the lead after falling behind after just five minutes, and they should have been 3-1 in front two minutes before half-time when Bastian Schweinsteiger stepped up to the penalty spot, only to crash his kick against the post.

Bayern had dominated the first half and should really have been out of sight, but two quick goals from promising youngster Marco Reus and Belgian striker Igor de Camargo turned the match completely on its head. From nowhere, Gladbach were suddenly back in front. In the end, it was up to skipper Philipp Lahm to save the match for the Bavarians, his right-footed effort snatching a precious point just six minutes from full time.

The draw against 'Gladbach was followed by a solid 3-0 win over Nürnberg, and a combative 1-1 draw at the BayArena against third-placed Leverkusen was backed up with a 4-1 thrashing of seventh-placed Eintracht Frankfurt – only for things to collapse in a heap again with a dismal 2-0 slump against relegation-threatened Schalke 04, coached by former coach Felix Magath.

A comprehensive 3-0 win over strugglers FC St. Pauli lifted the Bavarians into sixth place, and they would sneak into fifth spot in the final game before the *Winterpause* – a curious encounter against second-from-bottom VfB Stuttgart that saw in-form striker Gómez register a stunning hat-trick against his former team mates at the Mercedes-Benz-Arena.

Gómez scored his first goal after thirty-one minutes, and two more from Thomas Müller and Franck Ribéry saw Bayern hold a comfortable advantage at half-time. Martin Harnik pulled one back for the home side five minutes after the break, but within four minutes Gómez looked to have wrapped it up with two goals in less than 120 seconds to complete his and Bayern's goalscoring work for the afternoon.

Bayern should have been away and clear, with Harnik's second four minutes after the hour mark little more than a consolation. However when Christian Gentner found the back of the Bayern net with nineteen minutes still remaining, there must have been a few jittery moments on the visitors' bench. Stuttgart's Russian striker Pavel Pogrebnyak could have easily pulled the score back to 5-4 six minutes from time, but in the end the Bavarians had done enough to claim all three points.

The men from Munich had slowly started to work their way up the table, but even at the half-way mark it was clear that they were going to have their work cut out in attempting to retain their Bundesliga title. Louis van Gaal's side would end the year a massive fourteen points adrift of runaway leaders Borussia Dortmund, and even the most die-hard Bayern fan had to concede that it would take nothing short of a miracle to overhaul Jürgen Klopp's side.

During the winter break Bayern looked to strengthen their midfield unit with the acquisition of the highly-rated Brazilian enforcer Luis Gustavo from Hoffenheim, but the slow exodus that had started in the summer continued. Hoffenheim in turn would take on the unsettled Dutchman Edson Braafheid on a free transfer and promising Austrian youngster David Alaba on a six-month loan spell, while just a week into the *Rückrunde* captain Mark van Bommel brought his four and a half year spell in Munich to an end with a free transfer move to AC Milan in Serie A. The winter break also saw the departure of Argentinian Martín Demichelis, who made the move to Spanish side Málaga CF.

The opening weekend of the *Rückrunde* saw Bayern take a point at mid-table Wolfsburg, but a convincing 5-1 win over Kaiserslautern fuelled by yet another Gómez hat-trick lifted them into fourth place – still fourteen points behind leaders Dortmund. A 3-1 come-from-behind victory in Bremen followed, only for things to turn around yet again. Gómez and

Hamit Altıntop would give Bayern a comfortable half-time lead at the RheinEnergieStadion against strugglers Köln, but a stunning comeback from *Die Geißböcke* condemned the visitors to their fifth defeat of the season. Christian Clemens had sparked the Köln comeback ten minutes into the second half, and a brace from Slovenian Milivoje Novaković in the space of nine minutes completed the dramatic turnaround.

The defeat in Köln saw Bayern drop back into fifth place – fifteen points off the lead – but the relatively poor form of the teams immediately above them meant that second place still remained a realistic target. Leaders Dortmund were running away from the chasing pack, but just three points separated the Bavarians from Bayer Leverkusen in second spot.

A resounding four-goal thrashing of Hoffenheim at the Allianz saw Bayern leapfrog surprise packages Hannover and Mainz into third place, and an equally convincing 3-1 win in Mainz would finally put some daylight between them and the men from the Palatinate.

Bayern had not managed to put together three straight victories all season, and they were thwarted yet again at the Allianz by high-flying Dortmund. A Luiz Gustavo strike in the sixteenth minute had cancelled out Lucas Barrios's ninth-minute opener for the visitors, but when Nuri Şahin restored Dortmund's lead just two minutes later there was no looking back for the men in yellow.

When former Bayern youth player Mats Hummels settled the issue on the hour mark, there were no remaining doubts as to where the title was heading. While Bayern's ongoing struggle to fight for a place in the top three places was taking another serious jolt, Dortmund were away and clear at the top.

As the season entered the final ten matches there was no let-off for Bayern, and their next game pitted them against third-placed Hannover, one of the many teams punching well above their weight in what was turning out to be a competitive battle for the remaining Champions League spots.

In a match that was effectively worth six points, the pressure was on both the coach and players to deliver, but in the end they collapsed in a sorry heap against Mirko Slomka's well-drilled collection of talented youngsters and seasoned journeymen. Bayern had all the big stars – Robben, Ribéry, Lahm, Müller, Kroos, Gómez – but they were left floundering by a Hannover side playing as a confident and well-drilled unit.

Norwegian international Mohammed Abdellaoue would give the 96ers the lead after sixteen minutes, and with Bayern unable to make any headway Konstantin Rausch doubled the lead for the hosts six minutes into the second half. Robben then gave his countryman van Gaal a sliver of hope just four minutes later, only for Portuguese winger Sérgio Pinto to send the visitors back to Munich empty-handed with a third two minutes past the hour. Bayern's misery was compounded by the dismissal of Breno seventeen minutes from time following a foolishly hot-headed bodycheck, and when the figures were all totted up they were back in fifth place – nineteen points behind Dortmund, but more crucially seven behind Leverkusen and five behind Hannover.

The 2-1 defeat in Hannover would signal the beginning of the end for Louis van Gaal, with the board making the decision to terminate his contract at the end of the season. The Dutchman's first season in Munich had almost resulted in an unprecedented trophy treble, but the inconsistent start in 2010/11 was clearly not at the standard expected by Messrs Hoeneß and Rummenigge.

Knowing that he was on his way out van Gaal could have decided to simply walk away there and then, but with the decision already made the pressure was pretty much off. After all, there wasn't much worse that could happen. With the lid now off, the team responded to the situation in the best way possible, and the brunt of the reaction was borne by their next opponents, Hamburger SV.

Armin Veh's side had been sitting in seventh place within reach of the Europa League qualifying places, and they must have felt that they were in with a chance against a Bayern side low on confidence and with a dead man walking as coach – but they were completely unprepared for what would happen once they had stepped onto the pitch in Munich.

Hamburg had managed to make it to the forty-minute mark with the score still at 0-0 – eliciting more than the odd catcall from the increasingly frustrated Bayern faithful towards the men in red. Arjen Robben finally ended the stalemate, but nobody could have seen what was coming next. As if stung by the criticism of their own fans, Robben would lead his teammates on a second half rampage. The Dutchman buried a free-kick two minutes into the second half to double the lead, and just eight minutes later completed a stunning fifteen-minute hat-trick with another sweep of that lethal left boot. Franck Ribéry and Thomas Müller both added to the growing tally, and the final insult came courtesy of an own goal five minutes from time from HSV skipper Heiko Westermann.

A tight 2-1 win in Freiburg settled by a Ribéry strike two minutes from time kept Bayern on the tail of third-placed Hannover, and a laboured 1-0 win over rock-bottom Mönchengladbach finally saw *Die Roten* climb into third place following 96's 4-1 beating in Dortmund, only to fall back behind again with a 1-1 stalement in Nürnberg. It was yet another miserable afternoon, crowned by a dreadful miscalculation by 'keeper Thomas Kraft and the dismissal of Robben – who had not even featured in the match – after the game had finished.

There was a sense of inevitability about what was going to happen next, and with Bayern once again slipping out of the top three the board finally lost patience with Louis van Gaal. By the end of the weekend he was gone, replaced by his assistant Andries Jonker.

While Jonker was tasked with guiding Bayern through their remaining five matches and securing a top three position, the new coach had already been named: on 25th March, the Bayern board announced that Jupp Heynckes, currently at rivals Bayer Leverkusen, would be returning to Munich for the third time.

At the time, I personally thought that van Gaal had been rather hard done by. Some of the performances were far from stellar, but it was an undeniable fact that the coach had done much to reshape and develop the team, particularly with his selection of younger players such as Thomas Müller, Holger Badstuber, Toni Kroos and David Alaba. Off the pitch, the Dutchman's abrasive personality did not do him any favours, but in truth this approach was little or no different from his high-profile contemporaries. Or so one might have thought.

Hoeneß and Bayern clearly knew what they were getting when they sought out van Gaal. An egotistical and authoritarian old school coach with old school methods, he was the polar opposite of the inexperienced Jürgen Klinsmann with his new age theories and holistic modern solutions that bordered on mollycoddling and yogic therapy. While not of the medicine ball and calisthenics brigade like Felix Magath, van Gaal shared *Quälix's* predilection for barking orders on the training ground and his use of old fashioned methods. He could be described as the managerial equivalent of castor oil.

Bayern had been after a swift antidote to Klinsmann's failure, and they surely must have known what the Dutchman would bring to Munich. They just didn't know how far it would actually go.

Here was a man who would always be addressed by his players with the formal *Sie*, rather than the more familiar *du*. He was not there to be the players' friend and confidante, but their coach. Not just their boss, but *the* boss. It was this attitude that had started to get under the skin of the Bayern hierarchy. Karl-Heinz Rummenigge was clear in saying that van Gaal's dismissal was "inevitable", while Uli Hoeneß made no attempt to hide the fact that the decision had been a long time in coming. It had all started so well, but the relationship between the club and the egotistical coach had quickly started to sour and curdle.

The problem was that like Magath before him, van Gaal had started to get under the skin of the powers that be at Bayern, to the point where even the results didn't matter. Between the initial announcement about his contract and his eventual dismissal, Bayern had won three games out of four, with the one draw against Nürnberg. This was hardly a reason for being given the boot. But the board had had enough; not just with van Gaal's stubbornness, intransigence and arrogant bloody-mindedness, but an almost dogmatic, formulaic style of football that was seen by many as ugly and out of tune.

Van Gaal's philosophy may have been breath of fresh air in the spring of 2010, but his unwillingness to adapt after that was to be his undoing. The mould had started to form, and it became clear that the coach was not going to listen to even friendly advice or pay heed to constructive criticism. He chose to automatically distrust some players, while throwing his entire weight behind others. While the likes of record signing Mario Gómez struggled to get off the substitutes' bench, the unfortunate Thomas Kraft was elevated to a position way beyond his actual ability and talent. Van Gaal was like a Rottweiler with a rubber quoit; once he had a firm grip of it in his jaws, he would simply refuse to let go.

Then there was the issue of van Gaal's idiosyncratic behaviour and constant interference, both on and off the pitch. Some of his tactical decisions had been suspect at best, but even more irksome were his candid opinions on issues that manifested themselves as divisions among the fans. The straw that arguably broke the camel's back was the unnecessary controversy over the proposed signing of Schalke 04's promising goalkeeper Manuel Neuer, which firmly placed van Gaal and Hoeneß in opposite corners of the ring. The coach's almost ideological opposition to Neuer was almost certainly driven by his unbridled and blind faith in Kraft; after all, as he already had the greatest young goalkeeper in Germany – in his opinion at least – why would he need some overrated kid from Gelsenkirchen?

The reactions to the "koan Neuer" issue could be seen in the stands at the Allianz Arena, with some supporters clearly voicing their criticism of Hoeneß – something hitherto unheard of at Bayern. Kraft was a local boy brought up through the youth system while Neuer was an outsider (and, to boot, a true blue Schalke loyalist), and while there were genuine grounds for dissatisfaction, van Gaal did much to whip things up to the point of hysteria. It was almost as if the Dutchman was trying to supplant Hoeneß as the Ultras' terrace hero.

Rummenigge quickly found himself playing the role of peacemaker as things started to come to a head, but the narcissistic van Gaal's inability to accept any sort of advice was always going to be a deal breaker. Hoeneß was unequivocal: the Dutchman had been instrumental in "ripping the club to pieces".

Van Gaal had boasted about his arrogance as if it was a badge of honour, but nobody had really taken him seriously. Up against the headstrong Hoeneß though, there was only going to be one winner.

Following the success of the 2009/10 season, van Gaal had appeared like a demigod on the balcony of the *Rathaus*, playing to an adoring crowd. He had also described himself as a *Feierbiest* – a literal translation of "party animal" that doesn't actually exist in the German language (but probably does now, along with Giovanni Trappatoni's *ich habe fertig*). At the time, everybody had been more than happy to bathe in the coach's success; nobody could have guessed how things would end, but in hindsight the signs were there for all to see.

Some time after van Gaal's dismissal, Hoeneß suggested that the Dutchman's problem was not his believing that he was God, but God's father – more powerful than God himself. *Bevor die Welt existierte, war Louis schon da.* "Before the world existed, Louis was there".

Louis van Gaal was on his way out of Munich, but there was still football to play, with plenty at stake. Match day thirty threw up another tough challenge for Bayern in the form of second-placed Bayer Leverkusen, who started the day five points behind leaders Dortmund. If the task of motivating the team was not hard enough a task, replacement coach Andries Jonker also had to make do without the suspended Arjen Robben.

Adding further spice to the encounter was Leverkusen coach Heynckes, who found himself in the curious position of playing the team he was set to coach the following season. To add another interesting little twist, Leverkusen's starting eleven also included former Bayern skipper Michael Ballack, who had made his way back to the Rhineland club after his successful if injury-hit spell in the English Premier League with Chelsea.

Die Werkself would come into the game on the back of an eight-match unbeaten run, and having won their previous five on the bounce were marginal favourites against an unstable Bayern side. On this day however, the Bavarians would wake up from their slumber. *Die Roten* had been largely defined by their inconsistency, but the form book was quickly thrown out of the window with what was arguably their most astonishing performance of an otherwise forgettable season.

It was scarcely credible, but by half-time Bayern were already four goals in front – shattering an opponent that had conceded just five in their previous eight matches. Leverkusen skipper Simon Rolfes would find the back of his own net to get things going after just seven minutes, setting the perfect platform for Mario Gómez to deliver his fourth hat-trick of the season.

Rolfes' own goal was the first of a series of defensive disasters for the visitors as he failed to clear a Franck Ribéry corner, but the second was little more than a comedy of errors as

Stefan Reinartz and then Chilean Arturo Vidal combined to set Gómez up for an easy tap-in from close range.

With just two minutes remaining until half-time, *Die Roten* inflicted a telling double blow to severely dent *Die Werkself's* title ambitions. Gómez's second goal came courtesy of another easy finish after a neat pass from Thomas Müller, and just a minute later Bastian Schweinsteiger found the ungainly but deadly striker in space just inside the penalty area. Gómez needed no second invitation to complete his hat-trick, blasting a right-footed effort straight through 'keeper René Adler and into the bottom left-hand corner of the net.

Swiss international Eren Derdiyok finally got the visitors on the scoreboard two minutes past the hour, but flying winger Ribéry would put the final gloss on a fine performance by *Die Roten* fifteen minutes from time. With Hannover picking up just the one point in Hamburg, Bayern swapped places with the team from Lower Saxony yet again.

With four matches remaining Borussia Dortmund were away and clear at the top, eight points clear of Leverkusen with Bayern a further six behind – and just one ahead of Hannover.

Andries Jonker could not have asked for a better start to his short tenure as Bayern coach, but the work was still far from over. The team continued to be infuriatingly inconsistent as they followed their 5-1 thrashing of high-flying Leverkusen with a scrappy 1-1 draw against relegation-threatened Eintracht Frankfurt. Bayern were lucky to even get away with a point, their goal coming one minute from time courtesy of a penalty from the in-form Gómez.

With Bayern struggling to maintain their form in Frankfurt, Hannover would come away with a 3-1 win in Freiburg to edge themselves back in front in the chase for the third Champions League slot. It had been the fifth week in a row that the two teams had swapped places, and as the season entered the final straight Mirko Slomka's side held the narrowest of advantages – just a single point.

	P	W	D	L	Goals	GD	Pts
BV 09 Borussia Dortmund	31	21	6	4	62:19	+43	69
Bayer 04 Leverkusen	31	19	7	5	62:41	+21	64
Hannover 96	31	18	3	10	45:41	+4	57
FC Bayern München	31	16	8	7	67:37	+30	56

Hannover would have a distinct advantage in facing struggling Mönchengladbach on match day thirty-one while Bayern hosted mid-table Schalke 04, but by the end of the day things had taken an interesting turn for Jonker's men. Playing in the evening match Bayern had expected to be four points behind Hannover at the kick-off, but just a couple of hours earlier a seventy-sixth minute strike from promising youngster Marco Reus had given Mönchengladbach an unlikely win as they continued to claw their way towards safety.

A point behind with a game in hand, Bayern knew what they had to do.

A frenetic start at the Allianz saw the returning Arjen Robben give Bayern the lead after six minutes only for Holger Badstuber to put through his own net at the other end, but Thomas Müller and the seemingly unstoppable goal machine Mario Gómez quickly opened up a comfortable two-goal cushion with less than twenty minutes on the clock. With the three points safely in the locker, man of the match Müller scored his second goal and Bayern's fourth in a far more sedate second half to complete a convincing 4-1 win.

The win over Schalke and Hannover's surprising slip-up against Mönchengladbach saw Bayern climb back into third place, two ahead of Hannover. Once again, they were masters of their own Champions League destiny. Elsewhere, victory for leaders Dortmund over Nürnberg and defeat for Leverkusen in Köln confirmed the destination of the *Meisterschale*, which would make the move from Munich to the Ruhr.

With two match days remaining Bayern simply had to keep winning to retain third place, and with it that precious berth in the Champions League. Their penultimate opponents were St. Pauli – who after a bright start to their first season back in the top flight had sunk with alarming rapidity to the foot of the table like a stone.

Over the course of their topsy-turvy season Bayern had made heavy weather of a number of seemingly weaker opponents, but they would show little mercy at the Millerntor, against a St. Pauli side that was clearly mentally prepared for a return to second division football.

St. Pauli's scant hopes of avoiding an instant return to the 2. Bundesliga had all but disappeared by half-time, as Bayern swept into a 2-0 lead with goals from Mario Gómez and Daniel van Buyten.

Gómez's opener followed a shocking piece of defending by centre-back Markus Thorandt whose attempted chest-back to 'keeper Thomas Kessler was intercepted by the alert Bayern striker, and the unfortunate Thorandt was also to blame for the second as he allowed van Buyten to rise above him at the near post to meet an Arjen Robben corner.

Bayern were in the comfort zone now, and their clinical first half display was little more than the prelude to an avalanche of goals. The doomed Buccaneers were all at sea, going through the motions in the second forty-five minutes as they were brutally taken apart.

Gómez netted his second goal seven minutes after the restart with a calm finish, and just two minutes later Robben added a fourth with a rare close-range tap-in. When Franck Ribéry took advantage of more comical defending to add a fifth with a quarter of an hour remaining, the floodgates were well and truly open. As the home side desperately looked to batten down the hatches, the Bayern players were storming the decks.

A well-executed set-piece header from Marcel Eger saw the home side break their duck, but further strikes from Robben, Gómez and Ribery in a frenetic final six minutes would complete the rout. Robben complemented his earlier tap-in with an even rarer header from the edge of the box, Gómez had enough time to almost fall over before thrashing the ball low into the gaping net, and the almost unplayable Ribéry rounded off the afternoon's entertainment with what was arguably the goal of the game – a delicious right-footed curler that flew into the top right-hand corner.

The 8-1 win would set a new record for the biggest victory away from home for FC Bayern, and Gómez' eighty-sixth minute strike completed his fifth league hat-trick of the season – another record.

The combination of Bayern's record-breaking win and Hannover's 2-1 defeat in Stuttgart was enough to secure third place for the Bavarians, making the unheralded Andries Jonker one of the most successful caretaker coaches at the club. Bayern had even managed to get to within three points of Jupp Heynckes' second-placed Leverkusen, meaning that they were still in with sliver of a chance of grabbing second place – and with it a direct berth in the group phase of the Champions League – in the final week of the season.

Victory was duly achieved against Stuttgart at the Allianz as Jonker finished with a record of four wins and one draw from his five games in charge – and a staggering twenty goals.

A twenty-fourth minute goal from Japanese international Shinji Okazaki had given Stuttgart the lead, but Bayern and the home crowd were not to be denied as *Die Roten* fought back to secure a hard-fought 2-1 victory. The unstoppable Gómez scored another goal against his former side to level the scores eight minutes before half-time, and Bastian Schweinsteiger clinched the points nineteen minutes before the final whistle.

A defeat for Bayer Leverkusen in Freiburg would have seen Bayern sneak into second place on goal difference, but a tight 1-0 win for the *Werkself* in Freiburg ensured that coach-in-waiting Jupp Heynckes would have the last laugh before his return to Munich. With Hannover finishing a seemingly distant five points behind Bayern, the final table would actually mask the reality of just how close the battle in the home straight for third place had been.

	P	W	D	L	Goals	GD	Pts
BV 09 Borussia Dortmund	34	23	6	5	67:22	+45	75
Bayer 04 Leverkusen	34	20	8	6	64:44	+20	68

FC Bayern München	34	19	8	7	81:40	+41	65
Hannover 96	34	19	3	12	49:45	+4	60

The defending Bundesliga champions had climbed no higher than third place during what had been a highly inconsistent season, and it was much the same story in the cup events with both the DFB-Pokal and Champions League campaigns meeting disappointing ends.

Having overcome amateur side Germania Windeck in the opening round of the domestic cup competition Bayern would then come from behind to defeat Werder Bremen at the Allianz, setting up a dramatic third-round encounter in Stuttgart that resulted in an avalanche of goals. Bayern were two goals up within the first eight minutes through Andreas Ottl and Mario Gómez, only for VfB to draw level right on the cusp of half-time. Miroslav Klose would restore the visitors' lead seven minutes after the break, and with the dismissal of Stuttgart hard man Khalid Boulahrouz after sixty-seven minutes Bayern were looking at seeing things out. Bruno Labbadia's side had other ideas however, and despite being a man down achieved parity once again with just thirteen minutes left through French full-back Matthieu Delpierre.

With Stuttgart just nine minutes away from taking the game into extra time at 3-3, the visitors finally put their foot down on the accelerator. In a trice, the Swabians were swept away as Bayern scored three quickfire goals to settle the issue. Thomas Müller grabbed the fourth to restore the lead for *Die Roten*, and his goal was quickly followed by further strikes from Klose and Franck Ribéry to transform what had been a tough and fairly even struggle into a rather flattering 6-3 victory. If just to rub salt into Stuttgart's smarting wounds, they also finished the match with nine men as goalscorer Delpierre also saw red.

A quarter-final journey to the Dutch border produced another flattering result as Bayern scored three goals in the final quarter of an hour to wrap up a four-goal win against second division Alemannia Aachen, setting up a semi-final at the Allianz Arena that pitted the Bavarians against a mid-table and in truth fairly ordinary Schalke 04 side.

Having seen their local rivals Dortmund stroll to an easy 3-1 league win over Bayern at the Allianz just four days earlier, *Die Knappen* must have sensed that they were more than in with a chance against the tournament favourites. They may have been struggling in the league, but the Gelsenkirchen side clearly saw the cup as a one-off opportunity to take something positive away from what had been a wretched season. Then there was *Trainer* Felix Magath, who clearly relished the opportunity to cock another snook at his former side.

Despite enthusiastic support from the home crowd, nothing went to plan for Bayern. Spanish legend Raúl would give the visitors the lead after a quarter of an hour, and despite throwing everything at their opponents in the second half the holders were unable to find a way back into the contest. With the *Meisterschale* already on its way to a new home, Bayern's hope of retaining the cup had also gone up in smoke.

In the final in Berlin, Schalke were never really tested against second division MSV Duisburg. The *Zebras* were comprehensively outplayed as the *Königsblauen* – kitted out in dark pink *Trikots* – waltzed to a comfortable 5-0 win. With Dortmund having claimed the Bundesliga title, it meant that both of Bayern's domestic trophies were set to spend the following year in the *Ruhrpott*.

The Champions League draw saw Bayern in a relatively easy group along with Italian side AS Roma, Swiss champions FC Basel and Romanian outsiders CFR Cluj. Despite the team's domestic travails things would begin well with a solid 2-0 win over Roma in Munich, and after coming from behind to beat a battling Basel 2-1 in Switzerland Bayern were clear at the top of the group.

After a surprisingly close 3-2 win over Cluj at the Allianz helped by two own goals from their opponents, the return fixture in Transylvania was a more straightforward affair. The Romanian champions were no match for a Bayern team inspired by Mario Gómez, who bagged yet another hat-trick before Thomas Müller added a fourth to round off a convicing victory.

With their place in the knockout stages already assured, Bayern could afford to be a little more relaxed as they travelled to Italy to take on Roma, and at half-time things were looking pretty much perfect. Once again the prolific Gómez was right the thick of the action, finding the back of the net twice in the space of five minutes to put Bayern on the path to a fifth successive Champions League victory. The home side had looked down and out at the break, but a fifty-ninth minute strike from Marco Boriello gave the Italians hope as they too chased a place in the knockout stages.

Bayern were still in front as the game entered the final ten minutes, but two sucker punches from Daniele de Rossi and local hero Francesco Totti turned things on their head. The game would have no real consequence for Bayern, but the hope of securing a perfect hundred percent group phase record for the first time had been unceremoniously quashed.

Some semblance of normality would return with the final group game against Basel, with Bayern overcoming a spirited start by the visitors to register their fifth victory of the campaign. Goals from Frank Ribéry and Anatoliy Tymoshchuk gave Bayern a comfortable lead at half-time, and unlike in Rome three weeks earlier there was no let off for the Swiss side. Ribéry scored his second four minutes into the second half to round off the scoring, and Bayern would march into the second round where they would be drawn against Internazionale – a repeat of the previous year's final in Madrid.

Bayern were out of form, but the defending champions were also a shadow of the side that had triumphed in the Bernabéu the previous season. Coach Jose Mourinho had departed for Chelsea, and despite their inconsistency in the Bundesliga Bayern clearly fancied their chances ahead of the first leg at the San Siro.

Young goalkeeper Thomas Kraft would hold firm in a fairly evenly contested first half, but over the course of the second forty-five minutes Bayern started to swing things in their direction. Arjen Robben struck the post in the fifty-third minute to almost give the visitors the lead, and at the other end Kraft denied both Houssine Kharja and Thiago Motta.

A goalless draw would have been a decent result, but the Bavarians wanted more. One final attack down the right saw Robben cut inside before unleashing a shot at Julio César in the Inter goal. The Brazilian was able to parry the shot, but the alert Mario Gómez was first to the rebound, tapping the ball past the stricken 'keeper to snatch an unlikely but deserved victory.

The return leg in Munich saw the home side given a massive jolt after just third minutes, as Carmeroonian striker Samuel Eto'o smartly slipped the ball under Kraft from close range to level things up on aggregate. It looked like all of hard work achieved in Italy had been undone, but the home fans only had to wait until the twenty-first minute for the equaliser. Another blunder from Julio César allowed Gómez to again find the back of the net, and when Thomas Müller netted Bayern's second just after the half-hour mark, Bayern had finally managed to put a bit of daylight between them and their opponents.

Gómez would go agonisingly close to adding a third just before half-time as he saw the ball hacked off the line, and moments later a close-range effort from Franck Ribéry's was brilliantly blocked by Esteban Cambiasso.

As the opening forty-five minutes came to a satisfactory conclusion, there was only one team in the contest. Despite taking an early lead, the visitors had been comprehensively outplayed.

At half-time Bayern were 3-1 ahead overall, with Inter needing at least two more goals to snatch the tie. Things had been ticking over nicely for Louis van Gaal's side as the game passed the hour mark, but a growing determination from the visitors allied with a sudden nervousness from the hosts would see things thrown back into the balance again.

Dutchman Wesley Sneijder's well-struck shot from just outside the box put the Italians within a goal of turning the tie around, and as the clock ticked by Bayern had been forced onto the back foot. The confident mood of the first sixty minutes had been turned into one of desperation. Having dominated the game for so long, Bayern were struggling to keep their revitalised opponents at bay. The momentum was with Inter, and with the Bayern defence looking increasingly shaky the visitors pressed even harder.

The final twenty minutes were a marked contrast to the closing stages of the first half, as Inter continued to press and create opportunities. With two minutes remaining the dangerous Eto'o beat Breno just inside the Bayern penalty area, before cutting back inside and laying the ball on a plate for Goran Pandev. The Macedonian made no mistake, blasting the ball past Kraft into the roof of the net.

It was like a nightmarish blur. Inter had hauled the aggregate score back to 3-3, putting themselves ahead on away goals. The Munich crowd was stunned into silence, and there was to be no second wind for the home side.

Yet again, another Champions League campaign had been ended with a painful sucker punch right at the death. Yet again, Bayern had lost a match that should have been put to bed before half-time.

As if to rub salt into Bayern's gaping wounds, just a few weeks later the same Inter side would meet Bundesliga rivals Schalke 04 in the quarter-finals – where they were completely taken apart. Felix Magath's side produced what was arguably their best performance of the season to destroy the Bayern's conquerors 5-2 at the San Siro, before wrapping up an emphatic 7-3 aggregate victory with a more sedate 2-1 victory in Gelsenkirchen.

After all of the rich promise of 2009/10 and Louis van Gaal's excellent first season in Munich, his second had been nothing short of a complete disaster. While on the pitch Bayern's form had wavered between the occasionally magnificent and the truly dreadful all year, off it the coach had continued to lose friends at an alarming rate with his general bloody-mindedness and haughty, standoffish attitude towards the media. At times, he simply could not help himself.

Then there was his relationship with Uli Hoeneß, which had started so brightly following the Dutchman's appointment in the summer of 2009. The outward red-cheeked joviality of both men suggested a friendly cooperation, but as time went on differences became more pronounced and the problems more acute. Behind the façade, both men knew where they stood. Despite the many attempts by the club to keep things together, the relationship between Hoeneß and van Gaal deteriorated so badly that by the end of the Dutchman's time in Munich it resembled a Venetian blood feud.

Louis van Gaal may have left Munich under a cloud, but there is no denying that his relatively short spell in charge would have a profound impact on the team's playing style. The traditionally patient approach remained, but it was now married to a far more disciplined and possession-based style of play with a greater emphasis on the development of tactical acumen.

While the club had clearly suffered during the latter part of the Dutchman's time in charge, many players would reap the benefits of his coaching. Philipp Lahm had clearly benefited from being given the responsibility of wearing captain's armband, and the transformation of Bastian Schweinsteiger from a hit-and-miss winger into a midfield dynamo had been nothing short of a revelation. The coach had also created the perfect working atmosphere for the fast-tracked development of the young Thomas Müller, whose footballing intelligence and on-field presence had been quickly identified.

Sadly, the negatives massively outweighed the positives. There was never any real chance of compromise; Louis van Gaal could only ever be Louis van Gaal. This, in the end, would ultimately seal his fate.

The Dutchman's replacement Jupp Heynckes was a complete contrast in personality, a listener rather than a talker and a coach who right from the beginning had the total trust of the Bayern board. Heynckes' initial task was not to go back to square one and undo all of van Gaal's work, but rather to hone it and add a greater level of flexibility. Off the pitch, Heynckes was also the perfect antidote to the fetid FC Hollywood atmosphere that had been rekindled by van Gaal.

The more questionable aspects of the mad Dutch scientist's rigid philosophy were cast aside for a far more flexible pragmatism both on and off the pitch, but not at any stage was there any risk of the baby being thrown out with the bathwater. Heynckes knew that the machinery at Bayern was in good order; there was no obvious need for any excessive tinkering.

After the static era of Felix Magath and the arguably madcap appointment of Jürgen Klinsmann, it finally looked as if Bayern were on the way to developing a genuine formula. The mission for the new coach was clear: to reestablish and solidify FC Bayern's position not just as the number one team in Germany, but among the world's footballing elite.

VIZE-, VIZE-, VIZEMEISTER

The return of Jupp Heynckes to FC Bayern in the summer of 2011 would bring a sense of calm back to the Säbenerstraße. As well as being highly respected by both his peers and the Bayern board, Heynckes was a much-loved figure among the entire fanbase in Munich; his arrival would signal the beginning of an end to the bitter feud that had been created by his predecessor Louis van Gaal.

Heynckes had spent a short time in Munich as caretaker coach during the spring and summer of 2009 following the dismissal of Jürgen Klinsmann, but his reappointment on a permanent basis in July 2011 would finally close the circle on a decision that had weighed heavily on general manager Uli Hoeneß for almost twenty years. In late 1991, in a move that Hoeneß would later describe to the German press as his "greatest mistake", Heynckes had parted ways with FC Bayern after four and a half years in charge. In July 2011, an older and wiser Hoeneß would welcome back a mellower and calmer Heynckes.

During his first spell in Munich, the former Borussia Mönchengladbach and Germany striker had been a harsh disciplinarian. Easily flustered, his bright red, angry face would earn him the nickname "Osram", after the famous German lighting company. Twenty years of coaching at the top level had turned Heynckes into a calmer but no less determined character, and the man who returned to Munich was a complete contrast to his ebullient and overbearing predecessor van Gaal. He was also a Champions League winner, an accolade achieved in 1998 as coach of Real Madrid.

As a Bayern supporter who had been a massive fan of Jupp Heynckes back in the late 1980s, I was comforted by his return. Louis van Gaal had done some excellent things during his two seasons in Munich, but for the first time since the departure of Ottmar Hitzfeld in 2008 I felt that the team was back in good and capable hands.

Bayern would make a number of bold moves on the transfer market, the biggest of which was the acquisition of German international goalkeeper Manuel Neuer from Schalke 04. This was the issue that had not only created a split among some sections of the fans in Munich, but had done much to exacerbate the high-profile dispute between former coach van Gaal and club general manager Uli Hoeneß.

While Neuer's quality, talent and future potential were all beyond question, a number of the more hardline *Südkurve* fan groups had been irritated by the club's decision to sign a player who from his early childhood had been a member of the established *Ultras* in Gelsenkirchen. The announcement of the planned transfer had led to some Bayern supporters brandishing large *koan Neuer* ("no to Neuer") banners in the stands at the Allianz Arena, while others even extended their criticism to Uli Hoeneß himself.

The debate had taken a distinctly political edge, with the complex and almost ideological issue of club loyalty competing against simple footballing economics. For many old school Bayern supporters, there could never be a place in Munich for a player like Neuer. For Uli Hoeneß on the other hand, it was all about bringing the best goalkeeper in the Bundesliga to the biggest and best football club in Germany.

The matter had been complicated further by Louis van Gaal, who had taken the decision to make Thomas Kraft, a product of the Bayern youth system, his chosen number one. The result was that the anti-Neuer section of the fan base ended up on the side of van Gaal against "Mr. Bayern" Hoeneß, even though the Dutchman's motives were more to do with his being proved right about Kraft rather than any sense of loyalty to the Bayern fans.

For van Gaal, it was a simple matter of defending his position at best, and coarse cynicism at worst.

There were, of course, reasonable grounds for the fans' hardline position. In addition to his established reputation as a long-time follower of *Die Knappen*, Neuer had made a clear and obvious impression on many Bayern supporters with his mocking imitation of the famous "corner flag" celebration by club legend Oliver Kahn after *Die Roten* had pipped Schalke to the Bundesliga title in 2001.

At the Allianz Arena in April 2009, Neuer repeated Kahn's memorable celebration almost move for move. Following his team's 1-0 win, the young goalkeeper charged to the touchline before uprooting the corner flag and waving it maniacally after sliding on his back. (It was described by some as "revenge" for 2001, but it is worth noting that Schalke have never won a Bundesliga title).

With significant sections of the Munich *Südkurve* having placed their feelings in open sight in throwing their weight behind Thomas Kraft, it was up to the new keeper to win the fans over and earn their support – not only on the pitch, but as a member of the team at Bayern. Neuer had arrived in Munich for the hefty price tag of €28 million, and right from the beginning almost every eye in the stands was focussed on him.

Right from the start, Neuer had a good idea what he was going to be up against. During a pre-season training match in the Italian resort of Trentino, he was roundly jeered by a large section of visiting Bayern fans. One banner declared that Neuer could catch as many balls as he liked, but he would never be accepted in the FC Bayern shirt. It was a tough place for a young player to be, more so given that many at his former club had no hesitation in branding him a "traitor".

Somewhat less controversial was the signing of a second young German international, Jérôme Boateng. The tall and powerful defender arrived in Bavaria after a short and somewhat disappointing spell for Premier League outfit Manchester City for €15 million, the same price that had seen him move to England from Hamburger SV the previous year.

The squad was also bolstered with a number of other signings. Former Schalke 04 utility man Rafinha arrived from Italian side FC Genoa for €8 million, promising young striker Nils Petersen made the long journey south from Werder Bremen for €5 million, and unknown Takashi Usami became the first Japanese player to sign for Bayern with a one and a half million Euro move from Gamba Osaka. Completing the picture was Austrian starlet David Alaba, who returned to Bavaria following his short loan spell at Hoffenheim.

Heading in the other direction, veteran striker Miroslav Klose moved to Serie A side S. S. Lazio for a bargain €5 million, Turkish international Hamit Altıntop made a potentially lucrative €6 million move to Spanish giants Real Madrid, while defender Andreas Ottl headed north-east to Berlin to join Hertha BSC along with 'keeper Thomas Kraft – who would see little future for himself in the first team at Bayern following the arrival of Manuel Neuer.

Before all of the proper stuff was set to start, Bayern were involved in two short pre-season mini-tournaments played over the final two weekends of July. While little more than glorified friendlies, it was the perfect opportunity to ease the new signings into the squad.

In the four-team Liga Total! Cup held at the Coface Arena in Mainz, a 2-1 reverse against Hamburger SV was followed by a penalty shootout defeat against the home team after a well-contested 2-2 draw. A week later in the more high-profile Audi Cup at the Allianz Arena, Bayern would edge out AC Milan on penalties after a 1-1 draw, before falling to a two-goal defeat in the final against Barcelona. In front of a crowd of just under seventy thousand, the match was settled by a goal in each half from a twenty year old prodigy: Thiago Alcântara do Nascimento.

The Bundesliga season would begin at the Allianz Arena against Borussia Mönchengladbach, a meeting that had plenty of significance for Jupp Heynckes. The Bayern *Trainer* had been one of the many stars of the great Gladbach side of the 1970s, before returning to coach *Die Fohlen* between 2006 and 2007.

It was not an especially auspicious start from two of the new boys. With just over an hour gone, the visitors thumped the ball high into the Bayern half, with Ivan de Camargo looking to chase the ball and escape from his marker Jérôme Boateng. What followed was like something from a comedy sketch. The Belgian stole a yard to get in front of the wrong-footed defender, but at the same time Manuel Neuer charged off his line before flapping aimlessly at thin air. Moments later the ball was in the back of the Bayern net, and the 'keeper had seemingly provided the loud and very visible *koan Neuer* brigade in the crowd with even more ammunition.

Bayern continued to look unconvincing the following week in Wolfsburg, but would finally get their season up and running with a last-minute goal from Luiz Gustavo. This provided the perfect boost, and the following week's meeting with Hamburger SV at the Allianz would finally give the fans something to cheer about. A real team performance saw *Die Roten* stroll to a 5-0 win, with five different players finding the back of the net.

Having scored a record five hat-tricks the previous season, Mario Gómez would get his first *Dreierpack* on the board for 2011/12 in a 3-0 defeat of perennial bogey team Kaiserslautern. It was the perfect springboard for the big striker, who went one better the following week with a spectacular four-goal show as Bayern demolished a hapless SC Freiburg 7-0. Bayern had scored sixteen goals without reply in four matches, were back at the top of the Bundesliga table, and it finally looked as though things had clicked into place.

The following week Bayern took on Schalke 04 at the Veltins-Arena, where a hostile *Nordkurve* reception awaited Manuel Neuer. With some of the travelling Bayern fans still voicing their displeasure at his being in a Bayern *Trikot*, the young goalkeeper would have had to experience the strange phenomenon of being booed at both ends of the ground. Not that it fazed him one bit.

The new Bayern 'keeper kept another clean sheet, and even without the prolific Gómez – absent with a thigh injury – the Bavarians easily claimed the points with goals either side of half-time from Nils Petersen and Thomas Müller. Since their opening day defeat, *Die Roten* had won five matches out of five and had scored eighteen unanswered goals. For Neuer, the wobbly start against Mönchengladbach had become little more than a fading memory. By keeping his head down and getting on with the task in hand, his critics had been given the perfect answer.

A dominant 3-0 win over a tired-looking Bayer Leverkusen saw Bayern extend their run in the league to six straight wins – ten in all competitions – but the perfect record would come to an end the following week at Hoffenheim, who blanked the Bavarian attack for the first time since the season opener against 'Gladbach.

While the attack failed to fire, the Bayern defence, and goalkeeper Neuer, held firm to register yet another shutout. After his opening day howler, Neuer had extended his record without conceding a goal to over a thousand minutes.

It would still take a little more time for Neuer to win over some of his harsher critics in the *Südkurve*, but nobody could deny that the former Schalke man was pulling out all of the stops. With every decent performance, the bristling negativity in the stands towards the young 'keeper had slowly started to dissipate. The *koan Neuer* banners gradually disappeared, and the fans' voices were again as one – cheering for FC Bayern.

Neuer extended his record further with another clean sheet as Bayern strolled to a 4-0 win over mid-table Hertha BSC with Gómez netting another brace, but like all good things it would eventually come to an end. After a staggering 1147 minutes, Neuer's record was finally ended in a 1-1 draw against Napoli in the Champions League. Even then, an opponent couldn't beat him: it would take an own goal from Holger Badstuber to finally breach the Bayern net.

Just five days later, Neuer's attempt to wrest the Bundesliga clean sheet record from Timo Hildebrand would come to an end in Hannover, where Bayern's long unbeaten run also came to an end with a 2-1 defeat. Heynckes' team would never really be in the contest against Mirko Slomka's energetic side, and with in-form Borussia Dortmund brushing aside Köln 5-0 the Bavarians saw their advantage at the top cut to just three points. A return to form came with a 4-0 thumping of Nürnberg as Gómez added two more goals to his growing tally, and a tighter than expected 2-1 win at new boys FC Augsburg saw Heynckes' men once again open up a five-point gap ahead of second-placed Dortmund.

Everything was set up perfectly for match day thirteen, which saw Bayern take on Dortmund at the Allianz, with a win almost certainly guaranteeing their winning the unofficial crown of *Herbstmeister*. The crowd was treated to a tense opening hour, but on sixty-five minutes the atmosphere was deflated by a goal that came out of almost nowhere for the visitors. Polish striker Robert Lewandowski charged towards the Bayern penalty area and found Mario Götze, who then traded passes with Shinji Kagawa before wriggling in front of Jérôme Boateng and stabbing a low shot past a wrong-footed Neuer.

Bayern's third defeat of the season saw Dortmund close the gap between the teams to just two points, and just like that the title race had been blown wide open.

Bayern could have been eight points ahead of Dortmund when they visited thirteenth-placed Mainz on match day fourteen, but the home defeat had clearly taken the wind out of their sails. Mainz would take an early lead, and although Daniel van Buyten evened things up eleven minutes into the second half, Thomas Tuchel's energetic side would hit the Bavarians twice in the space of ten minutes to put clear daylight between the two teams. A second goal from van Buyten eleven minutes from time gave Bayern hope of rescuing a point, but the home side held on to collect all three. The 3-2 defeat sent Bayern crashing down into third place, behind Dortmund and Mönchenglabach.

Bayern would return to the top the following week with a 4-1 win over Werder Bremen as the two leaders fought each other for a point apiece, and another brace the following week from Gómez in a tight 2-1 win against his former club VfB Stuttgart saw *Die Roten* edge back into a three point lead over Dortmund. With a significant goal difference advantage over the Ruhr side Bayern were guaranteed to go into the *Winterpause* as league leaders, and the advantage was retained the following week with an easy three-goal victory over Köln.

The opening *Hinrunde* fixture against Mönchengladbach at the Allianz Arena had seen the visitors scrape a somewhat fortunate 1-0 win, but the return at the Borussia-Park in January 2012 would see a far more convincing display from Lucien Favre's exciting young side against a tired-looking Bayern team that were unable to find any real rhythm. *Die Roten* were second best from the moment they were hit by Marco Reus's eleventh-minute strike, and two goals from German under-21 international Patrick Hermann either side of half-time effectively settled the issue before Bastian Schweinsteiger netted a late consolation.

Bayern's defeat in Mönchengladbach would tighten things up considerably at the top. Heynckes' men still led the way on thirty-seven points from eighteen games, but the following pack had all but eaten up the Bavarians' advantage. Only goal difference separated the Bayern from both Dortmund and a resurgent Schalke 04, with Gladbach just a point off the pace in fourth.

All of the top four sides would win the following week with Bayern registering a hard-fought 2-0 result against a workmanlike Wolfsburg outfit, but Bayern's biggest enemy was their dismal form away from home. A decent result at the Allianz Arena was often followed by a poor one on the road, with the dropped points allowing the chasing pack to inch their way closer.

By the beginning of February, the hunter had become the hunted. While Bayern were limping to an uninspiring 1-1 draw against mid-table Hamburger SV, a 2-0 win for Dortmund in Nürnberg would see Jürgen Klopp's in-form side climb back to the summit.

While Dortmund had started to gather some serious momentum in their quest to retain the Bundesliga title, Bayern continued to leak points away from their fortress in Munich. A workmanlike 2-0 win over Kaiserslautern was followed by a forgettably dire goalless draw against basement-dwellers SC Freiburg, and any encouragement that might have been taken from a convincing 2-0 win over fourth-placed Schalke 04 at the Allianz was almost immediately quashed by the same scoreline in reverse the following week in Leverkusen. To go back to the last time Bayern had managed to win away from home, one had to go back before the *Winterpause* and the 2-1 win in Stuttgart.

An emphatic 7-1 thrashing of tenth-placed Hoffenheim fuelled by a Mario Gómez hat-trick would help get things going again, and the following week in Berlin would see *Die Roten* finally secure their first away win of the *Rückrunde* against Hertha BSC. It was as if the pressure valve had been released, and poor Hertha would be left to face the resulting storm as they were subjected to a six-goal slaughter which included three penalties, including two for hat-trick hero Arjen Robben.

Bayern would make it three wins from three with a 2-1 win over eighth-placed Hannover, but title rivals Dortmund had shown few signs of exhaustion as they continued their charge towards the finishing line. Unbeaten in domestic competition since the previous September, Jürgen Klopp's team were five points in front of Bayern with just seven games remaining; the title was theirs to lose.

But this was the Bundesliga, where things wouldn't be quite the same without a little drama.

At the same time as *Die Roten* were battling hard to earn another three precious points with a 1-0 win in Nürnberg, Dortmund were held to a 4-4 draw by seventh-placed Stuttgart in a topsy-turvy encounter at the Signal Iduna Park. Jürgen Klopp's team had seen a comfortable two-goal lead turned into a 3-2 deficit in the space of just eight minutes deep into the second half, and after scoring two more themselves to retake the lead with just three minutes remaining, an equaliser two minutes into injury time from Christian Gentner ensured a share of the spoils for the visitors.

While the drama in Dortmund had provided plenty of excitement for the neutral, for Bayern fans it meant that the title was back again in their own hands. The deficit had been trimmed from five points to just three.

A brace from Mario Gómez was enough to secure a 2-1 win in the Bavarian derby against FC Augsburg, setting things up perfectly for the second crucial meeting with Dortmund at the Signal Iduna Park. Earlier in the season the Bavarians had blown the opportunity to go eight points clear of the defending champions as they fluffed their lines at the Allianz, but this time the boot was firmly on the other foot. This time it was Bayern doing the chasing as they looked to close down Dortmund's three point lead.

This was a genuine six-pointer *Spitzenspiel*: while a Bayern win would be enough to see them edge back in front of their rivals on goal difference, a defeat would stretch the deficit back out to six points and almost certainly see the *Meisterschale* remain in the *Ruhrpott*.

As in the first encounter in Munich, it was a tight and well-contested battle between two equally-matched teams. Dortmund would have the better of most of the first half with a flurry of attacks in the opening ten minutes and saw a Lewandowski header crash off the upright, but after the break the visitors would look increasingly dangerous.

Bayern were doing most of the running, but with just thirteen minutes remaining the home side broke the deadlock as Kevin Großkreutz set up Lewandowski to finish from some six yards.

Bayern simply had to throw everything forward now. With the Bundesliga shield starting to slip away, they upped the tempo. It almost came off. Right at the death, Arjen Robben was brought down in the box by Dortmund 'keeper Roman Weidenfeller, and referee Knut Kircher pointed to the penalty spot. Robben got back up to take the kick, but his effort was simply awful. Weak and without any real conviction, it looked like a soft backpass as it ended up in Weidenfeller's grateful arms. The lifeline had been lost, and with it a precious point – in fact, three points given that Dortmund collected all three instead of just the one.

The moments that followed would define the growing rivalry between the two teams. As Weidenfeller clutched the ball close to his chest, the home crowd served up a chorus of boos and whistles. While this was hardly unexpected, it was accompanied by a disgusting display of unsportsmanlike behaviour from Dortmund's Serbian defender Neven Subotić, who charged like an elephant towards Robben before placing himself inches away from the disconsolate Dutchman in a pointlessly aggressive face to face encounter.

Robben was seemingly oblivious to Subotić's bizarre verbal assault, but the players – and every Bayern fan – would remember the incident. I had as a young Bayern fan grown up with an antipathy towards Hamburger SV that had then been superseded by an almost visceral loathing of Werder Bremen, but Dortmund were quickly building a reputation as the latest team to hate. They seemed to exude this peculiar brand of malevolence that just made them easy to dislike, and with bellicose characters like Subotić, Kevin Großkreutz and Marco Reus they were quickly creating their own collection of unique folk-demons.

Robben had an opportunity to redeem himself right at the death, but only succeeded in blasting the ball over an empty net after Subotić's header against his own crossbar had caused all sorts of panic in the Dortmund defence. When the final whistle blew Bayern were a massive six points adrift, and with just four games remaining everybody knew it would take a miracle to not see Dortmund keep the *Meisterschale* for another year.

With Dortmund continuing their unbeaten charge towards the title a punch drunk Bayern could only manage a goalless draw at home to eleventh-placed Mainz, a result that left them with a rather ridiculous mathematical chance of claiming the title. Eight points adrift of the leaders with just three matches to play, it was fair to say that Heynckes' side had started to focus their attention on the upcoming Champions League meeting with old rivals Real Madrid. The Bundesliga campaign would end as a contest the following week, with Dortmund retaining the title with a 2-0 win over Mönchengladbach. Bayern's 2-1 win over Werder Bremen combined with third-placed Schalke's 1-1 draw in Augsburg was enough to secure second place, and with far more important games ahead they saw out the season with a functional 2-0 over Stuttgart and a 4-1 win in Köln.

Having been a game away from establishing an eight-point lead over Dortmund earlier in the season, Bayern eventually finished behind their rivals by the same margin. The season had started brilliantly and would end just as strongly for *Die Roten*, but the slack months in middle were crucial in deciding the final destination of the Bundesliga title.

Heynckes' side had won nine of their last ten matches, but nothing could stop a Dortmund side that had started to gather momentum half a dozen matches into the campaign. Having suffered three defeats in their first six games, Jürgen Klopp's side would go through their remaining twenty-eight undefeated – racking up twenty-five victories in the process to set a new Bundesliga record of eighty-one points. Not even Bayern could keep up with that.

	P	W	D	L	Goals	GD	Pts
BV 09 Borussia Dortmund	34	25	6	3	80:25	+55	81
FC Bayern München	34	23	4	7	77:22	+55	73
FC Schalke 04	34	20	4	10	74:44	+30	64

| Borussia Mönchengladbach | 34 | 17 | 9 | 8 | 49:24 | +25 | 60 |

Bayern's domestic cup campaign would start with a rather flattering 3-0 win at third division Eintract Braunschweig, with penalties from Mario Gómez and Bastian Schweinsteiger taking the Bavarians into a two-goal lead at half-time before Thomas Müller wrapped things up seven minutes from time. What was effectively a second eleven then destroyed fellow Bavarians FC Ingolstadt 04 6-0 at the Allianz, but things would be a lot tougher at second division VfL Bochum. Bayern had for a long time shared a fan friendship with the Ruhr outfit, but there was little charity on the pitch as Andreas Bergmann's men gave as good as they got in what was a surprisingly even contest.

The club known as *Die Unabsteigbaren* – literally, "the un-relegationables" – would take a slender 1-0 lead into the half-time break, and although Bayern levelled the scores through youngster Toni Kroos seven minutes after the restart it would take a last-minute strike from Arjen Robben to settle the issue.

A more straightforward 2-0 win in Stuttgart against VfB saw Bayern safely through to the last four with Mario Gómez continuing to rub salt into the wounds of his former teammates, and in the semi-final the free-scoring Bayern side were taken the distance by Borussia Mönchengladbach. Lucien Favre's side would shut things down effectively to keep the Bayern attack at bay, and there would be a sense of inevitability about the resulting penalty shootout after two hours of goalless football.

Bayern scored first as the first five kicks were scored, but with Gladbach trailing 3-2 Brazilian defender Danté blasted his effort high over the target. Toni Kroos kept his cool to put Bayern 4-2 in front, leaving defensive midfielder Håvard Nordtveit with the task of keeping his team in the shootout. The Norwegian saw his spot-kick saved by Manuel Neuer, sending Bayern into yet another Berlin showpiece – where they would face title rivals Dortmund.

Dortmund had won the Bundesliga title at something of a canter, but things could have been very different had Bayern managed to squeeze a little more from the two very close contests between the two sides. This could not be said of the DFB-Pokalfinale in Berlin, where a confident Dortmund side rounded off their season in grand style. Japanese international Shinji Kagawa would seize upon a sloppy error by Luis Gustavo to open the scoring in the third minute, and although Arjen Robben scored from the penalty spot to even things up on the twenty-five minute mark, a penalty at the other end would put Dortmund back on top. Manuel Neuer dived well to his left, but Mats Hummels' kick was just too good.

Bayern were still reeling when Robert Lewandowski netted his team's third right on the cusp of half-time, and thirteen minutes after the break the Polish marksman would add another following a fast break up the field and the perfect assist from Kevin Großkreutz. 4-1 down with just over half an hour remaining, the Bavarians needed a miracle, the most epic *Bayern-Dusel* yet.

The game opened up as Jupp Heynckes started to throw caution to the wind, and there was the merest sniff of hope when Franck Ribéry scored what was arguably the goal of the game a quarter of an hour from time. Another goal from *Die Roten* would have made things interesting, but just six minutes later Lewandowski would complete his hat-trick to hammer the final lurid yellow nail into the red coffin.

Dortmund's fifth goal pretty much summed up Bayern's performance. Neuer made a complete mess of what should have been a simple gather and collect exercise, and as the Bayern 'keeper desperately struggled to get back on his feet, Łukasz Piszczek had more than enough time to float in a cross for his fellow Pole to head home from close range. Bayern would have their chances, but there was no arguing that they had suffered a brutal thrashing.

With the *Meisterschale* and now the golden DFB-Pokal on their way to Dortmund, Bayern would have one last opportunity to make up for everything by claiming the biggest prize of all – the Champions League – on their home ground.

Having finished in third place in the Bundesliga the previous season, Bayern would have to qualify for the opening group phase of the Champions League, kicking off their campaign with a two-legged play-off against Swiss side FC Zürich. The opposition may not have been the most testing, but the mission for Heynckes' team was simple: get the job done, and then look forward to the knockout stages.

The 3-0 aggregate scoreline was both straightforward and unspectacular, and Bayern never really needed to get out of first gear against a highly defensive and toothless opponent. The Swiss league runners-up would manage to restrict Bayern to just the two goals in Munich, and in the return leg the following week a goal from Mario Gómez after just seven minutes would effectively settle the tie. Zürich were probably happy to keep the score down at a respectable level, and Bayern were able to cruise through to the finish without break into a sweat.

The draw for the group phase saw *Die Roten* thrown together with English Premier League side Manchester City, Spanish outfit Villareal CF and arguably the most testing of the three, SSC Napoli from Serie A. It was fair to say that while the group was not the toughest, there were no easy points either.

Match day one saw Bayern make a potentially tricky trip to Spain, and at Villareal's compact El Madrigal they once again settled any nerves with a seventh-minute strike. Franck Ribéry's effort gave Bayern a lead that they never looked like losing, and after second half substitute Nils Petersen had missed three good opportunites to make the game safe Brazilian Rafinha – an early replacement for Daniel van Buyten – secured the points fourteen minutes from the end.

Mario Gómez would take his free-scoring league form into Europe with a first-half brace as Manchester City were easily disposed of at the Allianz Arena, but the striker would miss the perfect opportunity to maintain Bayern's one hundred percent record in the competition with a missed second-half penalty in Napoli. Toni Kroos had found the back of the net as the Bavarians once again struck early, but the Italians somehow managed to fashion an equaliser six minutes before half-time when Christian Maggio's cross was turned into his own net by the unfortunate Holger Badstuber. Bayern's *Elfmeter* came four minutes after the restart courtesy of a handball from Paolo Cannavaro, but 'keeper Morgan de Sanctis made easy work of Gómez's well-struck but poorly-directed spot-kick.

Napoli's goal would bring Manuel Neuer's long unbeaten record to an end, a spell that had covered a dozen matches and a total of 1147 minutes stretching back to the Bundesliga opener against Mönchengladbach. Although the record would end in Italy, Neuer had to wait until Bayern's next Bundesliga game against Hannover 96 before being beaten by an opposition player.

Manuel Neuer's Clean Sheet Record

Date	Opponent	Competition	Result	Mins.
07/08/2011	Bor. Mönchengladbach (H)	Bundesliga	L 0:1	28
13/08/2011	VfL Wolfsburg (A)	Bundesliga	W 1:0	90
17/08/2011	FC Zürich (H)	Champions League	W 2:0	90
20/08/2011	Hamburger SV (H)	Bundesliga	W 5:0	90
23/08/2011	FC Zürich (A)	Champions League	W 1:0	90
27/08/2011	1. FC Kaiserslautern (A)	Bundesliga	W 3:0	90
10/09/2011	SC Freiburg (H)	Bundesliga	W 7:0	90
14/09/2011	Villareal CF (A)	Champions League	W 2:0	90
18/09/2011	FC Schalke 04 (A)	Bundesliga	W 2:0	90
24/09/2011	Bayer 04 Leverkusen (H)	Bundesliga	W 3:0	90

27/09/2011	Manchester City (H)	Champions League	W 2:0	90
01/10/2011	TSG 1899 Hoffenheim (A)	Bundesliga	D 0:0	90
15/10/2011	Hertha BSC Berlin (H)	Bundesliga	W 4:0	90
18/10/2011	SSC Napoli (A)	Champions League	D 1:1	39

The point in Italy would leave Bayern top of the group standings on seven points from their three games, two clear of City.

The return fixture against the Italian side in Munich saw Bayern stretch their advantage over their rivals with three more points, but the Bavarians would make heavy weather of things as they almost contrived to blow a three-goal lead. Mario Gómez – who could almost do no wrong in front of goal – looked to have wrapped things up before half-time with yet another outstanding hat-trick, but a goal at the stroke of half-time and a second eleven minutes from the end gave Napoli a sniff of an opportunity they hardly deserved. There were a few nervous moments for the capacity 69,000 crowd at the Allianz, but Bayern had done enough to collect all three points.

Bayern's place in the knock-out stages was confirmed in match day five against winless Villareal, with the Bavarians easing to a 3-1 win at the Allianz. The energetic Ribéry opened the scoring after just three minutes and Gómez doubled the advantage twenty minutes later, and although the Spanish side would pull a goal back Ribéry would score his second with just over twenty minutes remaining to round off yet another satisfactory evening.

The three points combined with Manchester City's defeat in Napoli confirmed Bayern's place at the top of the group. Although they would lose their undefeated record in the final group game against the Citizens at the Etihad Stadium, nobody was complaining too much. With the added incentive of playing the final at the Allianz Arena, everybody could relax until the tournament's resumption after the winter break.

The second round draw pitted Heynckes' side against Swiss champions FC Basel, a tie most fans would have happily picked with potential opponents like AC Milan and Lyon also in the second pot. Confidence was high ahead of the first leg in Switzerland, and it is fair to say that a number of supporters – including myself - would seriously underestimate the opposition. As a result, the rather numbing 1-0 defeat was something of a rude shock.

It was one of those evenings. Franck Ribéry was denied at close range by Yann Sommer with just three minutes on the clock, and after just nine minutes the Basel 'keeper foiled the Frenchman again as he kept out another close-range effort. It was not all one way traffic as the home side twice rattled the Bayern woodwork, but as the first half came to an end *Die Roten* had nothing to show for their efforts.

The second half followed a similar script. Bayern made most of the running, but every promising move seemed to break down in the final third. Goal machine Mario Gómez would have an uncharacteristically quiet evening, and both Ribéry and Arjen Robben were kept in check by the organised Basel defence. The Swiss champions clearly had a game plan, and they would execute it perfectly.

The telling blow would come four minutes from time, with substitutes Jacques Zoua and Valentin Stocker combining to unlock the Bayern defence. An array of black shirts were left standing like statues as Zoua was allowed to advance unhindered to the edge of the penalty area before sliding a smart diagonal ball for Stocker, who had made his way into the box unchecked. The Swiss international had plenty of time to hone in on the target, stroking a low left-footed shot that nutmegged Manuel Neuer from eight yards out.

Basel had taken four out of six points against former champions Manchester United to reach the knockout stages at the English side's expense, but nothing could remove the feeling of shock among fans of the more well-known "FCB".

Heiko Vogel's side would have no doubt harboured hopes of pulling off a shock result when the two teams met for the return leg in Munich, but this time Bayern – and Gómez in particular – were ready and waiting for them. In a game that made a mockery of their patchy performance in the first leg, the red Bavarian machine fired into action as their hapless opponents were not just overpowered, but completely eviscerated. If the Basel defence had resembled a secure Swiss bank vault in the first leg, in the face of a ferocious Bayern onslaught that same back line looked more like sweating Swiss cheese.

Having rediscovered their shooting boots at the weekend with the 7-1 demolition of Hoffenheim, Bayern were in no mood to offer any mercy to the Swiss champions. Any fears of a shock exit were quashed after just ten minutes, when Arjen Robben smartly beat the offside trap to collect a chipped pass from Toni Kroos and smash home the opener.

The 66,000 crowd had to wait more than half an hour for the second goal, but when it came it opened the floodgates. Goalscorer Robben would turn provider three minutes before half-time with a perfectly floated cross from the right that was hooked in at the near post by Thomas Müller, and just two minutes later roving full-back Holger Badstuber made his way to the byline before cutting the ball back inside for Gómez to tap in from close range.

Three goals to the good and having swung the tie firmly back in their favour at half-time, the home side put their foot on the pedal in the second half – with the hungry, prowling Gómez again sniffing Swiss blood. Franck Ribéry's mesmeric mazy run down the left would set things up nicely for the tall striker to stroke in a spectacular second on the volley, and a minute past the hour Gómez made it two *Dreierpacks* in as many matches with a close range header following another dazzling run and cross from Ribéry.

The quicksilver Frenchman was almost unplayable, Gómez was scoring goals for fun, and Bayern were rampant.

Ribéry couldn't get himself on the scoreboard, but his approach play was nothing short of lethal. Just six minutes later he and Gómez combined yet again, and in what was arguably the best move of the evening the Frenchman would again dance past, round and through a number of white shirts before cutting the ball back sharply into the middle of the penalty area. Completely unmarked, Gómez had more than enough time to take aim and fire the ball firmly into the top right-hand corner of the net with poor Sommer left completely stranded.

Having dared to entertain the idea of causing an upset, Basel had been taught a footballing lesson – but the torture was not quite over yet. With nine minutes remaining the Emmental defence was sliced wide open yet again, with substitute Bastian Schweinsteiger threading the perfect through ball for Robben. The Dutchman evaded the first desperate challenge and skipped around the floundering 'keeper, who was left crawling on the ground like a bright yellow crab as the ball was drilled past him for the seventh time.

It had been a truly world class display, and after the first leg hiccup the mission to reach the final – the *Finale Dahoam* – was back on.

The draw for the quarter-finals pitted Bayern against 1993 champions Olympique Marseille, a first-ever meeting between the two teams in European competition. The tie would see Franck Ribéry line up against some of his former colleagues, and having eliminated Bayern's 2010 and 2011 conquerors Internazionale in the second round the French side were not being taken lightly.

This was with good reason: while Marseille were far from invicible and would come into the game without a win in their previous eight competitive matches, Bayern had been little better on the road in their previous three Champions League matches – their last positive result being the 2-0 group stage victory at Villareal the previous September.

Heynckes' side would spend most of the first half trying to pry open their highly defensive opponents, and although the home side had forced Manuel Neuer into an early save they largely relied on the counterattack as *Die Roten* took a firm control of the midfield. Ironically, Marseille's first genuine foray forward in what was a rather scrappy and uneventful first half would result them being hit on the break themselves. A minute before the interval, Philipp Lahm won the ball for the visitors before combining with Arjen Robben to find the inevitable Mario Gómez.

Spanish referee Carlos Velasco Carballo ignored the home side's claims for an initial handball against the Bayern skipper, and Robben's perfect through ball found Gómez, whose shot was hit straight at 'keeper Elinton Andrade. Andrade looked to have got his body behind the ball, only to inexplicably deflect it into his own net. With regular 'keeper Steve Mandanda suspended after being sent off against Inter in the previous round, Marseille fans might have felt doubly aggrieved.

With a crucial away goal on the board, Bayern could afford to slow things down and tighten their grip on the match. As Didier Deschamps' side were forced to abandon their clean sheet strategy, things slowly started to open up. Marseille would create a couple of half-chances early in the second half, but it was the visitors who looked more likely to score. The Bavarians resembled a coiled snake; relaxed while squeezing the life out of the opposition, while at the same time remaining patient, poised and ready to strike.

With twenty-one minutes remaining, Bayern scored their second. There was nothing elaborate about the move, which was like watching a highly-skilled surgeon at work as the Marseille defence was sliced open with clinical ease. The twinkle-toed Robben ghosted down the right, played a smart one-two with Thomas Müller, and looked up for a split second before executing the perfect finish, slipping the ball under the sprawling Andrade.

With their two unanswered away goals Bayern could afford to take a more relaxed approach to the second leg in Munich, with Croatian Ivica Olić given an opportunity to start in place of top scorer Mario Gómez. Faced with the task of scoring at least twice at a packed and noisy Allianz Arena, the French side were completely overwhelmed as Olić capably filled Gómez's big boots up front.

The Croatian would look marginally offside as he stabbed home Franck Ribéry's cross after just thirteen minutes, but it was the least *Die Roten* deserved as they quickly stamped their authority on the game. Having returned from his one game suspension Steve Mandanda was back between the sticks for the French side, and he would keep Marseille in the game with a series of stunning saves to keep out Toni Kroos, Anatoliy Tymoshchuk, Olić and Müller in quick succession.

It could very easy have been three or four before half-time as a Kroos effort finally beat Mandanda only to crash against the woodwork, but the fun and games would come to an end with Olić's and Bayern's second eight minutes before the break. The goal would come following another lightning fast break from the men in red, with Ribéry and David Alaba combining to cover the entire length of the pitch down the left with the young Austrian providing the crucial assist.

With Marseille needing at least four second-half goals to progress Bayern could afford to slip back down a few gears and comfortably see things through to the end. Having claimed a place in the last four, just one team would separate the men from Munich from another Champions League final: old foes Real Madrid.

Even before a ball had been kicked, the semi-final was always going to be a classic. If the rich and glorious histories of both FC Bayern München and Real Madrid CF were not enough, their many encounters in both the European Cup and Champions League had become the stuff of legend for both sets of supporters. It was the ultimate gladiatorial contest: the much-fêted *Galacticos* from Madrid against the Bavarian giants, a team that had become known to supporters of the Spanish side as *La Bestia Negra* – the much-feared "black beast".

The spring of 2012 would see a meeting that threw together two contrasting teams: the well-drilled Bayern side under Jupp Heynckes – himself a former Champions League winning coach with Madrid – and José Mourinho's star-studded lineup that featured a host of Spain's World Cup winning side and the likes of Portuguese talisman Cristiano Ronaldo, spindly Argentinian maestro Ángel Di María, French marksman Karim Benzema and German duo Mesut Özil and Sami Khedira. While Bayern's squad featured a number of top names, Madrid's was more like a who's who of international superstars – managed by one of the most highly-rated (though some may say overrated) coaches in the world.

After a slightly suspect start to their Champions League campaign *Die Roten* had won their last three matches in the competition, but *Los Merengues* had been the team in top form and the ones to watch. Apart from conceding a late injury-time equaliser in Moscow in the first leg of their second round meeting with CSKA – they would win the second leg 4-1 to complete a confortable 5-2 aggregate victory – Mourinho's side had put together a flawless record, winning all six of their group phase matches and almost casually swatting aside surprise quarter-finalists APOEL Nicosia 8-2 on aggregate.

While Bayern's accumulated total of twenty-two goals in their ten Champions League games was far from shabby, Real had scored a staggering thirty-two; Mourinho's side would also have the advantage of playing the second leg at home, and when the two teams lined up for the opener at the Allianz Arena the scene was set for yet another titanic two-match tussle that would inevitably go all the way. All the way to the bitter end.

Over the years as a Bayern supporter, I had developed an almost pathological loathing of Real Madrid; a primitive, visceral feeling that seemed to acquire an additional layer with every encounter. It may have been different for others and I can only speak for myself, but I have always felt that in terms of European competition it just didn't get any better. *The history. The* needle. *The bubbling undercurrent. 1987, Lothar Matthäus and the head-stomping Juanito.* Even the likes of Barcelona, Internazionale, AC Milan and Manchester United pale into comparison.

Real Madrid had always provided the ultimate challenge not only for the team out on the pitch, but also the fans both in the stands and those many millions sitting anxiously behind a television set. I would actually describe it as a form of footballing masochism.

One cannot describe the sense of fear and nervous anticipation before each of these meetings, the exhausting roller-coaster ride during the game itself, and the thin edges of both sides of the emotional wedge right at the end. Victory over Real Madrid has felt and will always feel better than one over any one else – think of the joy of beating Borussia Dortmund multiplied by a factor of ten – while defeat always leaves a cavernous hole that takes the longest time to fill.

With just two matches standing between Bayern and the final on home soil in Munich, the incentive could not have been any greater for Heynckes' men, who made their way onto the pitch in a red and white atmosphere that was almost feverish. Any hopes of wresting the Bundesliga title from Dortmund had long since disappeared with the dismal goalless draw in Mainz at the weekend, and it was all about overcoming this final hurdle. It was as if every single pent-up emotion had been compressed into this one evening.

And what an evening it would be.

The game would start as expected, with both sides adopting a cautious approach while continually looking for that crucial opening. The visitors would have the first shot at goal and Manuel Neuer was more than equal to it, but after a close penalty shout the Allianz exploded into life as Bayern took the lead. Franck Ribéry looked to have had his shirt tugged in the area by Sergio Ramos only to have referee Howard Webb wave play on, but just two minutes later the Frenchman would make no mistake. With the men in white struggling to clear a Bayern corner, Ribéry latched on the loose ball before hammering it home from twelve yards.

It was just the start we all wanted.

While Real had dominated much of the opening quarter of an hour, the goal would see the momentum swing the other way. Bastian Schweinsteiger shot narrowly wide, and Arjen Robben started to assert himself down the right flank against a shaky-looking Madrid defence. Half-time arrived, with the home side in the ascendancy.

Bayern continued to play positively after the break, but moments after Robben had smacked another shot narrowly over the target, the home crowd was stunned into silence. Madrid's equaliser had come from nothing: a scuffed Ronaldo effort, a parry from Manuel

Neuer, a poor clearance, another Ronaldo shot. Then, from three yards out, the finish from Mesut Özil.

Urged on by the crowd, Bayern kept pressing. Robben continued to run, twist and weave, an audacious effort from David Alaba found the crowd from twenty-five yards, and Mario Gómez fluffed a golden opportunity from close range after being set up by Ramos. With Real seemingly content with the away goal the white shirts piled in behind the ball as the red wave continued to surge forward. We had seen this many times before.

As the clock ticked down the home side continued to press for the winner. Gómez directed a header straight at Iker Casillas, and moments later the big number thirty-three would go down in the box as both Ramos and Fábio Coentrão dived in. The latter challenge looked like a clear penalty, but the referee turned a blind eye. It was frenetic, it was chaotic; it was FC Bayern versus Real Madrid, and you really couldn't guess what was coming next.

As the game approached the end of the regulation ninety minutes, the capacity crowd at the Allianz roared the home team on for one last push. As if pulled forward by some invisible thread connecting him to the throbbing *Südkurve*, Philipp Lahm put his head down and broke into that familiar stride, charging past Coentrão and sending the ball hard and low into the six yard box. Gómez then arrived to bundle it in past Casillas.

In that one moment, all of the tension and frustration had been catalytically converted into something indescribable. The noise from the Allianz was deafening, and stadium announcer Stefan Lehmann could probably have been heard across the border in Austria. Meanwhile, I was going crazy in front of my television set. For a moment like this, all of the pain and suffering was worth it.

The goal was far from pretty, but thoroughly deserved. There had only ever been one team playing football for most of the second half, and to not head to Madrid with an advantage – no matter how slight – would have been a travesty and an injustice for a Bayern team that had been far more committed to winning the game rather than simply ekeing out a result. Once again this fixture had delivered everything that it had promised, and the tie was finely balanced on the sharpest of knife edges ahead of the second leg in the Spanish capital.

Before the kick off in Madrid, both Bayern and Real would already know their opponent in the final. In what was considered something of a surprise, Chelsea had somehow managed to overturn a deficit and survive a missed Lionel Messi penalty to see off tournament favourites Barcelona. There would be no *El Classico* in Munich, and one of Real or Bayern would face a Chelsea team that had triumphed not through great skill or élan, but a combination of mental fortitude and obdurate defense – the "parking of the bus".

Things couldn't have started any worse for Heynckes' side at a seething Santiago Bernabéu. With less than fifteen minutes played, Bayern's hard-earned 2-1 advantage from the first leg in Munich had been dramatically turned into a 3-2 deficit.

With less than five minutes on the clock Ángel Di María launched a shot straight at David Alaba, who had little time to recover from the impact before seeing Hungarian referee Viktor Kassai point to the penalty spot. It was clearly a case of ball to hand rather than the other way around, but the decision had been made. Cristiano Ronaldo did the rest, sending Manuel Neuer the wrong way to put the Spanish side level on aggregate but ahead in the tie on away goals. As if to twist the knife even further, the unfortunate Alaba also received a yellow card, excluding him from any potential final.

Bayern almost hit back immediately as Robben inexplicably lifted a shot over the crossbar from point-blank range, and Franck Ribéry was denied by a lunging Sami Khedira. However for all the threat from the visitors, the second goal of the game came at the other end. After collecting the ball just inside the Bayern half, Mesut Özil rolled it through to the onrushing Ronaldo, who made no mistake in wrong-footing Neuer to find the bottom left-hand corner. The Bavarians still needed one goal to level the scores on aggregate, but the momentum was firmly with José Mourinho's side.

A third goal for Real would have almost certainly killed the match, and Bayern hearts were in their mouths as Ronaldo, subdued in the opening leg but now seemingly back to his best, threatened to take the game away from the Bavarians. Yet just moments after the Portuguese star had been lining things up one at end, Mario Gómez made his way to the other and into the penalty area, only to be shoved in the back by Ronaldo's countryman Pepe.

Mr. Kassai immediately signalled for a penalty, and Robben grasped the lifeline with a low left-footed kick that just about beat the diving Iker Casillas. The 'keeper had dived full length to his right and got a hand on the ball, but was only able to push it against the inside of the upright. Bayern had somehow been able to get out of jail, and had found a way back in the match.

With the aggregate score now dead level at 2-2, it felt like the match had started all over again. In what was quickly turning into a yet another classic European evening, both sides continued to look for openings and press the other. Karim Benzema sent a shot wide for Real, while at the other end Casillas kept out a Gómez strike before a deflected free-kick from Robben forced him into an ever better save. Replays would show that the deflection had come off Pepe's hand, but in contrast to the harsh handball decision against Alaba the Portuguese defender somehow managed to get away with it.

After the breathless first half, the opening to the second was slightly scrappy. It was if both teams were looking to conserve their strength, knowing what was lying in store for them. Bayern looked the stronger as they continued to press for that crucial second away goal, but they couldn't find a way through or past a Madrid defence that had clearly been tightened up. Just like that, breathless excitement had become nervous tension. It was time to sit on one's hands again.

With extra time looming Bayern launched one final attack, as Robben and Ribéry combined brilliantly down the left to set up Gómez. A first-time shot from the striker might have tested Casillas in the Real goal, but Gómez's hesitation allowed Sergio Ramos to make the block. The ball was collected by the 'keeper, and the fleeting opportunity had gone. The whistle blew to signal the end of normal time.

The first period of extra time would not produce any great drama, but the accumulation of bookings soon started to bite for Bayern. Already on yellow cards before the match, both Luis Gustavo and Holger Badstuber were booked for clumsy challenges to join David Alaba on the banned list for the final. The second period of extra time seemed to float by as quickly as the first, and apart from a flurry from the home side in the final five minutes we were all set for the final act: the dreaded penalty shootout.

Manuel Neuer had been lucky to get away with grabbing a piece of Real substitute Esteban Granero's shirt with five minutes remaining, and some of the Bayern players would be showing serious signs of fatigue. Both Bastian Schweinsteiger and Jérôme Boateng were clearly suffering from cramp, but nothing was ever going to stop them, or the tie from going the distance.

After more than three and a half hours of football, everything would be decided from the *Elfmeterpunkt*.

Knowing that he would play no part in the final, Alaba would do his duty with a fine left-footed strike to get things underway. Casillas dived the wrong way, the ball nestled comfortably in the bottom right hand corner, and Bayern were on their way.

Things got even better just moments later, as Real's two-goal hero Ronaldo saw his penalty well saved by Neuer – a blur of lurid yellowish-green. The Portuguese had placed his kick to Neuer's left early in the game and decided to go for the opposite side, but the 'keeper did exactly as he had done earlier and dived to his right – making the save look easier than it was. Gómez then sent his spot-kick into the bottom left-hand corner to double Bayern's lead, and when Brazilian Kaká was also denied by the brilliant Neuer's right glove I finally found the time to take a deep breath. Surely, we couldn't lose it now.

But these things are never easy. Toni Kroos stepped up to give Bayern what would have been a three-goal lead, but his kick was weak and well saved by Casillas. Xabi Alonso then calmly lifted his shot down into the middle of the goal to get Madrid off the mark, and although Bayern held the advantage the nerves had quickly started to freeze up again. Philipp Lahm was up next, and it was heart back in mouth time as the skipper's poorly-directed kick was batted away by Casillas with his trailing right hand. Real had missed two in a row and had seemingly thrown things away, but in the merest blink of an eye the Spanish side were back in the contest, and one kick away from levelling things up.

Just one successful kick away from what would effectively have been sudden death, Madrid stalwart Sergio Ramos stepped up to face Manuel Neuer. The Bayern 'keeper would get nowhere near the ball as it fizzed straight past him, but then he didn't have to. Spain had never successfully launched a rocket or sent a craft into space, but with a firm swipe of his right foot Ramos launched his country's first spherical satellite into orbit as the ball sailed high over the crossbar and into the Madrid night.

Within minutes, a number of spoof videos and memes had started to circulate on Facebook and Twitter. One might ordinarily have felt even the slightest smidgeon of pity for a player in such an unfortunate situation, but with the opponent being Real Madrid and the player being the pantomime villain Ramos, one would have needed a heart of stone not to laugh.

But things were not over yet. Real had missed their chance to draw level, but Bayern still had to win it.

Despite having suffered from cramp late on in extra time, Bastian Schweinsteiger made his way forward for what would be the decisive kick. With Madrid coach Mourinho standing tight-lipped on the touchline, *Der Fussballgott* calmly strode up to the penalty spot, replacing the ball a number of times before assuming the position.

One could have frozen time there and then, and after what felt like an age Schweinsteiger struck the ball firmly with his right foot. Casillas dived the wrong way, the ball was in the back of the net, and the *Südkurve's* folk hero was on his way, shirt off, towards the corner flag. The loud jeers and whistles of the home fans had suddenly given way to the cheers of the small collection of travelling Bayern fans standing immediately behind the goal.

After a titanic struggle that will go down as one more glorious chapter in the long and rich history of FC Bayern München, *La Bestia Negra* had triumphed once again.

Bayern had made it to the final. At home, in Munich. *Finale Dahoam.*

Having tried and failed to get a ticket for the final, I decided to do the next best thing and head to Munich for a few days, if just to live through what promised to be one of the most memorable days in the club's history. It is not often that a team gets to play in the Champions League final on their own home ground, and when I arrived at my hotel a short walk from the Sendlinger Tor the atmosphere in the city was slowly starting to build.

As well as taking in the match the weekend would also see my meeting up with a number of people: my friends and fellow Bayern fans Chris and Denise had made their way over from Arizona to soak up some of the atmosphere in Munich, former work mate Danny had also travelled from England to sadly follow the blue team, and I would also be meeting my friend Wolfgang, who had offered to put me up in his flat in the north of the city for two of the three nights I planned to spend in the city.

I had dinner at a traditional restaurant just around the corner from the Marienplatz with Chris and Denise on the Friday evening, and already there was a palpable tension in the air with a number of Chelsea supporters making their presence felt. Having finished our meal we had to make our way out through a noisy and intimidating blue mass, and just for a moment it felt like the night before an away game in a foreign city. Having negotiated the crowd I made it back to the hotel, where I spent far too much time deciding on which of the four Bayern *Trikots* I was going to wear on the day of the final.

The following day I headed out of my hotel wearing my 2001 Champions League *Trikot*, and the Marienplatz was a seething sea of red and white. Having met Wolfgang at the Fischbrunnen and dropped off my bags at his flat I headed back into town to meet Danny for a drink. I generally don't have much time for Chelski fans – most of them to tend be of the bellicose plastic blue variety these days – but Danny is a genuine "shed end" era supporter who had heard of the likes of Eddie Niedzwiecki, Pat Nevin and Paul Canoville. After a fruitless search for a cold beer that resulted in our having a couple of glasses of rather rough dry white wine we parted with a traditional "good luck" – not that either of us meant a word of it.

I jumped back on the U6 and made my way back to Wolf's place, and the carriage was full of Bayern supporters in good voice on the way up to Fröttmaning. I joined them in singing a few songs before getting off at Münchner Freiheit to walk to the flat in Schwabing; it was less than an hour before kick-off.

Under the stewardship of former player and Italian international Roberto di Matteo, Chelsea had taken an almost miraculous path to the final. Before their stunning 3-2 aggregate win over Barcelona in the semi-final, the Blues had snatched victory from the jaws of defeat against Napoli in the second round before securing more workmanlike home and away victories over Portguese side Benfica in the quarter-finals.

For many pundits in England, it was as if the team had their name already etched on the famous jug-eared trophy, much like Manchester United in 1999. With commentators in Germany saying pretty much the same thing about Bayern and their path to the final on their own home turf, it was certain that something had to give.

It was a pleasant May evening in Munich, and with it officially being a reduced-capacity "neutral" venue the Allianz Arena had a somewhat strange look to it. The usual sea of red and white was restricted to just over half of the stadium, and unlike a normal home game there were plenty of Chelsea supporters in contrasting electric blue. It was a home game, but it wasn't. Nevertheless, Bayern were big favourites to lift a fifth European crown.

I was quietly confident ahead of the match, but past finals had shown that the better team on the night – usually Bayern – did not always win. My feelings were clearly shaped by the three finals in 1982, 1987 and 1999 where Bayern should have won, but didn't. Bayern supporters have often been described as arrogant, but these past failures had tempered any such feelings. Of course, I couldn't speak for those who might not have experienced these painful defeats.

After all of the buildup and the pre-match predictions, there was a sense of relief when Portuguese referee Pedro Proença blew his whistle to get things underway.

Bayern would dominate possession in the opening quarter of an hour without really threatening Petr Čech in the Chelsea goal, but as they gathered momentum and confidence the opportunities started to come. Mario Gómez would take too much time on the ball and allow Gary Cahill to foil what should have been a perfect goalscoring opportunity. Then, just after the twenty minute mark, Arjen Robben danced and wriggled into the penalty area and got a low shot on target from the tightest of angles, only to see Čech deflect it onto the outside of the post.

Heynckes' side started to crank up the pressure and their opponents were struggling to cope, but the scoreboard remained static. With every minute that ticked by, frustration among the Bayern fans started to grow; discussions were already starting in front of the television in between the bites of chocolate *Torte* and sips of *Weißbier*.

The half-chances kept coming: Robben scuffed a shot straight at Čech, Müller skipped past his marker only to shoot wide, and after Manuel Neuer had his gloves gently warmed by Solomon Kalou, Gómez was guilty of blowing yet another gilt-edged opportunity. After a fine buildup from Franck Ribéry and the energetic Robben, Gómez had failed to control the ball properly with the goal in his sights. The big striker had been scoring goals at will all season, but at that moment it looked as though he had run into a brick wall.

Three minutes before half-time, Gómez spurned yet another chance, possibly the best of the lot. After Thomas Müller looked to have been fouled by David Luiz in the penalty area, the ball rolled perfectly to where the big striker was lurking. Gómez did all the hard work as he smartly side-stepped Cahill, but then, with the goal at his mercy, thrashed a truly ugly shot high over the target and into the crowd. The crowd groaned. We all groaned.

The tall man in the number thirty-three shirt clearly had to be an impostor, and it seemed that the free-scoring Gómez had suddenly been transformed into the bumbling comedy character that had made such a poor impression in front of goal for Germany at Euro 2008. Well either that or Fernando Torres had secretly spirited himself away from the Chelsea bench, dyed his hair black and pulled on a FC Bayern *Trikot*.

The statistics at half-time would show that Bayern had bossed the possession and had produced sixteen shots at goal to Chelsea's two. On any other day, things would have already been wrapped up with the trophy already on its way to the Säbenerstraße. With di Matteo's men piling everybody behind the ball to resist the red tide, I thought back to the European Cup final in 1982 against Aston Villa – where both the statistics and Bayern's dominance over the entire course of the ninety minutes had counted for nothing.

The second half would start as the first had ended, with Bayern well on top. A Robben shot was blocked by Ashley Cole, and when an effort from Toni Kroos was deflected wide for yet another corner it surely was a case of when rather than if the first goal would come.

In the fifty-third minute, the busy Čech was unable to hold onto another Robben effort, and Franck Ribéry pounced on the loose ball to break the deadlock. The Frenchman wheeled away in celebration and we were all off our seats, but the referee's assistant quickly brought an end to all that. The replays at the time were far from conclusive, but Ribéry had been flagged for offside. Surely this couldn't go on for much longer.

The relentless red tide continued to smash against that blue wall. Cole again denied Robben with a desperate block, and when the England left-back looked to have handled the ball in the penalty area just minutes later the Portuguese referee Pedro Proença just waved play on. Was it going to be one of those nights again? There was only one team trying to actually win the game, but the other, somehow, were still in it.

With the scoreboard still goalless, Bayern's superior work-rate, possession and a number of corners had counted for absolutely nothing. David Luiz would get in the way of a Kroos effort before Chelsea launched a rare and all too brief foray in the Bayern half, but the play switched back to the other end, culminating in another poor Bayern corner. They might as well have given the ball back to the opposition.

As the match entered the final ten minutes with extra time being the major topic of conversation, the ball was again in the back of the Chelsea net. This time there was no heroic defensive block, no flag and no whistle: Ribéry's looping cross from the left missed Gómez completely, and the unmarked Müller stole in at the far post to send a downward header that bounced sharply over Čech before gently bulging the back of the net. As Müller ran off in celebration, I half expected a whistle, a flag, something to spoil to moment. Not this time. Bayern were in front.

Endlich! The pressure had paid off, and surely it was all over now. Having been on the defensive for the entire match, there was no chance Chelsea could get back into this now. Or at least none of us could see how they could. All *Die Roten* had to do was to maintain the pace and momentum, play like they had done for the remaining seven minutes and see things through. The crowd roared, we were all off the sofa dancing about like mad people, and Müller was engulfed by his happy team mates.

When Chelsea coach Mourinho sent on Fernando Torres for Kalou – scotching any idea that the Spaniard might have been sporting a dark wig and masquerading as a Bayern centre-forward – it was surely going to be the last desperate act for a Chelsea team that had added nothing whatsoever to the spectacle. With the clock ticking down, all the men in red had to do was keep their cool: everybody still remembered the Camp Nou in 1999, and nobody wanted to make a mistake now.

With just four minutes of normal time remaining, goalscorer Müller made way for centre-back Daniel van Buyten. *Der Raumdeuter* was cheered by the Bayern fans as he slowly and deliberately made his way off the pitch and towards the dugout, but Wolf and I looked at each other, clearly thinking the same thing. After taking the lead the best tactic would have simply been to see things through to the end without making any changes to the tactics or the formation, but with just four minutes remaining Jupp Heynckes was clearly looking to shut things down – effectively inviting the opposition to attack. With the men in blue now having nothing to lose, this was simply asking for trouble.

And so it proved. With just three minutes remaining, Chelsea won their first corner of the match. Wary of Bayern's weakness at these set pieces and with a centre-back who had only been on the pitch for less than a couple of minutes, we sat there hoping that Juan Mata would overcook his delivery and allow for a swift punt back down the pitch.

It was not to be.

The Spaniard's delivery was far better than anything Bayern had produced from the hatful of *Eckbälle* they had been provided with that evening, and there was an awful sense of inevitability as Didier Drogba found space ahead of the hitherto untested Jérôme Boateng to power a header from just outside the six-yard box into the top right hand corner past Neuer.

Chelsea had done nothing all game. Nothing. Yet here we were with the score at 1-1 with just seconds remaining. Memories of 1999 came flooding back as Bayern suddenly found themselves floundering and hoping for the final whistle just to recover from the shock. I could only think of Thomas Müller, now sitting helplessly on the bench as his team mates clung on for dear life in the hope of stretching things out for a further thirty minutes.

In a flash, everything had been turned on its head with the English side looking more likely to snatch a winner. Right at the death, Bayern hearts were in their mouths as a Drogba free-kick fizzed high over the crossbar.

The final whistle could not come soon enough, and the best Heynckes could do was to help his team regroup and re-establish their composure. The *Henkelpott* had been snatched away from under Bayern's nose just as the red and white ribbons were being tied to its large handles, but unlike in 1999 they would at least have the opportunity to take it back again.

Chelsea would pick up where they had left off at the start of extra time, but just three minutes in Heynckes' men finally got a break. Having just saved Chelsea with his equaliser two minutes from time, Drogba clumsily hacked at Ribéry's ankle in the eighteen-yard box, leaving the referee no option but to point to the penalty spot. The decision now was who would take the kick. The reliable Müller was on the bench, Gómez had had a nightmare in front of goal, Ribéry was still hobbling badly after Drogba's challenge, and Robben's last spot-kick against Dortmund had seen him hit it straight at the 'keeper.

In the end the Dutchman picked up the ball and placed it on the spot, with an opportunity to give Bayern the lead for the second time. His kick was struck well enough, but was poorly placed. Čech almost dived too far to his left, only for the ball to hit his legs. The Chelsea 'keeper collected the rebound, and the chance had gone. Just to make matters worse, the injured Ribéry could no longer continue and was forced to make way for Croatian Ivica Olić.

Half-time in extra time came and went in what felt like a blur, and the second fifteen-minute period saw Bayern continue to press forward for a winner. Just three minutes after the restart a swashbuckling run presented Olić with another chance to win it, but the Croatian would spend far too much time deciding whether to shoot or pass to Gómez before sending his shot wide. It was as if someone wanted to see this nightmare stretched out for as long as possible.

And so it continued. Taking more risks in pressing forward, Lahm almost found Gómez in front of goal only to see the ball blocked by a flying Cahill. Just moments later, the skipper combined with Robben only for the Dutchman to spray his shot well wide of the target. The banging on the door of the big blue bus continued and Bayern had notched up a staggering twenty corners, but there was no way through.

The final whistle blew. It would all come down to a penalty shootout.

The talk had always been of German teams being the best in the world at penalty shootouts, but there were lingering doubts about this Bayern team. They had successfully seen things through against Real Madrid in the semi-final, but there was plenty of serious debate as to who would step up and take responsibility. Both Lahm and Toni Kroos had fluffed their lines in Madrid, the trusted Müller and Ribéry were both off the pitch, Gómez couldn't hit a barn door from ten yards let alone twelve, and Robben was surely going to be a bag of nerves.

Even in this footballing game of chance, Bayern were handed the slight advantage with the shootout taking place in front of their own supporters. With nerves of steel, Lahm brushed aside his miss in Madrid and opened the scoring, sending his kick just to the right of the flying Čech, whose fingertip touch was not enough. Mata then stepped up for Chelsea, and once again we were given reason to hope as his poor effort was well covered by Neuer. Clearly unaffected by his series of glaring misses in open play, Gómez confidently drilled his penalty low into the bottom right-hand corner to double Bayern's lead. Even though David Luiz would get Chelsea on the board with a thumping thunderbolt, Bayern had their fate in their own hands. So long as they kept finding the target, the trophy was theirs.

The first psychological wobble came when the next Bayern player stepped up. We had expected Toni Kroos to take the third penalty, and the first thing we would ask ourselves is whether he had bottled it. Instead we saw Manuel Neuer, the man with the massive *Eier* and nerves of steel. Čech again dived the right way, but Neuer's penalty was hit firmly into the bottom left-hand corner to restore Bayern's two goal advantage and maintain their course. Frank Lampard then smashed his spot-kick straight down the middle to pull the score in the shootout back to 3-2.

There was no Kroos for the fourth Bayern penalty, with substitute Ivica Olić taking the responsibility. The Croatian's side-footed effort was neither firm nor well placed, and it was easy for Čech as he dived to his left. When Ashley Cole thumped his kick past Neuer to level the scores at 3-3, it had come down to sudden death.

Bastian Schweinsteiger had always been one of Bayern's go-to men from the penalty spot, and as we continued in our ongoing commentary there was little fear of him not repeating what he had done in the semi-final against Madrid. This was Basti, der *Fußballgott*. If you were to pick one man to be trusted from eleven metres (or twelve yards), it was the man in the number 31 shirt.

Schweinsteiger's shot was not the firmest, but it was well placed and surely heading for the bottom right-hand corner – only to ping sharply off the base of the upright. What looked like the impossible was only confirmed by the replay, which showed that Čech had got his outstretched fingertips on the ball and do enough to push it away from the goal and low onto the post. On another day, the 'keeper might have dived the wrong way and Bayern would have been in front. But this was one of those evenings. It was a truly fantastic save.

Suddenly, everything had been turned on its head. A 3-1 lead in the shootout had been whittled away, *Der Fussballgott* had failed to find the back of the net, and Didier Drogba – in his last game for Chelsea – stepped up to take his team's final kick. Drogba had been the major protagonist in the latter stages of the match; it was he who had pulled the match out of the fire with his late equaliser, it was he who had brought down Ribéry for Bayern's penalty in extra time, and now it was he would make his way to take Chelsea's final kick.

We were all crossing our fingers and hoping for either a smashed effort over the crossbar or yet another big glove from Neuer, but countering this was a gloomy sense of inevitability about what was coming next. Bayern's *Finale Dahoam* was something that could have been written in the stars, but instead it proved to be the final act in Drogba's own personal fairytale. With a firm stroke of his right boot, the Ivorian sent the ball to the left of the goal, sending Neuer the wrong way.

The victorious Chelsea players charged towards Drogba, and for Bayern the dream of a hometown celebration was over. For us, there was no cheering to hear out in the streets. The remaining beer was left in the fridge.

After a speechless and rather surreal few minutes after the final whistle Wolf and I immediately initiated the healing process. It was a wound that needed to be bandaged quickly. They say talking helps, and having a fellow Bayern fan sitting next to me at this moment was in marked contrast to 1999, when I had been left staring at the ceiling in silence. The television had already been switched off, with neither of us wanting to face the sight of the Chelsea players parading around the Allianz Arena with the trophy – the trophy that by rights should have been Bayern's. There were more questions than answers, and the usual selection of what-ifs.

What if Mario Gómez had got at least one of his shots on target? What if Franck Ribéry had not been flagged offside when he put the ball in the net? What if we had not switched into defensive ten-men-behind-the-ball mode after taking the lead so late on in the game? What if Thomas Müller had not been substituted? What if we had done better with our twenty corners? What if Arjen Robben had gone the other way with his penalty in extra time? What if Franck Ribéry had not been injured? What if Bastian Schweinsteiger had placed his shootout spot-kick just a fraction more to Petr Čech's left?

And so on. *What if, what if, what if.*

The media post-mortem was similarly long and protracted. The same questions were asked, and time and again one ended up looking at the statistics, wondering how Bayern had managed to lose. It really was head-scratching stuff: they had bossed the possession for the entire 120 minutes. They had created the better opportunities. They had been awarded twenty corners to Chelsea's one. In fact, the more one analysed the statistics the more frustrating the entire exercise became. After a while, it felt like picking at a scab.

In my thirty-years as a supporter of FC Bayern, I had encountered many painful moments, yet the late evening of May 19th 2012 easily goes down as the worst. In 1982, Bayern had been mugged on an off day by underdogs Aston Villa. In 1987 they had been beaten by two moments of brilliance by an ultimately more deserving FC Porto. In 1999 against Manchester United they had been tripped up within sight of the finishing tape before being punched in the solar plexus, but at least it was all over quickly.

In 2012 they had simply been tortured in their own back yard by a team that had been relentless in their dullness.

Having dominated for more than eighty minutes Bayern had deservedly taken the lead, only to have it wiped out almost immediately following their opponents' first and only corner of the match. In extra time they had another chance from the penalty spot, only to be denied. Even in the penalty shootout they were ahead after the first half-dozen kicks, only to implode right at the end. Every glimpse of that shining light at the end of the tunnel had been followed by a firm kick to the guts; it was simply horrible.

The result will always be the result and their name will always be in the record books, but it is fair to say that Chelsea had been one of the most underserving winners in the long and rich history of Europe's premier tournament. The thought of their team – including the suspended John Terry – parading *our* trophy in *our* home ground was something that made me feel almost physically sick, and to this day it continues to do so.

While I had slowly become more comfortable in coping with the trauma of Manchester United's two late goals in 1999, I doubt I will ever be able to watch the 2012 final in its entirety ever again. Just looking at the lowlights for the purpose of writing this chapter was painful enough.

Following on from their second place in the Bundesliga and the defeat in final of the DFB-Pokal by Borussia Dortmund, being overturned in the Champions League final had completed an unwanted treble for Jupp Heynckes' side – one that matched Bayer Leverkusen's infamous 2001/02 season. The Bayern players had been psychologically shot to pieces, and this would continue during Euro 2012 the following month – when after a solid enough start Germany's campaign came to a messy end in a forgettable semi-final against old rivals Italy.

For me, my long weekend in Munich continued with a quiet Sunday afternoon at a local *Biergarten* with Wolf, his father and girlfriend Lindita, accompanied by the promise not to talk about football – a promise that we couldn't keep for long.

On the following Monday, I spent all morning and much of the afternoon at a table at the Viktualienmarkt, and a number of *Weizens* later I was ready to make my way home. Even the sight of some returning Chelsea fans at the airport didn't disturb me any more, though I made a point of not wearing any Bayern colours on the way back. The last thing I wanted was to have some smug blue-clad goon singing loudly in my face.

The Bayern players would finally get the opportunity to recharge their batteries after what had been an emotionally bruising season, but they would have less than two months before things started all over again. Established members of the squad such as Bastian Schweinsteiger and Philipp Lahm had been described by some sections of the German press as being burnt out and lacking the right mental fortitude when it really mattered, while Arjen Robben was on the end of some particularly vocal criticism both from the media and the stands. During a friendly match between Bayern and the Netherlands the week after the Champions League final, the Dutchman was roundly jeered by some sections of the Munich crowd.

With his career at what was arguably its lowest ebb, Robben then had to endure an even worse Euro 2012 tournament with a pitifully poor Dutch team – leading to much media chatter and talk of his making his way to the exit door at the Säbenerstraße.

Nobody would have blamed the players for any loss of focus as they prepared for the new season, but there was something brewing in Munich. The pain, misery and broken hearts of

2012 would not lead to yet more navel-gazing, but a steely determination not to let the same thing happen again – and with it the desire to push themselves even harder.

OANS, ZWOA, DREI, GWUNNA!

The pain of 2012 had cut deep, but we all knew that in Munich there was a team capable of recapturing the glory days and restoring their position as the best football team in Europe. The summer of 2012 would see plenty of changes in personnel as Jupp Heynckes looked to hone the side that had come so close into a winning outfit, and a number of names made their way to the Säbenerstraße.

By far the biggest purchase was twenty-three year old Spaniard Javi Martínez, a tall midfield engine turned defensive midfielder who arrived in Munich from Athletic Bilbao with the hefty price tag of forty million Euros – a new transfer record in the fifty-year history of the Bundesliga.

Despite playing only a handful of international matches for his country, the highly-rated and versatile Martínez had been sought after by a number of clubs across Europe, and Bayern always knew that they would have to dig deep into their pockets to secure his services with a five-year contract. As soon as the announcement of his arrival had been made, Bayern fans were looking at a new-look defensive partnership of the new boy and established old head Bastian Schweinsteiger.

Martínez was joined by a number of others who had impressed the previous season. FC Basel's promising winger Xherdan Shaqiri would arrive at Bayern for just short of twelve million Euros, while two players who had played starring roles for other Bundesliga teams in 2012 also made their way to Bavaria. VfL Wolfsburg's hard-working Croatian striker Mario Mandžukić had impressed at the Euros and was snapped up for thirteen million Euros, while powerful Brazilian centre-back Danté followed a highly successful season with Borussia Mönchengladbach with a move south to Munich.

Youngster Mitchell Weiser completed the summer spending with an 800,000 Euro move from the Köln youth setup, and the squad was boosted further with the arrival of a number of players on free transfers. Two goalkeepers at different stages of their careers arrived in the form of Hoffenheim veteran Tom Starke and Schalke 04 youngster Lukas Raeder, while fans' hearts were gently warmed with the news of the return of the much-loved Peruvian striker Claudio Pizarro from Werder Bremen.

Bayern didn't make any massive sales to match their high-value purchases, but a number of players would leave Munich in the summer. Goalkeeper Hans-Jörg Butt retired from club football after what had been an exciting end to his career in Munich, while Croatians Ivica Olić and Danijel Pranjić would leave on free transfers to join Wolfsburg and Portuguese side Sporting Lisbon respectively. The largely unused Takashi Usami moved back to Japan, while underused striker Nils Petersen moved up north to Werder Bremen on loan.

One of the most publicised arrivals however was not a member of the playing staff, but former German international Matthias Sammer – who arrived in Munich at the beginning of July 2012 as Bayern's new Director of Sport.

One of the few former East Germans to succeed in the *Nationalmannschaft* after reunification 1990, Sammer had earned a reputation as a tactically astute and hard-working player, and after four years as coach of Borussia Dortmund and one with VfB Stuttgart he had been appointed as technical director with the DFB in the months prior to the 2006 FIFA World Cup. The wide-ranging role had seen him work closely with *Nationaltrainer* Joachim Löw, and in 2010 Sammer was also closely involved with the ongoing development of the highly successful youth system.

After completing his initial five-year contract Sammer had been linked with a move north to Hamburger SV, but instead extended his agreement for another five years with the DFB. However, when the role in Munich became vacant in 2012 it was too good an opportunity to turn down.

While many sceptics may have seen Sammer as more of a Dortmund man given his long and largely successful spells at the *Ruhrpott* outfit both as a player and coach, the businesslike Dresdener was a perfect fit for the Bayern board.

After Bayern's unbeaten start in 2011/12 Dortmund had dominated the season to win the domestic double, and the two teams would meet in early August 2012 for the annual DFL-Supercup. The match itself was little more than a pre-season showcase, but at a packed Allianz Arena Bayern would finally manage to get a victory on the board against a team they had failed to beat since February 2010 – a barren spell of five straight league and cup defeats spanning 912 days.

New signing Mandžukić and Thomas Müller would put Bayern two goals in inside the opening eleven minutes, and although Robert Lewandowski pulled a goal back fifteen minutes from time, a major psychological blow had been struck against Jürgen Klopp's side.

The Bundesliga campaign would begin less than two weeks later at newly promoted SpVgg Greuther Fürth, and the short journey up the Autobahn A9 to Franconia was rewarded with a solid 3-0 victory. The three points put Bayern at the top of the Bundesliga table for the first time since January, and this was followed by a 6-1 demolition of a hapless VfB Stuttgart as things got off to a flying start at the Allianz. With nine goals in their first two matches *Die Roten* had laid down the challenge to defending champions Dortmund, and a 3-1 win against Mainz would make it three from three.

All of these first three victories had been genuine team efforts. The goals against both Fürth and Mainz had been scored by three different players, and the half-dozen against Stuttgart had been shared by five with Thomas Müller netting a brace. Despite the previous season's top scorer Mario Gómez being out injured, the FC Bayern goal machine was firing on all cylinders. Toni Kroos and Müller would split the scoring as Bayern maintained their one-hundred percent start at Schalke, and after four matches *Die Roten* and surprise team Eintracht Frankfurt were already five points clear of the chasing pack.

With Eintracht being held to a 3-3 draw by Dortmund, an easy 3-0 win over Wolfsburg would see Bayern open a two-point lead at the top, and the goalscoring form of Mandžukić had more than compensated for the absence of Gómez. Including his goal in the Super Cup the Croatian had notched up six goals and three assists in six games; it was simple a case of one Super Mario being replaced by another.

Bayern would leave things late in Bremen with two goals in the last ten minutes as Mandžukić maintained his goal per game strike rate, and a Franck Ribéry brace against Hoffenheim saw *Die Roten* edge away from the pack as Franfurt finally succumbed to their first defeat of the season in Mönchengladbach.

Match day eight saw newly-promoted Fortuna Düsseldorf entertain the league leaders, and although Norbert Meier's side would start the day in seventh place they would be no match for Bayern's superior firepower. Mandžukić would get the show on the road just short of the half-hour mark, with Luiz Gustavo doubling the advantage nine minutes before the break. Thomas Müller added a third ten minutes into the second half, and although the home side would provide some stout resistance, Müller and Rafinha would round things off nicely with two goals in two minutes right at the end.

Bayern were looking unbeatable with eight wins from their opening eight matches, but things would come to a sticky and rather unlucky end the following week at home to fifth-placed Bayer Leverkusen. There was a flat look to the Bayern side with both Gómez and Ribéry out injured and the out of favour Arjen Robben on the bench, but the defence had looked solid enough against an unthreatening Leverkusen team – until half-time, when a Philipp Lahm clearance took a unfortunate bounce off the shin of Stefan Kießling and past a helpless Manuel Neuer.

There was only be one side in it for much of the second half, and when Mandžukić's header finally beat Bernd Leno in the seventy-seventh minute it looked as though there was only going to be one winner. The Croatian and Claudio Pizarro combined to make a complete mess of a golden opportunity just two minutes later, and just as Bayern looked to have found some momentum Leverkusen scored another freakish goal to claim the points. With seven minutes left on the clock the visitors broke down the right, and Gonzalo Castro's cross towards Sidney Sam saw the winger's header take an unfortunate deflection off Jérôme Boateng that left Neuer completely wrong-footed.

The first defeat of the season allowed Schalke 04 to get within four points of Bayern at the top as they overhauled Frankfurt, but the following week the gap was stretched back out to seven with Schalke losing in Hoffenheim and Bayern strolling to a 3-0 win over mid-table Hamburger SV with all three goals coming in a frantic thirteen minute spell either side of half-time.

Early threats Frankfurt were calmly seen off at the Allianz with goals from Ribéry and David Alaba, and although Bayern were held to a 1-1 draw the following week in Nürnberg, their lead at the end of match day twelve was a healthly eight points. The lead was stretched to nine the following week as defending champions Dortmund edged into second place, with Bayern subjecting a poor Hannover 96 to a mauling at the Allianz. The game had seen the welcome return of striker Mario Gómez, who after coming on as a sixty-sixth minute substitute wrapped up a 5-0 win – with the other goals being spread around again as Martínez, Kroos, Ribéry and Danté all found the back of the net.

A 2-0 win in Freiburg secured the title of *Herbstmeister* and put Bayern ten points clear, and just under half way through the season Dortmund's record points tally was already under threat. If the Bavarians' *Rückrunde* was as any good as their *Hinrunde*, the record was there for the taking.

The previous season Bayern had blown a five-point advantage over Borussia Dortmund as Jürgen Klopp's side embarked on a relentless charge for the title, but when the two clubs met at the Allianz on matchday fourteen the advantage was significantly healthier. As expected, it was a hard-fought affair. Toni Kroos would give the home side the lead on sixty-seven minutes, an advantage that was cancelled out by Mario Götze just seven minutes later.

Dortmund had started the day in third place – a point behind Leverkusen and eleven points adrift of top spot – and although they had fought hard to earn a point at the Allianz Arena even the most optimistic Dortmund fan knew that their team were pretty much out of the title race.

A 2-0 win in Augsburg coupled with defeats for both Leverkusen and Dortmund saw Bayern extend their advantage to a massive eleven points, and although two dropped points at home to Mönchengladbach would see the lead trimmed back down to nine, it would be a case of Bayern having to lose the title rather than anyone else winning it as the *Hinrunde* came to an end. Apart from the late October blip against Leverkusen, it had been the perfect half season: thirteen wins, three draws and just that one defeat.

Bayern would embark on their now traditional winter tour during the latter part of the *Winterpause*, but by the middle of January the biggest story for years had slowly started to brew in Munich. Former Barcelona coach Josep "Pep" Guardiola had decided to take a year long sabbatical in New York City after resigning from the Catalan giants at the end of the 2011/12 season, and soon rumours were starting to spread about his arrival in the Bavarian capital.

On 16th January 2013, all of the media speculation would finally come to an end. After a number of successful meetings with Uli Hoeneß and Karl-Heinz Rummenigge, Guardiola officially signed a three-year contract with Bayern that would see him take the reigns at the start of the 2013/14 season.

Bayern's courting of Guardiola had been conducted in the cleanest way possible, but given the extent of media interest and the timing of his appointment it was always going to generate a degree of controversy – particularly given the status of current coach Heynckes. The official line was that Heynckes was all set to retire at the end of the season regardless, but some commentators were quick to suggest that the veteran coach had been gently ushered towards making this decision.

The decision to not extend Heynckes' contract was not an easy one, especially for his long-time friend Hoeneß. Not long after the news had been released, the Bayern president informed the media that while Heynckes had been looking at an extension, the chance to snare the man dubbed by many as one of the greatest coaches of the modern era was just too big an opportunity to miss. Once Hoeneß and Rummenigge had their fish on the end of the hook, the decision to cast out the net and complete the catch was a no-brainer.

Jupp Heynckes and Uli Hoeneß had been close friends for many years since the coach's first spell at Bayern in the late 1980s and early 1990s, and the decision must have been a severe wrench for the Bayern president. Ultimately, the long-term future of FC Bayern München came first – and the professional Heynckes took it on the chin with his customary good grace. If anything, the decision made him even more determined to right all of the wrongs of the previous season. Furthermore, if he was to be followed by the much-fêted *Supertrainer* Guardiola, he would make it a point to raise the bar even higher for his successor.

The massive story that had developed off the pitch would not affect Bayern's form after the winter break, and a straightforward 2-0 victory over bottom side SpVgg Greuther Fürth was followed by wins by the same scoreline in both Stuttgart and Mainz. After their initial climb up the table Schalke 04 had sunk back down to sixth place, and their visit to the Allianz would find the home side in a particularly uncharitable mood. David Alaba struck twice as Bayern strolled to an easy 4-0 win, and at the end of the day Bayern were a staggering fifteen points clear of Dortmund in second place.

With thirteen games remaining it had become not a matter if Bayern were going to claim back the *Meisterschale*, but when. Wolfsburg were clinically brushed aside 2-0 as Bayern took their goal difference to +50, and Werder Bremen's visit to the Allianz at the end of February would turn into another goalfest. Bayern would concede their first goal in six matches and only their eighth in the twenty-three games played, but not before they had smashed in a round half dozen against their hapless opponents.

Having spent nearly all of the 1980s and much of the 1990s struggling to score against Bremen, it was rather pleasant to see them being hit for six. No more memories of Wynton Rufer or Bernd Hobsch. Bayern's advantage at the top had been extended to a massive seventeen points, and Dortmund were left needing a mathematic miracle – and a complete meltdown in Munich – to even have the slightest sniff of retaining their title.

A tough match in Hoffenheim was settled by a Gómez goal as Bayern notched up their twentieth win of the season, and a surprisingly competitive encounter against strugglers Fortuna Düsseldorf saw Heynckes' side come back from 2-1 down with Jérôme Boateng grabbing the winner just four minutes from time. As the chasing pack continued to falter the lead was stretched out to a massive twenty points. With nine matches remaining, Dortmund's record of eighty-one points, set only in the previous season, was clearly in sight.

Bayern's only defeat had been the unlucky 2-1 reverse at home to Leverkusen earlier in the season, and the return saw the Bavarians exact sweet revenge at the BayArena. Mario Gómez would open the scoring late in the first half, but as the visitors began to show distinct signs of tiredness the home side drew level through Simon Rolfes fifteen minutes from time. But this time the luck was with Bayern as the game entered the final straight, and the freak own goal they had conceded in the *Hinrunde* was paid back in full when Bastian Schweinsteiger's free-kick three minutes from the end took a nasty deflection off defender Philipp Wollscheid.

Bayern were now strolling serenely towards a twenty-third domestic league title, and what was arguably their most noteworthy performance would come at home to eighth-placed Hamburger SV. Here the purring Munich machine switched up another gear, powering into overdrive as their once-great rivals from the late 1970s and early 1980s were simply torn to pieces and roundly humiliated in front of a full house at the Allianz.

Both of the Marios were missing from Bayern's staring lineup along with Franck Ribéry and Thomas Müller, not that it made a shred of difference. Fringe player Xherdan Shaqiri opened the scoring in the first five minutes with a well-struck long-range skidder and Schweinsteiger added a second with a near-post header after nineteen minutes, and right on the half-hour mark veteran striker Claudio Pizarro – making a rare start in the absence of the two super Marios – would get on the end of a Robben corner that had been nodded on by Javi Martínez.

Bayern could have already been six goals in front as they created chance after chance, and just three minutes later Robben and Pizarro combined brilliantly with the Dutchman slipping the ball low into the bottom right-hand corner past the shellshocked HSV 'keeper René Adler. With the game starting to look like a training exercise, Pizarro stroked in his second right on the brink of half-time after Shaqiri had seen his effort crash off the upright.

Hamburg may not have been the greatest opposition in the world, but this was just a joy to watch. It was pure, free-flowing, precise, glorious total football – like an artist sweeping freely across the canvas with smooth, wide brush strokes.

There was no respite for the beleaguered *Rothosen* after half-time as Bayern simply picked up from where they had left off before the break. Robben was now in his element, firing on all cylinders and running freely at terrified defenders, leaving them trailing in his wake.

Seven minutes after the restart, the sprightly Dutchman collected Schweinsteiger's beautifully weighted looping pass and took the ball from just inside the opposition half all the way to the byline, where his sharp cross back into the six-yard box was tucked away by Pizarro to complete his hat-trick. This was no ordinary tap-in, but a smartly executed backheel that left Adler completely flatfooted. It was the sort of goal you could watch again and again.

Hamburg were by now running on empty, and less than a minute later after Bayern's sixth goal defender Jeffrey Bruma was robbed by Pizarro, who this time turned provider for Robben's second. Adler again had little chance, charging out only to see the ball smartly dinked over him and into the net.

Robben and Shaqiri finally made their way off after sixty-four minutes, but anybody who thought that this was act of mercy on Jupp Heynckes' part was seriously mistaken. Robben's exit was met with loud applause from the home crowd, and on would come Thomas Müller and Franck Ribéry as the Bayern coach looked to turn the screw even tighter.

It would take less than five minutes for both substitutes to make an impact, as Ribéry found Müller in the box with a low, defence-splitting pass. Having made his way to the byline Müller would cut the ball sharply back into the box, where Pizarro arrived to tap in his fourth and Bayern's eighth. Adler could only look up at the sky with a glazed expression, while an exasperated HSV skipper Heiko Westermann berated his colleagues. With more than twenty minutes remaining, double figures were surely on the cards.

Hamburg snatched what looked like a consolation when Bruma rose above Danté to head the ball past Manuel Neuer – once again exposing Bayern's frailities in dealing with corner kicks – but order was quickly restored at the other end just a minute later when Ribéry cut in from the left into the penalty area before drilling in goal number nine.

Four minutes from time Hamburg would win another corner out on the right. With what was almost a carbon copy of their first goal, Westermann arrived unhindered to nod the ball home. The 9-2 scoreline flattered the visitors, and their coach and former Bayern man Thorsten Fink was left tight-lipped on the sidelines. A flying Adler palmed away Luiz Gustavo's cross-cum-shot with Pizarro lurking as Bayern looked for number ten, but Hamburg would at least be spared that ignominy. It had been a spectacular display, the defining moment when Bayern's machine was transformed into an unstoppable juggernaut destroying everything in its path.

Match Day twenty-eight saw Bayern travel to Frankfurt, where a victory would not only guarantee them the *Meisterschale*, but also the record for the fastest-ever Bundesliga title in the competition's fifty-year history. Fifth-placed Eintracht were far from a pushover, and so it would prove in a tough match that was eventually decided by a truly memorable goal.

Seven minutes into the second half in the Commerzbank-Arena, a clearance from veteran Frankfurt 'keeper Oka Nikolov was intercepted by Thomas Müller, setting up a fast break down the right involving Arjen Robben and Philipp Lahm. The skipper's perfectly delivered cross into the six yard box was timed perfectly for the arrival of the fast-approaching Bastian Schweinsteiger, whose finish was as magical as it was inspired. With the deftest of backheels the ball was in the back of the Frankfurt net.

It was the sort of goal one could watch time and again, the fast-paced counterattack and perfect picture-book finish that summarised a style that had been honed to perfection. That the move was finished by terrace hero Schweinsteiger was the icing on the cake; Bayern had reclaimed the title with six games to spare, and were only six points away from equalling Dortmund's points record.

There were plenty of celebrations the following week at the Allianz against old Bavarian rivals Nürnberg, and right from the kick-off there was little mercy shown by Jupp Heynckes' men. The Bayern coach had picked a starting eleven with only a handful of the regular names on show, but this would make little difference as Jérôme Boateng, Mario Gómez and Rafinha effectively wrapped things up by half-time.

Bayern started to wind things down in the second half, but not before Xherdan Shaqiri had scored a fourth as a Nürnberg side that had come into the game off the back of an impressive nine-game unbeaten run were swatted aside with minimum fuss.

Bayern were by now charging inexorably towards a new points record, and the next team to suffer at the hands of the marauding *Münch'ner* were poor Hannover 96. Sitting fairly comfortably in tenth place, the team from Lower Saxony were far from relegation-threatened cannon fodder, but they too would join the long list of teams to be outthought, outgunned and simply outclassed as they were put to the sword in front of their own fans at the AWD-Arena by a rampant Bayern.

An own goal from Lars Stindl early on would open the floodgates, with Claudio Pizarro taking over from there to show that whatever the two Marios could do, he could do just as well. The popular Peruvian scored two goals and provided two assists as the Bavarians notched up another half-dozen to match Dortmund's record of 81 points – with four matches to spare.

The remainder of the season was little more than a procession, with perhaps the only disappointment being the failure to reach the landmark figure of a hundred goals – some disappointment! Fifth-placed Freiburg were beaten by a reserve side and a well-taken goal by teenage starlet Emre Can, while in a game with much pride at stake, Dortmund ended

Bayern's run of fourteen straight Bundesliga victories with a hard-earned 1-1 draw at the Signal Iduna Park.

There was little love lost between the sets of players, and after an exchange of goals inside the first twenty-five minutes the busiest man on the pitch was referee Peter Gagelmann. Manuel Neuer would keep out a Robert Lewandowski penalty after a handball decision against Jérôme Boateng, and amid a flurry of cards Rafinha was dismissed with twenty-five minutes remaining. While Dortmund would have taken some pride in stalling the Bayern machine, they wouldn't have wanted to look at a Bundesliga table that had them a massive twenty points behind the champions elect.

With far more important matches lying around the corner, Bayern would take their foot off the gas. Local rivals FC Augsburg would do well to keep a full-strength team at bay for close to seventy minutes at the Allianz, before Die Roten flicked on the switch to deliver a decisive three-goal salvo.

In what would turn into an emotional and almost surreal final Bundesliga match for Jupp Heynckes against his former side Borussia Mönchengladbach, Bayern would flirt with disaster before providing the ultimate champagne finish to what had been a spectacular season at a packed Borussia-Park.

Right from the start, it was a crazy game. After Bayern had fluffed a decent chance in the opening minute, some comedic defending allowed the home side to storm into a shock two goal lead. Juan Arango's floated free-kick evaded the static Bayern defence, and Austrian Martin Stranzl headed the ball past Manuel Neuer from close range with just three minutes on the clock. Then, just two minutes later, Branimir Hrgota intercepted a dreadful pass from former Gladbach man Danté. The Swede calmly found Mike Hanke, who did the rest with a well-struck angled shot.

Javi Martínez would pull a goal back just two minutes later after charging through the opposition defence and slotting the ball neatly past 'keeper Marc-André ter Stegen, but the craziness continued almost immediately as Norwegian Havard Nordtveit – looking a little like Zorro in a black protective mask – collected a defence-splitting pass from Patrick Hermann before restoring Gladbach's two-goal cushion with a composed finish.

The Bayern defence was all over the place, and it was hard to imagine that this was the same team that had destroyed nearly everything in its path since the turn of the year. Jupp Heynckes, meanwhile, remained poker-faced and tight-lipped on the touchline.

Within nine minutes, Franck Ribéry pulled Bayern back into the contest after beating ter Stegen at his near post with a well-struck shot, completing a crazy nineteen minute spell that had yielded five goals. With both defences looking shaky, one must have wondered where the next mistake was coming from.

There were no more goals before half-time, and the second half would see a far more composed performance from the Bavarians as things were visibly tightened up at the back. With Gladbach looking far less adventurous, the balance gradually tipped towards the visitors. Just before the hour mark, two goals in the space of six minutes would settle the issue and complete an astonishing turnaround.

The equaliser was more than fitting for the occasion. Arjen Robben would set things in motion, sprinting down the right towards the byline before pulling the ball back for Philipp Lahm, and the skipper's rather innocuous looping ball towards the left side of the opposition penalty area was struck with considerable interest by Ribéry. Meeting it full on the volley, the Frenchman sent the ball fizzing into the top right-hand corner with a smooth swing of his right foot.

Having scored what was a clear candidate for goal of the season, the irrepressible Ribéry then turned provider a minute short of the hour mark, sending in a nicely-floated cross across the six-yard box for Robben to sweep home on the volley from close range.

Gladbach still had just over half an hour to get back into the game, but they were completely spent. As the threat from the home side started to ebb away, Mario Mandžukić almost scored a fifth for Bayern. The tall Croatian was on target with a towering near-post header, only to see his effort spectacularly blocked by the flailing ter Stegen. Another goal would have certainly added a gloss to the comeback, but it was fair to say that a 5-3 scoreline would have been flattering for Heynckes men.

It had been a completely bizarre encounter, but as a season-ending spectacle it could not have been any better. Having dominated all comers for most of the season it was the perfect opportunity to show that Bayern had not lost any of their fighting qualities. To put Gladbach's three goals into perspective, *Die Roten* had conceded just eighteen in the Bundesliga all season.

	P	W	D	L	Goals	GD	Pts
FC Bayern München	34	29	4	1	98:18	+80	91
BV 09 Borussia Dortmund	34	19	9	6	81:42	+39	66
Bayer 04 Leverkusen	34	19	8	7	65:39	+26	65
FC Schalke 04	34	16	7	11	58:50	+8	55

With the exception of the bizarre home defeat against Leverkusen seven months earlier, it had been an almost perfect season for Jupp Heynckes' men. Undefeated away from home, twenty-nine wins from thirty-four matches, ninety-eight goals with a scarely believable goal difference of +80, and a total of ninety-one points; ten more than Dortmund's record. From the opening week of the season when they assumed the number one spot, Bayern were not headed at any stage.

In the wake of their winning the Bundesliga in 2012, Borussia Dortmund had commissioned a number of novelty fan items brandishing the number "81". Within the space of a year, they had been made to eat their own hats, scarves, t-shirts and posters.

Bayern's quest to reclaim the DFB-Pokal would begin in August, some 120 kilometres north of München in the city of Regensburg. Rather than the usual lower tier outfit the first round draw pitted *Die Roten* against SSV Jahn, newly promoted to the 2. Bundesliga.

With nothing to lose in front of a crowd of twelve and a half thousand packed into the small Jahn-Stadion, the second division side had managed to keep a strong Bayern side at bay for the opening thirty minutes before being cracked open by Mario Mandžukić. Even then, they managed to hold their own until past the hour mark, when Bayern substitute Xherdan Shaqiri took control to engineer what was in truth a flattering 4-0 win. After finding the back of the net from a direct free kick to double the advantage, the Swiss international then provided assists for Mandžukić and Claudio Pizarro.

The second round saw Bayern drawn against another second division side, but unlike SSV Jahn Regensburg this opponent was one with a more distinguished pedigree. For a long time one of Bayern's bogey teams in the top flight, Kaiserslautern would have relished the chance to relive the old days as they took on the Bavarian giants at a packed Allianz Arena. There were few surprises however as Bayern took command early through Pizarro, and although the home side had to wait until four minutes after the break to double their lead, it was plain sailing after that. Pizarro completed his brace, and a double from Arjen Robben completed another comprehensive 4-0 result for the Bavarians.

A tough 2-0 win in a chilly Augsburg would see Bayern through to the last eight as Mario Gómez and Xherdan Shaqiri found the net either side of half-time, and following the draw for the quarter-finals, everything was perfectly set up for what was quickly billed as the match of the round: a repeat of the previous year's final against Borussia Dortmund.

When the two teams had met in the Pokalefinale in 2012, Dortmund had already been crowned Bundesliga champions with a then record tally of eighty-one points. At the end of

February 2013, the situation was markedly different. Bayern were seventeen points clear of their rivals at the top, and had not been beaten since October. Nevertheless, this was a good old-fashioned cup-tie, a one-off; with the Bundesliga shield slipping out of their grasp, it was the perfect opportunity for Jürgen Klopp's side to bite back. Or at least have a nibble.

The balance before the match was almost perfect. Although dominant in the league, Bayern would have to look back to 2010 for their last competitive victory over Dortmund – a barren run of six matches. They had beaten the Ruhr outfit in the pre-season DFL-Supercup, but we all knew that this didn't really count. So while Bayern were the form team coming into the match, their opponents would hold the statistical edge – and with it a slight psychological advantage. In a one-off cup tie past records and current form meant nothing of course, and any talk of the cup being a minor competition of minimal importance was quickly put aside.

Despite missing the suspended Franck Ribéry, Bayern dominated the early exchanges, roared on by the 71,000 capacity crowd at the Allianz Arena. There were a few testing moments for Dortmund 'keeper Roman Weidenfeller, but nothing what could be described as genuine opportunities. As half-time approached, the visitors would have been more than happy to see things out at 0-0. However, two minutes before the break would come one of those moments of magic. A moment that, as a fan, you will always remember.

In all my years following FC Bayern I have seen some great players, but for continually producing those magical moments Arjen Robben was right up there at the top of the list. Having put the horrors of 2012 firmly behind him, the flying Dutch winger was looking more dangerous than ever: the lithe, balding, dancing, weaving, almost ghostlike master of trickery.

As the clock ticked down towards half-time, Robben engineered a move down the right with Philipp Lahm, only to be foiled by a yellow-shirted defender. However as Dortmund failed to clear Lahm quickly recovered the ball from a floundering Marcel Schmelzer, rolling it back to Robben who was lurking just outside the penalty area. Without a second thought, the Dutchman swung that special left foot, launching the ball as if firing a sling. It appeared to accelerate as it moved through the air, fizzing past the outstretched right arm of Roman Weidenfeller before crashing into the top left-hand corner of the Dortmund net.

Dortmund would throw everything forward in the opening fifteen minutes of the second half, but the Bayern back line held firm. Having weathered the storm, Heynckes' men settled down far better to see things through to the end. When the final whistle blew, there was a distinct feeling of relief among the Bayern fans. This was far from the dispirited outfit that had conceded five goals in Berlin; I for one felt that a massive yellow millstone had finally been lifted off the players' necks.

The previous season's bugbears were out, Bayern were into the last four, and the cup was there to be won.

The semi-final against VfL Wolfsburg was in contrast a far less fraught affair. After a mildly competitive first half, Bayern simply turned on the afterburners to destroy their opponents – with Mario Gómez running onto the pitch as a late substitute to deliver a stunning six-minute hat-trick. Perhaps it is not surprising given Bayern's catalogue of success in the late spring of 2013, but not many people can remember Gomez's quick-fire hat-trick. For me, however, it was one of the defining moments of the season. It was when Heynckes' team truly realised that they could destroy almost any opponent at will.

Robben had set up Mario Mandžukić after seventeen minutes and the Dutch winger doubled Bayern's advantage ten minutes before the break, but Brazilian Diego's stunning shot right on the brink of half-time would give Wolfsburg hope.

However, any threat of a Wolfsburg comeback was quickly quashed five minutes after the restart. Xherdan Shakiri restored Bayern's two-goal cushion, and Bayern were able to relax again. As the game entered its final quarter of an hour, Heynckes' side looked all set to complete a quiet final amble towards the final whistle.

Thirteen minutes from time, one Mario was on for another, with Gómez replacing Mandžukić. The substitute only had to wait three minutes before making his mark, executing the easiest of tap-ins after an excellent assist from the energetic Shaqiri. It was the beginning of a six-minute spell that turned what was already a well-worked win into a mauling for the unfortunate Wolves.

Just three minutes after netting Bayern's fourth goal, Bastian Schweinsteiger's slide-rule pass was matched by Gómez' equally cool finish as he rolled the ball into the bottom left-hand corner past 'keeper Diego Benaglio for number five. Bayern were home and dry, but Gómez was not quite done yet. Another three minutes later, he completed his hat-trick with what was almost a carbon copy of his previous effort. Collecting another defence-splitting pass from Schweinsteiger, the big striker executed the calmest of finishes to notch up Bayern's half-dozen.

Having already clinched the Bundesliga title, Bayern remained firmly on track for yet another domestic league and cup double. Their opponents in the final would be VfB Stuttgart, who had reached the final after beating regional rivals SC Freiburg by the odd goal in three. This, however, was set to be the final dish in this three-course meal. A week before the cup final in Berlin against their southern rivals, Bayern would be playing their biggest game of the season.

After the traumatic events of 2012 and the shattered homecoming dream, Bayern's quest for a fifth Champions League crown had become the one defining mission. No group of players had wanted it so badly, with the painful memory of the penalty shootout defeat by Chelsea at the Allianz only helping to spur them on to greater efforts. The Bayern juggernaut had destroyed everything in its path domestically, and now it was time for the rest of Europe to reap the whirlwind.

The 2012/13 European campaign would start slowly, only to develop in a way that few Bayern supporters had experienced before. There had been plenty of great moments in the past, but nothing could have prepared us for what was about to happen. For me, it was the crowning glory in my thirty-three years as a supporter of this great football club. It was a story of glorious football, high emotion, and, ultimately, redemption.

Bayern's opening group would provide interesting if not particularly testing opponents, with the stiffest test – on paper at least – provided by 2001 final opponents Valencia CF. French side OSC Lille were something of an unknown quantity, while Belarussian champions BATE Borisov were the group's unknown mystery team.

A smart angled finish from Bastian Schweinsteiger and a long-distance cracker from Toni Kroos had given Bayern a two-goal lead over Valencia in Munich, but an otherwise comfortable evening would end in a bit of a flurry. A goal in the final minute from former Bremen and Dortmund striker Nelson Valdez would put the visitors on the scoreboard, and just moments afterwards Valencia's Adil Rami was shown a second yellow card for a foul on Arjen Robben in the penalty area. Mario Mandžukić stepped up to take the spot-kick, only to hit it straight at 'keeper Diego Alves. It was as if Bayern's penalty-taking malaise at the Allianz had picked up just where it had left off against Chelsea the previous season.

A trip to Belarus for a first-ever meeting with BATE Borisov followed, and in what was a rather bizarre match Bayern would have one of "those" evenings against what was arguably the weakest team in the group. Jupp Heynckes' side dominated the early proceedings in Minsk's Dinamo Stadium as Kroos hit the post early on and Mandžukić had a goal disallowed for offside, only for the home side to open the scoring against the run of play through striker Aleksandr Pavlov after twenty-three minutes. The Bayern defence were caught napping, Pavlov was left completely unmarked in the middle of the penalty area, and had plenty of time to send a low right-footed shot into the middle of the goal past Manuel Neuer.

Bayern continued to dominate in search of the elusive equaliser, but the combination of 'keeper Andrei Gorbunov, poor finishing and even poorer luck added to their growing sense of frustration. When BATE scored their second twelve minutes from time, it was no great surprise. The script had clearly been written for the occasion, and Vitali Rodionov made no mistake as he was allowed to dance into the Bayern box before beating Neuer at his near post.

With little choice but to keeping pressing on, it was then Franck Ribéry's turn to hit the woodwork, but just moments later the Frenchman would give the visitors a lifeline with a well-taken finish. The sniff of a comeback was shortlived however, as BATE once again found space on the counterattack. With the Bayern defence caught completely out of position, Brazilian Renan Bressan put an end to what had been a miserable evening for the men from Munich.

Having been shaken by the shock reverse in Belarus, the pressure was back on for the double-header against Lille. Having lost their opening two matches the French side were fighting hard to keep their chances of making the knockout stages alive, and only a twentieth-minute penalty from Thomas Müller could separate the two teams at the Stade Métropole. There was little to write home about in a scrappy match that produced eight yellow cards, but the three crucial points would get Bayern's campaign firmly back on track.

The return meeting a fortnight later couldn't have been more different. A fifth-minute free-kick from Bastian Schweinsteiger would get things off to a great start, and by half-time Bayern had raced into a 5-0 lead with Claudio Pizarro snaring a fifteen-minute hat-trick. It was the perfect antidote to the two previous matches, and although Lille would pull a goal back in the second half, Toni Kroos rounded things off nicely with goal number six. Bayern were back in business, and joined Valencia at the top of the group table with nine points. Having beaten the Spaniards in their opening match, *Die Roten* knew that a draw in Spain and a win over BATE would be enough to see them finish top of the group.

Having beaten Valencia in Munich, Bayern knew that a draw at the Estadio de Mestalla would be enough to keep them in front of the *La Liga* side – and confirm their place in the second round. BATE's surprise defeat earlier in the evening at home to bottom side Lille had guaranteed Valencia's place in the last sixteen, leaving Bayern just a point short of a place in the knockout stages.

With the Bavarians needing a draw and Valencia prepared to bide their time, it made for a cagey encounter at the Mestalla. Although both sides created chances, the game remained locked at 0-0 as the clock ticked into the final quarter of an hour.

Bayern had been more than good value for the point and seemed to be cruising through to a quiet finish that would have benefited both sides, but it would take yet another moment of ill fortune to put us all on edge. Algerian winger Sofiane Féghouli cut inside from the right and embarked on a mazy run towards the Bayern box, unleashing a shot that looked to be going just wide of the target before taking a wicked deflection off the body of Danté. Unable to get himself out the way, the big-haired Brazilian could only deflect the ball past the helpless Manuel Neuer.

Suddenly, BATE's surprise defeat earlier in the evening had taken on a far greater significance. At the start of the day Bayern had been just three points ahead of the Belarussian side; had things gone to form in Minsk, a defeat in Valencia would have left *Die Roten* in third place – with BATE just needing a draw in Munich to secure second spot and send Bayern spinning into the reject pool of the Europa League. However as things stood Valencia were guaranteed first place, leaving Bayern with the task of avoiding defeat in their final match against BATE to secure the runners-up spot.

Although they were behind with just thirteen minutes remaining, Jupp Heynckes had already done his maths homework. The Bayern coach knew that even if his side were to concede a second goal or even a third, it would make no difference to the overall group standings. It was a well-calculated risk, and Heynckes immediately switched to a more attacking 4-4-2 formation as he looked to secure the point that would be enough to pip Valencia on head to head record – and with it guarantee a place in the knockout stage of the competition. As the teams headed back to the centre circle for the restart, Mario Gómez – match fit and raring to go again after a frustrating three-month absence – was already waiting on the touchline.

Gómez had only been on the pitch for three minutes when Philipp Lahm collected the ball on the right, sending in a well-timed cross that appeared to evade all of the white-shirted defenders camped in the penalty area. The substitute flicked a leg at the ball, providing the perfect backheeled pass for Thomas Müller who lashed it past 'keeper Vicente Guaita. Bayern were back in the driver's seat.

Bastian Schweinsteiger then hit the post as *Die Roten* almost snatched a late win, but the 1-1 draw was enough to put both Bayern and Valencia four points ahead of third-placed BATE, with just one match day remaining. It needed just one more solid performance at the Allianz to secure top spot.

Heynckes' men would quickly put their defeat in Minsk behind them for BATE's visit to the Allianz, and after Mario Gómez had opened the scoring midway through the first half there was only ever going to be one winner. The Belarussian champions managed to keep the Bavarians down to the one goal at half-time, but after the restart Müller, Xherdan Shaqiri and David Alaba all found the target as the home team threatened to run riot. BATE would blot the copybook with a late consolation goal, but the 4-1 win confirmed Bayern's position ahead of Valencia at the top of the group table.

Second round opponents Arsenal had barely scraped into the last sixteen behind Bayern's Bundesliga rivals Schalke 04, and ahead of the first leg at the Emirates Stadium there would be little to fear from Arsène Wenger's side. The Premiership team had looked unimpressive in losing 2-0 at home to Schalke – who themselves had been subjected to a 4-0 thrashing at the Allianz Arena just days before Bayern's trip to London. Jupp Heynckes' side had hit a rich vein of form in the Bundesliga, and unlike previous meetings with the Gunners I was able to sit down to watch the match in a confident mood.

My confidence was justified after just seven minutes when Toni Kroos put Bayern in front from Thomas Müller's cross, and when Müller smashed the ball into the roof of the net from close range with not even a quarter of the game gone there was only one team in the contest. With two away goals already banked, the visitors were seriously threatening to overrun the home side and get things over and done with by half-time.

Mario Mandžukić would head just over the bar in the dying seconds of the first half, but it had been a wholly satisfactory first half for the visitors – with the exception of a yellow card for Bastian Schweinsteiger that would result in his missing the second leg in Munich.

Apart from a brief flurry at the beginning, Arsenal had offered next to nothing. But once again, Bayern would let their opponents back into the game when everything should have been done and dusted. Out of nowhere, Arsenal found a lifeline ten minutes into the second half. Once again Bayern's weakness at corners was badly exposed, as Jack Wilshere's kick was allowed to float into the box and bounce among a crowd of uncoordinated black shirts. Manuel Neuer was left helpless as former Bayern man Lukas Podolski calmly nodded the ball into the net to give his side a goal they hardly deserved

Suddenly, Heynckes' side were right up against it. Arsenal had managed to find a second gear, and both Podolski and Olivier Giroud had excellent opportunities to pull the score back to 2-2.

As Arsenal continued to press, they were increasingly vulnerable to Bayern's lethal counterattack. Thirteen minutes from time, *Die Roten* struck the decisive blow. The break was executed brilliantly, but the finish was bizarre to say the least. A long cross ball from Schweinsteiger found Arjen Robben, who in turn combined down the right with Philipp Lahm. The skipper's cross floated into towards the six yard box and was just in front of the fast advancing Mandžukić, but somehow the ball managed to hit the back of the Croatian's legs before taking a curious arc over 'keeper Wojciech Szczęsny.

Arsenal fans might have felt very hard done by, but the final 3-1 scoreline reflected a match where Bayern had been supremely dominant. With three away goals, Bayern were clear favourites to progress into the last eight.

If the first leg in London had been an exercise in rhythm and control, the return match in Munich – billed by the majority of commentators before the game as little more than a walk in the park – provided what was arguably the biggest scare of the season.

Bayern were missing the suspended Schweinsteiger and the injured Franck Ribéry, but with Arsenal also missing a number of regulars including Wilshere and first leg scorer Podolski, there was little for the home fans to fear – until the celebratory atmosphere inside the packed stadium was almost immediately punctured by Giroud's third-minute strike. An unfortunate stumble by left-back David Alaba allowed Theo Walcott to find space down the right, and the England winger's low cross nutmegged a panicking Danté before finding the French striker – who made no mistake from a yard out at the far post.

Giroud's strike gave Arsenal the perfect early fillip, and with Jupp Heynckes unsure as to stick or twist, the pressure was firmly back on Bayern. Arsène Wenger's side still needed at least two more goals, but there was no doubt that they were right back in the contest. Bayern's confidence from the first leg had been completely sucked out, and they would spend the remainder of the first half on the defensive as their opponents bided their time before upping the ante.

It still looked like a mountainous task for the visitors, but memories of the 3-2 defeat just two years earlier at the hands of Inter Milan started to play on my mind as I watched the men in red gradually retreat into their shell. Suddenly, it was like watching another team altogether.

The second half was a bizarre and cagey affair, with Bayern unwilling to risk conceding a second and Arsenal continuing to wait patiently until it was almost too late. A fortunate offside call against Theo Walcott had the anxious home fans sitting on their hands, and missed chances from Luis Gustavo and Arjen Robben only heightened the sense of tension in an increasingly nervous Allianz Arena. With eight minutes remaining Thomas Müller had a great opportunity to put the tie beyond doubt, but within three minutes Bayern were again left to look at their inability to cope with opposition corners.

There was a dark sense of inevitability as Santi Cazorla's kick curled into the Bayern box, and amidst the crowd of red shirts Gunners' fullback Laurent Koscielny headed home – prompting a bizarre pile-up in the goalmouth as Manuel Neuer made a ridiculously comical attempt to prevent the visitors from quickly returning the ball to the centre circle.

With the tie now hanging by a thread, Bavarian nerves were jangling. As the clock ticked into stoppage time, Arsenal threw every man forward in search of what would surely have been the winning goal. It was hard to believe that the Bayern team now looking like a collective bag of nerves had been unbeaten in any competitive fixture since the previous October, and at that moment nobody in the stadium would have been surprised had the visitors managed to breach the Bayern defence for a third time. When the final whistle blew, the sense of collective relief was palpable.

Rather than a worrying sign, the shock of defeat would prove to be the perfect wake-up call for Heynckes' men. From that point on, things would only get better – and then after that, better still.

Bayern's opponents in the quarter-finals were Italian giants Juventus, at the time riding high at top of the Serie A table. Having disposed of Scottish champions Glasgow Celtic in the second round, Antonio Conte's side made their way to Munich in positive mood, while Bayern were in top form having thrashed Hamburg 9-2 the previous weekend. The Bavarian juggernaut had started to roll with purpose, and the midweek meeting with the Italian champions would finally see the last piece of the puzzle put into place – at the expense of another.

The start could not have been more emphatic. No sooner had English referee Mark Clattenburg signalled the start in front of a packed Allianz Arena, Bayern were in front. With less then twenty-five seconds played, David Alaba found space just outside the Juventus penalty area before unleashing a left-footed shot towards goal. Taking a nasty deflection off the foot of Chilean Arturo Vidal, the ball travelled towards the bottom right-hand corner, with wrongfooted 'keeper Gianluigi Buffon unable to make up the ground to keep it out. The coach couldn't have asked for a more perfect start.

Both playmaker Andrea Pirlo and that combative Vidal would go close for the Italians as they looked to recover from Bayern's early strike, but with just under a quarter of an hour gone Toni Kroos started to hobble badly. With the young midfielder unable to continue, Arjen Robben made his way onto the pitch. So early on, it was a major blow – or so we all thought at the time.

Seen by some as Bayern's forgotten man and by others as the villain of the previous season's failure, the Dutchman was the final piece of the puzzle. Having not expected to play a major role in the campaign, Robben's arrival against Juventus would signal the beginning of his redemption. The previous season's woes, ongoing injury problems and being the pantomime villain for a number of the Bayern faithful had clearly wounded him, but the mercurial and at times fragile winger would make the most of this opportunity to re-establish his place in the team.

On that early April evening in Munich, the rejuvenated Robben played like a man possessed. With Frank Ribéry also on the pitch, Bayern upped the tempo – and the chances quickly started to come. It was like the good old days, with "Robbéry" running rings around the opposition; Ribéry sent a snapshot narrowly wide, Robben warmed Buffon's gloves as he fashioned a shooting chance, and Bastian Schweinsteiger sent a well-struck effort narrowly over the crossbar.

The opportunities kept coming in the second half. Mario Mandžukić was denied by Buffon and Alaba shot narrowly wide, and with Bayern looking increasingly dangerous it was only a matter of time until they scored their second. Just after the hour they received just reward for their endeavours. Robben's run down the right opened the space inside to the left for Luiz Gustavo, whose left-footed shot was only parried by Buffon. The ball fell to Mandžukić, who unselfishly rolled it inside for Thomas Müller to complete an easy finish from two yards. The 2-0 scoreline probably flattered the Italians, who knew their work would be cut out in the second leg in Turin.

There was plenty of noise coming from Turin ahead of the second leg, and there was plenty of physicality from Juventus as they looked to claw back the two-goal deficit. Despite a tough first half Bayern maintained their clean sheet, though the coach would again be forced into making an early unplanned substitution. This time, a groggy Daniel van Buyten had to make way for Jérôme Boateng ten minutes before the break.

Both sides had their chances, with both goalkeepers warming their gloves. Gigi Buffon did well to deny Mario Mandžukić, and at other end Manuel Neuer produced an excellent save to keep out a well-directed Andrea Pirlo free-kick. Having to chase the game, Juventus were far more positive than they had been in Munich.

The early stages of the second half saw the home side create the better opportunities, but it was the visitors who would land the first blow after sixty-four minutes – effectively killing off Juve's already slim chances. Buffon had done well to keep out Javí Martinez's attempted toe-poke after the Spaniard had got on the end of a curling free-kick from Bastian Schweinsteiger, but the veteran 'keeper could do nothing as Mandžukić quickly made his way forward to meet the rebound, sending the ball into the back of the net with a stooping dive.

Three goals in front and with an away goal safely on the board, Bayern could finally relax, safe in the knowledge that Juve had to score four times in less than half an hour. To their credit Conte's side kept plugging away, but with time ticking away they knew their cause was becoming increasingly forlorn. As the home side's enthusiasm for the fight gradually began to wane, *Die Roten* turned on the style – and the chances started to come. Müller sent one shot over the crossbar before striking the upright, and the tirelessly impressive Robben scampered straight down the centre of the pitch before forcing the 'keeper into another fine save. With their place in the last four assured, Schweinsteiger's perfect pass set up substitute Claudio Pizarro, who beat Buffon with the coolest of finishes to apply the gloss right at the end of the ninety minutes.

Juventus had dominated their domestic league, but apart from a few sparks had been completely outthought and outplayed by a Bayern side that had finally taken their dominant domestic form onto the European stage. Even with the likes of long-established and always menacing powerhouses Real Madrid and Barcelona still in the draw, we could finally dare to dream.

The semi-final draw saw the two Spanish giants joined by Bayern and another Bundesliga team – Borussia Dortmund. While nobody in Munich would have complained about a semi-final against Jürgen Klopp's side, the thought of playing the *Schwarzgelben* on the famous Wembley turf was too good a thought to pass by. When the names were drawn out of the pot in UEFA's headquarters in Nyon, we would get what we wanted. BVB were paired with Real Madrid, while Bayern were pitted against Barcelona – the great team that had been transformed into an even greater one by Bayern's incoming coach Pep Guardiola.

The pre-match buildup ahead of the semi-final would see plenty of media gossip about Jupp Heynckes getting inside information about the Barca team from his soon to be successor, but director of sport Matthias Sammer was quick to quash such rumours. Heynckes was a man with more than five decades of experience in the game as both a player and coach, and the last thing he would have wanted was help from anybody else – especially the young Catalan pretender.

Bayern's last European encounter with Barcelona – the Champions League quarter-final in 2009 – had resulted in a humiliating four-goal drubbing that would mark the end of Jürgen Klinsmann's short and unsuccessful spell as coach. Over the following four years *Die Roten's* style had been first transformed by Louis van Gaal and then fine-tuned by Jupp Heynckes, and hopes were high in the buildup to the first leg of the semi-final against the *Blaugrana* at the Allianz Arena. However, nobody even in their wildest dreams could have seen what would come next: ninety minutes of football that for many commentators would signal the end of one era and the beginning of a new one.

With both Toni Kroos and Holger Badstuber absent through injury and Mario Mandžukić suspended for two yellow cards against Juventus, there was a slightly fragile look about Bayern's starting eleven, but things would soon settle down on what was a pleasant late April evening in Munich. Barca 'keeper Victor Valdés would keep out an Arjen Robben effort after just two minutes, and Gerard Pique was lucky not to be called for handball in the penalty area as the clock passed the quarter of an hour mark.

With twenty-four minutes gone, Bayern opened the scoring. A slightly overhit corner from Franck Ribéry resulted in the ball floating out towards the right edge of the penalty area where it was collected by Arjen Robben. After an exchange of passes with Thomas Müller, Robben looped a pass into the box towards Danté. Rising above Dani Alves with ease, the tall Brazilian looped the ball back towards the far post, where *Raumdeuter* Müller – unmarked and unwatched – ghosted in towards the far post before nodding the ball down, straight through the flapping Valdés and over the line in a style reminiscent of his strike against Chelsea the previous May.

The crowd in the packed Allianz Arena were rocking now; a noisy, seething sea of red and white. In front of my television meanwhile, I tried my best to remain in my seat. After all, I had seen it all before.

Despite controlling almost two thirds of the possession, Barcelona had offered little in the way of a serious threat in front of goal. While the time spent on the ball by the Catalans was an impressive statistic, Bayern had been the more dynamic of the two teams, and were in complete control of the game.

The Catalans were far from their best and superstar Lionel Messi was clearly out of form, but Bayern were serving up the perfect combination of suffocating defensive play and swift counterattacks. The Bavarians were winning all of the key battles in the middle of the pitch, completely neutralising the likes of Messi, Xavi Hernández and Andrés Iniesta. When Bayern did have control of the ball, their forays into the opposition half were swift, incisive and menacing.

Barcelona would make it to half-time just the one goal down, but the buoyant home crowd wouldn't have to wait long after that for the second goal. Just three minutes into the second half, Robben and Müller combined again to set up Mario Gómez. After the Dutchman's right-sided corner had been headed back across goal by Müller, Gómez arrived to sweep the ball into the back of the net from close range.

Bayern's lack of productivity from corners had been the coach's curse for a long time, but the team looked to have got things right in exploiting a Barcelona team that was lacking in height and noticeably weak against set pieces. With Tito Vilanova's side looking increasingly fragile, Heynckes' men simply cranked up the pressure.

From that point on, it was all Bayern. There were chances aplenty. Müller sent a shot wide, and Ribéry narrowly missed the target after being perfectly set up by the marauding Robben. The visitors meanwhile would make a complete mess of the few opportunities to come their way. Manuel Neuer had to wait sixty-even minutes before he had to make a save, but even then he didn't have to do much to keep out Marc Bartra's weak effort.

With seventeen minutes remaining any remaining fears of a Barca comeback completely evaporated, as Müller and Robben conjured up Bayern's third. On another evening the goal may well have been chalked off, but this evening was always destined to be special. Capping off an excellent individual performance, Robben collected Bastian Schweinsteiger's pass and sprinted down the right, before cutting inside Jordi Alba and rolling a low shot past Valdés into the bottom left-hand corner. Meanwhile, *Raumdeuter* Müller had ghosted into the area to conveniently block off Alba's path as Robben set himself to take aim with that lethal left foot. Hungarian referee Viktor Kassai found himself surrounded by an irate mass of claret and dark blue, but the goal stood.

Nobody was going to spoil this evening, and it was only going to get better. Less than ten minutes later, the remaining ghosts of the 4-0 defeat in 2009 had been banished as Müller hit Bayern's fourth. After some slick combination play down the left from Ribéry and David Alaba, the young Austrian's cross was perfectly set up for Müller, who timed his slide perfectly to stab it home. The chastened looks on the faces of the Barcelona players as they trudged off after the final whistle would say it all.

In all my years following FC Bayern in Europe I must have watched hundreds of matches, but this spring evening at the Allianz was right up there as one of the greatest moments in the club's history. Barcelona had not just been beaten, but completely destroyed. They had been hung, drawn, quartered, boiled, roasted and flambéed in ninety epoch-changing minutes.

Suddenly, Bayern were big news – and having trailed for so many years in the wake of the likes of Real Madrid, Barcelona and AC Milan it felt slightly strange to be a supporter of a club now being dubbed as the best in the world. With the imminent arrival of Borussia Dortmund starlet Mario Götze – announced just the day before the semi-final – and coach Pep Guardiola, it felt like Bayern had taken a quantum leap. When one scoured the football pages for international club news it had always been a steady diet of *La Liga* and *Serie A*, but almost everything would now be about the Bundesliga.

Following Dortmund's 4-1 demolition of Real Madrid in the first leg of the other semi-final the following evening, the talk of *El Classico* at Wembley had all but disappeared; it was now about *Der Klassiker*. Not Real Madrid versus Barcelona, but FC Bayern München versus Borussia Dortmund.

Munich's finest had almost single-handedly dominated European football during the mid-1970s and the Bundesliga had been right up there with the English First Division during the late 1970s and early 1980s, but this would be a first in the modern commercial era. Thanks to the tactically astute Jupp Heynckes, Dortmund's excitable hipster coach Jürgen Klopp and foreign journalists' sudden discovery of the long-standing 50+1 rule, German *Fußball* was not only successful, but had become both fashionable and marketable.

It was easy to be swept along: despite my long-held dislike for all things *Schwarz-Gelb*, I found myself rooting enthusiastically for Dortmund – though it did help that they were playing Madrid. The second leg of the other semi-final was played the evening before Bayern's meeting with Barcelona, and despite a late rally from the Spanish side at the Bernabéu, Dortmund booked their place in the final.

It was now up to Bayern to see things through and take Germany's biggest football fixture to Wembley.

No club had thrown away a 4-0 lead in the long history of the European Cup and Champions League, but after their shaky 2-0 defeat in the second leg of their second round match against Arsenal that had seen them flirt with elimination, Bayern were taking no chances. Barcelona were out for revenge after their first leg humiliation in Munich, but with their talisman Lionel Messi half-fit and on the bench there was little chance of the *Blaugrana* repeating their four-goal triumph of 2009. All Bayern had to do was maintain their shape and keep their heads.

Perhaps the biggest concern for Bayern were the players on yellow cards, which included Philipp Lahm, Bastian Schweinsteiger and Javi Martínez; one rash tackle or poor refereeing decision would rule them out of the final.

As in the first leg, Barcelona quickly took control of the ball, but with most of their neat passing moves taking place in their own half this mattered little. With every minute that ticked by, the home side's task would keep getting harder. As the match passed the fifteen-minute mark, Bayern were looking the more dangerous of the two teams with Barcelona's defence looking just as wobbly as it had done in Munich. So long as the visitors remained patient, the time to strike would come.

It didn't take long for Heynckes' side to settle. Just short of twenty minutes *Die Roten* would have an excellent claim for a penalty turned down as Lahm appeared to have been brought down by Gerard Piqué, and 'keeper Victor Valdés was all at sea as he just about managed to stifle a swift counterattack engineered by Thomas Müller and Mario Mandžukić.

Barcelona's game on the other hand was summed up perfectly when the usually unflappable Xavi carved an effort from close range high over the target, and with Bayern sticking to their solid defensive tactics every opposition attack was quickly closed down. As half-time approached, Dani Alves' crude challenge on Bastian Schweinsteiger was the best the *Blaugrana* could offer.

While the tie had arguably been settled in Munich, it would take just three minutes of the second half for Bayern to put things beyond all doubt. An early break saw Müller spurn an opportunity to open the scoring, but just moments later Arjen Robben would produce another moment of genius. With the Barcelona defence almost evaporating in front of him, the Dutchman collected David Alaba's looping long ball and cut inside Adriano, before finding the top right-hand corner of the net with one of those famous left-footed curlers. Valdés dived valiantly, but in truth he could have spared himself the effort.

A goal up on the night and 5-0 ahead on aggregate, Bayern could finally afford to open their shoulders. The calm and patient approach had paid off, and now it was time for Heynckes' men to flex their muscles and drive their opponents into the ground.

While the Barcelona players probably wished that the ground would swallow them up, the men in red were making the most of their evening in Catalonia. They passed the ball around with an almost arrogant nonchalance, and there were loud shouts of *Olé* from the visiting *Südkurve*. It was ever so slightly surreal; after all, this was not a Saturday afternoon shooting show at the Volksparkstadion in Hamburg or the Weserstadion in Bremen, but a Champions League semi-final at the famous Camp Nou.

It was only just a matter of time before Heynckes' men decided to dispense with the showboating and score their second, and if just to rub it in Franck Ribéry's sharp cross was brilliantly volleyed into the back of his own net by the unfortunate Piqué with eighteen minutes left. Yes, Bayern had finally allowed a Barcelona player to get his name on the scoreboard.

Just four minutes later Ribéry raced down the left again, sending a high looping cross that floated over the hapless Valdés to Müller – who rose majestically above his marker with consummate ease to nod home Bayern's third at the far post. Substitute Rafinha found the side netting as Bayern threatened to score a fourth and rub even more salt into Catalan wounds, and the full-time whistle couldn't come soon enough for their battered, bruised and broken opponents.

This wasn't just a win, but a result for the ages. If the four-goal thrashing of Barcelona in Munich had been outstanding, the arguably more convincing 3-0 triumph in front of close to a hundred-thousand supporters at the famous Camp Nou was even sweeter. Bayern were through to the final. Only Bundesliga rivals Borussia Dortmund would stand between Bayern and a fifth European crown.

When the date of 2013 Champions League final at Wembley was announced, it didn't really bother me that much. The last Saturday in May, still a long way away. Then at the end of 2012, we received an invitation to the wedding of two of our friends. The venue: the small Spanish coastal town of Ametlla de Mar, around 150 kilometres south of Barcelona.

The date: 26th May 2013, the day after the Champions League final.

I continued to think nothing of it: the competition was still in the group phase at that point, and Bayern were still a long way from the Wembley final. However as the date slowly but surely began to close in and an increasingly dominant Bayern just kept on winning, the chances of my being close to Barcelona – of all places – while the final was being played just ten miles from home at Wembley were increasing on an almost exponential basis.

Soon after Bayern had defeated Arsenal to reach the last eight, there was an opportunity to apply for tickets to the big event. The chances of actually getting a seat were as slim as finding the proverbial needle in a haystack after stumbling across a basket full of hens' teeth, but I just had to have a go. Then the chain of events began to unfold: victory over Juventus, followed by that famous 7-0 aggregate thrashing of Barcelona, the very city I would be visiting just a month later.

After Bayern's 4-0 victory in the first leg of the semi-final, I seriously started to consider all sorts of mad plans. If I did manage to get hold of a ticket, how was I going to get myself over to Spain in time for the following afternoon?

Was such a plan even possible, short of chartering a private jet and landing right on the beach outside the hotel?

There were no convenient flights to Barcelona on the Saturday night, with almost everything involving a stopover in some out of the way location such as Bucharest, Moscow or Istanbul. Then there were the eyewatering prices, with these truly awful flights costing upwards of £500. I had nightmares about ending up stuck in some soulless airport at the back of beyond and messing up the entire weekend completely, or the match going to extra time and penalties and my not being able to make it to the airport in time. In short, it was completely ridiculous.

My friend Gary – the groom – would immediately offer his apologies when we met for his stag evening in early May. In fact, before we had even exchanged greetings on the tube platform I could see his furrowed brow as he walked towards me. I simply said "well mate, so long as Bayern win".

In a way I was massively relieved when I found out that I had missed out on getting a ticket to the match. We spent our first three days in Barcelona as planned, before taking the two-hour or so drive south for the wedding at the weekend.

Once we reached the hotel in the resort of Ametlla de Mar early on the Saturday afternoon after a pleasant drive down the scenic Costa Dorada, I vaguely played around with the idea of corralling a bunch of people in the early evening and heading off into nearby Salou to watch the match – but with the wedding the following day there were never going to be many enthusiastic takers. In the end, I'd watch the match from the slightly sterile hotel lobby on a standard television screen with Spanish commentary.

I was the only FC Bayern fan in the room. Well, the only obvious one at least. The majority if not all of those around me were supporting Dortmund, including a small group of people from Recklinghausen – a city known to me only for its association with Adam Opel AG, Bayern's former shirt sponsors.

One of the younger German lads would be particularly interested in my 2001 Champions League *Trikot* with "21 – Zickler" on the back. "Why Zickler?" he asked in English, clearly surprised at my shirt not being adorned with the name of someone more famous like Stefan Effenberg, Mehmet Scholl or Giovane Élber. I had no real answer, save the fact that having Zickler's name on the back actually made people more interested in the shirt than they might have otherwise been. I did tell him about some of my other numbered shirts which did include some of the more internationally well-known Bayern players from the previous twenty or so seasons – including "31 – Schweinsteiger" and "7 – Ribéry" – but for some reason he found "20 – Salihamidžić" *sehr cool*.

I just wish I had received my new customised Thomas Müller "25 – Raumdeuter" *Trikot* before leaving home – that would have certainly got everybody talking.

After a spectacular but slightly bizarre opening ceremony where the pitch was invaded by two rather kitsch armies of mediaeval knights and archers kitted out in the red and white of FC Bayern and the yellow and black of Dortmund, the famous *Henkelpott* appeared – carried on by Bayern legend Paul Breitner and former Dortmund star Lars Ricken, scorer of the third goal in BVB's 3-1 defeat of Juventus in Munich in 1997.

Bizarrely, both men stepped out onto the pitch in elaborate fancy dress, with Breitner wearing a red and white military uniform with a shining breastplate and the younger Ricken looking like a nineteenth-century duke in black jacket and pale yellow breeches. Breitner's pitch walk-on at Wembley was a striking contrast to the previous year, when he had carried the famous trophy out onto the pitch at the Allianz Arena dressed in a far more formal suit.

After a mock skirmish between the two "armies" in the centre circle, it was finally time for the real battle to begin. Meanwhile on what was a bright and calm evening in southern Catalonia, I settled down in front of the television set with a chilled *Estrella Damm*.

On a pleasant evening under the big arch in north-west London, it was the underdogs who got off to the better start, with a fast-paced opening that threatened to take the game away from Jupp Heynckes' side. Polish international striker Robert Lewandowski provided the biggest danger, sending one effort over the crossbar before forcing Manuel Neuer into a sharp save. As the clock reached the fifteen-minute mark the Bayern 'keeper had to pull off another stop, this time to deny Jakub Błaszczykowski - another one of Dortmund's triumvirate of Polish stars - who rifled in a shot from eight yards out.

The BVB supporters around me were in good voice, while I just sat there gripping my beer glass waiting for the early yellow squall to blow over. I had been unable to take as much as a sip, worried by the complete disappearance of the Bayern team that had walked over Juventus and mercilessly shredded Barcelona. I had momentary flashbacks to 1987, 1999 and as Dortmund continued to press high up the pitch and chase every fifty-fifty ball, swooping on the men in red shirts like a swarm of angry wasps.

Both Marco Reus and Sven Bender warmed Neuer's gloves again as Jürgen Klopp's side maintained the pressure, and for Bayern it was a simple case of maintaining their composure and weathering the yellow storm. The game had passed the twenty-five minute mark before the Bavarians had even created their their first genuine opportunity: a cross from the hitherto well-shackled Franck Ribéry, a firm header by Mario Mandžukić, and a fine reaction save from Dortmund 'keeper Roman Weidenfeller. Jupp Heynckes' side looked to have recovered their poise, but ten minutes before half-time Neuer had to be on hand again to foil the dangerous Lewandowski.

Bayern had clearly been second best for most of the first half, and slowly started to find their feet. Arjen Robben made a complete mess of one goalscoring opportunity as he tried to get the ball onto his favoured left foot, and just two minutes before the break the Dutchman finally managed to get a shot on target. His thumping shot was on target, only to hit the advancing Weidenfeller square in the face. The whistle blew for half-time.

At that stage all I wanted to do was take a breath of fresh sea air outside as the sun was slowly starting to set. Dortmund had showed in forty-five minutes that they were far more of a threat than either Juventus or Barcelona, and although I remained confident it was clear that the rest of the evening was not going to be an easy ride for the men in red.

The opening ten minutes of the second half saw Jürgen Klopp's side pick up where they had left off at the end of the first forty-five minutes, with Bayern content to simply soak things up and offer little or nothing in return. As the game approached the hour mark Dortmund had started to slow down, and things started to turn a little scrappy. At this point, Bayern changed gears. Right on sixty minutes, the Bavarians struck against the general run of play.

Robben made the initial burst down the left before finding Franck Ribéry, with the Frenchman's perfectly timed return pass beating both the offside trap and all three of the yellow-shirted defenders closing in on him. Having made his way to the byline, Robben then skipped outside Weidenfeller before slipping the ball sharply back into the six-yard box, where Marcel Schmelzer's botched attempted clearance fell perfectly for Mandžukić. As Schmelzer struggled to undo his error and close down the space, the Croatian had plenty of time to execute a textbook left-footed finish, sweeping the ball into the net from just over a yard to put Bayern in front.

With those immediately around me slipping into silence as the ball rolled into the Dortmund net, my almost silent "Ja!" was accompanied by a controlled clenched fist and some polite applause from hidden pockets of support dotted around the room. There were no other red shirts, but at least I knew I wasn't alone. Having seen Bayern take the lead in European finals so many times only to stumble and fall right at the end, I wasn't going to celebrate quite yet: past experiences had taught me to keep things firmly in check until the final whistle.

Within ten minutes, my pessimism proved to be well-founded. Danté - already on a yellow card for an earlier mistimed tackle - clumsily bundled into Marco Reus, who crashed to the ground. Italian referee Nicola Rizzoli immediately pointed at the penalty spot, and it was surely only a matter of seconds before Danté was going to see a second *Gelb* flashed in his direction. Inexplicably - and to my huge relief - the official chose to keep his cards in his pocket. İlkay Gündoğan sent Neuer the wrong way to bring the Ruhr side level, but it could have been far worse.

The game suddenly burst into life, with Dortmund's equaliser the catalyst. Bayern upped another gear, as if offended by the opposition's temerity to breach a defence that had been unsullied for a touch over seven hours in Champions League competition.

With eighteen minutes remaining, the Dortmund defence was torn wide open as *Die Roten* broke at speed. Thomas Müller rounded Weidenfeller and sent the ball towards the far corner, and I was off my seat as Robben charged in to apply the finishing touch. Rather than slide in to meet the ball, the Dutchman attempted to chase it down before tapping it in. It gave his *bête noire* Neven Subotić just enough time to slide in and execute a miraculous challenge.

The gloves were off now. Just two minutes after Subotić's goal-saving challenge, an audacious long-range effort from Lewandowski flew into the Bayern net. The whistle had already gone for handball against the Pole. I didn't know what to think: Bayern had come so close to retaking the lead, but that little bit of luck usually required to tip the balance in these closely-fought encounters also seemed to have deserted their opponents.

With both teams providing the perfect advertisement for this new brand of German football in front of the watching world, Bayern started to tighten the screw. David Alaba's firmly-struck effort was well parried by the suddenly busy Weidenfeller, and Mandžukić hit the side netting. Desperate to avoid a repeat of the previous season's penalty shootout agony against Chelsea, Bastian Schweinsteiger launched a speculative effort high into the crowd. Meanwhile, Lewandowski was lucky to escape a straight red card for a petulant stamp on Jérôme Boateng that went unseen by the officials. Dortmund should have been down to ten men, but after Danté's lucky escape just minutes earlier, there were no real grounds for complaint. Everything had been balanced out.

This was perfect entertainment for the neutral, the action swinging from end to end with both teams slugging it out like two heavyweight boxers. The chances kept coming: Boateng showed his strength to stave off a Dortmund assault before initiating another fast counterattack, and Weidenfeller again came to his side's rescue with a fine save to deny the determined Schweinsteiger.

With the score still locked at 1-1 and things all set to go into extra time, there would be one final twist to this dramatic script. A year earlier, Arjen Robben had been at the lowest point of his career: having missed that crucial extra-time spot-kick against Chelsea, he had even been jeered by his own supporters. His evening at Wembley had not been too great either, and despite his determination and energy he had nothing to show for it save a number of scuffed shots and near misses. Nearly every other tweet, text or Facebook message I received from fellow supporters as the final whistle approached demanded the Dutch winger's replacement.

It seems silly to say it now, more than a year after the event, but I had this strange feeling that things were going to change. I firmly suggested to the Robben-haters that they remained patient. Somehow, I just knew he was going to come good when it really mattered. For all the tension, I somehow managed to maintain a zen-like calm. After all, the fear of conceding a last-minute goal against Borussia Dortmund could not have been any worse than conceding a last minute equaliser, missing an extra-time penalty, and then blowing out completely in an *Elfmeterschießen* on one's home ground.

With just over a minute of normal time remaining, a hopeful punt deep into the Dortmund half was seized upon by Ribéry, whose crafty backheel through the yellow and black stripy-shirted defence found Robben. The pain of 2012 was wiped away in an instant and his misses on the night were immediately forgotten, as the fleet-footed Dutchman almost tiptoed his way past a static Mats Hummels and into a shooting position before tapping the ball with his left foot past the wrong-footed Weidenfeller. The Dortmund 'keeper could only watch as the ball rolled into the bottom right-hand corner of the net.

As Robben charged towards the touchline with his team mates in tow, I was finally able release all of those pent-up emotions. It must have been quite a sight to watch me there, the only red-clad madman in a lightly-crowded room of people cheering for the other side. The feeling was indescribable. After years of suffering from late sucker punches in big European finals, Bayern had finally delivered one of their own. There was no way back for Dortmund now.

This wasn't just about beating Dortmund of course, but exorcising the previous year's painful episode against Chelsea as well. Part of it was also for Arjen Robben, and the fact that I had never wavered in my faith in him to deliver when it mattered. As the game entered the final minute of injury time Jupp Heynckes made two changes, with Luiz Gustavo and Mario Gómez coming on for Ribéry and Mandžukić.

Dortmund substitute Julian Schieber managed to get a tame shot on goal that ended up in the secure hands of Neuer, but unlike the year before in Munich, there was no further drama. Four minutes of injury time were safely played out, and when the final whistle blew it brought an end to one more glorious evening in the long and rich history of FC Bayern München.

As skipper Philipp Lahm received the famous silver jug-eared trophy and held it aloft, I just sat there and took it all in. Twelve years after the victory in Milan against Valencia, Bayern were European champions again.

The locals started to filter out, and the Dortmund fans from Recklinghausen offered a gracious "well played" in English before quietly retreating back to their rooms. Then, my partner Caroline suddenly appeared with a face like thunder. I had completely forgotten about dinner, and even in Spain it was far too late in the evening to venture out for something to eat.

It had been a close run thing, but in the end all of the statistics favoured Bayern. They had dominated possession with more than sixty percent of the ball, and over the course of the ninety minutes had managed to accumulate more corners and get more shots on target. Dortmund may have started brightly and may have threatened to take the game by the scruff of the neck, but in the end Bayern would have the extra quality to tip the balance in their favour.

The wedding the following afternoon completed what was a truly wonderful weekend, capped off by a fantastic four-course banquet and copious amounts of tapas and *vino*. I may not have been at Wembley to witness the final, but this had been my most memorable moment as a supporter of FC Bayern München. Having retreated back to our room late in the evening, I began to put together a few ideas about a post-match article. I had no idea at the time what it would eventually turn into.

The Bayern players arrived back in Munich and were given a wonderful welcome in the pouring rain as they showed off the gleaming silver trophy, but there would be one final challenge awaiting them. With both the *Meisterschale* and *Helkelpott* safely locked away in the trophy cabinet at the Säbenerstraße, history beckoned as the team headed to the Olympiastadion in Berlin for the final of the DFB-Pokal the following Saturday.

Die Roten needed just one more victory to secure a unique treble, and just one obstacle remained: VfB Stuttgart.

Bayern had beaten the Swabians 6-1 and 2-0 earlier in the season, and after the easy stroll to the Bundesliga title and the glorious triumph at Wembley this was always going to be the easy bit – on paper, at least. Stuttgart however had other ideas. Bayern may have been chasing an historic treble, but for Bruno Labbadia's side it was their one and only chance to claim some silverware in what had been a truly disappointing season.

Die Roten would be massive favourites in Berlin, but there was no way that their less heralded opponents were simply going to lie down and take another thrashing.

Coach Jupp Heynckes would make just two changes for the cup final, with Daniel van Buyten coming in for Danté in the centre of the defence and Mario Mandžukić making way for Mario Gómez – in what would turn out to be the striker's final game for FC Bayern.

Gómez would eventually move to Serie A side Fiorentina the following month, but as the season came to an end most Bayern fans already knew that he was heading towards the door in Munich. Having endured a disappointing and injury-troubled season Gómez had found himself slowly shunted down in the pecking order behind Mandžukić, and there was no little coincidence in his being picked to start against his former side in Berlin. It was the perfect opportunity for the big striker to say farewell, and sign off in style.

Bayern started the game confidently, and were quickly into their stride. Wembley hero Arjen Robben flashed a shot narrowly wide after some good approach play by Franck Ribéry, and it looked as though the Bavarians were going to score another half-dozen. But there was no early goal, as the first half an hour would see Stuttgart defy expectations.

The same team that had finished down in twelfth place in the Bundesliga – a staggering forty-eight points behind Bayern – looked anything but a team prepared to tamely roll over. Far from piling men behind the ball and parking the bus, Labbadia's team took a positive approach. Romanian midfielder Alexandru Maxim shot wide, and Manuel Neuer was forced into action to keep out a teasing free-kick from Georg Niedermeier. At the other end, Niedermeier would come to his team's rescue, beating Mario Gómez to the ball with the striker just two yards out from goal and poised to strike.

Just as Stuttgart had started to look threatening, Bayern flicked that familiar switch. Having started slowly, they were now leaving their opponents chasing shadows as they swept majestically up and across the pitch. Stuttgart 'keeper Sven Ulreich did well to close down David Alaba and referee Manuel Gräfe waved play on after Robben had gone down in the penalty area, but it was a simple case of if rather than when Bayern were going to open the scoring.

Some eight minutes before half-time, Bayern's pressure on the Stuttgart backline finally told. Skipper Philipp Lahm embarked on a typically swashbuckling run down the right flank and into the penalty area, only to be clumsily shoved in the back by Ibrahima Traoré. Herr Gräfe pointed to the penalty spot, and the unflappable Thomas Müller stepped up to send Ulreich the wrong way. The wheels were rolling.

As half-time approached Gómez did brilliantly to collect the ball before twisting on a sixpence to shoot narrowly over the target, and the whistle would blow just as Jupp Heynckes' side looked to put their foot on the pedal. Stuttgart had belied their lowly league position to offer a worthy challenge, but having scored the crucial opening goal it was now up to the men in red to turn on the afterburners.

It would take just three minutes of play in the second half for Bayern to double their lead. Robben and Müller combined brilliantly down the right, and with the Stuttgart defence in complete disarray Lahm's low cross was turned in from close range by Gómez. The finish was a scrappy one as Gómez' right-footed effort cannoned off his left knee before nestling in the goal, but in getting on the scoresheet the big striker had more than justified his being in the starting lineup.

As the clock ticked past the hour mark Gómez would score a much better second, smartly directing the ball past Ulreich after another well-timed right-wing cross, this time from Müller.

Three goals to the good with just under half an hour to play, some Bayern fans started to celebrate. However, their opponents were not ready to give up the ghost quite yet. With Heynckes' men starting to look just a little complacent, Japanese international Gōtoku Sakai's floated cross into the Bayern box was well met by the unmarked Martin Harnik, whose well-directed header beat Neuer before flying into the top left-hand corner.

Harnik's goal was surely no more than a consolation, but Labbadia's men still had enough time to turn things on their head. Looking far more confident, the Swabians threw everything forward as they sought the impossible. Shinji Okazaki created an opening only to hit a weak shot straight at Neuer, and with the Bayern defence looking more than a little rattled the referee waved play on after the ball looked to have struck Jérôme Boateng's hand in the penalty area.

Stuttgart could easily have folded after that, but their bold play was again rewarded nine minutes from time. After Bayern failed to clear a corner, Okazaki drilled a nineteen-yard effort that crashed off the inside of the upright, and from the rebound Harnik's shot was brilliantly parried by Neuer. The ball could have gone almost anywhere, but landed right back at the feet of the Austrian – who made no mistake with his second attempt. A slight deflection off Bastian Schweinsteiger took the ball away from the Bayern goalkeeper, and a match that had looked done and dusted just ten minutes earlier was suddenly right back in the balance.

A rare Bayern attack saw Robben blaze a shot high over the crossbar, but right at the death the underdogs continued to press in search of the goal to take the two teams into extra time. Deep into injury time a floated free-kick from Sakai made its way into the Bayern box, and Bayern again managed to get away with it. Okazaki would get to the ball first, only to completely lose his bearings as his header skewed towards the corner flag. Meanwhile, the referee completely missed Boateng grabbing a handful of Vedad Ibišević's shirt. With the Bayern players and fans now desperate to hear the sound of the final whistle, the clock ticked agonisingly into a fifth minute of additional time.

There would be one more chance for the Swabians as they fought bravely to the last, but skipper Serdar Tasci's header was gratefully clutched by Neuer. Just seconds later as the ball made its way back into the Stuttgart half, the final whistle blew to end a dramatic cup final – and with it signal the greatest achievement in the history of FC Bayern München. *Jetzt is das Spiel vorbei! FC Bayern holt das Triple!*

There had been plenty of hairy moments in those final ten minutes, but history had been made. In thirty-three years I had been through it all following FC Bayern, but this was an achievement that would surely never be surpassed. In 1999, Bayern had reached the Champions League and DFB-Pokal finals after clinching the Bundesliga title, only to fall short in both matches. In 2010, they had fallen against Internazionale at the final hurdle after claiming the domestic double. In 2013, a year after the heartbreak of the *Finale Dahoam*, the pieces had finally all fallen into place for a team that could rightly claim to be the best in Europe.

Bayern had made history, and every fan of *Die Roten* could finally forget about Chelsea, Dortmund and the pain of 2012. For the post-treble photoshoot, the team all wore special t-shirts, adorned with the slogan *Oans, Zwoa, Drei, Gwunna!* – Bavarian for "one, two, three, winners!"

Much-loved *Trainer* Jupp Heynckes had gone out on a high, setting the benchmark for everybody else to follow. There may come a day when Bayern wins another treble, but only one coach can ever claim to be the first. Having already won a Champions League title with Real Madrid in 1998, Heynckes joined Ernst Happel, Ottmar Hitzfeld, Carlo Ancelotti and José Mourinho as the only coaches to win the *Henkelpott* with two different clubs.

After the summer break, the Chelsea bugbear would also be addressed in the UEFA Super Cup under new coach Pep Guardiola. One could hardly call it "revenge" for 2012, but there was something particularly sweet about beating the London side in a penalty shootout after a dramatic 2-2 draw after extra time.

Chelsea must have felt that they had won the match after taking the lead three minutes into extra time, only for Javi Martínez to score a dramatic equaliser when the referee was poised to blow the final whistle. Bayern scored all five of their penalties, Belgian striker

Romelu Lukaku missed Chelsea's final kick, and *Die Roten* had won the Super Cup for the first time after three previous failures in 1975, 1976 and 2001.

The victory in Prague confirmed Bayern's position as the best team in Europe, and by the end of 2013 their triumph at the FIFA World Club Cup in Morocco had solidified their claim to be the best football club in the world.

PROJECT PEP

I had initially planned to close off this story at the end of the triumphant 2012/13 season, but in taking so long to put things together, the next three years seemed to float straight past me. When you can only spare a few hours here and there outside of normal working hours at the office, time does appear to fly a lot faster.

When I first started to put this book together in the summer of 2013, Pep Guardiola had just been unveiled as FC Bayern's new coach. As the Catalan's three years in Munich was coming to an end, I too was fast approaching the finishing line. Somehow, the timing felt appropriate.

I have considered writing another in-depth piece on Guardiola's three years in charge at FC Bayern, but felt that something needed to be said here in this closing chapter, if just to make a few points about a period that had initially been billed as the beginning of a new era in Munich.

There is no doubt that Guardiola has had a massive impact at FC Bayern. The club has increased its presence as a major global brand, and now stands alongside the likes of Barcelona, Real Madrid and Manchester United as one of the biggest and most marketable sporting organisations in the world.

The reality was that it could have been a whole lot better. Bayern continued to develop their profile and international appeal, but the results on the pitch never quite matched the marketing hype off it.

Of course, everything is relative, and the matter of whether "Project Pep" was a success or not will continue to remain a matter of heated debate both among Bayern fans and football pundits. On the one hand, Jupp Heynckes had left behind a fantastic team that had secured a first-ever treble; it was not massively unfair to have hoped that with the arrival of one of the world's most talked about coaches, Bayern would have built on that success. On the other hand, the Bavarians were far from looking like treble-winning material when the news first broke about Guardiola's arrival in January 2013. Nobody, least of all Guardiola himself, would have expected to inherit such a heavy burden of expectation.

As things got better for *Die Roten* during the spring of 2013, the weight of the millstone that the Catalan would have to put around his neck had started to increase. When the treble was secured after the cup final victory in Berlin, the coach-in-waiting knew that he would have his work cut out to even match Heynckes' historic achievement.

For the club's supporters, however, it was all about the end game. In simple terms, the best team in the world with the best coach in the world had failed to win the Champions League during Guardiola's three years at the helm. Meanwhile, bitter rivals Real Madrid would win the trophy twice in the same period.

Domestically, there were few issues with the coach. Bayern were just as dominant as they had been in Heynckes' final season, and every other week one could hope to witness an avalanche of goals at the Allianz Arena. It was nice to see old rivals from the 1980s such as Hamburger SV and Werder Bremen being given a tonking. For a while, this dominance carried over into Europe too.

Guardiola's first season in charge in Munich had started with a stutter as Borussia Dortmund exacted a small matter of revenge in the Super Cup, but by the turn of the year things could not have been running any smoother for the new coach. Bayern were unbeaten in the league, with their only reverse coming in the group phase of the Champions League against Manchester City at the Allianz. The result was more of a statistical annoyance more than anything else; having already secured top spot with five straight victories, Bayern had stormed into a two-goal lead after twelve minutes only to be hauled back by a resilient opponent desperate for the points.

After the blip against City, normal service was resumed with the beginning of another unbeaten run. By the final week of March 2014, the Bundesliga title was wrapped up in record time with a 3-1 win in Berlin against Hertha. Bayern were still unbeaten in the league, and had made serene progress in both cup competitions; for many, they were big favourites to secure back to back trebles.

Guardiola's men had pushed Barcelona aside as the team to watch, and Bayern fans started to believe.

Then, the wheels slowly started to come off. What should have been a celebration at the Allianz was almost ruined by an enthusiastic Hoffenheim side, in a match that saw Bayern throw away a 3-1 lead and almost lose it at the death. As Guardiola started tinkering around with the starting lineup, Bayern's fifty-three match unbeaten run in the Bundesliga – a record stretching back to November 2012 – came to an end against unheralded Bavarian rivals FC Augsburg. The following week, a disjointed and disorientated team collapsed to a 3-0 defeat at home to Dortmund.

While it was easy to dismiss the sudden drop in form on the coach's policy of rotation or even simple old-fashioned complacency, the signs were there even before the Bundesliga title had been secured. A 2-0 win against a hard-working Mainz in the middle of March had flattered Guardiola's side, and there were signs that opponents had started to identify Bayern's weaknesses. Of course, the same thing had happened to Guardiola's clearly superior Barcelona team in 2012 against Chelsea, when the Catalan had been outthought and outwitted by the inexperienced Roberto di Matteo.

A 5-1 hammering of former bogey team Kaiserslautern saw Bayern safely through to the final of the DFB-Pokal, but for everybody the season would hinge on *Die Roten's* defence of the *Henkelpott*. Having made smooth progress through to the last four, Bayern were drawn against old foes Real Madrid.

The first leg at the always atmospheric Santiago Bernabéu could have gone either way, and Bayern were unlucky not to come away with at least one away goal. In the end the match would be settled by Karim Benzema's strike in the nineteenth minute, but Bayern fans were left rueing Mario Götze's missed opportunity to equalise just six minutes from time.

Bayern had never lost to *Los Merengues* at home and were the bookmakers' favourites ahead of the second leg in Munich, but for me there was plenty to be worried about. Just three days earlier, I had witnessed the team's weaknesses for myself against Werder Bremen – my first-ever live match at the Allianz Arena. Bayern had come back from 2-1 down at half-time to eventually win an exciting encounter 5-2, but the fact that a team as ordinary as Bremen had twice been able to outflank and penetrate the previously impervious Bayern defence was concerning.

These fears were ultimately realised against Real Madrid, where the coach appeared to play straight into the hands of opposition coach Carlo Ancelotti, rather than work with his own team's many strengths. It took just sixteen minutes for the visitors to take the lead in Munich, and just four minutes later they had doubled their advantage. The goals were straightforward, simple, training ground executions: two well-delivered crosses, and two accurate headed finishes from defender and 2012 penalty-fluffer Sergio Ramos. Good old-fashioned stuff.

It was safe to say that the match was already over after that, and Cristiano Ronaldo added a third for Ancelotti's side before half-time. In the space of eighteen painful minutes, Bayern's hopes of retaining the *Henkelpott* had spectacularly collapsed around them. Their long and proud unbeaten home record against Real had been destroyed, and with it the myth of *La Bestia Negra*.

Real were not quite finished, and a second Ronaldo goal a minute from time was one more dagger in the heart for the despondent home crowd. The coach, in his own words, had "fucked up"; was this a moment of clarity, even contrition? Not a bit of it, in that he went on to qualify his failure by blaming the players for persuading him to be more attacking. The bitter truth was that Guardiola had been outthought, outwitted and ultimately outgunned by the more experienced Ancelotti.

The defeat against Real had clearly overshadowed Bayern's glorious march to the Bundesliga title, and it would take an emotional extra-time victory over Dortmund in the DFB-Pokal final to restore hope in the coach. It probably sounds a little strange to complain about "only" winning the league and cup double, but it is difficult to describe the amount of emotional investment that had been lost in the wake of the Champions League semi-final defeat. No, scratch that – semi-final embarrassment.

Although Bayern had already wrapped up the league title in record-breaking time, the collapse in form at the end of the season was particularly dispiriting. Bayern had been unbeaten for well over three-quarters of the season and had looked well on course to surpass the recently-set record of ninety-one points, but six dropped points in their final six matches ensured that they would finish a single point short of the mark set by the treble-winning squad.

For many, this was just as well; it meant that the record was still the property of Jupp Heynckes' Bayern side.

The 2014/15 season followed much the same pattern as 2013/14. Bayern were again the dominant force in the Bundesliga, but it is fair to say that many of the better teams had started to get the measure of Guardiola and his tactics. *Die Roten* would win their twenty-fifth league title and finish a convincing ten points clear of second-placed VfL Wolfsburg, but the comfortable margin between Bayern and the rest of the pack masked a fundamental weakness.

A closer analysis of the results would show that Bayern had registered a record of twenty-two victories, one draw and one defeat against teams outside the top six, but a far more patchy three wins, three draws and four defeats in their ten matches against their five closest rivals. Despite their clear and obvious dominance, Guardiola's men could very easily have been described as flat track bullies; had those immediately below them been able to achieve a similar level of consistency in dispatching the cannon fodder, the race for the title would have been far more competitive.

There was to be no repeat of the domestic double as Bayern – quite literally – slipped out of the DFB-Pokal after a penalty shootout defeat against Dortmund (yes, them again) in the semi-finals, and another Champions League journey would be ended by Spanish opposition (yes, again).

I had managed to see Bayern play live on a number of occasions during the 2014/15 season, including three Champions League away matches. The first against AS Roma would provide one of my most memorable evenings as a Bayern fan, as the team tore the Italian side to shreds in front of their own crowd at the Stadio Olimpico. Next up was a 3-2 dead-rubber defeat against Manchester City at the Etihad Stadium, where Bayern fought gamely with ten men, only to succumb at the death to two late Sergio Agüero strikes.

My third and final journey of the season was to the Camp Nou, for the first leg of the semi-final against Barcelona. In the previous knockout rounds Bayern had hammered Shakhtar Donetsk 7-0 on aggregate before destroying 1987 final conquerors FC Porto 6-1 at the Allianz, having lost an error-riddled first leg 3-1.

Bayern had constantly battled with injuries all season, and things finally came to a head after the defeat in Portugal. The post-match discussion would not only focus on the team's shoddy defensive showing that had resulted in their conceding three soft goals, but the sudden departure of the entire medical team, including long-time specialist Dr. Hans-Wilhelm Müller-Wohlfahrt.

Nobody had any idea what was actually going on behind the scenes. While Müller-Wohlfahrt claimed that his decision to resign had been motivated by the medical team being blamed for Bayern's defeat, sporting director Matthias Sammer was quick to suggest otherwise. Regardless of who was to blame, it quickly became apparent that the doctor had clashed with the coach on a number of issues regarding player fitness, with Karl-Heinz Rummenigge also getting involved.

To put things in perspective, Müller-Wohlfahrt had worked with Bayern for thirty-eight years since his appointment in April 1977, apart from a temporary hiatus during the short reign of Jürgen Klinsmann. During this time, he had worked with no fewer than sixteen different coaches. After not even two seasons working with Guardiola, he was packing his bags.

It was like a bizarre circus act, made worse by the timing of it all.

There was more than a whiff of FC Hollywood about Bayern again; the media were focussed on problems off the pitch rather than on it, and matters were certainly not helped by Guardiola's inability to be straight about his contractual situation. The media focus on the coach was a cause of constant distraction, and once again rumours had started to circulate about instability and disagreements behind the scenes. While the Bayern board made it clear that they were firmly behind the coach, many fans of the club were starting to get more than a little tired of the ongoing shenanigans.

It was not the best setting for a Champions League semi-final, but Bayern would do well to hold Barcelona at bay until deep into the second half. Then, they imploded spectacularly. Rather than shutting up shop after Lionel Messi had given the *Blaugrana* the lead thirteen minutes from time, Guardiola's men took on the form of headless chickens. A 1-0 defeat would have been considered a workable escape, but two more Barcelona goals in the final ten minutes left Bayern with a mountain to climb in the second leg in Munich. The buildup to the match and most of the match had seen us in good voice, but the mood when making out way out of the ground was depressing to say the least.

Following the defeat, Guardiola's tactics were closely scrutinised again. Yes, there were ongoing injury problems. But this couldn't justify the team's implosion or, for that matter, the coach's decision to leave talisman Thomas Müller on the bench for what arguably the most important game of the season.

Bayern did manage to win the second leg 3-2, restoring some of their battered pride. Centre-back Medhi Benatia's seventh-minute opening goal had provided a brief spark of hope, which was just as quickly extinguished by Neymar just eight minutes later. The away goal for Barcelona meant that Bayern had to score at least four more, and from that point on it was all about putting up a decent show for the home crowd.

That they did, coming back from 2-1 behind to finish the campaign with a win.

The pattern didn't change during Guardiola's third and final season at Bayern. Another comfortable amble to the Bundesliga title, victory in Berlin to secure a second domestic league and cup double in three years, and another Champions League campaign where Bayern flattered to deceive before stumbling against Spanish semi-final opponents for the third year in a row. The defeat in 2016 completed the set: after Real Madrid in 2014 and Barcelona in 2015, this time it was the turn of the less heralded Atlético de Madrid.

Again, one could look at the coach and his tactics for the first leg in Spain, where not for the first time he appeared to base his tactics around the opposition rather than his own team's strengths. One might have thought that he would have learned from the dramatic quarter-final against Juventus where Bayern had clawed an unlikely 6-4 aggregate victory from the jaws of defeat, but the questionable tactics in Madrid simply played into the hands of Diego Simeone and his capable but hardly world-beating side. Perhaps the most bizarre decision, however, was to leave talisman Thomas Müller on the bench.

It was a tight game at a feverish Estadio Vicente Calderón, and Bayern would have their fair share of opportunities. But as in 2014 against Real, they returned from the Spanish capital a goal in arrears.

Like many long time Bayern supporters, I had been intensely critical of Guardiola from the beginning, but the second leg at the Allianz Arena was arguably one of the best matches in his three years in Munich. On that evening, Bayern were simply outstanding – but it was still not quite enough to take them over the line and claim what would have been a deserved place in the final.

The coach had finally hit the right note, but in the end it was a case of too little, too late. As a spectacle, the match was perfect for the neutral, but ultimately heartbreaking for a Bayern team that was, truth be told, a considerable distance ahead of the opponents in terms of both ability and quality. Ultimately, the Bayern supercoach had been undone by a cannier rival with more limited resources at his disposal.

Bayern would never really have the rub of the green in the second leg, but it is fair to say that they had their opportunities to take command of the tie. Having levelled the aggregate score through Xabi Alonso just after half an hour, *Die Roten* had the perfect opportunity to take the lead just minutes later when they were awarded a penalty, only for the usually reliable Thomas Müller to see his weak effort kept out by Atléti 'keeper Jan Oblak.

It was a crucial moment in the match; the game had swung heavily towards Bayern in those frantic five minutes, and with the Atlético coach and players almost boiling over, a second goal could have easily seen the emotionally fragile Spaniards fall apart at the seams. Simeone would admit after the match that Müller's missed penalty had "given his team life".

Atlético should have been two behind and psychologically on a knife's edge, but they recovered their poise to weather the red storm. When Antoine Griezmann scored a goal on the break eight minutes into the second half, Bayern were back under the cosh again.

Oh how they tried. In a breathless rearguard action that reminded me of the heroic semi-final failure against AC Milan in a soggy Olympiastadion more than a quarter of a century earlier, Bayern threw everything and the kitchen sink at their opponents. Every player ran his heart out, and when the tireless Arturo Vidal teed up Robert Lewandowski with seventeen minutes left to retake the lead, there was renewed sense of hope among the capacity crowd.

When Griezmann then missed a penalty that had been awarded for a foul well outside the box, some may have felt that destiny was calling Bayern to the final in Milan, site of their fourth Champions League title in 2001. But there was no way through. Atlético held their ground brilliantly against an almost relentless flood of Bayern attacks, and Oblak was outstanding.

2-1 was the final score, and Bayern were out on away goals.

Bayern would have thirty-three shots to Atlético's seven, with eleven on target. Twelve corners to two, and a staggering seventy-three percent possession. On any other day, they would have wiped the floor with their opponents. One can only speculate, but if Müller's penalty had gone in we might have been talking about another treble rather than yet another missed opportunity. With Atlético on the brink of a meltdown, Bayern could possibly have finished winners by three or four against ten men.

Pep Guardiola would bid farewell in Berlin as Bayern edged to a penalty shootout victory over Dortmund after a hard-fought goalless draw, but he had always known that his time in Munich was going to be judged by his success or failure in the Champions League. He had already committed himself to a new contract in England with Manchester City, a move that he was quick to describe as a new "challenge". This was an interesting choice of words, given the prerequisite to taking up a new challenge is usually succeeding in the previous one.

There is no doubt that Guardiola brought a certain something to Bayern. Some players – Jérôme Boateng, David Alaba and Joshua Kimmich to name but three – had clearly improved during his three years in charge, and the team had clearly undergone a transformation. But the net result was that the combination of super team and super coach – to use one of the Catalan's favourite words, *super* – hadn't really hit the mark. Some of the more vociferous defenders of "Project Pep" have argued that his mission was simply to improve the team and leave it in good shape for his successor, but I think we could all call nonsense on that.

For many, the three years under Guardiola was like a brief hedonistic experience. There were many great moments, but not much else. Granted, he had won two domestic doubles in three seasons, but even then he had been unable to match Felix Magath's back to back doubles achieved with a far weaker team a decade earlier. Perhaps this is being overly harsh, but it probably reflects the feelings of many long-term Bayern supporters. In the final analysis, one could argue that it was a case of the emperor's new clothes.

Another issue with Guardiola, along with his spiky cohabitation with the media and strange relationship with the Bayern medical experts, was his connection with the Bayern fans – or apparent lack of it. Unlike many of his predecessors, Guardiola appeared to look uncomfortable with the Bayern culture – even though he did manage to pull off the right look when wearing *Tracht*.

Unlike the likes of Ottmar Hitzfeld, Jupp Heynckes or the overly enthusiastic Louis van Gaal, there was something not quite right with the images of Guardiola in Lederhosen or when holding a foamy *Maß* in front of the cameras. It was like he didn't want to be there. One got this vision of Pep wanting to take off the itchy socks as soon as he was out of eyeshot, or asking to replace the inconviently large mug of foaming Bavarian beer for a glass of gently sparkling organic water distilled from the tears of unicorns only found in the mountains of Bhutan.

Of course, this was never going to go down well with the majority of Bayern fans, for whom the concept of *Mia san Mia* is everything. The coach, like the players, is seen as part of the fabric of the club, and with it the larger Bayern family.

While neither Hitzfeld nor Heynckes were born south of the fictional *Weißwurstäquator*, they were natural fits in Munich; even Louis van Gaal, for all his sins, made a concerted effort to knit himself into the Bayern fabric and make a connection with the supporters. The more guarded Guardiola, in stark contrast, made sure that he was seen only where he needed to be seen – while maintaining a safe distance.

Then there were issues concerning the development of the squad, which appeared to veer in a completely different direction. Louis van Gaal had been responsible for developing a number of younger players from the Bayern academy, a policy that was followed by Jupp Heynckes. This seemed to fall away after Guardiola's appointment. When the Catalan coach was keen to develop some of the younger players already in the squad, little time was shown for those on the fringe.

Between 2009 and 2013, Thomas Müller, David Alaba, Holger Badstuber and Toni Kroos had been able to make the smooth transition from the reserves to the first team. After that, it was little more than a disappointing procession, with the likes of Julian Green, Emre Can, Pierre-Emile Højbjerg, Gianluca Gaudino and Lucas Scholl all getting short airings before being ushered out of the back door or shunted back into the reserves.

The coach's clear preference was for young players from outside Germany, particularly his home country; meanwhile, whether through unfortunate accident or nefarious design, the Bavarian core of the German national team that had triumphed at the World Cup in 2014 was slowly whittled away.

Perhaps the biggest issue concerned a player who had not only been a driving force behind the *Nationalmannschaft's* triumph in Brazil, but part of the furniture in Munich for the best part of two decades. Bastian Schweinsteiger had been at the club since the age of fourteen was the fans' *Fußballgott*, but within a year of Guardiola's arrival he was little more than a dead man walking. A long catalogue of injuries didn't help Schweinsteiger's cause, but it was pretty clear to even the most casual observer that he was not part of the Catalan chemist's long-term vision. While no one player is bigger than any club, it was a truly heartbreaking moment to see the much-loved "Basti" leave Munich – and to go to Manchester United, of all places.

All of this, and Guardiola's decision to leave Bayern to "fulfil his ambition" of coaching in the English Premier League, suggested that he never really wanted to be part of the fabric at Bayern. To those whose relationship with the club runs deep, it was little more than a punch in the guts. Guardiola is an excellent coach and motivator, but was never the best fit in Bavaria. He is a project manager, a chemist, a psychologist, a tinkerer, a crazy chef; elsewhere, I have described him as being football's molecular gastronomist – easily understood by those who share and appreciate his vision, but something of an unfathomable mystery to everybody else.

While Guardiola will always be respected as a professional practitioner who delivered successive Bundesliga titles in Munich, he is unlikely to be on the list of those genuinely loved by Bayern fans. That special accolade will always be reserved for the likes of Ottmar Hitzfeld, Jupp Heynckes, and older coaching legends such as Udo Lattek and Dettmar Cramer.

Coaches and players have come and gone, football has seen massive changes, and FC Bayern München have been transformed from one of the leading clubs in Germany to a major player on the world stage. Thirty-six years is a long time. Yet today I am as much a fan of FC Bayern as I was when I first discovered them as a nine year old in the spring of 1981.

There will be more struggles to endure, and more trophies and titles to win; more pain, and with it, more glory. Meanwhile, my own red odyssey will continue.

Printed in Great Britain
by Amazon